McCALL'S

ESSENTIAL GUIDE TO SEWING

McCALL'S®

ESSENTIAL GUIDE TO SEWING

Tools • Supplies
Techniques • Fabrics • Patterns
Garments • Home Décor

BRIGITTE BINDER • JUTTA KÜHNLE • KARIN ROSER

sixth&spring books
NEW YORK

Contents

ALL ABOUT PATTERNS

PREPARING TO SEW

CREATING A GARMENT

TECHNIQUES FOR HOME DÉCOR

PATCHES AND REPAIRS

USEFUL KNOWLEDGE

DEAR READER,

Some books stay with us for a lifetime because they offer a wealth of knowledge at our fingertips. *McCall's Essential Guide to Sewing* is one of those books. For beginners and experienced sewers alike, this colossal reference provides detailed instructions and information on every sewing topic, from the operation of your sewing machine to basic stitching techniques to making pattern alterations like an expert.

The world of sewing is becoming not only more innovative, but also more international. Websites, sewing portals, and online purchasing opportunities provide a spectrum of sources, inspiration, and instruction in many languages. *McCall's Essential Guide to Sewing* takes advantage of this global sewing community, offering a world of expertise in a single volume.

The Internet also offers a variety of avenues for making money from your sewing. Perhaps you'd like to sell your designs online: our "Marketing" chapter guides you through the e-tailing process, explaining what to do and watch out for, beyond just the legalities.

We hope that this book will be your go-to reference for years to come and will prove to be a helpful partner in your sewing endeavors!

Yours,

B F Binder

Kerri Roser

Justin Hinkle

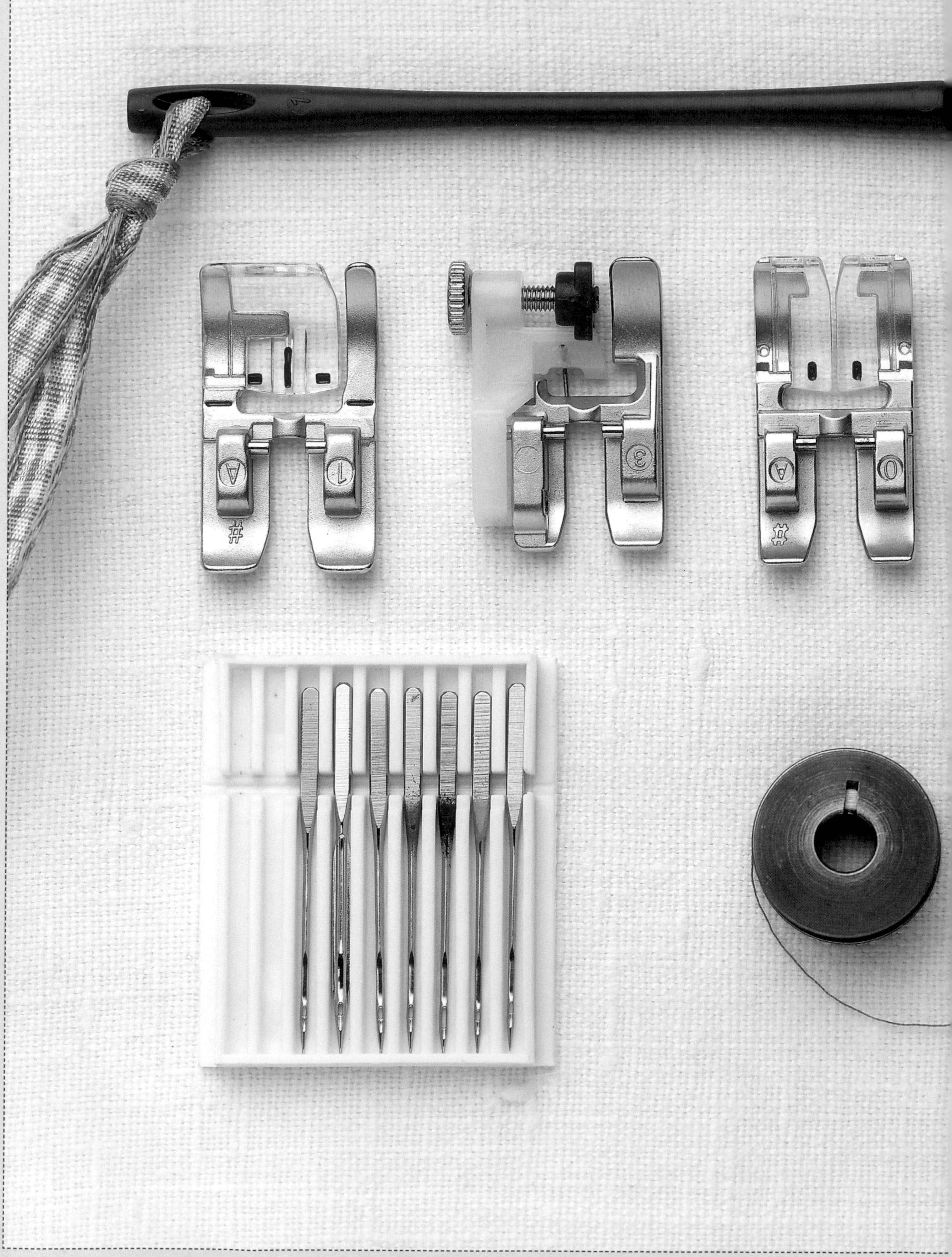

sewing machines

BEFORE BEGINNING TO SEW, YOU NEED TO BECOME WELL ACQUAINTED WITH YOUR SEWING MACHINE AND ITS CAPABILITIES. PROPER CARE OF YOUR MACHINE PLAYS AN IMPORTANT ROLE AS WELL. A WIDE ARRAY OF PRESSER FEET MAKES IT EASIER TO ACHIEVE PROFESSIONAL-LOOKING WORK, AND THE RIGHT CHOICE WILL LEAD TO MYRIAD CREATIVE POSSIBILITIES AND PERFECT SEWING RESULTS.

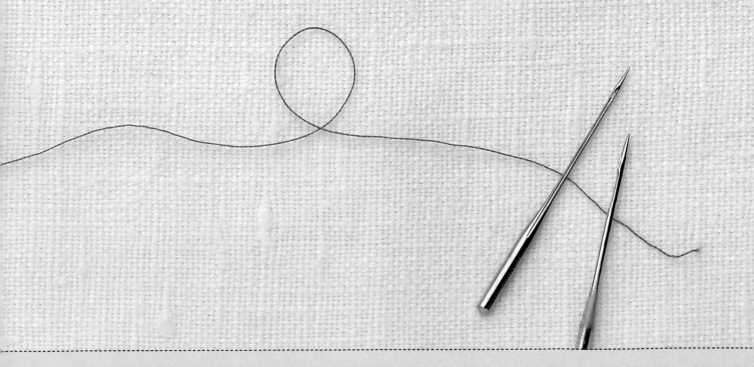

sew
many possibilities

Quite simply, it is great fun to be able to realize your own designs out of fabric and thread, and to design and sew customized clothing! For that you need just a sewing machine, needles, thread, fabric, a few accessories, and good instructions—with those items in hand, your creativity will know no bounds.

SEWING MACHINE OVERVIEW

Not all sewing machines are created equal. These days a large selection of innovative sewing machines, embroidery machines, and other specialty sewing machines are available on the market, with varying features and capabilities. Take a look at all the currently available machines—you may not be familiar with all of them. Whether you are already a prolific sewer or just getting your feet wet, such a survey will help you determine which machine is the best fit for you and your needs.

1a

1b

2

3

5

6

7

1 MECHANICAL SEWING MACHINES

For occasional clothing repairs and to sew simple textile items for the home, a basic electric utility sewing machine will suffice. In addition to a straight stitch, it should be equipped with a zigzag stitch that is adjustable in length and width (1a). An elastic stitch, or stretch stitch, is helpful for sewing stretchy fabrics, as is a free arm for sewing sleeves and pant cuffs. A buttonhole function is essential. Occasionally these basic machines are also capable of a limited number of decorative stitches (1b).

----

2 COMPUTER-CONTROLLED SEWING MACHINES

Experienced sewers who frequently work with a machine and want to create decorative and creative projects, and who value helpful functionality, will find this type of machine a good fit. Via a touch screen, buttons, or knobs, you can select preprogrammed stitches, stitch modifications, automatic buttonholes, and much more.

----

3 EMBROIDERY MACHINES

One unusual specialty sewing machine is the computerized embroidery machine. These machines are computer controlled and have an additional module to create professional-looking embroidery patterns. Compact embroidery machines can embroider at commercial quality and are suited for samplers and swatches, one-of-a-kind designs, and small batches of items.

----

4 SERGERS/OVERLOCK MACHINES

A serger is a special machine that originated in the textile industry; it stitches, trims, and finishes seams in one pass. The seam finishing resembles that of ready-to-wear clothing.
Some sewing projects can be worked completely with a serger. But a serger does not replace a sewing machine; it's a supplement to it. A serger can't sew in a zipper or make buttonholes, but it is ideal for elastic materials. Its special carriage prevents seams from stretching as you stitch (see page 16).

----

5 QUILTING MACHINES

These machines are characterized by an especially generous opening for fabric pieces to pass through. Special preprogrammed quilting stitches and patchwork programs simplify the task. Some machines are equipped with a special attachment for a quilting frame, which makes it possible to quilt fabric pieces more than 3¼ yards (3 meters) wide.

----

6 FELTING MACHINES

A felting machine may look like a normal sewing machine, but it operates without a top or bottom thread. Instead, it's equipped with three, five, or twelve specialized felting needles that have tiny hooks and are grouped together in a holder. Depending on how firmly the foot pedal is depressed, the needles move faster or slower.
With a felting machine you can create textiles with structure. It can alter the color and form of fabric, work yarn and string into fabrics, shrink thin fabrics, and even create seams without thread. It is ideal for creating stylish accessories and clothing, and for felting home décor textiles.

----

7 SASHIKO MACHINES

These machines imitate the ancient Japanese technique of hand sewing with the sashiko stitch. A special thread-feeding system creates a sashiko stitch that looks like a handsewn running stitch where one stitch is skipped and the next one is worked double. Sashiko stitching is suitable for decorative work on clothing, home accessories, and quilts.

» The ABILITY TO MANUALLY ADJUST NEEDLE POSITIONS is extremely helpful, even on mechanical sewing machines.

! Computerized sewing machines provide the ability to COMBINE DECORATIVE STITCHES TO CREATE NEW PATTERNS or to use programmed alphabets to create SIGNATURES AND MONOGRAMS.

functions *of the* sewing machine

The basic functioning of all sewing machines is quite similar, but standard functions are located in different places on different models of machine. Your machine's user manual will tell you the locations of all your machine's functions.

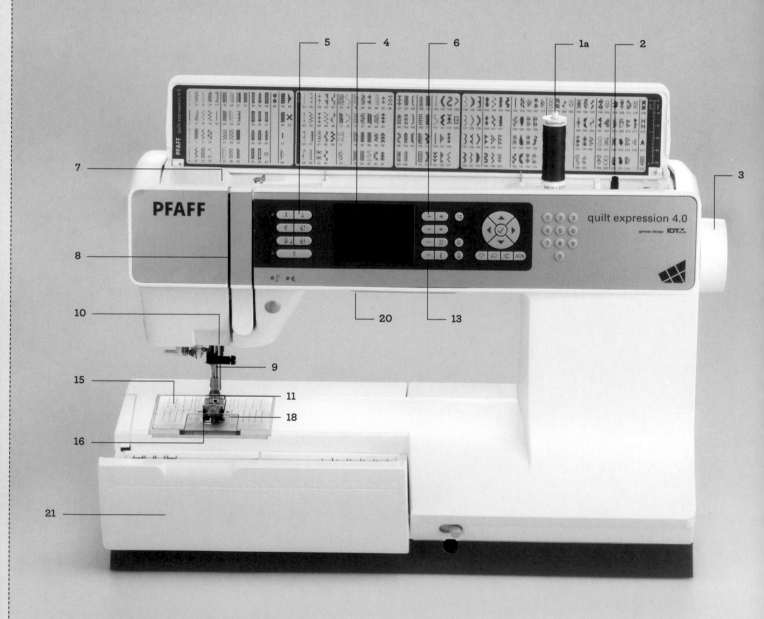

1 **SPOOL PINS** with spool caps *(see page 18, number 7)* guarantee smooth thread feeding and give the spool of thread itself a foothold. Many machines have both vertical (1a) and horizontal spool pins *(see page 14, number 1b)* that can be selectively engaged depending on the size of the spool, the way it is wrapped, and the sewing technique being used. The spool cap is pushed up against the spool on horizontal spool pins.
A machine that is outfitted with two spool pins enables the use of a twin needle for certain creative stitching techniques. There are also spool holder stands that can be set up next to a machine. They are used for large spools (cones) of thread that will not fit on a normal spool pin *(see page 19, number 5)*.

2 **THE BOBBIN WINDER**, as the name suggests, is for winding bobbins. Every machine will have a somewhat different mechanism, which will be explained in the user manual. The winder may be situated on the top, side, or front of the machine. Often the sewing mechanism must be shut off during bobbin winding and automatically reengages when the bobbin is removed.

3 **THE HANDWHEEL** is found on the right side of the machine. The main uses of the handwheel are to manually raise and lower the needle, to help coordinate the movement of fabric with the formation of stitches, and to enable precise placement of stitches on a piece of sewing.

4 **DISPLAY WITH SELECTION BUTTONS** is for utility and decorative stitches and various additional functions, such as buttonhole making, button attachment, et cetera.

5 **THE REVERSE/REINFORCEMENT STITCH BUTTON** is for sewing reverse stitches, usually to reinforce the ends of a seam.

6 **STITCH ADJUSTMENT BUTTONS** regulate stitch length and width. Newer machines have electronic keys or a touch screen display for making these selections.

7 **THE THREAD TAKE-UP LEVER** pulls the thread from the spool and is an important component when threading the machine. When the lever is lowered, as during stitching, the thread tension is taut. The lever must be in the completely raised position whenever you place or remove your piece of sewing.

8 **THE THREAD GUIDE** stabilizes the thread. The direction in which it is threaded is usually indicated on the housing of the machine.

9 **PRESSER FOOT HOLDER** with needle, needle threader, and thread cutter. The thread cutter may be found on the housing of some models.

10 **THE NEEDLE THREADER** helps to quickly and easily thread the needle.

11 **THE PRESSER FOOT,** when lowered, holds fabric flat during sewing. Presser feet typically have a clamp mechanism for attachment and removal.

12 **PRESSER FOOT LEVER** (on the back of the machine) is for raising and lowering the presser foot. Thread tension is activated when the lever is lowered.

13 **THREAD TENSION** is adjusted from the outside of the machine via a knob or button. On modern machines the tension may be adjusted via a display panel.

14 **PRESSER FOOT PRESSURE CONTROLLER** (not pictured) increases or decreases the pressure exerted by the presser foot on the fabric. If the fabric is not held tightly enough or is held too tightly by the presser foot, the pressure must be increased or decreased to achieve proper stitching.

15 **NEEDLE PLATE** has grooved seam guides and an opening for the feed dogs to help move the fabric during sewing. There are straight-stitch needle plates with round openings that can be used only for straight stitching. The opening is small and circular and guarantees precise stitch formation so that fabric cannot easily be caught and pulled down through the needle plate into the bobbin holder—particularly advantageous when working with lighter-weight fabrics. Some machines have a transparent needle plate, allowing you to monitor the need for a fresh bobbin.

16 **FEED DOGS** move the fabric underneath the presser foot during sewing as you provide gentle guidance. They regulate stitch length via the amount of fabric allowed to pass under the presser foot during sewing. The feed dogs can be lowered to allow free movement of the fabric in any direction, which is essential when doing freehand sewing or appliqué.

! OLDER MACHINES have a SMALLER, INTERNAL WHEEL on the handwheel (3) that can be loosened to disengage the needle mechanism of the machine while winding bobbins.

! ON MANY SEWING MACHINES the decorative stitches will be PRINTED ON THE HOUSING OR COVER OF THE MACHINE and executed via a selection knob or selection buttons rather than with direct push buttons.

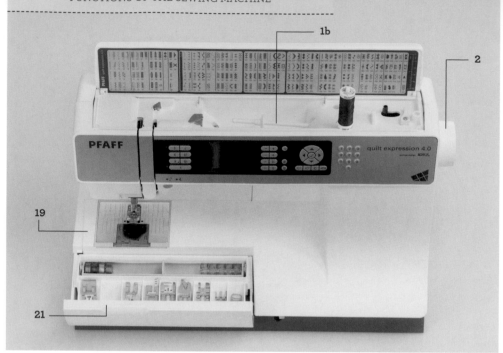

17 **AN INTEGRATED WALKING FOOT** (not pictured) ensures precise fabric motion, **evenly feeding the fabric from both the top and the bottom** so the fabric layers cannot shift. This feature can be deactivated.

18 **BOBBIN CASE** is used with bobbins that sit under the slide plate. There are some machines that operate without a bobbin case; the bobbin is **dropped from above** into the holder, which has a transparent cover.

! FOR SAFETY REASONS, use only the **POWER CORD THAT WAS SUPPLIED WITH YOUR MACHINE.**

19 **A FREE ARM** allows for problem-free sewing of tube-shaped pieces (such as pant legs, sleeves, cuffs, and neck openings). On most machines you must **remove the accessory case (21)** to utilize the free arm.

20 **A SEWING LIGHT** illuminates your work space; there are also user-adjustable LEDs available for this purpose. LED lights are shadow free, and their intensity and color are adjustable according to your fabric and the amount of ambient light.

21 **ACCESSORY CASE** is for bobbins, extra presser feet, cleaning brush, machine oil, et cetera.

22 **THE MOTOR** is built into the machine and therefore not visible. On old machines you may see motors that are attached to the outside housing.

23 **A FOOT PEDAL** regulates the speed of sewing. Usually foot pedals are placed on the floor. The farther the pedal is depressed, the faster the machine will sew.

24 **A KNEE LEVER** may replace the foot pedal, depending on manufacturer, and serves the same function. New machines can also be stopped and started with the push of a button, with the speed regulated directly on the machine. This allows people with certain disabilities to use a sewing machine more easily.

25 **AN ELECTRICAL CABLE** supplies power. Use only the cord that was provided with your machine.

MACHINE CARE AND MAINTENANCE

Regular cleaning, care, and servicing of your machine will extend its life span and proper functioning. Frequently, skipped stitches or looped stitches are caused by pieces of thread under the feed dogs or in between the tension discs.

OIL REGULARLY

Sewing machine oil is specific to sewing machines and the only kind of oil you should use on your machine; other oils will gum up over time. You can purchase sewing machine oil at your local sewing store or online. Your machine's user manual will provide specific instructions as to the points where oil should be applied to your machine.

REMOVE DUST AND LINT

Dust and lint from fabric and thread are generated while sewing and collect inside the machine. Regularly removing dust and lint from the bobbin area, underneath the needle plate, inside the bobbin case, the feed dogs, and in between the tension discs will help prevent thread breakage, broken needles, and defective seams.

- Use a small, soft brush to remove dust and lint from in between the tension discs.
- Remove the needle plate in order to clean the feed dogs and bobbin case.
- Occasionally wipe the machine housing with a damp cloth; do not use harsh cleaning products.
- Remove bits of adhesive from thread spools from the spool pin.
- Keep the ventilation slits for the motor free from dust, to ensure uninterrupted airflow and prevent the motor from overheating.

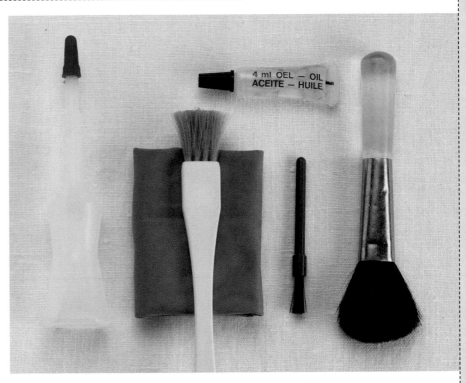

YOUR USER MANUAL

It is important to become familiar with your machine's user manual in order to get to know and understand your machine and its capabilities. You will find advice about caring for your machine, troubleshooting tips, a list of available accessories and their uses, as well as everything about your machine's available stitches and how to adjust them.

Beyond that, you should be able to correctly name the various parts of your sewing machine so that you will fully understand troubleshooting advice you may receive—whether over the phone, via e-mail, or on the Internet. You'll need to be certain of which part is being referenced and what its function is.

! IT IS BEST to get in the habit of cleaning your machine AFTER EVERY SEWING PROJECT.

! BEFORE CLEANING AND OILING, unplug the power cord!

» Clean the sewing machine housing and displays with a damp MICROFIBER CLOTH.

! REGULAR OILING will help prevent labored, noisy, and irregular sewing.

! THE NEWEST MACHINES typically don't require oiling. Refer to the user manual for your particular machine for more information.

» AFTER OILING, place a scrap of cloth on the machine without any thread, needle, needle plate, presser foot, or bobbin and "sew" a few stitches to catch any EXCESS OIL and any dust and thread remnants that may have been left by a previous project.

professional finishing

For professional finishing, a serger (also called an overlock or coverlock machine) comes into play. The seam finishing on these machines rivals that on commercially produced items. A serger is the perfect supplement to a standard machine. And anyone who works frequently with knitted and jersey fabrics will love these machines.

SERGER FEATURES

Depending on the model, sergers use a number of looper threads and needle threads: 4-thread serger seams have two looper and two needle threads, while 5-thread serger seams are worked with three looper and two needle threads. The machines are equipped with upper and lower cutting knives that trim away fabric edges as you stitch. Seams worked on a serger have cleanly trimmed and finished edges that look professional. Coverstitch machines can sew 2- or 3-needle topstitched seams as well as chain stitching; they do not sew serged seams. Combination machines, called coverlocks, can sew both serged and topstitched seams.

! SPECIAL ACCESSORIES AND PRESSER FEET. Sergers, like sewing machines, have a wide spectrum of specialized accessories and presser feet. Advice about which ones to choose can be found in the user manual for a given machine.

! OVERLOCK THREAD is sold on cones of 1,000–5,500 yards (approximately 1,000–5,000 meters), because sergers require more thread than standard sewing machines.

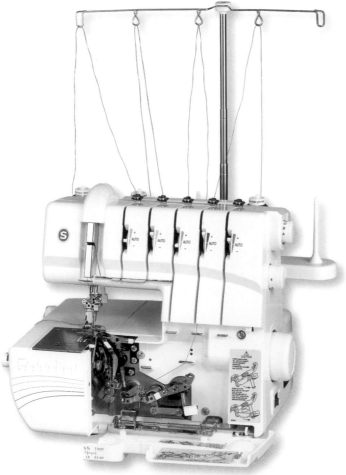

SERGERS

This machine's specialty is doing everything at once. With every stitch, a serger handles **multiple tasks simultaneously:** it sews two fabric pieces together, cuts off the excess fabric, and clean finishes the edges. Some sergers can even create a hem at the same time. Serger seams are extremely durable and flexible. Sheer, light, or stretchy materials are easy to work on a serger thanks to its **even fabric feeding.** Even thin, delicate fabrics such as chiffon can be sewn and finished without a problem.

SERGER FUNCTIONALITY

Standard serger features are positioned differently depending on the serger model. Check your user manual for the location of yours. But the **mechanics of every serger** are fundamentally the same.

COVERSTITCH MACHINES

These machines, in contrast to sergers, can sew 2- and 3-needle topstitched seams in varying widths but cannot sew serged seams. They can also create chainstitching.

COVERLOCK MACHINES

A coverlock is a combination of a serger and a coverstitch machine. While a coverlock is space saving (you need one machine, not two), it does have to be converted when used for topstitching. (On newer models this conversion is quite simple.)
A coverlock machine can work both a topstitched seam and chainstitching. A topstitched seam works as an elastic seam finish on T-shirts, sweatshirts, and sportswear. Chainstitching, which is part of 4- and 5-needle safety-stitched seams, can also serve as a seam closure. The stitch is attractive on both sides of the fabric and works very well as a decorative stitch.

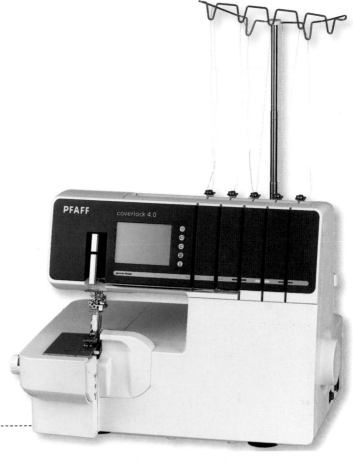

TYPICAL SEAMS

Typical seams on sergers and coverlock machines are 4- or 5-thread safety-stitched seams, 3- and 4-thread overcast seams, 4-thread assembly seams, 2- and 3-thread rolled hems, and flatlock seams, plus topstitching and chainstitching.

THE 3- AND 4-THREAD SERGED SEAM

This is a safety-stitched seam used for the simultaneous sewing together and finishing of regular and lightly stretchy fabrics, as well as for superfine weaves, such as organza.

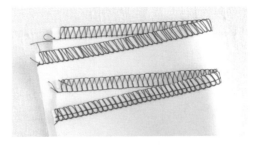

TOPSTITCHING

You will find this professional seam finish on T-shirts, sweatshirts, and all types of elastic fabrics.

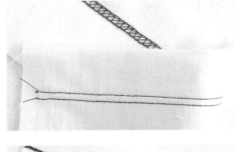

CHAINSTITCHING

Well suited for **sewing hems,** this can also be used as a decorative stitch. Chainstitching is attractive on both sides of the fabric.

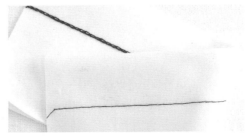

! CREATE A DECORATIVE CHAINSTITCH by using a specialty thread in the looper.

sewing machine accessories

In addition to the standard accessories—including numerous basic presser feet—that come with a sewing machine, there are myriad special accessories and specialized presser feet that can greatly increase the capabilities of a machine. Many styling techniques and creative touches are possible only with specialized accessories.

STANDARD SEWING ACCESSORIES

>> WHEN PURCHASING a sewing machine, try to get one with the most **COMPREHENSIVE SET OF STANDARD ACCESSORIES** possible, as additional accessories add additional cost.

All the items on the following illustrated list of standard accessories are easily obtainable for any sewing machine. Many machines include these basic accessories with the machine at purchase.

1 **NEEDLE SET** with sewing machine needles in various sizes and needle points for various types of fabric.

2 **SPOOL PINS** for attaching spools of thread.

3 **SCREWDRIVER**

4 **SEWING MACHINE OIL** for care of the machine.

5 **CLEANING BRUSH** for removal of dust and thread clippings from the machine.

6 **SEAM RIPPER** *(see page 31, number 4)*, used to undo stitches and seams.

7 **SPOOL CAPS** to secure spools of thread. These allow for a **smooth spooling of the thread** during sewing.

8 **UNIVERSAL TOOL AND PRESSER FOOT HEIGHT EQUALIZER** for sewing fabrics with **varying thickness**, as on a jeans seam where the fabric is folded on itself multiple times and **the presser foot must sew at different "heights."** A height equalizer **supports the presser foot and allows for an even feeding of fabric** and the achievement of the proper seam. It can also be helpful for **sewing on buttons with shanks.**

9 **BULB-CHANGING TOOL** for changing the machine's lightbulb(s).

10 **STANDARD PRESSER FEET** *(see page 20).*

11 **BOBBINS** hold and unwind the lower thread. They may be made of **metal or plastic** and come in varying sizes.

12 **USER MANUAL** illustrates and explains **the functionality of the machine.** Some also offer sewing tips and troubleshooting advice.

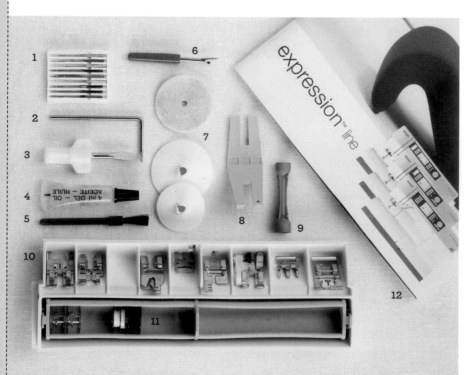

SPECIALIZED SEWING ACCESSORIES

Specialized accessories for sewing machines make sewing more pleasant, make certain sewing projects easier, and even make some possible to do at all. You can find **information about specialty accessories** on the Internet, in sewing magazines, at sewing conventions, or at your local sewing store.

1 **AN EXTENSION TABLE** increases your work space and provides **extra room when sewing** large projects, such as quilts, curtains, bed linens, blankets, and tablecloths. **Printed inch and centimeter markings** on many extensions make it easier to sew accurately.

2 **A STRAIGHT STITCH PLATE** ensures smooth feeding of fabric at the beginnings and ends of seams, without the risk that the fabric will get pulled into the needle plate. This is **especially advantageous when working with thin, fine, or delicate fabrics.** When using the straight stitch plate, set the needle position to the center to avoid damaging the needle, the presser foot, and the needle plate. A straight stitch needle plate used in combination with a straight stitch presser foot is **ideal for quilting and patchwork sewing.**

3 **SPECIALTY BOBBIN CASE** is for working with bulky ornamental threads.

4 **BOBBIN RING**, made from silicone, is for storing threaded bobbins without the bothersome unwinding of the threads.

5 **A SPOOL HOLDER** sits on top of the machine and has pegs for up to eight spools of thread. The pegs are numbered to simplify **thread changes.**

6 **SEWING MACHINE BAG/CADDY** (not pictured) is for the easy and comfortable **transporting of your machine** to sewing and quilting classes, to service appointments, or in and out of storage.

! DECORATIVE, ORNAMENTAL, AND BULKY THREADS often won't fit through the eye of a sewing machine needle. But they can be HAND WOUND ONTO THE BOBBIN, which in turn is placed in a special bobbin case. Regular sewing thread is used as the top thread. You then stitch with the wrong side facing up, so that the ORNAMENTAL STITCHING IS VISIBLE ON THE RIGHT SIDE OF THE FABRIC.

» TO ACHIEVE EVEN MOVEMENT OF YOUR FABRIC when sewing multiple layers together, the stitch length must be increased.

» TO PREVENT BOBBINS FROM SLIDING OUT OF A SILICONE RING, the ring can be reshaped to the bobbin's width by dipping it in boiling water for about 20 seconds. Remove the ring from the water, SQUEEZE THE SIDES TOGETHER TO EQUAL THE BOBBIN WIDTH, then allow the ring to cool in cold water.

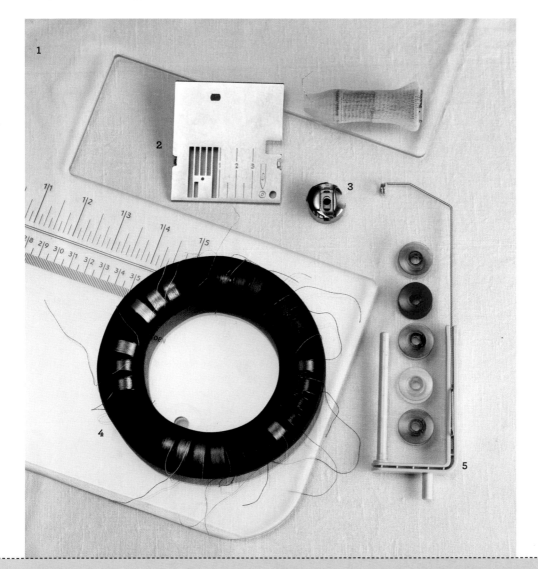

BASIC PRESSER FEET

All sewing machines are equipped with a basic set of presser feet that are crucial for performing fundamental sewing tasks such as seaming, hemming, and stitching buttonholes or zippers.

! THE BLIND STITCH FOOT can be used as an OVERCAST FOOT for serger-like seaming. When using the blind stitch foot, position the peg of the foot along the edge of the fabric to prevent puckering.

! PERFECT SEAMING is guaranteed by a combination of a STRAIGHT STITCH FOOT WITH A ROUND OPENING TOGETHER WITH A STRAIGHT STITCH NEEDLE PLATE, and also facilitates sewing along edges (TOPSTITCHING) as well as quilting and patchwork sewing.

» The rolled hem foot helps you stitch a perfect, narrow rolled hem and is also useful FOR DECORATIVE AND CREATIVE STITCHING.

» Use the ZIGZAG STITCH FOR NARROW SEAMS on thin or stretchy fabrics. The seam will lie better than it would if sewn with a straight stitch.

! FOR IMPROVED FEEDING OF FABRIC at the start of a hem, place tearaway or dissolving stabilizer underneath the fabric. Use a 2mm rolled hem foot for lightweight fabrics and a 3mm to 6mm rolled hem foot for midweight fabrics.

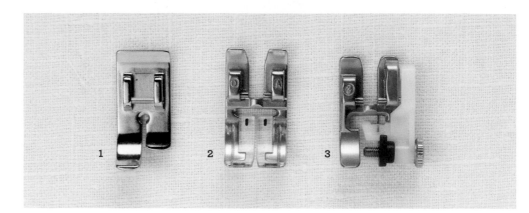

1 STRAIGHT STITCH FOOT with round opening is for sewing simple straight stitches and is ideal for quilting and patchwork. Using this foot in combination with a straight stitch needle plate with a small, round opening in its center ensures a perfect line of stitching, as when topstitching edges. The foot has a smooth underside that provides even pressure against the feed dogs, so it feeds the fabric evenly.

2 ZIGZAG FOOT, or standard foot, is the most commonly used presser foot for general sewing and is sometimes referred to as an all-purpose foot. It can be used for all kinds of stitches, including decorative stitching, and works with the majority of fabrics. It may be made of metal or plastic and has a large, centrally placed oval opening, so that the needle can be used in any position. The zigzag foot is appropriate for use with twin and triple needles.

3 BLIND STITCH FOOT is for sewing invisible seam finishes. The guide edge on the foot allows you to maintain a consistent distance from the fabric edge, and accommodates narrow spaces when sewing along edges. It is also suitable for sewing and finishing stretchy fabrics. The stitches are formed over the peg on the inner edge, allowing each stitch to receive additional thread.

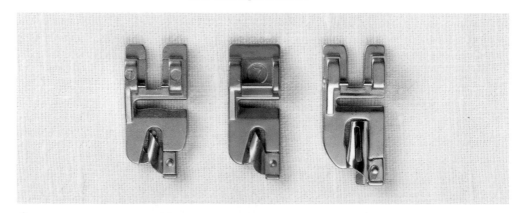

4 ROLLED HEM FOOT—also called a hemming foot—is used for hemming light- to medium-weight fabrics without having to iron or baste the entire hem. It comes in different inch and millimeter sizes for hem widths of ⅛", ³⁄₁₆", ¼", ⅜", ⅝", ⅞", 2mm, 3mm, 4mm, and 6mm. It has a twisted, snail-shaped opening into which the fabric is guided as you stitch.

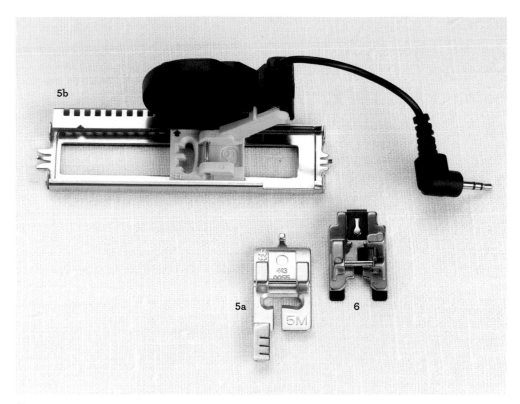

5 **BUTTONHOLE FEET** come in many types. Depending on the machine and model, there are different styles for all the various ways of fashioning buttonholes: standard buttonhole feet (5a), feet with integrated rulers (not pictured), feet where the buttons are placed inside to determine the length of the hole (not pictured), and feet with a cable that attaches to the machine that electronically conveys information about the predetermined buttonhole length (5b).

6 **BUTTON ATTACHMENT FOOT** offers the trouble-free attachment of two- or four-hole buttons of varying sizes. The foot clamps the button between a metal shaft and the foot itself and holds it in the desired position. When the shaft is removed, shank buttons can also be sewn.

7 **ZIPPER FOOT** is primarily for sewing in zippers. It can be set into the presser foot holder in either left or right position to allow you to sew closely along each side of the zipper teeth. Zipper feet can look very different from each other, depending on the manufacturer.

8 **ZIPPER FOOT for invisible zippers** allows you to insert invisible zippers within a seam so that the zipper is undetectable from the outside; it looks like a regular seam. The zipper is sewn onto the seam allowance, not through the seam allowance and outer fabric. When purchasing the zipper, be sure to choose one that is designated as an invisible zipper.

>> FOR OPTIMAL BUTTONHOLES, add ⅛" (3mm) to the button measurement. FOR A SPECIAL DESIGN FEATURE, stitch your buttonholes with contrasting thread.

>> TO CREATE SLIGHTLY RAISED BUTTONHOLES, use buttonhole twist thread.

>> BUTTONS CAN BE SEWN ON WITHOUT USING A PRESSER FOOT, but the presser foot holder must be in the lowered position. To ACTIVATE THREAD TENSION, lower the feed dogs, SET THE STITCH LENGTH TO 0, and adjust the zigzag width to match the width between the holes in the button. To finish, pull the starting and ending threads to the underside of the item and knot them.

! HOOKS, EYES, AND SNAPS can also be sewn on using a buttonhole foot.

! INVISIBLE ZIPPERS have their teeth on the back (under) side of the zipper. They are sewn onto THE SEAM ALLOWANCES ONLY, so that no stitching is visible from the front.

>> A BUTTONHOLE FOOT is also well suited for sewing CORDING OR PIPING, as well as for attaching beaded strips or decorative braids with thicker edges.

SPECIALIZED PRESSER FEET

In addition to basic presser feet, sewing machine manufacturers offer a number of feet designed for special sewing techniques. These feet simplify your work by creating pleats, sewing within seams, sewing and topstitching at precise angles, sewing with difficult materials such as leather or tarpaulin, creating borders, or creating cording and piping. These feet must be **compatible** with your machine's model and can be purchased from the manufacturer.

1

2

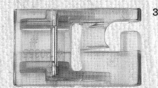

3

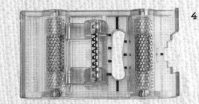

4

! Transparent BOXES DESIGNED FOR STORING HARDWARE SCREWS are perfect for organizing presser feet.

» A ROLLER FOOT in combination with decorative thread *(see page 43)* can generate lovely results on leather and vinyl.

1 **EDGE STITCH FOOT** simplifies sewing along narrow edges, such as when working on pockets, collars, and cuffs. The foot makes techniques like stitching in the ditch and joining abutted fabric pieces simple and straightforward.

2 **BORDER GUIDE FOOT** is for applying decorative trims on clothing, lingerie, and home décor pieces. This foot allows you to sew the main fabric and a decorative fabric (such as tulle, lace, or a ruffle) in one pass.

3 **FELLING FOOT** (also known as a LAP SEAM FOOT) is for sewing especially durable flat felled seams such as those found on jeans. The foot has a deep groove on the underside and a lip on the top, which folds over the protruding fabric so that it can be stitched down. Felling feet are available in two widths (equaling the finished seam width), 4mm and 6mm. Some machines accommodate an 8mm felling foot that can sew an 8mm-wide flat felled seam in two steps. Using contrasting thread can achieve decorative effects.

4 **ROLLER FOOT** with two metal (or plastic) rollers is for handling difficult materials such as leather, faux leather, vinyl, and plastic sheeting. Heavy woolen fabrics, such as boiled wool (walk) or loden cloth, can also be worked perfectly with this foot.

5 **BINDER FOOT** is for the quick and easy finishing of fabric edges. This specialty foot simultaneously folds a binding strip and attaches it to the fabric edge. It has a channel on the top into which the unfolded binding fabric is fed.

5

6 **SHIRRING FOOT** is designed specifically to create ruffles on pillows and drapes or for shirred stitching (false smocking) on children's clothing. It is available in metal and plastic. Using this foot, you can simultaneously shirr fabric while attaching it to another piece of fabric.

6

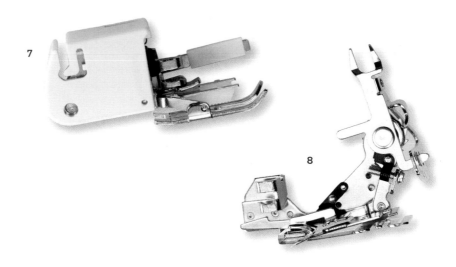

7 **WALKING FOOT** is for machines that do not have an integrated version. A walking foot is larger than, and looks quite different from, a typical presser foot, but it's attached to the machine in the same manner. It holds and evenly feeds multiple layers of fabric, preventing them from shifting or pulling out of shape as you sew. This foot is especially useful when **sewing together fabrics of different types and weights,** such as silk charmeuse and felted wool.

The walking foot is very helpful for **quilting,** as it holds together the quilt layers and keeps them aligned while sewing. **Straight stitching, wavy stitching, ornamental stitching, and stitching in the ditch** are all made easier using this foot, because its large opening offers a clear view as you sew.

A walking foot is also very well suited to sewing **stretch and jersey fabrics** in combination with a twin needle and topstitching. An optional ruler grid can be attached to the foot to help you maintain even distances between stitching lines.

8 **RUFFLER** is for creating **evenly spaced pleats.** It can be set to one, six, or twelve pleats and can also establish the depth of the pleats. It simultaneously creates pleats while sewing one piece of fabric onto another.

9 **ELASTIC FOOT** is for simultaneously guiding, stretching, and attaching **various types of elastic.** It has an adjustable peg (or screw) on the top and a channel for the elastic band.

10 **CORDING/DOUBLE-CORD FOOT** is for sewing cording. Cording is frequently used as a border treatment or embellishment on home décor items such as pillows and cushions. The cording foot (10b) is used for simple cording and the double-cord foot (10a) for double-cord welting.

11 **PIPING FOOT** is for sewing piping. Piping feet look like cording feet and are used similarly, but are significantly thinner and more delicate and are used for **decorative touches** on pant and jacket pockets, collars, cuffs, and seams. You can also sew **ready-made piping** with this foot.

» A ruffler is a real **TIME SAVER** because it takes care of the marking, dividing, and measuring of pleats for you. At the medium pleat setting 6 (one pleat every six stitches), you will **NEED DOUBLE THE FABRIC LENGTH** of the desired finished size.

! Piping and cording can also be attached using a **ZIPPER FOOT.**

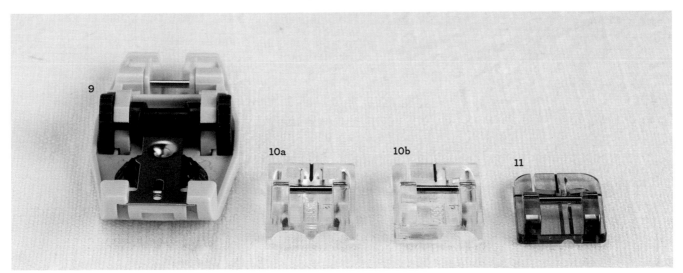

PRESSER FEET FOR CREATIVE SEWING

In addition to basic and specialty presser feet, there are feet designed for creative techniques such as appliqué, freehand stitching, sewing braid and fringe, and much more. These **unusual feet** can be used to embellish fabrics with beads, sequins, ribbon, or string.

>> LOTS OF INSPIRATION AND IDEAS for creative sewing can be found in MAGAZINES AND BOOKS, ON THE INTERNET, or at your local sewing shop.

>> Use DOUBLE-SIDED ADHESIVE STABILIZER to attach APPLIQUÉS. This helps prevent the appliqué from shifting during sewing.

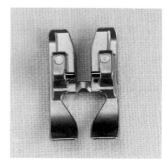

1 SATIN STITCH FOOT is made of plastic or metal and offers a clear view of your stitching. Its markings allow for **precise sewing and appliquéing**, using the satin stitch or other ornamental stitches along edges or following guidelines. Satin stitches pass easily through the groove on the underside of the foot.

2 APPLIQUÉ FOOT, on account of its small size, is very good for satin stitching in **tightly spaced rows or around curves.** The groove on its underside provides space for thicker satin stitching, and its **transparency allows for precise stitching along** the edges of appliqués.

3 CANDLEWICKING FOOT is for sewing pre-marked **motifs or monograms** with a candlewicking embroidery stitch. It has a deep groove on the underside to allow better passage of bulky stitches.

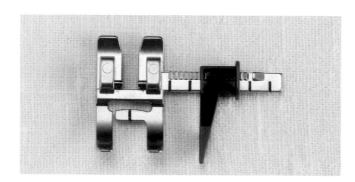

4 SEAM GUIDE FOOT has an adjustable ruler that can be placed along any guideline in order to keep a **consistent distance between seam lines.** The guide can be aligned with the fabric edge or a seam to create a perfectly straight topstitched seam. This foot is suitable for straight stitching as well as decorative stitching and is ideal for **sewing parallel lines.**

5 BI-LEVEL FOOT ensures the even feeding of fabric when **topstitching over uneven fabric thicknesses** and when sewing borders with multiple layers.

6 NONSTICK FOOT has a special coating on the underside for sewing "sticky" materials such as leather, vinyl, and coated fabrics.

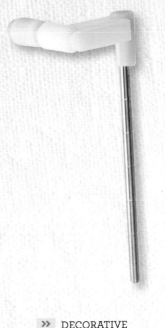

7 RIBBON FOOT is used for flat ribbons, string, novelty yarns, embroidery thread, and so on, which are threaded through the channels and/or holes in the foot. Ribbon feet allow you to create lovely decorative features.

8 SEWING STAR FOOT is for wide decorative stitches; it minimizes puckering during stitching.

9 BEADING FOOT is for attaching strings of beads, sequins, lacing, and cording.

10 EMBROIDERY/DARNING FOOT is for freehand sewing and embroidery, usually in conjunction with an embroidery hoop to hold fabric taut.

11 OPEN FREEHAND FOOT/OPEN TOE WALKING FOOT, with its extra-large opening, offers an optimal view during freehand sewing, embroidery, and quilting (11a).

12 CIRCULAR FOOT (not pictured) is for sewing decorative stitches in a circular pattern. Different manufacturers offer various types of circular feet. Before sewing, the fabric must be pulled taut in an embroidery hoop and reinforced with fusible interfacing.

》 DECORATIVE RIBBON will stand out better from the background material if it is sewn with thread that matches the ribbon. Use transparent thread along seams and borders.

! Thread ribbons, yarns, et cetera through the ribbon foot **BEFORE ATTACHING IT TO THE MACHINE.** A needle threader can be useful here.

! **STRING BEADS BEFORE SEWING** and coordinate the bead size with your fabric type. Thinner fabric works best with smaller beads, while heavy fabric can support larger ones.

! **DARNING** should always be done using an embroidery hoop; place the damaged area **WITHIN THE HOOP AND PULL IT TAUT.**

》 Use a beading foot or ribbon foot in combination with a circular foot. At the start and end of the circle, **LEAVE LONG HANGING THREADS,** pull them to the wrong side of the fabric, and tie in a knot.

7

7

7

8

9

9

11

10

11a

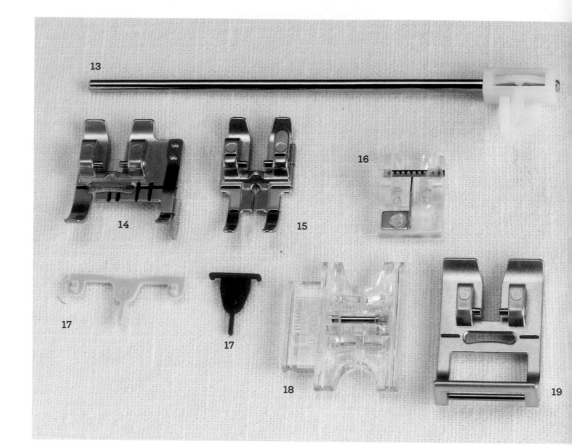

! SOME QUILTING SEAM GUIDES can be attached only on the right side of the presser foot.

» A SEAM GUIDE FOOT eliminates the need for time-consuming marking of stitching lines and seam allowances. The metal runner is ⅝" (1.5cm) away from the central needle position.

! TO CREATE LOOSE STITCHES, decrease the tension on the upper thread and stabilize the fabric with tearaway or dissolvable stabilizer.

» FRINGE MAKES A PRETTY BORDER for pocket openings when contrasting or variegated thread is used.

! MAKE PINTUCKS BEFORE CUTTING THE FABRIC, since this will reduce the width of your piece as you sew. Plan to use about 2⅜" (6cm) of fabric for each pintuck; this will vary based on the fabric type. You can thread thin cording or crochet yarn through the needle plate or use a separate cording guide IN PLACE OF A CORDING TONGUE.

» PINTUCKS MADE FROM LIGHTWEIGHT FABRIC can be sewn with a double needle with up to ¹⁄₁₆" (2mm) of separation between pintucks; medium-weight fabrics can have up to ³⁄₁₆" (4mm) of separation.

» FOR SEWING FABRIC STRIPS with a chenille foot, select a straight stitch length of approx. ⅛" (3–3.5mm). You may want to reduce the presser foot pressure.

! Use a chenille foot to apply decorative ribbons or to EMBELLISH SIMPLE COTTON TAPE WITH EMBROIDERY STITCHES.

13 QUILTING SEAM GUIDE is particularly helpful for sewing straight stitching or quilting lines. The marked quilting guide can be mounted to the left or right of the presser foot.

14 SEAM GUIDE FOOT keeps seams at a consistent width with the help of a metal guide built into the foot. It is marked, in inches and/or mm, for a range of seam sizes.

15 QUILTING OR PATCHWORK FOOT with inch markings (here ¼") is very helpful for quilting and patchwork, because it allows you to always stitch at precisely the same distance from the fabric edge or from a seam.

16 FRINGE/LOOPING FOOT has a metal bar down the center over which a zigzag stitch is formed. The resulting stitches are very loose on the right side of the fabric. This foot can be used for embellishing terrycloth or velvet. When snipped, the loops can become a fringed border trim. It can be used to mark sewing and cutting lines, eliminating the need to do so by hand.

17 CORDING TONGUE, which is attached to the needle plate, makes pintucks even more three-dimensional.

18 PINTUCK FOOT makes pintucks, the narrow, raised ridges sewn with double needles and commonly found on blouses, dresses, and bed linens. The grooves on the bottom of the pintuck foot allow you to create tight groupings of multiple pintucks. There are pintuck feet with three, five, and seven grooves and feet with spacing between the grooves to allow for subsequent decorative embroidery.

19 CHENILLE FOOT with a large opening allows up to eight strips of bias-cut fabric to pass through at once. These multiple layers of bias-cut strips sewn onto the main fabric will, after washing and drying, create a soft, velvety effect known as chenille.

CONSIDERATIONS FOR PURCHASE

Before purchasing a sewing machine, think carefully about the purposes for which you will be using it. Will straight and zigzag stitching suffice? Should it be capable of small decorative stitches or able to sew motifs? Will it be used by a beginner or by an experienced hobbyist? Or will it be used most often for quilting?

» If you enjoy sewing and plan to do a lot of it, DON'T PURCHASE THE SIMPLEST MACHINE AVAILABLE. You will very QUICKLY PUSH THE BOUNDARIES OF THE BASIC MACHINE'S CAPABILITIES.

! Before buying a machine, consider where you will set up your SEWING AREA. Your SPACE CONSTRAINTS may affect your choice of machine.

WHICH SEWING MACHINE FOR WHOM?

For **beginners,** an electric free arm machine with utility stitches is most suitable. In addition to a **straight stitch,** it should also be capable of making **zigzag stitches** that are adjustable in length and width. It is also an advantage to have an **elastic or stretch stitch** capability. An **adjustable needle position** and a buttonhole function (one- or four-step buttonholes) are helpful. A straight stitch foot *(see page 20),* zipper foot *(see page 21),* and buttonhole foot *(see page 21)* should be among the standard accessories. The ability to **lower the feed dogs** allows for freehand embroidery and creative sewing.

For **experienced sewers** and accomplished hobbyists, there are a multitude of computer-driven machines with myriad functions, such as creating automatic buttonholes, fastening off and trimming threads, needle stop, **programmed utility and decorative stitches,** tapering for perfect corners, the ability to create your own embroidery and stitch combinations, integrated walking feet, adjustable work lights, and much more. The **sewing comfort level** of these machines is high and, of course, comes at a price.

CONSIDERATIONS BEFORE PURCHASE

If one is located nearby, there are many advantages to having a local **sewing machine dealer** to advise you on your purchase, provide instructions, take care of any eventual repairs, and offer supplemental or replacement parts.
When purchasing a machine **online,** especially from discounters, you should inquire as to any available customer service and whether **replacement parts and a warranty** are offered.

It's often a good idea to buy a **machine directly from a specialized dealer, which is the only way** you can try out a machine in person!

Test all of the functions on your desired machine at the dealership. See how it sews on difficult fabrics and pay attention to its **ease of operation and handling**—things such as simple threading and simple stitch selection and adjustment. Does the presser foot lift high enough to allow for thicker fabrics to pass without a problem between the foot and the needle plate? Can the needle position be adjusted? Can presser feet and needles be easily swapped out? Does it come with supplemental presser feet? The functional value of even a very basic machine can be increased by its having these features. The size and weight of a machine are also important considerations if you frequently attend sewing groups and carry your machine with you.

sewing equipment

HAVING THE RIGHT EQUIPMENT PLAYS A BIG ROLE IN SUCCESSFUL SEWING. IN THIS CHAPTER YOU'LL GET THE BROAD PICTURE OF THE WIDE RANGE OF TOOLS AVAILABLE, GOING FAR BEYOND JUST SCISSORS, NEEDLES, AND THREAD. A BASIC SET OF SEWING SUPPLIES WILL INCLUDE THE ESSENTIALS, BUT SPECIAL AND SUPPLEMENTAL TOOLS OFFER A BIT OF LUXURY TO TOP IT OFF, AND MAKE SEWING EVEN MORE FUN.

essential
equipment

In order for sewing to be truly enjoyable and productive, equipment such as scissors, rulers, et cetera should be of high quality. Skillful, accurate sewing can be undermined if your thread is continually breaking. And while most households certainly contain one or another tool that can be used for sewing—such as kitchen scissors or straight pins left over from some packaging—these items won't really contribute to the successful completion of sewing projects.

>> SCISSORS WITH BLADES THAT ARE SCREWED TOGETHER will cut through thick and multi-layered fabrics better than scissors that are only riveted. With an ADJUSTING NUT you can tune the blade pressure to your fabrics.

TAILOR'S TOOLS

A pair of scissors is your most important piece of equipment when sewing. They should be sharp and cut along the entirety of their blades. Scissors come in varying sizes, shapes, and materials. There are **steel scissors and scissors made of aluminum alloy**. Steel scissors are heavier than aluminum scissors and can cut through multiple layers of fabric without a problem, and they can be sharpened. That said, they are more expensive than aluminum scissors. In the following pages you'll find scissors and other cutting tools of various types and sizes. They are designed for specific tasks and can very much lighten your workload.

1 **THREAD SCISSORS/EMBROIDERY SCISSORS** have short, pointed blades and are handy and ideal for smaller cutting jobs, such as **trimming corners, clipping or notching curves, and trimming thread ends.** We recommend you keep a pair next to your sewing machine.

2 **PAPER SCISSORS** are for cutting paper patterns and templates. Don't use fabric scissors to cut paper; it will dull the blades for fabric.

3 **FABRIC SHEARS** are asymmetrical, so that the lower blade rests flat on the cutting surface when in use; this way the fabric is not lifted and the **cutting line stays straight and precise.** They are assembled and sharpened so that fabric will not get crimped in the blades.
Fabric shears may have plastic-covered grips, with a smaller "eye" for the thumb and a larger opening for the remaining fingers. They are available for both **right- and left-handed users.**

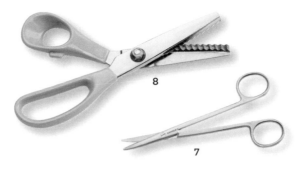

8

7

4 SEAM RIPPERS are useful for opening up seams and cutting buttonholes. The blade with its tiny hook quickly rips open seams and the fabric inside the buttonhole. When removing stitching, the hook lifts each stitch so it is easy to slice through. The (usually colored) ballpoint tip on the hook guards against inadvertent damage to fabric.

5 CUTTING SHEARS are heavier than fabric shears and are good for **cutting heavy or multilayered fabrics.**

6 TWEEZER SCISSORS have a spring mechanism and are either flat or curved upward. Use these to snip threads very close to the fabric and keep seams looking clean and tidy.

7 APPLIQUÉ SCISSORS have **curved blades** that can easily trim off excess fabric from around appliqués.

8 PINKING SHEARS are suitable for cutting seams and hemlines on fabric that does not fray easily, such as woolens and lining fabrics. **Edges cut with pinking shears do not require further finishing.** Pinking shears are also ideal for cutting felt and thin leather. The resulting jagged edge provides an additional **decorative element.**

❗ USE FABRIC SHEARS exclusively for cutting fabric—**NOT EVEN FOR THREAD**—because other materials such as paper or cardboard will **DULL THE BLADES.** The cut edges of your fabric will then start to look ragged.

» You should keep a pair of embroidery scissors or thread snippers **NEXT TO THE SEWING MACHINE. TWEEZER SCISSORS** are well suited for cutting threads when doing machine embroidery.

» **FABRICS ARE EASIER** to cut with a circle cutter when they have **TEAR-AWAY STABILIZER** ironed onto the back. Stabilizers can be ironed on and reused several times.

9 CHENILLE CUTTERS, similar to rotary cutters, have four differently sized channel guides to allow for the **precise cutting of varying widths of strips** *(see page 125).*

10 ROTARY CUTTERS are available in various sizes, with smooth or wave-like blades that are interchangeable. The blades can **cut through multiple layers of fabric at once** and are ideal for cutting long strips of fabric and **millimeter-precise patchwork and quilting pieces.** Because the blades are extremely sharp, cut edges are very accurate and can be sewn together precisely.

11 CIRCLE CUTTERS allow you to **cut out precise circles of fabric** that have a clean, smooth edge. The cutter works somewhat like a **compass,** and the circle diameter can be set to any size up to 8½" (22cm). It's helpful to stabilize your fabric first when using a circle cutter.

12 HOBBY KNIVES (also known as craft knives and scalpels) are extremely sharp knives that are primarily intended for cutting leather, fur, film, cardboard, and paper. They use blades that can be retracted after use and replaced when they become dull.

13 CUTTING MATS should always be used when working with rotary cutters and hobby knives, to **prevent damage to your table or work surface.** Cutting mats have grids with inch and centimeter markings on the front and back; they come in various sizes.

14 AWLS (not pictured) are designed to punch holes in fabric and leather, as well as to punch out sewn eyelets.

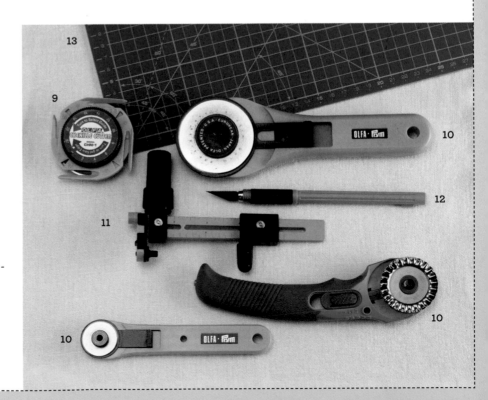

MEASURING AIDS

Precise and well-constructed measuring aids are indispensable for precisely fitting work. Whether you're creating narrow hems, measuring seam allowances, or measuring pieces of fabric, for every task there is a corresponding tool.

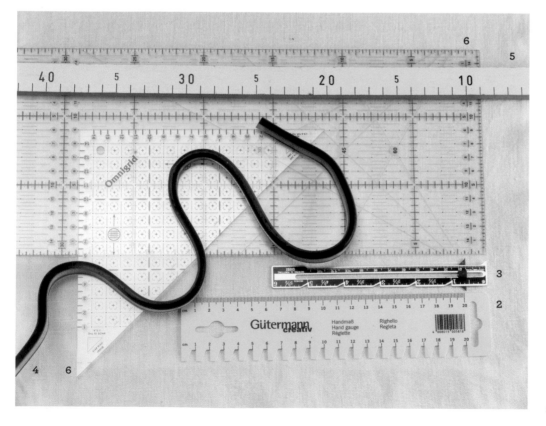

1 **TAPE MEASURES, with or without sliders**, are made of coated linen or plastic and should be flexible, but not stretchy. Their total length is generally 60" (150cm), making them useful for measuring larger fabric pieces, and they are usually about ⅝" (1.5 to 2cm) wide. They can be used to take body measurements and to more accurately measure curved lines, due to their flexibility. Tape measures with both inch and centimeter indicators, and a slider to record your measurements, are ideal.

2 **SMALL RULERS** are handy for **measuring and marking hems and topstitching lines, seam allowances, buttonholes, pleats, and darts**. They are made of plastic and are about 8" (20cm) long.

3 **HEM-MEASURING TOOLS** are used to **measure and mark hems, seam allowances, buttonholes, pleats, and darts**. A desired measurement can be marked with the slider, making it easier to, for example, ensure **consistent buttonhole placement or pleat depth**. They are made of aluminum and have a movable slider, and are marked with both inches and centimeters.

4 **CURVED RULERS** make it easier to **mark and transfer round and curved shapes**. They are made of flexible plastic that can be bent into the desired shape and are about 20" (50cm) long.

5 **WOODEN YARDSTICKS** are 36" (91cm) long and are useful for measuring long lengths of fabric.

6 **OMNIGRID RULERS** are all-purpose measuring tools that work for both right- and left-handed users. They are made of transparent plastic and have gridlines marked in either inches or centimeters. They are ideal for marking and **cutting longer edges and angles of 30, 45, and 60 degrees**; for marking the placement of darts, pintucks, pleats, or zippers; and for cutting along slanted lines. They are also useful for **checking fabric grain and for guiding rotary cutters**. Omnigrid rulers are available in multiple sizes; 6" x 18" (15 x 60cm) is an especially practical size for multi uses.

>> **A TAPE MEASURE SHOULD NEVER BE TIGHTLY ROLLED UP**, because it can stretch out of shape and render its markings inaccurate. Instead, wrap it loosely around two fingers.

>> Attach small **ANTI-SLIP PADS** to the **BACK OF A LONG RULER** to discourage slippage when using a rotary cutter.

FABRIC MARKERS

Markings made on fabric with the help of various types of markers are **helpful for both cutting and sewing.** Markings make it easier to position sleeves, collars, pockets, buttonholes, et cetera. Modern marking tools replace the time-consuming **pierced transfer of pattern markings** and hemline depths (using tracing paper and a tracing wheel) onto fabric.

1 **WATER-SOLUBLE MARKER,** a water-soluble ink felt pen **with a standard tip** is suited for marking and tracing sewing and cutting lines.

2 **DISAPPEARING-INK MARKER** is a **self-erasing pen** for transferring markings, sewing lines, and cutting lines. The markings disappear within forty-eight hours, with some fabrics requiring more time than others. It is used for sewing, quilting, embroidery, and patchwork.

3 **MARKING PENS** are **permanent markers** for tiny markings and for stenciling on fabric. For the latter, lay the stencil on the fabric and use the pen to trace around the stencil; the resulting line is later sewn over by hand or by machine. Marking pens can also be used to **label linens and clothing.**

4 **TRANSFER PENS** are used to create **patterns on paper** that **can then be ironed onto fabric.** The patterns are drawn as mirror images and transferred (by ironing) onto the fabric and can then be sewn or embroidered.

5 **TAILOR'S CHALK** comes in blocks, triangles, or sticks and is available in various colors. It is used to **transfer seam lines, markings, assembly points, et cetera** onto fabric. It should always be used on the reverse side of the fabric! Tailor's chalk markings can be subsequently brushed out.

6 **WONDER TAPE** is a transparent, double-sided sticky tape for the temporary bonding of fabric, ribbon, borders, lace, or zippers. It is water-soluble—in other words, it washes out. For **difficult-to-handle fabrics** that slip easily and need to be precisely positioned, it is indispensable.

7 **CHALK PENCILS** with erasers are suited for **temporary markings on textiles.** They come in various colors. Markings can be removed with the eraser tip.

8 **TRACING WHEELS** are used to transfer markings from paper patterns onto fabric in combination with tracing paper. They are made of metal or plastic, with serrated or smooth wheel edges, and should be **chosen according to fabric type.** For example, use a plastic wheel and/or a smooth wheel for knitted or embroidered fabrics, to prevent threads from snagging.

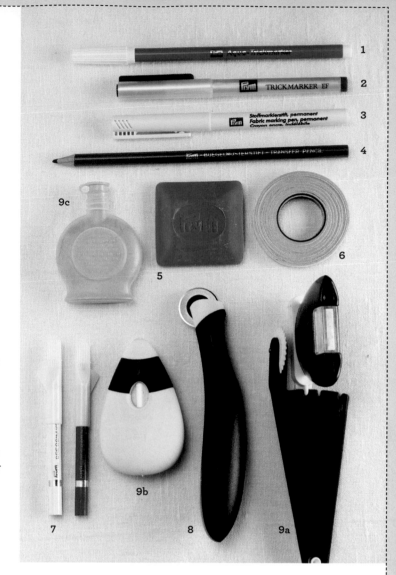

9 **DOUBLE TRACING WHEELS (9a)** or double chalk wheels (9b) use chalk powder (9c) and simultaneously mark the sewing line and the cutting line. This eliminates the need to separately mark seam allowances. They can be set to various widths, from .4" to 1½" (10 to 30mm).

10 **CHALK HEM MARKERS** (not pictured) are used to mark dress, skirt, or pant hems evenly around with chalk.

» **TEST YOUR DISAPPEARING-INK MARKER** on a scrap of the fabric you'll be working with before you mark with it.

! **TAKE CARE** when using colored chalk. Test first on a scrap of fabric to make sure it can be **REMOVED WITHOUT LEAVING RESIDUE.**

types of needles

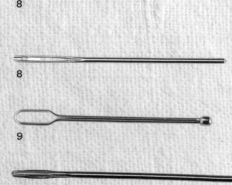

1

1

2

3

4

5

6

7

7

8

8

9

10

10

There are differences among hand, machine, and embroidery needles, which come in different styles and are made from varying materials. Using the right needle will make a noticeable difference in your work and will save you a lot of frustration. Faulty machine stitches, damaged fabrics resulting from dull or bent needles, or holes created when embroidering specialty fabrics are just a few possible pitfalls. It is a good idea to keep an assortment of different hand and machine needles at the ready, so that a defective needle can be swiftly replaced.

HAND SEWING NEEDLES

Hand sewing needles come in different lengths and with eye openings of various sizes.

1 **SEWING NEEDLES/Sharps** come in regular and half lengths, in different thicknesses and with large and small eyes.

2 **QUILTING NEEDLES/Between needles** are especially sharp, thin needles with small eyes that slip very easily through fabric layers and are good for creating small, short quilting stitches.

3 **SELF-THREADING NEEDLES** are helpful when threading, especially for those with vision impairment. The thread is pulled into the eye from the top through a small slot opening.

4 **DARNING NEEDLES**, or finishing needles, are very long and sharp, to bridge longer distances. The eye is large enough to accommodate darning thread or thin yarn.

5 **BEADING NEEDLES** are especially long and thin, and able to hold a large number of even the tiniest beads.

6 **LEATHER NEEDLES** have a sharp, triangular tip that cuts easily through leather, vinyl, or canvas.

7 **BLUNT EMBROIDERY NEEDLES** (also called tapestry needles) are intended for counted embroidery on cross-stitch fabric. They can also be used for sewing knitwear pieces together, as the blunt end glides between knitted stitches rather than through them. Sharp embroidery needles are designed to embroider over marked patterns (stencils, iron-on designs, et cetera) or whitework embroidery on densely woven fabric. The needle thickness must be coordinated with the fabric type and the thickness of thread used.

8 **DOUBLE EYE NEEDLES** make it possible to sew with two different threads simultaneously, in various color and thread type combinations. These needles also come with blunt ends for embroidery.

9 **BODKIN NEEDLES**, also called ballpoints, are thick needles with a ball end and a large eye, used to pull elastic bands, ribbons, and thicker yarns through casings. They come in both round and flat versions, and with enlarged or flattened tips. They also work well for pushing out sewn corner points.

10 **CURVED OR UPHOLSTERY NEEDLES** are semicircular and helpful when sewing hard-to-reach areas on dolls, stuffed animals, cushions, hassocks, et cetera.

11 BALL POINT NEEDLES (not pictured) are suited for work with **stretch fabrics**, such as knits and jersey, as well as for **lightly woven textiles**. (You could also use a thin tapestry needle.) The ball point of the needle does not pierce the threads while sewing, but rather pushes them aside and slips through the resulting opening.

12 MILLINERY NEEDLES (not pictured) are **extra-long needles with round eyes**, used for sewing hats as well as for smocking and pleating.

13 NEEDLE THREADERS assist with pulling thread through the eyes of hand needles. They come in various styles.

14 THIMBLES have tiny indentations and protect the tip of the middle finger while hand sewing; during sewing, the needle is held between the thumb and index finger while the middle finger presses on the needle eye, pushing the needle through the fabric. Thimbles come in various sizes and materials. For some people they are also beloved **collector's items**. Ring thimbles (not pictured) can also be used.

13

14

» PINCUSHIONS make popular gifts. Some can be worn on the wrist, and they may be fashioned in the form of animals, toadstools, muffins, or similar forms.

! PIN LENGTHS vary between ¾" and 1¾" (or 1.2 and 7.5cm) and are selected **ACCORDING TO FABRIC THICKNESS AND SEWING TECHNIQUE.**

! THE QUALITY of pins is important and should be taken into consideration. **A GOOD PIN MAY BEND SLIGHTLY DURING USE, BUT WILL NOT BEND PERMANENTLY OUT OF SHAPE.** Cheap pins are often dull, their plastic heads fall off quickly, and the pins become rusted. Don't be tempted by the cheerful, colorful assortment of pins in discount stores; you will be better served by higher-quality pins.

PINS

Pins are useful in numerous ways for all types of work with textiles. They secure **pattern pieces to the fabric** and fasten fabric pieces, seams, and hems together, and can be used to **mark** cutting points, assembly points, and much more. There are many varieties of pin heads.

1 PINCUSHIONS are a practical way to store needles and pins. They are usually filled with batting, fabric remnants, or sand. Pins are easily accessible during sewing, and injuries caused by inadvertently grabbing into the pins are avoided.

2 GLASS HEAD PINS are easy to see and grasp, and come in a variety of colors and lengths.

3 PLASTIC HEAD PINS may melt if ironed.

4 METAL HEAD PINS can be ironed, but are difficult to grasp and can be hard to see on patterned fabrics.

5 FLAT HEAD/flower head pins are suitable for fine, netlike, and openwork fabrics such as tulle, lace, or netting, since the flat heads **cannot slip through the fabric**. The heads come in flower or heart shapes. Flat head pins are 2" to 2½" (5 to 6cm) long and have sharp points. The heads are often non-melt.

6 QUILT CLIPS hold patchwork fabric edges together so they do not slip during quilting.

1

7 SAFETY PINS can quickly secure a seam or hem and are useful for **pulling cording through a casing**. They can also be used like straight pins in cases where straight pins would slide out of slippery or loosely woven fabric. Safety pins come in different types of metal and in various sizes and colors.

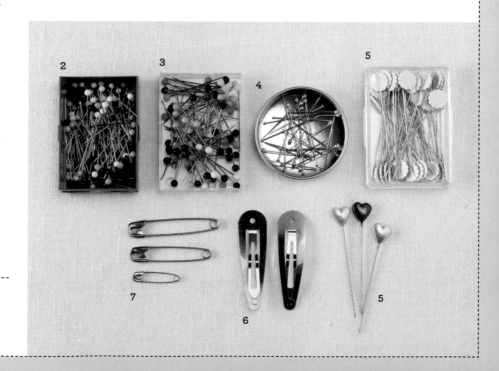

2   3   4   5

7   6   5

machine needles

Machine sewing needles also come in many types, appropriate for different sewing machines, sewing techniques, fabrics, and thread. Machine needles need to be exchanged frequently, because the quality and look of a sewn piece depends greatly on the right needle choice. Machine sewing and embroidery needles come in varying thicknesses and systems.

ANATOMY OF A NEEDLE

Household sewing machines usually work with the 130/705 H system. These are **flat shank needles**, where the "H" stands for "hollow." This type of needle has a flattened shaft that is easily inserted into the machine. On machines with a spool pin mounted on the side (usually the left), the flat side of the needle faces right. Most machines, though, have the spool pin on the front or top, in which case the **flat side of the needle faces the back.**

There are also needles with round shafts (often found on very old machines) and special needles with threaded or grooved shafts, but as these are not suited for normal household machines, they are not discussed here.

>> Keep **USED NEEDLES** in the original packaging when not in use. Turn the flat edge of the needle shaft toward the front to indicate that the needle has been used. **NEW NEEDLES ARE PACKAGED WITH THE ROUNDED SIDE OF THE SHAFT FACING OUTWARD.**

! Needles that have residue on them from **SPRAY ADHESIVES** or adhesive stabilizers should be cleaned with turpentine substitute.

Both the American and European needle size can be found on the flat part of the shaft.
- For thin, delicate fabrics, use needle sizes 8/60, 10/70, and 11/75.
- For cottons and mid-weight fabrics, use size 12/80 or 14/90.
- For thick and heavy fabrics, sizes 16/100, 18/110, and 19/120 are best.

It's not just the size of the needle that's important for getting good results, but also the **shape of the needle point**. Depending on the manufacturer, machine needles may be **color coded** (with a small ring at the shoulder). The various types are then easier to differentiate.

Frequent needle replacement is the first step toward solving many sewing problems. Dull, bent, or overused needles can cause **fabric damage, broken thread, skipped stitches, or uneven seams.**

All home machine needles have the same basic structure. The difference lies in the **shape and sharpness of the tip, the needle size, and the size of the eye.** With an all-purpose needle you can sew many materials easily and without any problem.

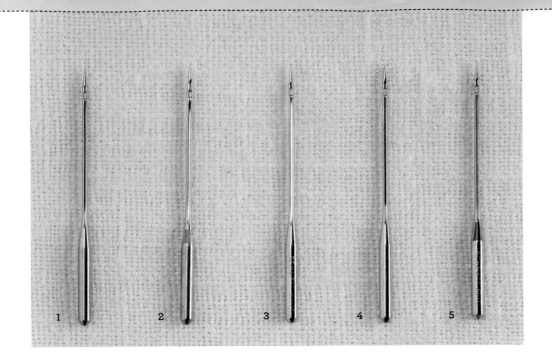

1 **UNIVERSAL NEEDLE** system 130/705 H, also called a standard needle, is **appropriate for all standard sewing work** and will pierce almost all fabric types and weights. The tip is lightly rounded. Universal needles come in sizes 8/60 to 19/120 and have no color coding.

2 **STRETCH AND SUPER STRETCH NEEDLE** system 130/705 H-S ("S" signifies stretch) is for **extremely elastic fabrics**; for example, jersey velour and silk jersey. The ball point of this needle, its special concave shape, and its special eye prevent badly formed and skipped stitches. Stretch and super stretch needles are available in sizes 9/65, 11/75, and 14/90 and have a yellow color coding.

3 **LEATHER NEEDLE** system 130/705 H-LL ("LL" signifies a leather tip) has a honed cutting tip. It easily pierces through **leather, faux leather, and similar materials** but is not suitable for woven or knitted fabrics. Needle sizes range from 10/70 to 19/120 and have no color coding.

4 **BALL POINT NEEDLE** system 130/705 H-SUK ("SUK" signifies medium ball point), with a ball point, is intended for **knitted fabrics**. The ball point slips between stitches and **prevents piercing of the knitted threads themselves**. Needle sizes range from 10/70 to 16/100 and have no color coding.

5 **DENIM NEEDLE** system 130/705 H-J ("J" signifies jeans) is for **jeans, sailcloth, and very dense woven fabrics**. It is especially sharp and has a **fortified shaft** to prevent bending, breaking, and skipped stitches. Needle sizes range from 10/70 to 18/110, and it has a blue color coding.

6 **MICROTEX NEEDLE** system 130/705 H-M ("M" signifies microtex) is for **silk, satin, microfiber, organza, coated fabrics, films, and faux leather**. This needle is especially sharp and thin, so that it will not cause pulled threads in delicate fabrics such as silk. Needle sizes range from 8/60 to 18/110, and it has a purple color coding.

7 **QUICK-THREADING NEEDLES** (not pictured) have a **small slit** on the side, to allow the thread to slip easily into the eye. Threading this needle on the machine is thus much simpler, which can be especially helpful for those with impaired vision. Needle sizes range from 12/80 and 14/90, and they have no color coding.

» You can **TEST A NEEDLE'S POINT** by using it to pierce a piece of **NYLON PANTYHOSE**. If any stitches are pulled, the needle should be replaced.

» **ON VERY THICK FABRIC** it is advisable to sew slowly with a denim needle. You may even want to form **INDIVIDUAL STITCHES USING THE HANDWHEEL** and keep some pressure on the fabric, to keep the thick layers feeding evenly.

» **WITH A MICROTEX NEEDLE** it is advisable to **ALSO USE A NONSTICK OR ROLLER FOOT** when working with coated materials, films, or faux leather.

6

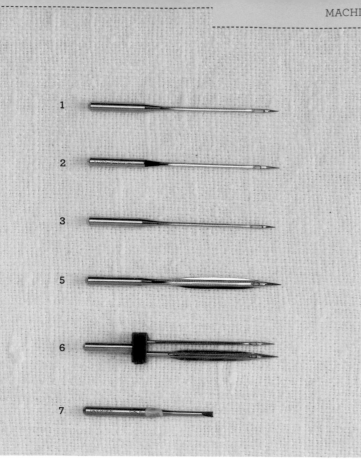

MACHINE NEEDLES FOR DECORATIVE SEWING

1 TOPSTITCHING NEEDLE system 130/705 N has an especially large eye and an extra sharp point. These are used for **embellishment and topstitching** with thicker sewing and embroidery threads. Needle sizes range from 12/80 to 16/100.

2 EMBROIDERY NEEDLE system 130/705 H-E ("E" signifies embroidery) is especially **designed for embroidery** or embellishment with machine embroidery and decorative threads. A large, wide eye and a wide **THREAD GROOVE** prevent twisting of thicker embroidery threads. It is appropriate for embroidery work and trims. Needle sizes are 11/75 and 14/90, with red color coding.

3 METALLIC NEEDLE is for embroidering and sewing with metallic thread. A large, smoothly ground eye prevents twisting and tearing of the thread.

4 TOPSTITCH OR QUILT NEEDLE system 130/705 H-Q ("Q" signifies quilting; not pictured) has an unusually thin, lightly rounded tip that can effortlessly sew through multiple layers of fabric and batting without damaging fabric. Appropriate for quilting and patchwork as well as topstitching. Needle sizes are 11/75 and 14/90, with a green color coding.

» Choose the SMALLEST POSSIBLE NEEDLE SIZE that will work with your fabric, to avoid ending up with noticeable holes.

» SEW OR EMBROIDER SLOWLY with metallic threads, which can be very delicate.

» A CONSISTENT SEWING SPEED helps prevent needle breakage when freehand quilting.

» A WING NEEDLE lets you create holes in lightweight fabrics (for example, near the edges) to form a FOUNDATION FOR CROCHETED EDGINGS.

5 WING NEEDLE system 130/705 H-WING has a sword-like shaft that spreads fabric threads apart to create a visible point of entry, which becomes a hole that is then emphasized with the corresponding stitch. Appropriate for hem stitching, entredeux work, and decorative seams in lightweight wovens, such as batiste and linen. Needle sizes are 16/100 and 19/120.

6 DOUBLE WING NEEDLE works on the same principle as the wing needle, except **a standard row of stitches is created parallel to the row of holes.** The standard stitching can be emphasized by using contrasting thread.

7 CUTWORK NEEDLES have tips that are **shaped like tiny knives.** Sewing/embroidering with them creates a perforated outline, so that the section within the perforations can later be easily removed from the fabric.

8 SPRING NEEDLE SYSTEM 130/705 H-SPR has a spring that sits around the needle and takes on the role of a presser foot. This needle is always used with lowered feed dogs and without a presser foot and is appropriate **for freehand embroidery with an embroidery hoop,** darning, and needle painting.

9 DOUBLE EYE NEEDLE SYSTEM 705 DE has two eyes, one above the other. It can be threaded with two of the same or two different threads, which can lead to interesting effects. The stitching is more distinct than when two threads are threaded through a single hole.

10 TWIN/TRIPLE NEEDLE SYSTEM 130/175 H-ZWI NE 1.6 will work only on machines with a zigzag needle plate, and a second spool pin is required. Twin needles are available for almost all types of sewing. The characteristics of the needles are the same as with single needles. Appropriate for single- and multicolored decorative topstitching, trims, and hems.

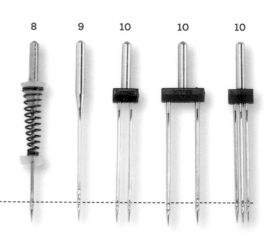

Twin needles come in various sizes and spacings. The abbreviation "NE" corresponds to the spacing between the two needles. If twin needles have a spacing of ⅟₁₆" (1.6mm), the needle packaging will say NE 1.6.

NEEDLE SPACINGS AND NEEDLE SIZES

Spacing NE 1.6	Sizes 10/70 and 12/80
Spacing NE 2.0	Size 12/80
Spacing NE 2.5	Size 12/80
Spacing NE 3.0	Size 14/90
Spacing NE 4.0	Sizes 12/80 to 16/100

NEEDLE PACKAGING

Sewing machine needles are sold in five packs or ten packs. Some may contain a variety of needle sizes and types. The packaging provides information about the characteristics of the needles, such as size and application.

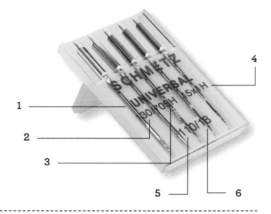

1 Universal = needle type
2 130/705 = indicates a needle for household machines
3 H = hollow shaft
4 15x1 H = another code for system 130/705
5 110 = European needle size
6 18 = American needle size

NEEDLE SIZE CODING FOR MACHINE NEEDLES

European	American
60	8
65	9
70	10
75	11
80	12
90	14
100	16
110	18
120	19

COLOR CODING FOR MACHINE NEEDLES

Needle type	Color coding
Universal	none
Stretch	yellow
Jersey	none
Leather	none
Denim	blue
Microtex	purple
Embroidery	red
Quilting	green
Superstretch	orange

NEEDLE SYSTEM CODING FOR MACHINE NEEDLES

Needle system code	Needle type
H	Universal
H ZWI NE …	Twin
N	Topstitching
H-S	Stretch
H-S ZWI NE 2.5 or NE 4.0	Twin-stretch
H SUK	Jersey
H-J	Denim
J ZWI NE 4	Twin-denim
H LL	Leather
H-M	Microtex
H-E	Embroidery
H-E ZWI NE 2.5	Twin-embroidery
MET	Metallic
MET ZWI NE 2.5	Twin-metallic
H-Q	Quilting
H WING	Wing
H ZWHO	Twin
H ZWI NE …	Twin
H ZWI BR NE 6.0 or NE 8.0	Twin-universal with extra-wide spacing
H-S ZWI NE …	Twin-stretch
H DRI NE 2.5 or NE 3.0	Triple
H SPR	Spring
DE	Double eye
HDK	Quick thread

❗ Needles should always be replaced after each **LARGER SEWING PROJECT**. The passage of the thread and the movement of the needle through fabric cause imperceptible damage to the eye and tip, and this can **AFFECT YOUR SEWING RESULTS.**

❗ **GOOD RESULTS** also depend on the correct needle choice. Different fabrics have various characteristics that need to be considered when **CHOOSING THE APPROPRIATE NEEDLE.**

types of thread

Thread is available for purchase in various qualities, compositions, and colors, and with assorted properties. For every sewing or embroidery technique, there is appropriate thread that will have a definite influence on your finished product.

THE RIGHT THREAD

Not every thread is right for every technique or every fabric. Whether a thread is better for hand or machine sewing will depend on its weight and composition. Thread weight should always be matched to material, sewing technique, and desired decorative effect. The general rule is, **the higher the thread number, the thinner the thread**—and therefore the lower its break resistance. (The thread number is based on the length of a piece of thread of a given weight.) A 30-weight thread is significantly thicker and stronger than an 80-weight thread. Thread comes in many colors, and may be made from natural fibers, such as silk, cotton, linen, or rayon, or from synthetics, such as polyamide or polyester.

STANDARD COTTON THREADS made of pure cotton are appropriate for sewing **cotton and linen fabrics** and come in a wide array of colors.
- 80 weight for lightweight, delicate fabrics, cotton batiste, and fine linens and blouses
- 60 weight for lighter-weight cotton and dress fabrics, for regular and topstitched seams, and for buttonholes
- 50 weight for midweight cotton and dress fabrics, for regular and topstitched seams, and for buttonholes on bed linens
- 40 weight for dense, thick fabrics, denim, and home décor fabrics
- 30 weight for dense cottons, twills, work wear, and awning cloth

SILK SEWING THREAD is made of pure silk and is appropriate for both hand and machine sewing. It is strong and slightly stretchy, and has an elegant sheen. It is used for **tailoring and haute couture, as well as with silk and satin fabrics, wool, and cashmere.** It is available in a wide array of colors.
- 100 weight for thin, delicate silk or satin fabrics and delicate decorative stitching
- 40 weight for decorative stitching and hand-sewn eyelet buttonholes
- 30 weight for topstitching and buttonholes in heavy woolens

⚠ QUALITY THREAD **IS A GUARANTOR** of successful results. Threads that break during sewing are an irritant and take the fun out of your work. Cheap deals on thread are best avoided; often these products are made from **SHORT STAPLE FIBERS THAT TEND TO KNOT UP** and unravel quickly during machine sewing. Also critical is whether a thread is **FADE RESISTANT AND COLORFAST.**

⚠ **THREAD IS ALSO A DECORATIVE ELEMENT,** and thread weight should be chosen to complement your material. **FOR HIGH PILE AND PLUSH FABRICS,** for example, opt for a thicker thread, so that decorative seams will stand out; with lighter-weight fabric, use thinner thread. But every rule has an exception— heavy thread can sometimes create an interesting textural effect on thin fabric. For these projects the fabric should be reinforced with stabilizer, to reduce the chance of puckering.

POLYESTER THREAD, known as **all-purpose or universal thread,** can be used for both hand and machine sewing. It is made of 100% polyester fibers, is appropriate for all fabrics and seam types, is slightly elastic, and is **highly resistant to breakage and wear.**

- 120 weight for seams and topstitching on lightweight fabrics; appropriate for regular and overlock machines
- 100 weight for seams and topstitching, buttonholes, attaching buttons, and embellishment stitching and decorative seams
- 40 weight, a heavy-duty thread for heavily stressed seams, jeans, work clothes, and heavyweight wovens and canvas
- 30 weight for topstitching, decorative topstitching, and quilting seams, hand-sewn buttonholes, work clothes, and cushions

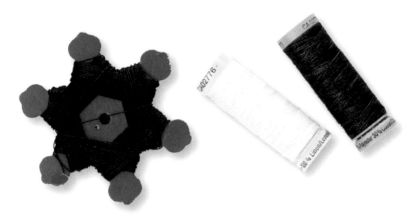

PEARL COTTON is a strong and very break-resistant thread for hand sewing and is used for backpacks, bags, leather belts, and craft projects. It is **100% cotton** and is available in multiple colors.

PEARL LINEN is a strong and very break-resistant thread for hand sewing and is used for backpacks, bags, leather belts, and craft projects. It is **100% linen** and is available in multiple colors.

DENIM THREAD, depending on the manufacturer, is made of some mixture of cotton and polyester; it is highly break-resistant and is used for hand or machine sewing of **densely woven fabrics and seams,** and for decorative seams and topstitching.

! FOR HIGHLY STRESSED SEAMS, use extra-strength thread, which is available in sewing stores. It is 100% polyester and is appropriate for heavy, densely woven fabrics.

SERGER THREAD is made of 100% polyester or cotton, or some blend of the two. It is designed especially for sergers. Since these machines require more thread than standard machines, the thread is sold in larger quantities: 1,000 to 5,500 yards (or 1,000, 2,000, or 5000 meters) on cones/spools.

» A supplemental spool holder is needed when using **LARGE CONES** of thread (*see page 19, number 5*). Alternatively, cones may be placed **IN A TALL DRINKING GLASS BEHIND THE MACHINE.**

>> Use a standard size 16/100–19/120 needle FOR BUTTONHOLE THREAD.

>> ELASTIC THREAD can be used as a carry-along thread for knitting and crochet.

>> WATER-SOLUBLE BASTING THREAD can be used for machine basting as well. Use the basting stitch setting, if available, or alternatively a STRAIGHT STITCH WITH A ¼" (6MM) LENGTH. Loosen the thread tension slightly, and sew slowly.

1 **BUTTONHOLE THREAD**, also known as decorative thread, is a 30-weight polyester thread. It is used for decorative stitching, topstitching, decorative seams, and hand-sewn buttonholes in heavy fabrics. It has a silky sheen, is slightly elastic, and is available in many colors.

2 **EMBROIDERY AND DARNING THREAD** is made of 100% cotton and is used to repair clothing, for machine darning, and for machine-made buttonholes in lighter-weight fabrics. It is available in many colors.

3 **QUILTING THREAD** is available for machine and hand sewing. It is made of cotton or a blend of cotton and polyester, and is especially break- and wear-resistant. Hand quilting thread is often waxed, in order to glide more easily through fabric layers. Hand quilting thread cannot be used for machine quilting, nor vice versa.

4 **BASTING THREAD** is made of cotton or synthetic fibers and is thin and not very break-resistant. It is used for basting or marking provisional seams.

5 **ELASTIC THREAD** is a stretchy thread made of a blend of polyester and polyurethane. It is used as the bobbin thread in machine sewing, and for ruching, gathering, and smocking.

6 **TRANSPARENT THREAD** is made of 100% polyester, is very delicate, and matches invisibly to all fabrics. It is used for sewing multicolored fabrics or for seams that are intended to be invisible, as well as for sewing beads, trims, and sequins, for transparent embroidery, or for topstitching over printed images.

7 **WATER-SOLUBLE (WASH-AWAY) BASTING THREAD** is ideal for any temporary seams. The need to remove your basting is eliminated, as the thread dissolves in contact with water or steam.

embroidery and novelty threads

The use of specialty threads, such as machine embroidery thread and novelty thread, allows you to achieve colorful, lustrous, and textural effects on fabric or textile backgrounds. Embroidery with the right thread adds elegance to clothing and home décor pieces and elevates them beyond everyday textiles.

MACHINE EMBROIDERY THREAD

Machine embroidery thread is used for creating logos and other motifs, for sewing decorative borders, and for freehand machine embroidery. It is available in different fiber contents and myriad colors and color combinations.

1   2   3a   3b   4   5

1 **POLYESTER EMBROIDERY THREAD** is made of 100% polyester, is available in many colors, has a high luster, and is very break-resistant. Embroidery made with polyester thread is **washable, colorfast, and wear-resistant.** This is a particular advantage for embroidered work clothes that are frequently washed and may be exposed to bleaching agents.

2 **VISCOSE OR RAYON EMBROIDERY THREAD** is made of 100% viscose and is sometimes called artificial silk. Viscose embroidery thread has a high sheen and is available in many colors. It is primarily **designed for embroidery patterns** but may also be used for decorative borders or machine quilting. Embroidery using viscose thread is softer than that using polyester thread. Viscose thread may be washed in water up to 200°F (95°C) and is dryer-safe and colorfast. It can be used with almost all fabric types.

3 **COTTON EMBROIDERY THREAD** is available in many colors (3a) as well as in multicolors (3b). It is appropriate for **embroidery with a matte finish** on boiled wool (walk), felt, linen, or corduroy, as well as for cottage-style decorative borders and stitches. It is ideal for machine quilting. When used as looper thread in a serger, it can create decorative seams.

4 **BOBBIN THREAD** comes in 150 weight and is made of 100% polyester. It is a **break-resistant, thin, uniform lower thread** and is used for machine embroidery.

5 **PREWOUND BOBBIN THREAD** feeds evenly off the spool and contains **more yardage than a self-wound bobbin.** The extra yardage is especially practical for embroidery motifs with high stitch counts, as it eliminates the need for frequent bobbin changes.

❗ COTTON EMBROIDERY THREAD may be brushed after sewing with a stiff brush to create a **PLUSH EFFECT.**

NOVELTY THREADS

Novelty threads, threads for special effects, and other decorative threads might have **slubs**, **be thick-and-thin, or possess various other characteristics** that are created during the thread manufacturing process.

>> Place spools **VERTICALLY** on the spool pin.

! When **WORKING WITH METALLIC THREAD**, the upper tension should be decreased and a **MESH SLEEVE PULLED OVER THE SPOOL** so that the thread will feed out evenly. Reducing the machine speed, **SEWING SLOWLY**, and using a special **NEEDLE DESIGNED FOR USE WITH METALLIC THREAD** *(page 38)* will guarantee you glistening results.

1 **METALLIC THREADS** are shiny, lustrous, and intended for **stitching up special effects in glimmering colors**. They are well suited for decorative stitches and ornamental seams, or for embroidery on everything from festive garments to purses or accessory items. They are composed of up to 60% polyamide and up to 40% polyester, and are available in many colors in addition to silver and gold.

2 **FLAT METALLIC THREADS** are suited for creating **striking glittery and sparkling effects** in embroidery motifs and satin stitching. They are composed of 60% polyamide and 40% polyester.

3 **HOLOGRAPHIC THREADS (HOLOSHIMMER)** are similarly intended **for striking glittery and iridescent effects** in embroidery; they are composed of up to 60% polyamide and up to 40% polyester.

4 **SOLAR** thread is the chameleon of the sewing world: it starts out white but **changes color when exposed to sunlight.** This amazing effect is created by the interaction between a **special coating** on the thread and ultraviolet light, allowing decorative seams and stitching to become suddenly visible. Solar is made of 100% polyester and is available in a number of pastel colors.

5 **GLOWY,** or glow-in-the-dark, thread is able to store sunlight, UV light, or artificial light and later **glow in the dark.** The duration of its exposure to light determines the intensity of its glowing power. This thread is **useful for adding logos or other designs for safety purposes.** It is made of 100% polyester and is available in several colors.

>> Using different **SERGER THREADS** in combination with various stitches can create interesting effects.

6 **DECORATIVE SERGER THREADS** are especially soft threads that are comfortable against the skin and can be used in serger/overlock machines. Ornamental versions are made of **rayon or cotton, as well as in metallics.** These are threaded not through a needle but rather through the serger's thread guides. With a regular sewing machine, these decorative threads can be employed using the *couching technique (see page 131)* or using *specialized presser feet (see pages 24 and 26).* They can also be wound on bobbins to be used as the bottom thread.

YOUR BASIC EQUIPMENT

Here is a collection of the **most important items** that are **indispensable** for marking, pinning, cutting, and sewing.

! As you are assembling your basic equipment, focus on acquiring **HIGH-QUALITY PRODUCTS**.

1 Buttons

2 Safety pins

3 Bodkin

4 Seam ripper

5 Hand sewing needles

6 Tracing wheel

7 Embroidery scissors

8 Pincushion and pins

9 All-purpose thread in various colors

10 Disappearing-ink marker

11 Fabric shears

12 Tacking thread

13 Ruler

14 Measuring tape

helpful
extras

Sewing is even more fun with the right equipment, as various construction steps can be achieved more quickly and efficiently. The best way to put together the ideal set of equipment for your sewing needs is through trial and error. Your personal work style will determine what is most useful and advantageous for you.

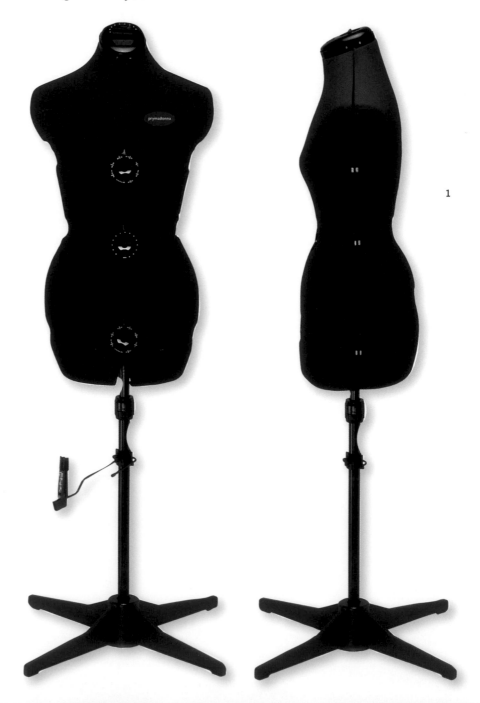

1

1 **DRESS FORMS** are practical for **custom-made pieces.** Dress forms come in male and female models, and some can be adjusted to a person's individual measurements. They are usually covered with a foam lining, allowing pins to be stuck into them—ideal for **fitting and draping fabric pieces prior to sewing.**

2 **POINT TURNERS/ SEAM CREASERS** feature a pointed end to **push out and shape turned corners,** as well as a rounded end for curved edges and seams. The **specially designed shape** of the tip prevents the inadvertent piercing of corners.

3 **TURNING TOOLS** such as loop turners (3a) and turning rods (3b) assist with *turning narrow fabric tubes (see page 261)* for belts, bag handles, straps, carriers, et cetera.

4 **BIAS TAPE MAKERS** come in different sizes for making various-sized bias strips. The tool helps to *precisely fold the edges of pre-cut strips (see page 259).* The resulting bias strips **may be used for decorative edge finishing.**

5 **HOLE PUNCHERS AND AWLS** are needed to **create eyelets in textiles, leather, foils,** et cetera. A hole punch (5a) can make six different holes in sizes ranging from ⅛"–½" (2.5–5mm). The tapered, pointed metal tip of an awl (5b) can create small holes (for example, eyelet buttonholes) or can increase the size of existing holes.

6 **EYELET PLIERS** can quickly **punch holes** ⅛", ³⁄₁₆", and ¼" (3mm, 4mm, and 8mm) in diameter or can be used for the machine-free application of grommets, eyelets, and snaps. This practical tool ensures an even application of pressure and **eliminates the need for a hammer.**

7 **A DARNING EGG,** also available in a mushroom shape, simplifies repairs by **spreading fabric taut.** For darning, the damaged area is laid over the egg.

essential
notions

Small items used in sewing, such as trims and fasteners, are collectively referred to as notions. They are required, in addition to fabric and thread, to complete a sewing project, whether for practical or purely decorative purposes.

FASTENERS

Zippers and fastening tapes are standard fasteners that can be found everywhere. For special clothing pieces and chic accessories, there are also **specialty fasteners** to fulfill various needs.

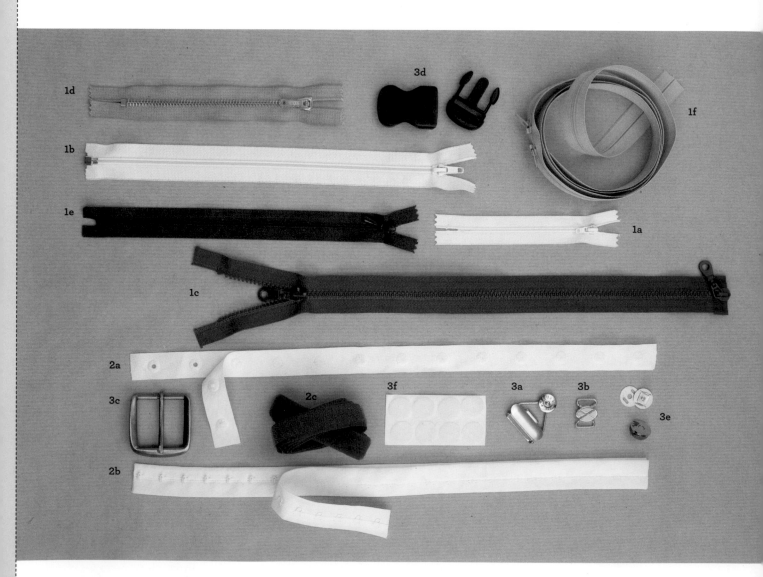

1 ZIPPERS

Zippers come in **various types, lengths, colors, and weights.** They are made with **either a plastic coil/spiral fastener or metal or plastic teeth** and come in an assortment of widths. The tapes are made from cotton, a cotton blend, or polyester and should be coordinated with the fabric weight and care instructions of the finished sewing project. For light- to midweight fabrics, skirts, and dresses, a coil (or spiral) fastener is preferable, because it will be considerably lighter and more flexible than a zipper with metal teeth (though also less sturdy). There are different ways of *sewing in zippers (see pages 241–247).* In addition to fashionable **novelty zippers,** a typical sewing store will carry the following zipper types:

Standard zippers (1a) are closed at the bottom, i.e., are not separable, and come with coil (spiral) closures or teeth. They are used for pants, pullover tops, skirts, and dresses, as well as for pillows and handbags. They can be set in with one or both sides covered.

Separating zippers (1b) can be opened at the bottom, and **two-way separating zippers (1c)** with teeth and a double pull can be opened and closed at both ends. Zippers with heavier coils (spirals) or larger teeth, typically in long lengths, are for garments that open all the way, such as jackets and coats. They are also ideal for children's clothing and sportswear.

Durable pant zippers (1d) with metal teeth are usually used with a fly opening. **A small safety hook** on the back of the pull prevents the zipper from coming open on its own.

On an **invisible zipper (1e)** the coil (spiral) sits behind the bands, so it does not add bulk. The zipper can be concealed in a seam and the attachment stitching is not visible from the right side.

So-called **endless zippers** are sold **by the yard (1f)** and are economical and easy to use. They are available as basic zippers or with plastic coil (spiral) closures, and the number of pulls is selectable. Various longer required lengths, for bed linens, bags, cushions, and cushion covers, for example, **can be cut exactly to size.**

2 FASTENING BANDS

Fastening bands always consist of two halves and are available with a variety of fasteners.

Snap bands (2a) are practical because the snaps are already sewn onto the band at regular intervals. They are more flexible than hook and loop fasteners (such as Velcro) and are **suitable for lapped closures** on baby clothes, corsets, and bed linens, as well as for removable linings and décor pieces.

Hook and eye bands (2b) are suitable for abutted closing edges; for example, on foundation garments.

Hook and loop bands (tape) (2c) are suitable for lapped closures. They come in various widths and colors and may be **self-adhesive or sewn on.** Hook and loop bands (tape) hold together when pressed and are used, for example, on **removable linings and shoulder pads,** on maternity wear, and as **easy-to-use fasteners** on children's clothing and handbags.

3 SPECIALTY FASTENERS

These are special-purpose fasteners, such as **overall buckles (3a), bikini hooks (3b), belt buckles (3c),** and **quick-release buckles (3d)** for backpacks, hip packs, and shoulder bags. Four-piece **magnetic snaps (3e)** consist of two pronged magnetic disks, one male and one female, each of which is attached using a second, interlocking disk. Magnetic snaps are useful for wallets, handbags, totes, and backpacks.

Self-adhesive snap fasteners (3f) suffice as simple fastenings at low-stress points.

! THE LENGTH on a zipper does not refer to the length of the tape, but rather to the LENGTH OF THE TEETH OR SPIRAL.

! MAGNETIC CLOSURES should not be worn over pacemakers and should not be allowed to make DIRECT CONTACT WITH CARDS WITH MAGNETIC STRIPS, such as credit cards.

1

BUTTONS, HOOKS, AND EYES

Take care when choosing fasteners for your projects—you may want them to be subtle, in a matching shade, or decorative in a contrast color. They should be tailored to their **intended use,** including consideration of the amount of stress they will have to withstand and the care requirements of the fabric they will be used with. It is sometimes important when attaching fasteners to first reinforce the attachment point with an appropriate **stabilizer** or *interfacing material (see page 60).*

1 **BUTTONS** are usually made of plastic, shell, wood, metal, coconut, glass, leather, or horn. Some materials, such as wood and glass, are delicate; for example, wood buttons should not be washed, to prevent them from swelling, and glass buttons can easily crack when they encounter a hot iron.

The weight of a button should match the weight of the fabric it is used on, especially with more delicate fabrics. There are **holed buttons,** usually with two or four holes through which thread is pulled when sewing them onto an item, and **shank buttons,** with a small shank or metal eye on the back. A shank leaves a sufficient distance between the button and thick fabrics, allowing for easier use.

2 **COVERED BUTTONS** consist of **two-piece blanks** in various sizes, made of metal or plastic, the *top part of which may be covered with fabric (see page 233).* When matching or coordinating buttons are not available, these allow you to easily create matching buttons yourself.

3 **LAUNDRY BUTTONS** are usually white and made of linen, twill, or plastic. They are **machine-washable in hot water, safe for ironing,** and appropriate for all types of home textiles. Linen and twill versions may be **dyed or colored with fabric pens** to match your fabric.

>> COLLECTING AND RECYCLING BUTTONS is fun and saves money. When discarding old clothes, remove and save all buttons. To help with organization, ALWAYS STRING IDENTICAL BUTTONS ONTO ONE THREAD and store them in a box or jar.

>> It's best to INCLUDE REPLACEMENT BUTTONS in any button purchase, as it can potentially be difficult to find matching buttons at a later time.

2

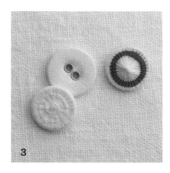

3

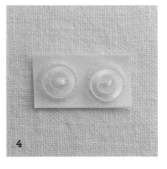

4

4 SEW-FREE BUTTONS are particularly useful while traveling, when there may be no time or opportunity to sew on a replacement button. These **self-adhesive buttons** offer a temporary fix.

5 BACKING BUTTONS are small and flat, and are simultaneously **sewn to the reverse side of the fabric along with the featured button,** so that the primary, visible **button has more stability.** Backing buttons should be used with large and heavy buttons, and also for any buttons on leather and faux leather or on delicate fabrics. The use of backing buttons will help **prevent these fabrics from tearing.**

5

6

6 FROG CLOSURES are sewn onto garment opening edges with tiny hand stitches along the cording. These **decorative fasteners made of cord loops** may be used on clothing, accessories, uniforms, and various creative projects. You can also make your own frog closures *(see page 235).*

7 DENIM SNAP FASTENERS are used primarily on jeans and other denim wear. The two-part snaps are **quick and easy to attach by hand.**

8 SEW-ON SNAPS have two pieces—a lower half with an indent and an upper half with a small peg. They are often used at necklines or as supplementary fasteners. Plastic snaps can withstand only light pulling and are thus suited for **light synthetics and thin fabrics.**

9 NO-SEW/SEW-FREE SNAPS (9a) are more durable than sew-on snaps and are especially well suited for **baby clothes, children's clothes, and sports and leisure wear.** The snaps have four parts and are best applied with *eyelet pliers (see page 47).* There are special snaps (9b) for use with **jersey;** these have pronged backs and close easily.

10 RIVETS are used to connect perforated pieces or can serve as a fashionable **decorative element;** for example, on jeans. They are also useful for tacking down the folded ends of bag handles and belts. Applying rivets is easily done with the help of special eyelet pliers *(see page 47).*

11 GROMMETS (11a) are used in small diameters for clothing pieces with laced closures (to give just one example) and in large diameters for home textile pieces, such as curtains. Eyelets (11b) are suited for various tasks, including reinforcing the holes in leather belts.

12 HOOKS AND EYES often serve as **secondary fasteners;** for example, just above a zipper. They can be sewn on so as not to be visible from the right side.
The shape of the eyes can vary: straight eyes (not pictured) are used on overlapping edges, whereas curved eyes are preferable for abutted edges. Larger, thread-wrapped hooks and eyes (not pictured) are typically used on jackets and coats, as well as on clothing made from fur or plush fabric, where the fastener can be seen when the garment is worn open.

13 SKIRT HOOKS AND EYES are a special type of hook and eye that is used on skirt and pant waistbands **in place of a button.** The special form of the hook prevents it from slipping out of the eye. Depending on the style they may be **riveted and visible** (13a) or **sewn on invisibly** (13b).

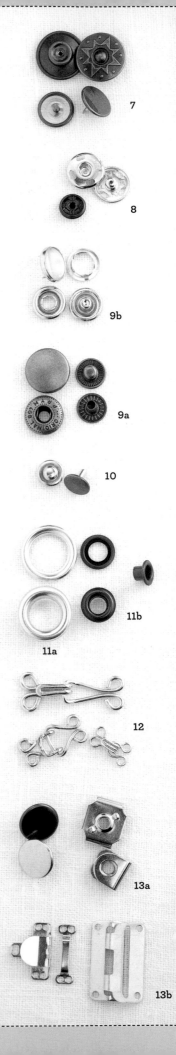

7

8

9b

9a

10

11b

11a

12

13a

13b

TAPES AND TRIMS

Those who would like to add creative touches to functional sewing will find plenty of inspiration in the assortment of available tapes and trims on the market. Many trims are **sold off the roll.** There are various colors, widths, and types to choose from, but always make sure the **care properties are matched to your fabric.** Depending on the style, they may be sewn into seams, stitched onto fabric edges, or used as decoration or for lacing pieces together. Trims with straight edges are easily inserted between two pieces of fabric.

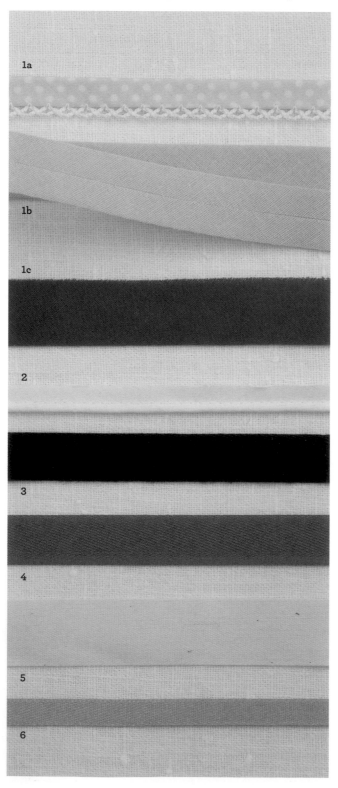

1 **BIAS TAPE** comes in many varieties, in solid colors or patterned with delicate lace (1a), and is usually made from cotton or polyester. It is used for **edging and finishing exposed fabric edges;** for example, on seam and quilt edges, aprons, children's clothing, and tablecloths. Because of its bias cut it can easily follow curves. It comes pre-folded (1b) or flat (1c) and can also be made from scratch with the help of a *bias tape maker* (*see page 259*).

2 **PIPING** is used on **home décor** items, such as pillows and slipcovers, and is sewn between layers of fabric to create attractive edges. On clothing it may be used to **trim necklines,** pocket openings, collars, et cetera. Flat piping consists of a long, folded strip of fabric, while regular piping has cording incorporated to create a rounded edge. You can also make piping yourself (*see page 120*).

3 **SEAM BINDING** is usually made of cotton, has a dense weave, and is suited for reinforcing seams that might otherwise stretch. It is useful for hem edgings as well as for **loops and ties.**

4 **HEM FACING** is sewn to the hem from the inside and **protects and strengthens the lower edge of the hem.**

5 **TWILL TAPE** is a multipurpose cotton tape that **has a variety of uses.** It is suitable for stabilizing seams and hems, edging household linens, creating apron ties, and, in narrower widths, making hanging loops for dish and bath towels.

6 **HANGING RIBBON** is used to create hanging loops for skirts, pants, and outerwear such as blazers and jackets. It is usually made of **viscose or polyester.**

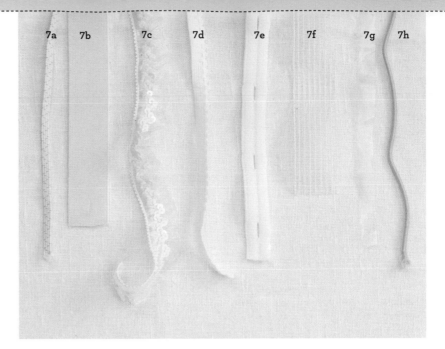

7a 7b 7c 7d 7e 7f 7g 7h

7 ELASTIC BANDS AND CORD ELASTIC come in a variety of types and widths. Non-roll elastic (7a and 7b) is particularly suited for pulling through casings; other types, for example those with **decorative edgings** (7c), are sewn onto fabric edges as finishing. Buttonhole elastic (7e) has evenly spaced buttonholes and allows waistbands to be adjusted on children's clothing and maternity wear. Transparent elastic tape (7f and 7g) can be used to gather delicate and lightweight fabrics, as straps on camisoles, or as a finish on lingerie. Cord elastic (7h) comes in different weights. Thin elastic cord, also called shirring elastic, is often used as a bobbin thread to create stretchy, gathered fabric pieces; thicker cord elastic is suitable for use in casings.

8 CORDING comes in a variety of widths. It is **twisted or braided** out of multiple strands in one or more colors. Anorak cord is used as a draw cord for outerwear. Decorative cording can be used with casings on drawstring bags or applied as a pretty accent on home décor items.

9 RIBBON AND LACE TRIMS add an individual touch to clothing pieces, bags, and home décor items. Examples include **pompom trim, rickrack, sequin tape, woven and printed ribbon, velvet ribbon, beaded trim, ruffled elastic,** and more. These decorative trims can be used in many ways. Bobbin lace, scalloped lace, and lingerie lace are used for evening and bridal wear and are available in various colors and styles. They may be adorned with beads, sequins, rhinestones, et cetera. Elastic lace is a pretty trim for lingerie. Simple trims may be sewn on with a machine, while others are better applied with careful hand stitches.

8 + 9

EMBELLISHMENTS

! You can also make your own **APPLIQUÉS** (*see pages 123–124*).

Hand-sewn items such as bags, clothing, and other textiles often get a final flourish from the addition of eye-catching embellishments. You can also get striking results by embellishing ready-made items. It's especially easy with **embellishments that can be ironed on or sewn on by hand.**

1 **APPLIQUÉS** (or, more simply, patches) are solid or multicolored fabric pieces that can serve to repair or reinforce heavily stressed areas, or as decorative accents. Appliqués might be anything from leather elbow patches to more strictly fashionable accents, which can be made quite striking through the addition of beads, rhinestones, or sequins. Some **ready-made appliqués come with an iron-on backing.** For added security you can reinforce these afterward with machine or hand stitching; on delicate fabrics they should be sewn on directly, without ironing.

2 **RHINESTONES** come in many shapes, colors, and sizes. They might be **stuck, glued, sewn, or ironed** onto fabric. Embellishment goes especially quickly with stick-on rhinestones.

3 **BEADS** can be applied in subtle tone-on-tone shades or in eye-catching contrast colors. Some of the most common beads are seed beads and faux pearls; bugle beads and paillettes are also quite popular (*see page 79*).

! WHEN CHOOSING DECORATIVE MATERIALS, check to see whether they are washable; they must be compatible with the care properties of your primary fabric.

» SHOULDER PADS on blouses and sweaters are best applied with hook and loop strips. They can then easily be removed when the garment is washed.

SPECIALTY NOTIONS

Among available notions are ready-made products that **have particular characteristics** that enhance your finished design; some help give shape to an item.

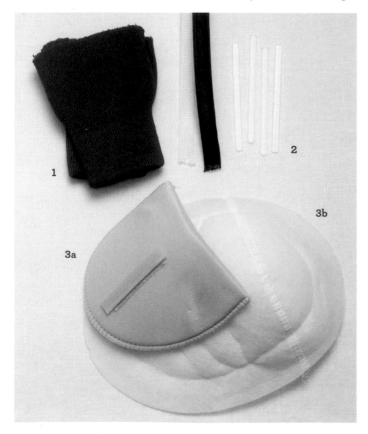

1 **KNITTED CUFFS** are primarily intended for tops made of jersey, sweatshirt material, and knitted fabric. The prefinished, elastic material allows you to make quick work of sleeve openings.

2 **BONING AND TWILL BONING** both come in assorted lengths and widths, and are made of various materials such as polyester, nylon, and metal. On some purses and corsets they are used to **stabilize the item's shape and are fed through channels built into the design.** Polyester twill boning can be sewn through.

3 **SHOULDER PADS** need to work with both the shape of the sleeve and the width of the shoulders. Standard **half-moon shoulder pads (3a)** are designed to work with set-in sleeves on blouses and lightweight jackets. **Oval pads (3b)** are for raglan and close-fitting sleeve shapes. Covered pads may be sewn by hand directly into unlined garments; **unfinished pads are intended to be sewn in between the main fabric and a lining,** or otherwise must first be covered.

4 **BAG HARDWARE** for straps on hand-sewn purses and tote bags is easy to attach. The **screw closure** helps you quickly add your handles.

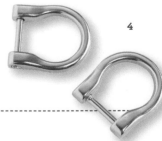

GLUES AND ADHESIVES

Some steps during sewing can be made easier or less time-consuming through the use of adhesive products. Before beginning to sew, be sure to **read the manufacturer's instructions.** It's advisable to test a product on a scrap of fabric first, or to begin in an area that will not be visible on the finished article.

PERMANENT ADHESIVES

Fabric glues are good for **quick and lasting adhesion of small pieces,** such as appliqués, if they are made of appropriate fabrics. Fray check is a clear gel that binds and strengthens woven surfaces and thus inhibits fraying at fabric edges. Apply the gel in a thin layer on the cut edges of fabric and allow it to dry; afterward you can sew seams even very close to the edges. Fray check is also helpful for working with extremely small fabric pieces.

TEMPORARY ADHESIVES

Spray adhesives, textile adhesive sticks, and double-sided basting tape allow for **temporary adhesion without pins or basting stitches** and prevent fabric from shifting during sewing. They are also useful when working with appliqués, patch pockets, belt loops, decorative trims, and zippers. The adhesives are water-soluble and do not leave behind any residue.

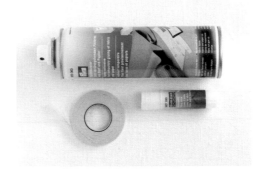

! When using **BASTING TAPE, CLEAN YOUR NEEDLE** after each seam to eliminate any sticky residue.

BONDING WITH AN IRON

Hemming tape (a) is a double-sided, iron-on adhesive tape. It allows you to quickly create a long-lasting hem finish. The tape comes with or without backing paper.
Fusible webbing (b) **will bond two fabric pieces permanently.** It is appropriate for use with all fabrics, including leather (using a low iron setting). It can even bond appliqués onto surfaces such as wood or cardboard.
Fusible film (c) is coated on both sides and can be used to **permanently bond appliqués** and fabric collages onto textile backgrounds.
Powdered bonding agent (d) is used to create a **quick but lasting bond for patches without the use of needle and thread.** The powder is sprinkled on the damaged area, and then the patch is laid on top and ironed. The powder melts and binds the two fabric pieces together.

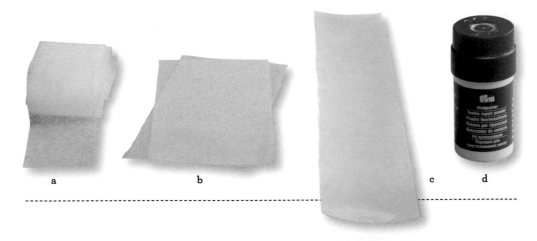

a   b   c   d

helpful
stabilizers

All sewing stabilizers are nonwoven and thus will neither rip apart nor dull machine needles, as would be the case with paper products. Stabilizers support machine sewing and embroidery and make it easier to manage. They are even used for traditional embroidery of decorative stitches, along with quilting and patchwork. They are useful for all kinds of creative projects.

SEWING AND EMBROIDERY STABILIZERS

Sewing and embroidery stabilizers are sold by a number of manufacturers and are available under various names.

These stabilizers are indispensable aids for professional-looking sewing and embroidery results. **An abundance of fabric types and sewing techniques** means there is also an **abundance of stabilizers.** Traditionally, stabilizers are placed under the main fabric in order to strengthen it. Sometimes stabilizers are placed **on top of the fabric** when the fabric is plush—as with velvet, terrycloth, fleece, or similar.

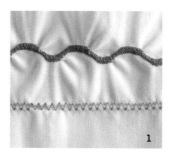
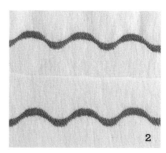
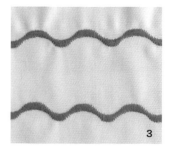

Stabilizers **prevent fabric from wrinkling, stretching, or puckering** (1, without stabilizer) during sewing or embroidery. **Evenness of stitches and embroidery** is also guaranteed when using stabilizers, as they prevent imprecise stitching and the sinking of stitches into the fabric (2, reverse side of fabric, top with one layer of stabilizer, bottom with two layers; 3, fabric as seen from right side). Some stabilizers can be drawn or printed on and therefore can work as templates. For hand embroidery using a hoop, the stabilizer can be stretched inside the hoop, ironed on, or bonded with spray adhesive, depending on the project.

! Cut STABILIZERS with all-purpose scissors.

» STABILIZER SCRAPS can be reused on smaller projects.

TEAR-AWAY STABILIZERS

Tear-away stabilizers are the most commonly used type of stabilizer. They prevent lightweight fabrics from being pulled into the feed dogs, **puckering during sewing, and/or ending up with uneven seams or uneven rows of embroidery.**
Tear-away stabilizer is applied to the back of fabric either with temporary spray adhesive or with **basting stitches;** when sewing is complete, the stabilizer can be carefully torn away.

APPLIQUÉS

Tear-away stabilizer can also be useful for working with appliqués. Place the stabilizer under the main fabric and apply the appliqué. The stabilizer ensures **wrinkle-free movement of fabric** and prevents the edges of the appliqué from pulling on the main fabric. When sewing is complete, the stabilizer can be carefully torn away up to the border of the appliqué.

FREEHAND EMBROIDERY

For freehand embroidery, the stabilizer is stretched in the frame underneath to **reinforce** the main fabric and carefully ripped away once the embroidery is complete.

SELF-ADHESIVE, TEAR-AWAY STABILIZER

This type of stabilizer has a paper backing that covers the adhesive coating. It is helpful with **awkward-to-handle textile pieces** (braids, ribbons) or for areas that are too small to be stretched into an embroidery frame (collar tips, cuffs, ties, napkin corners, et cetera). It is also **ideal for fabrics that cannot be stretched** because the frame would leave behind marks (velvet, corduroy, fleece, silk).
Pull the backing off the stabilizer, **press the fabric, ribbons, et cetera onto the adhesive,** then sew or embroider as usual. Because of its adhesive properties, this stabilizer is useful for many creative sewing projects.

RIBBON PATCHWORK

Satin ribbons are **placed edge to edge onto adhesive stabilizer** and then sewn down with novelty threads and/or decorative stitches.

>> WITH LIGHTWEIGHT FABRICS or closely spaced rows of embroidery, use TWO OR THREE LAYERS OF STABILIZER.

! THE RIBBON PATCHWORK TECHNIQUE is ideal for sewing together fabric and ribbon scraps in order to create new projects.

IRON-ON, TEAR-AWAY STABILIZER

This type of stabilizer is ironed on and is easy to tear away. When applied to **stretch fabrics**, it prevents them from getting stretched out of shape during sewing or embroidery work. Making buttonholes in stretch fabrics is also problem-free with this type of stabilizer, as the holes cannot pull out of shape. **Prior to sewing, iron** the stabilizer onto the back of the buttonhole placket. Once the buttonholes are completed, the stabilizer can be torn away.

>> **FABRIC-BACKED WITH IRON-ON STABILIZER** can be used in your printer—perfect for creative projects such as fabric greeting cards, gift tags, bags, boxes, et cetera.

>> **STABILIZER CAN ALSO BE USED TO MAKE CUTTING EASIER.** Slippery, delicate fabrics that are difficult to cut and whose **EDGES TEND TO ROLL INWARD** can be reinforced with iron-on stabilizer and cut like paper.

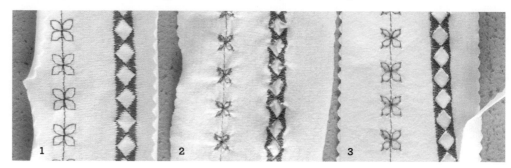

Fabric without stabilizer: The edges roll inward (1) or the embroidery is uneven and the fabric puckers (2). **An optimal result** can be achieved when an iron-on stabilizer is applied (3).

IRON-ON, HEAVY-DUTY STABILIZER

This stabilizer is extra strong, has a coated side for ironing on, and among many other uses can be employed as an interfacing on valances, as it lends fabrics a **lasting heft.** The stabilizer remains in the finished item in bags, backpacks, fabric boxes, and textile hangings, to provide permanent stability.

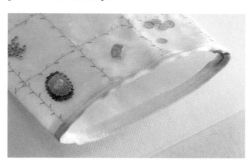

Iron the stabilizer, **coated side down, onto the wrong side of your fabric** (following manufacturer's instructions), then continue sewing per your instructions.

HEAT-SENSITIVE STABILIZER

This product is heat sensitive and disintegrates when ironed, leaving behind no residue. It is used on **sheer, thin fabrics and on unlined textiles** when the wrong side of the fabric will be visible on the finished product. It can be torn off after use, and any small leftover pieces can then be ironed away.

! Do not use **HEAT-SENSITIVE STABILIZER** on plush fabrics.

This stabilizer is placed **underneath the working fabric.** It can be basted in place or, with larger pieces, stretched in an embroidery frame.

WATER-SOLUBLE EMBROIDERY FILMS

These water-soluble stabilizers are transparent and available in different weights. Thick films can replace or reinforce working fabric, while thin films are used only as supporting layers.

THIN, WATER-SOLUBLE EMBROIDERY FILM

Thin, transparent, water-soluble film can be used when embellishing the surfaces of plush fabrics such as terrycloth, woolens, fleece, or faux fur, as well as fabrics with uneven textures such as French terry, velvet corduroy, piqué, bouclé, coarse linen, and certain knits. Decorative elements such as embroidered borders, motifs, or appliqués on the surface of these fabrics will maintain a clear, even stitch pattern and will not sink into plush textures or "wiggle" on piqué or velvet corduroy.

Very thin fabrics such as silk may be placed in between two sheets of thin, water-soluble film to be worked on more easily, as the film supports the fabric. The film becomes perforated by the stitching and is easy to remove later.

 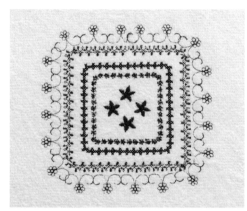

> **!** WATER-SOLUBLE STABILIZERS are EASILY WASHED OUT in lukewarm water; ANY REMNANTS, for example, in between embroidery rows, CAN BE DABBED AWAY WITH A WET COTTON SWAB.

THICK AND EXTRA-THICK WATER-SOLUBLE EMBROIDERY FILM

Thick, transparent, water-soluble film is used for sewing and embroidery work on delicate fabrics such as chiffon, organza, or tulle to create free-form machine embroidery and lacework. It can also be used like a working fabric and is helpful for freehand embroidery.

The film may be drawn on with a marker, and the drawing lines can then be sewn or embroidered, as for freehand monogram embroidery. Creative techniques such as textile collage and felting in the washing machine can be done with help from extra-thick water-soluble film.

Thread and fabric remnants can be arranged (sandwiched) between two layers of thick film, and this sandwich can be densely sewn over with either free-form stitching or straight lines. Dissolve the film in lukewarm water, tidy any errant threads using an embroidery needle, and allow to dry flat on a towel.

> **!** FABRICS used in combination WITH WATER-SOLUBLE STABILIZER must be WASHABLE.

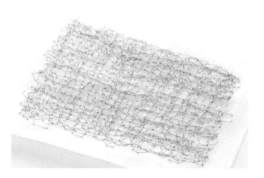 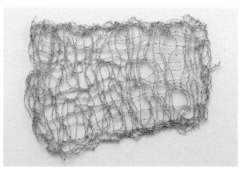

interfacings

A wide assortment of interfacings is available to choose from. They are used to provide shape and substance in strategic locations on garments or other textile creations.

! PATTERN INSTRUCTIONS typically will provide exact specifications for WHAT TYPE OF INTERFACING SHOULD BE USED IN WHICH AREAS.

INTERFACING OPTIONS

There are both woven and nonwoven interfacings that can be sewn in or ironed on (the latter type is usually called fusible interfacing). Most interfacings come in neutral colors such as white, beige, gray, or black. When choosing an interfacing, you must consider the **type of fabric you are using as well as its care properties and its ability to withstand ironing;** the interfacing's color must also be compatible with your chosen fabric. Fusible interfacings are especially popular for home sewing, as they will not fray, are easy to use, and are appropriate for most fabrics.

1 **FUSIBLE INTERFACING STRIPS** come in several styles:
Waistband interfacing (1a): This is available in varying widths and, despite the name, can be used for **cuffs as well as skirt and pant waistbands.** The premade folding and sewing lines allow for precise application without needing to mark the fabric; this is a great time saver.
Narrow waistband interfacing (1b): This punched band is helpful for creating crisp button plackets, narrow cuffs, pockets, and hems on jackets, coats, et cetera. It is ironed on with the perforated line along the fold line of the fabric. **Narrower hem facing (1c)** is reinforced with lengthwise fibers and is used to stabilize closing edges, pocket openings, sleeve slits, and lapels on jackets and coats.
Bonding web (1d): strengthens **high-stress seams** and is especially good for reinforcing seams on soft and stretchy fabrics such as jersey at shoulders, necklines, and sleeve openings. It also minimizes fraying at fabric edges.
Fusible bias tape (1e): This diagonally cut strip is used to **reinforce slanted or rounded edges** and may have an incorporated sewing guideline. In the latter case, it is important to make sure the sewing line is placed along the planned seam line when applying the tape.

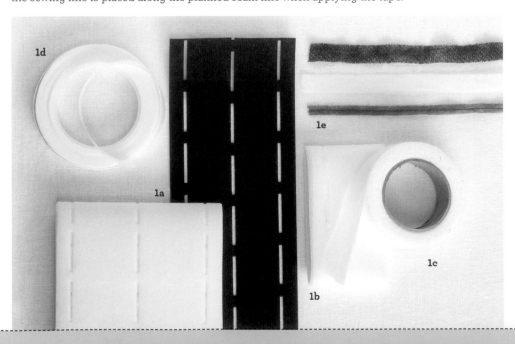

2 NONWOVEN FUSIBLE INTERFACINGS

consist of **synthetic fibers** and are available in many types. Depending on their weight, they are appropriate for delicate fabrics such as silk or viscose, lightweight fabrics such as cotton and polyester, or midweight fabrics such as wool and raw silk.

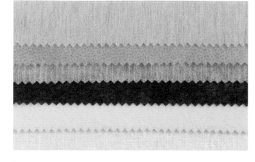

Stretchy interfacings are recommended for fabrics such as jersey, while there are special leather interfacings for heat-sensitive materials such as suede, leather, and faux fur. For light- to midweight fabrics, flexible interfacing with reinforcement fibers running lengthwise is used. Denser, more stable interfacing can also be used with light- to midweight fabrics and is useful for reinforcing belts, bags, hats, and fabric boxes.

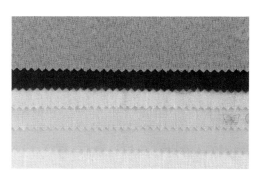

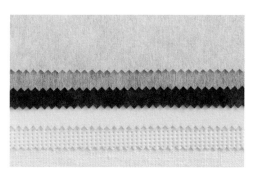

3 WOVEN FUSIBLE INTERFACINGS,

depending on type (sheer, light, medium, or heavy), are appropriate for **small areas on blouses and shirts made of woven fabrics,** but also for other textile projects. **Two-way stretch interfacing** will stretch both length- and widthwise and is primarily for use with **elastic** and **stretch fabrics,** such as cotton and polyester jersey, as it will not hinder their flexibility.

4 SEW-IN INTERFACINGS are used for

fabrics that cannot stand hot ironing, for example, plissé, crushed fabric, terry, and fabrics with printed coatings. It is especially good for small areas such as cuffs and collars on blouses, dresses, jackets, et cetera, as well as for hobby projects.

! IRONING **INSTRUCTIONS** for interfacing are printed **ON ITS EDGES** or on accompanying packaging, but you should always do a test first on a scrap of fabric. Per the manufacturer's instructions, lightly press for a few seconds on every part of the interfacing. Allow interfaced pieces to **COOL OFF COMPLETELY** before continuing work.

! **MID- AND HEAVYWEIGHT** interfacings are usually cut without seam allowances, so that finished seams and edges do not become bulky.

5 FLEECE INTERFACING comes in both

sewn-in and fusible versions and is often manufactured to resist pulling apart. Different thicknesses, from thin to highly plush and voluminous, are available. It can work like **batting in patchwork and quilt projects** and can give bags and fabric boxes a firm and even surface. It is also useful for warm clothing and three-dimensional embroidery effects.

recommended
ironing equipment

Ironing is one of the most important aspects of tailoring and sewing. The thorough pressing of seams allows for better working of further seams and makes an important contribution toward the shape of your finished project.

BASIC EQUIPMENT

The absolute minimum equipment for pressing and ironing consists of an iron, an ironing board, and a sleeve board. These should always be close by and at the ready while you are sewing.

1 **IRON** with **variable steam control and steam burst capability is best.** A standard, not-too-lightweight household iron that is comfortable to hold is recommended. **Nonstick soleplates** glide well and are easy to clean, preferably with a special cleaner designed for that purpose and available from your sewing store.
For large quantities of fabric or plush materials sensitive to ironing, such as velvet, corduroy, et cetera, a **fabric steamer** (not pictured) can be very helpful. It has a separate water container and can generate a large amount of steam even at lower temperatures.

2 **SLEEVE BOARD**, with different-sized ends, is padded and helps with ironing small or **difficult to reach areas,** such as necklines, narrow fabric tubes, and sleeve and pant cuffs.

3 **IRONING BOARD**, well padded and **height adjustable** (not pictured), is a must. Ironing comfort increases with various features; some boards have their own electrical outlet for the iron as well as a cord minder. For large pieces of fabric, an ironing board is indispensable.

>> IT IS BEST NOT TO USE a colored press cloth, as it could transfer dye. A press cloth should also have as smooth a surface as possible; TEXTURE PATTERNS CAN GET PRESSED INTO THE MAIN FABRIC.

HANDY HELPERS

Every household should have an iron and ironing board. The following small gadgets and accessories can further lighten a home sewing enthusiast's workload.

4 **IRONING MITT** for quick ironing of **sleeves, collars, lapels, pockets, and ties.** The strap on the back of the mitt can go over your hand or over the narrow end of a sleeve board.

5 **PRESS CLOTH**, placed between iron and fabric, **prevents delicate fabrics such as silk and wool blends from becoming shiny.** A press cloth made of translucent cotton batiste, silk, or organza is especially practical, since you can see through the cloth to the fabric being ironed. When additional steam is required, the cloth may be dampened.

6 **CLOTHES BRUSH** is for removing **chalk marks,** preferably before ironing. It is also useful when ironing **plush fabrics,** to immediately fluff up the surface while it is still warm.

7 **TAILOR'S HAM** is for steaming shaped or curved areas such as shoulders, necklines, collars, hip curves, and darts. It is **egg-shaped and firmly stuffed.** It is sometimes **outfitted with a strap or belt** on one side, so it can be fastened to the narrow end of an ironing board, with either the more pointed or the blunter end facing outward, as needed.

8 **SEAM ROLL** (*see page 64, number 1*), **for ironing seams,** is about 12"–14" (30–35cm) long and firmly stuffed, and is especially useful with fabrics that tend to show ironing marks. The round shape helps prevent seam allowances from creating an impression visible on the right side of the fabric.

9 **PATCHWORK IRON/QUILTING IRON** is designed especially for small fabric pieces and very narrow spaces where a normal iron cannot reach. It simplifies ironing on patchwork and quilt projects, as well as on doll clothing, and can be used for ironing bias tape, appliqués, et cetera. Depending on the manufacturer, interchangeable heads in various shapes may be available.

9

pretty and practical

Alongside your indispensable equipment, there are a number of accessories that can support your creative endeavors and make certain tasks go more quickly and easily. And it's truly fun to work with beautiful gear, even if it's not put into use as often as your scissors and measuring tape. These so-called luxury items also assist in generating precise and beautiful results, making the extra effort well worth it.

1   Seam roll for ironing seams

2   Retractable tape measure for taking body measurements

3a Decorative thimble, probably less suited for actual sewing

3b Thimble made from comfortable rubber

4   Needle case with built-in threader

5   Decorative pin cushion with whimsical pins

6   Magnetic pin collector

7   Mini steam iron for ironing seams

8   Needle threader for effortless threading

9   Seam ripper with built-in magnifier

10 Seam ripper with built-in tweezers

11 Magnetic pin cushion

12 Tweezer scissors with spring action

13 Tweezers for pulling threads

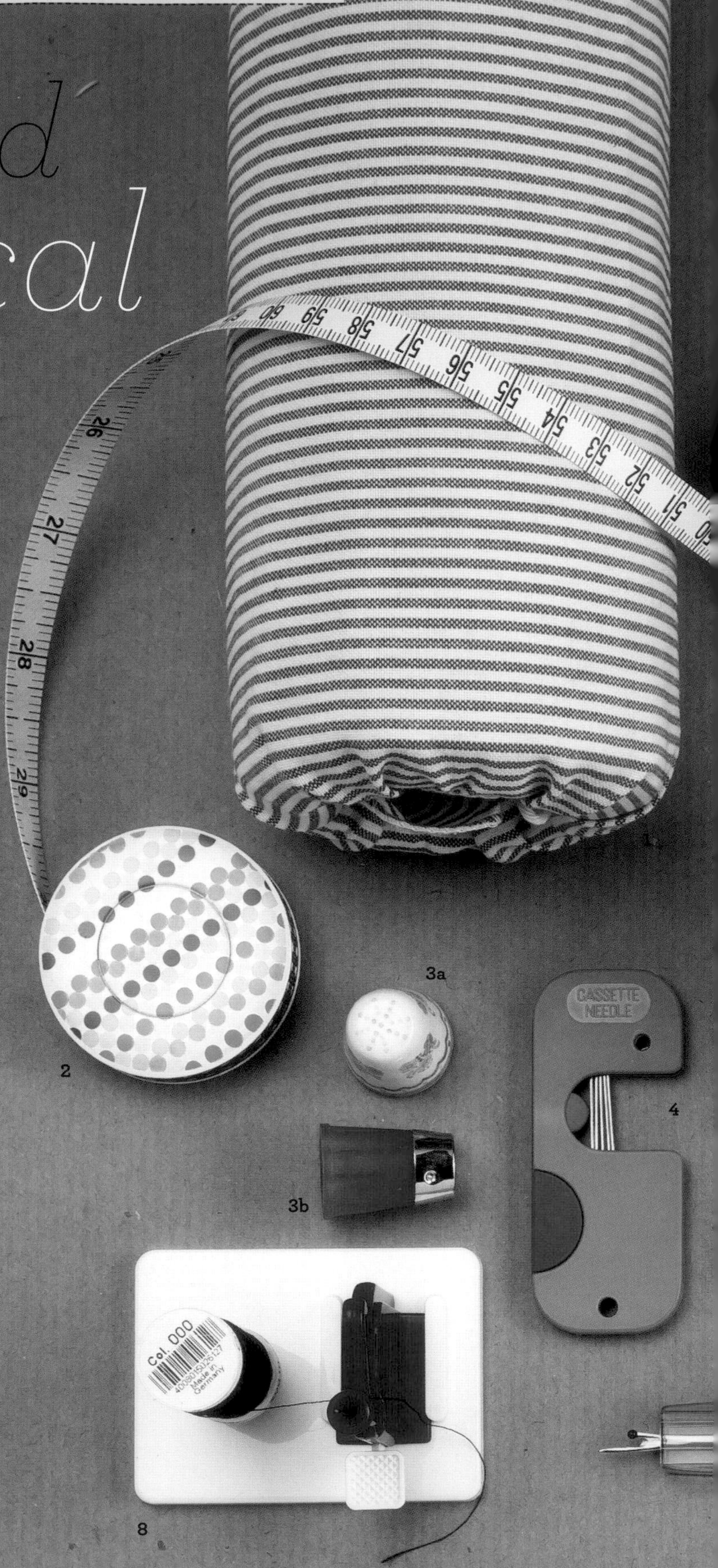

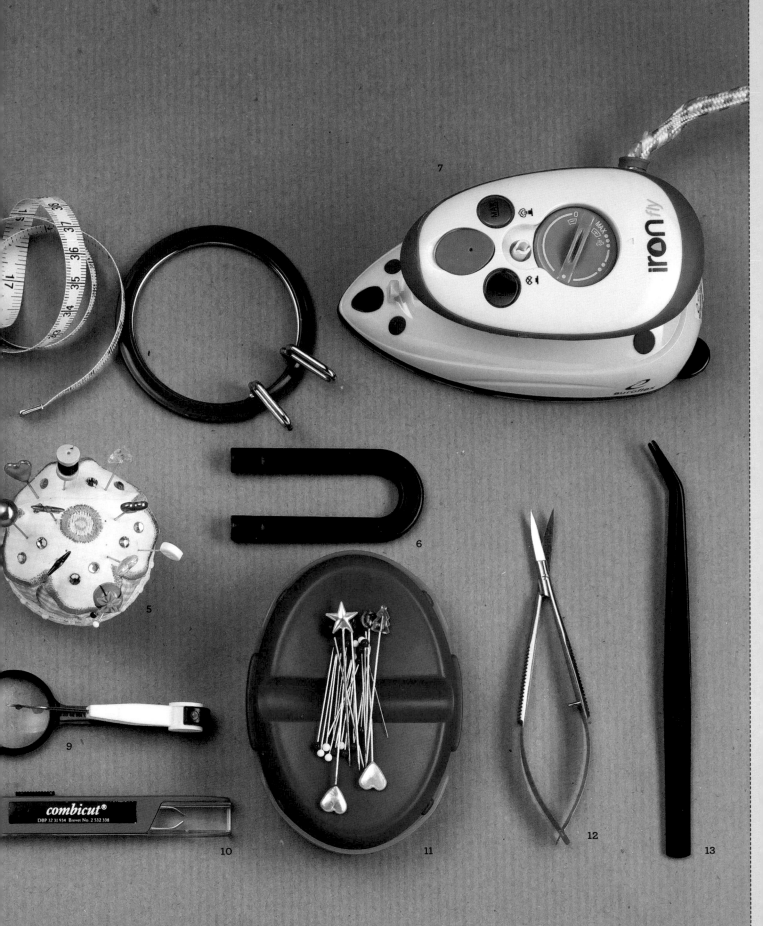

7

6

5

9

combicut®
DBP 32 31 934 Brevet No. 2 532 338

10

11

12

13

sewing techniques

MANY ROADS LEAD TO BEAUTIFUL FINISHED SEWING PROJECTS. STILL, SOME FABRICS CALL FOR SPECIFIC THREAD TYPES OR SPECIFIC SEWING TECHNIQUES. BOTH UTILITY STITCHES AND DECORATIVE STITCHES CAN BE WORKED BY HAND OR WITH A MACHINE. BUTTONHOLES, HEMS, AND EDGINGS CAN BE FASHIONED IN VARIOUS WAYS. EMBELLISHMENT TECHNIQUES OFFER A COLORFUL HOST OF FURTHER POSSIBILITIES.

sewing by hand

Sewing by hand has become less common in the age of modern sewing machines, but certain hand stitches are still useful. The so-called utility stitches are used to hold together layers of fabric when making garments, home décor items, or other sewing projects. Decorative stitches serve as pretty accents and add individuality to hand sewn items.

HANDSEWING NEEDLES

Since every different fabric and technique requires an appropriate *sewing needle (see page 34)*, we recommend that you have a small assortment on hand in **different lengths and sizes,** and with **various types of tips.** For small stitches a short needle is practical, while for larger stitches a long one is preferable. A general rule: the more delicate the fabric, the thinner the needle. **Darning and embroidery needles** have bigger eyes, so that heavier threads can be used.

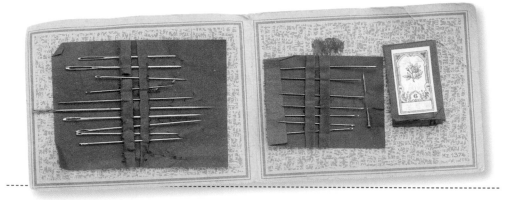

THREAD TYPES

Your thread should be matched to your fabric type and the intended use of your project. For **utility stitching,** *standard/universal sewing thread (see page 40)* is typically used; for **decorative stitching,** use thicker *embroidery thread (see page 69)*. Stitches will be subtle when made with thread matching your fabric or in a slightly darker or lighter shade, while strongly contrasting thread will create striking accents. As a rule, utility stitches are made with a **single thread,** but for certain applications, such as attaching fasteners, a **doubled thread** will supply greater stability *(see page 71, lower right)*.

! THE CORRECT THREAD TENSION—as with your choice of thread and needle—is just as important when handsewing as when machine sewing. You should PULL THE THREAD EQUALLY TAUT AFTER EVERY STITCH, so that it is neither too tight nor too loose, and so that it works with your fabric.

! A DURABLE SEAM is achieved through short stitches, not long ones. Stitching lines and contours may be DRAWN ON THE FABRIC BEFOREHAND WITH A WATER-SOLUBLE MARKING PEN. Left-handers should follow given instructions in mirror image.

OVERVIEW OF THE MOST COMMON EMBROIDERY THREADS

Embroidery thread comes in **various weights** and is put up in tiny hanks or balls. Multi-ply thread can be divided to create thinner stitches. **The heavier the embroidery thread, the more three-dimensional the stitching will be.** Your fabric can be pulled taut in an **embroidery hoop** to help the stitches come out nice and even.

» 100% SYNTHETIC AND SYNTHETIC-BLEND THREADS tend to twist. To discourage this, keep your THREAD LENGTH ON THE SHORTER SIDE.

1 **EMBROIDERY FLOSS** has six strands and is appropriate for many kinds of embroidery and fabrics, whether used **as is** or **divided** into fewer strands. Because of the versatility of having multiple strands and its general utility, it is the most popular kind of embroidery thread. Embroidery floss is washable in water up to 200°F (95°C).

2 **FOUR-STRAND EMBROIDERY FLOSS** is a classic all-purpose embroidery thread that works with numerous techniques. It is made from slightly shiny cotton fibers and is available in multiple weights. Soft, durable **matte embroidery cotton** (not pictured) works well with coarser fabric types and is characterized by a light, matte sheen. It is lightly twisted from five plies and is easy to work with. Both the 4-ply and 5-ply are washable in water up to 200°F (95°C).

3 **PEARL COTTON** (also called perle cotton) is a 2-ply, lightly twisted yarn with a **silky look** (3a), which, on account of its even stitch formation, works well for all kinds of embroidery projects. It is **washable in water up to 200°F (95°C)**. Metallic pearl cotton (3b) is made of a combination of cotton and metallic threads and can be **washed in water up to 85°F (30°C)**.

4 **MULTICOLOR** embroidery thread is cheerfully variegated and **available as floss or pearl cotton**. Depending on the type, it is washable in water up to 140–200°F (60–95°C).

5 **METALLIC EMBROIDERY THREAD** is characterized by its brilliant metallic shine and can be used anywhere a **pronounced**

glittering effect is desired, such as on embroidered holiday items. It is often used in combination with embroidery floss. **This thread is washable in water up to 85°F (30°C).**

6 **EMBROIDERY HOOPS** are primarily useful for decorative embroidery. Fabric is clamped between the two rings so that it is taut and stitches can be **evenly formed**. The two-piece hoops come in many sizes and are also available with stands.

preparations for *handsewing*

Regardless of whether you are sewing by machine or by hand, if you want good results you must take sufficient time for each step in the process. It is also important not only to have the right tools, but also to know how to use them correctly.

THREADING HAND NEEDLES

Use sharp scissors to cut a piece of thread to the desired length; it **should not be longer than about 24" (60cm)**. Thread that is too long can quickly become knotted and tangled, more so with every pull through the fabric. Threading is easier when the thread is **cut on the diagonal** and the **end is dampened**.

SINGLE THREAD END
Insert one end of your thread through the eye of an appropriate embroidery or *handsewing needle (see page 68)*, pulling through about a **quarter of the thread's length**. When choosing your needle, pay attention to whether **the size of the eye suits the weight of your thread**: an eye that is too small will make threading difficult, while an eye that is too large allows thread to slip out easily.

FOLDED THREAD END
This technique is advisable for use with **darning thread and multi-ply** thread that tends to fray apart at the ends.

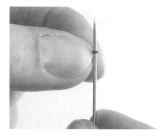 

1 Fold the thread firmly over the needle. Pull the needle downward and out of the ensuing tiny loop; **do not let go of the loop.**

2 Insert the tip of the loop in the eye and pull through.

USING A THREADER
Threaders are especially helpful with **delicate needles and thin thread.**

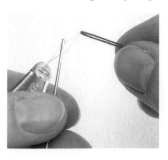 

1 Insert the wire loop of the threader into the eye of the needle and **draw the thread through the loop.**

2 **Pull the threader back out through the eye**, along with the short end of the thread.

» THREAD BECOMES MORE DURABLE, is less likely to twist, and glides better through fabric if it is waxed before use. To wax thread, DRAW IT THROUGH A PIECE OF BEESWAX, lay it between two pieces of paper toweling, and briefly iron. The wax will be distributed evenly into the thread, and any extra will be absorbed by the paper towels.

! BEFORE YOU THREAD YOUR NEEDLE, check whether it is clean and has a sound point. You need an unblemished needle to achieve good results.

» SELF-THREADING NEEDLES can be very helpful. The eye has a slotted top, across which the thread is draped. The thread then slips into the eye with a gentle tug.

SECURING A HANDSEWN SEAM

Thread ends must be secured at the start of a seam, preferably as unobtrusively as possible on the back (or wrong) side of the fabric, either with a knot or with backstitches. A small, double backstitch is appropriate for securing a permanent seam. For provisional seams, such as for basting or for holding opening edges of a garment together, place a knot at the end of your thread so it cannot slip through the fabric.

>> There are several ways to TIE A KNOT; with every method, it will be EASIER IF THE THREAD END IS DAMPENED.

LOOPED KNOTS

For provisional seams a knot is typically used. Make a loop at the end of the thread and pull the end through to make a **knot.** Depending on the weight and type of thread you are using, you may want to make a second knot at the same point to help **prevent the thread from slipping through the fabric later.**

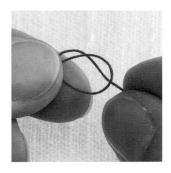

ROLLED KNOTS

Knots can be made quickly using the rolled technique. With a little practice and nimble fingers, rolled knots will soon be effortless.

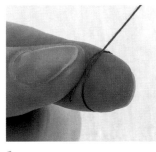 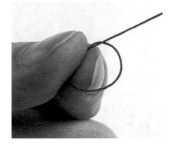 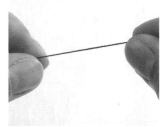

1 Wrap **one thread end** around the tip of your index finger (= loop); hold the other end of the thread with your free hand.

2 Use the **tip of your thumb** to roll the thread off of your index finger, so that the **end of the thread goes into the loop;** do not let go of the thread.

3 Hold the loop with the help of your middle finger and release your index finger, while at the same time pulling with your other hand **so that a knot results** at the thread end. Trim any extra thread remaining beyond the knot.

! WHEN WORKING WITH DOUBLED THREAD, lay both ends next to each other and knot them together (bottom left).

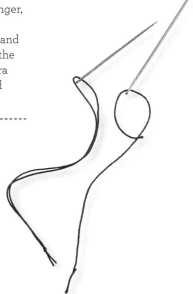

SECURING THE START OF A SEAM

It is particularly important on permanent seams to secure your thread at the beginning. There are different ways to achieve this, but it is always done starting in the seam allowance or at the back (or wrong side) of the fabric.

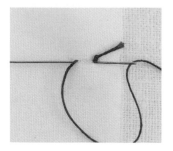

KNOT PLUS BACKSTITCH

The following is good for **securing both basting seams and permanent seams:** first *make a knot* at the long end of your thread *(see page 71, lower right).* Stick the needle into the fabric and out again about ⅛" (3mm) away. Then insert the needle again next to the knot and pull through to the top at the first exit point.

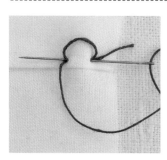

DOUBLED BACKSTITCH

This method is for **securing permanent seams,** particularly with sheer materials. Without knotting the thread, insert the needle into the fabric from above and up again about ⅛" (3mm) away, leaving a tail of thread approximately ⅝" (1.5cm) long. Then insert and exit again at the same spots, creating a small loop. Make a second backstitch at the same spot, pull the needle through the loop, and pull taut.

SECURING THE END OF A SEAM

» ON VERY THIN AND DELICATE FABRICS, as well as in any spot where a knot would be likely to pull through, it is advisable to secure a seam at both ends WITH TWO OVERLAPPING BACKSTITCHES.

A seam must be secured at the end just as at the beginning. If your remaining thread isn't long enough to make a knot or backstitch, it can be secured with fabric glue.

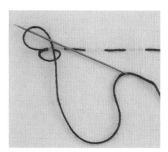

BACKSTITCH PLUS KNOT

This technique creates a **very secure seam closure.** At the end of your row of stitching, make a small backstitch, leaving a tiny loop. Stick the needle through this loop, allow a second loop to form, and pull the needle through that loop as well. Pull the ends tight and trim the remaining thread end.

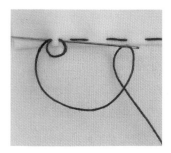

DOUBLED BACKSTITCH

This method is used to **secure permanent seams,** particularly with sheer materials. At the end of the seam, make a small backstitch, leaving a loop behind. At the same spot, make a second backstitch and insert the needle through the loop from the first stitch. Pull the thread taut and trim the remaining thread end.

assorted hand stitches

Choose the most fitting stitch type for your sewing project. The following lays out the most important hand stitches, as well as some specialized utility stitches and what they are used for.

UTILITY AND DECORATIVE STITCHES

For utility stitches, which ideally should be barely noticeable, thread should be **color matched** to your fabric and used in a straightforward way. The more precise your stitching, the prettier and more durable your seams will be. **Decorative stitches,** in contrast, do not need to be rendered precisely in every instance; indeed, some embroidery works best with irregular stitching, which can lend a **whimsical charm.**

BASTING

Basting with special basting thread serves to **temporarily hold together fabric layers** so that they will not shift during sewing. Contrasting thread is best for this use, so that the stitches are easily visible. When the basting seam is no longer needed, the **thread is easy to pull out.**
As if weaving, insert the needle into the fabric from top to bottom, and then a short distance later bring it back through to the top. Stitch **length and distance between stitches should be equal on both sides,** usually about ¼"–½" (5–10mm). For quick basting where accuracy is less important, the stitch length may be as long as ¼" (6mm) and the distance between stitches up to 1" (25mm).

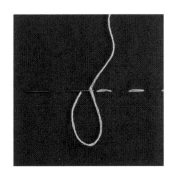

DIAGONAL BASTING

With this large stitch—approximately 1" (2.5cm) long—also **called tailor basting, large pieces can be quickly tacked together,** as when securing interfacing or lining onto a main fabric. Short, closely set diagonal stitches are used in cases where fabric layers must not shift; for example, when **seam edges must be kept flat** for topstitching on heavy fabrics, or when pleats need to be established before ironing. The needle should always exit at the left. Then insert it again at some distance above and to the right, making a horizontal stitch from right to left. The shorter and closer the stitches, the stronger the hold.

>> WATER-SOLUBLE BASTING THREAD is a helpful time saver. It is used like normal thread but dissolves upon contact with water or steam, leaving no residue. It is especially practical when working with SLIPPERY FABRICS, since you can sew directly on top of the basting stitches. This thread should be used only on FABRICS THAT WILL NOT BE DAMAGED BY WATER.

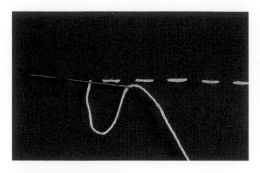

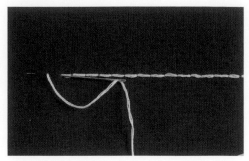

RUNNING STITCH

This is used as a **decorative stitch** to **accent contours**, edges, and borders, and is **also used for gathering**. For the latter, usually two parallel rows of stitching are worked, with the individual stitches lined up and parallel, and the start and end of the stitching are not secured.

The **running stitch** is worked like the basting stitch, but the stitches are shorter. Insert the needle into the fabric from the top to the bottom, and then a short distance later bring it back through to the top. The **stitch length** should be correlated with how strong the seam needs to be—**the shorter the stitch, the stronger it is.** The stitches may be of equal size on both sides of the fabric, or longer on the top.

BACKSTITCH

Backstitching **resembles machine stitching** and creates a **stable handsewn seam**. It is used for repair work as well as for decorative accents. **The stitches are twice as long on the back side of the fabric as on the front.** Short, individual backstitches can also be used at the beginnings and ends of seams to secure them.

To start, insert the needle through the fabric from the bottom to the top. Then insert the needle a half stitch length ¹⁄₁₆" (2–3mm) behind the exit point and bring it back to the top a half stitch length ¹⁄₁₆" (2–3mm) beyond the exit point. For every following stitch, the insertion point is the exit point of the previous stitch.

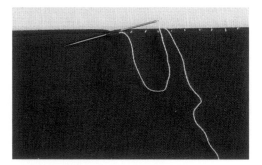

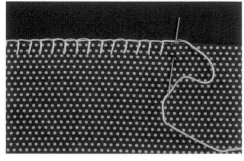

WHIPSTITCH

This practically invisible stitch (when worked with matching thread) is used to connect two finished, folded-over edges or to attach appliqués.

To start, bring the needle out through the front folded edge and then insert it **directly across** into the rear folded edge. Guide the needle diagonally toward the front through the fabric and bring it out again, catching just a thread or two on the front folded edge.

BLANKET STITCH

The blanket stitch creates a chain of stitching along a fabric edge. It is good for **finishing the edges of fraying fabrics, decorative finishing of wool and fleece fabrics,** and sewing on appliqués and ribbons. It may be worked with alternating shorter and taller stitches for variation.

Insert the needle into the fabric ¼" (5–6mm) or so below the edge and guide it vertically to the edge. **Lay the thread along the edge of the fabric for the desired stitch distance and insert the needle again from below, as shown, creating a loop; then pass the needle up through the loop.** Pull the thread gently taut so that it will lie evenly along the edge of the fabric.

⚠ RUMMAGE AROUND YOUR HOUSE, in your cabinets and drawers—there are so many items that lend themselves to embroidery. Dish towels, curtains, fabric shoes, bags, or fabric lampshades can be **TRANSFORMED WITH JUST A FEW STITCHES.**

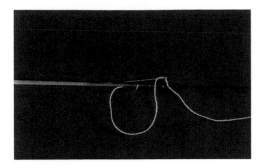

SLIPSTITCH

The invisible slipstitch is particularly good **for sewing two folded edges together**; for example, a short opening in a seam that is accessible only from the front. Slipstitching is often used for **sewing in linings**. Appliqués can also be sewn on with this stitch.
Bring the needle through the fold of the lower fabric. Insert the needle directly across from that exit point into the other fold, then exit the fold after a stitch length of about ¼" (6mm). **The next stitch is made directly opposite that exit point in the lower fold,** then pulled through and out again after an identical stitch length. Pull the thread taut every few stitches so that the edges pull together.

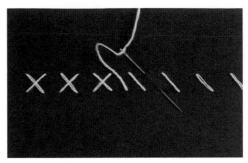

CROSS-STITCH

The well-known, simple cross-stitch is very versatile and can be used to outline motifs, create borders, or fill empty areas, to give just a few examples. Usually the stitches are made **without spaces in between**. Gingham is a popular background for cross-stitching, as its grid pattern allows for the easy creation of even cross-stitches without any added markings required.
In general the bottom stitch is made from lower right to upper left. The thread is guided underneath the fabric, and the top stitch is made from lower left to upper right. When multiple cross-stitches are worked in a row, **first work all the bottom stitches, and on the return path work all the top stitches.** Entire stitches can also be made one by one, but this will use slightly more thread.

» TO AVOID KNOTS on the back of an embroidery piece, begin your work by pulling all but about 1" (2–3cm) of the thread through from back to front. **CATCH THE THREAD TAIL UNDER THE FIRST FEW STITCHES, THUS COVERING IT UP ON THE BACK OF THE FABRIC.** When finishing with a length of thread, feed it under a few of the existing stitches on the back.

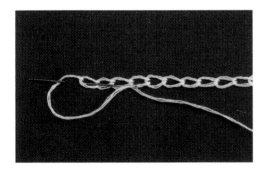

CHAINSTITCH

So named because the line of loops in this stitch **resembles the links in a chain**, the chainstitch is used mainly to create outlines and decorative borders.
Bring the needle through the fabric from behind (the bottom) to the front and **create a loop.** Insert the needle directly next to the exit point and exit again one stitch distance away, being careful to **bring the needle out through the loop.** Pull the thread through and tug gently taut to create a link in the chain.

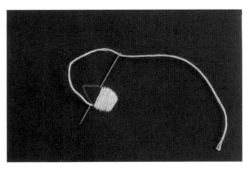

FLAT STITCH

The densely worked flat stitch serves to **fill in small surface areas** and is often combined with other embroidery stitches; for example, stitches that emphasize the outline of the filled shape.
To start, insert the needle at one marked edge through the fabric from underneath. Insert the needle into the directly opposite marked edge from top to bottom and bring to the top again **directly adjacent to the first exit point.**

» WITH AN IRON-ON TRANSFER PEN you can transfer patterns onto your fabric using tracing paper and an iron. If you want to draw freehand designs or trace around a stencil, you can use a **DISAPPEARING-INK MARKER.** Always test markers first on a scrap of fabric.

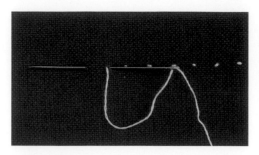

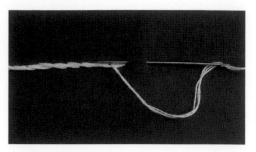

>> If you are just becoming familiar with decorative stitches and would like to practice, **EMBROIDER A VARIETY** of them onto a piece of plain fabric—you will end up with a decorative **SAMPLER**.

DOT STITCH

These stitches appear on the **right side of the fabric as small dots** and are almost invisible when worked in matching thread. They are created like the backstitch, but with shorter stitches. Dot stitches are **well suited for sewing in zippers on delicate fabrics.** A *shallow* dot stitch is worked only on the top layer of fabric, so that the stitching is not visible on the **underside**; for example, when embellishing collar edges.

Bring the needle through the fabric from the back to the front, then insert the needle one or two fabric threads behind the exit point; bring the needle back to the front about ⅛"–¼" (3–5mm) from the previous exit point.

STEM STITCH

This stitch is frequently used for **outlining and to create stems of embroidered leaves and flowers.** The stitches lie slightly slanted along a line. When accurately formed, they will look like a row of backstitches on the reverse side of the fabric. To create a wider line, hold the needle at more of a diagonal.

Work from left to right; the needle points left. To start, insert needle through fabric from the bottom to the top. At one stitch length, or about ¼" (5mm), insert needle from top to bottom and then back to top **at the midpoint between the exit and insertion points.** As you continue, always insert the needle after a stitch length and come back up at the end of the previous stitch. Keep the thread running below the sewing line.

! FEATHER STITCH was originally used for smocking. Now it is often used to embellish edges and seams, and is popular for use **WITH APPLIQUÉS**.

FEATHER STITCH

The feather stitch is good for **sewing abutted edges together**, as on patchwork; for applying ribbon trims; and as a decorative stitch. To create consistent stitches, it is best to draw **four equally spaced parallel lines** beforehand.

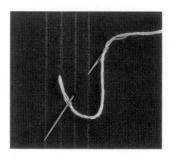

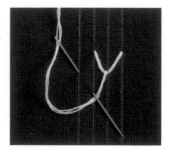

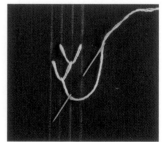

1 Bring the needle from the back to the front on the second line from the left and **form the thread into a loop.** Insert the needle into the rightmost line horizontally across from the exit point, then bring the needle up again **midway between the two points** but slightly lower down, making sure the loop is under the needle. Pull the thread through to **create a V shape.**

2 Insert the needle at the same height on the far left line, then bring the needle to the front lower down on the second line from the left. **This creates a second V.**

3 Now insert the needle again on the rightmost line and come back up through the second line from the right.

4 The simultaneously looped and open form of the completed stitch **resembles a feather.**

FRENCH KNOTS

This three-dimensional decorative stitch resembles a small bead and can be made as an individual accent or clustered together. It is a good choice for the centers of embroidered flowers.

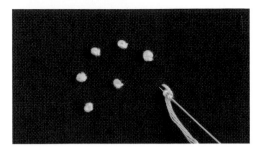 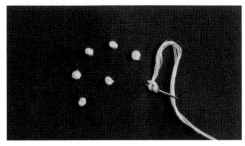

1 Bring the needle through the fabric from the bottom to the top, then wrap the thread one to three times around the needle, depending on thread thickness and the desired finished size of the knot.

2 Insert the needle into the same spot it came out, holding the wrapped thread onto the surface of the fabric, if needed, and pull the thread through to create a knot.

>> ALWAYS TAKE CARE WHEN IRONING EMBROIDERY. Raised and three-dimensional stitches SHOULD NOT BE PRESSED FLAT. If the fabric requires ironing, use a thick, soft cloth as a base and PROTECT THE EMBROIDERY WITH A PRESS CLOTH.

SPECIAL UTILITY STITCHES

Alongside the standard utility and decorative stitches, which in some cases are very versatile and can be used for numerous purposes, there are also **special utility stitches with very particular functions.**

THREAD TRACING/THREAD MARKING STITCH

On sheer and delicate or thick and soft or plush fabrics, it is sometimes difficult to transfer pattern markings using tailor's chalk or copy paper. In these cases you can use thread tracing (marking), a **precise method** borrowed from classic tailoring that **creates thread marks simultaneously on both sides of the fabric, even through multiple layers.** Depending on the type of fabric, a coarse thread may be preferable, as it will not as easily slip out of the fabric. **For sheer and delicate fabrics, it is better to use standard sewing thread and a thin needle.** Always use **contrasting thread,** so that it will be easy to see.

1 With the thread doubled, stitch along the lines and markings to be transferred **through the pattern paper and all layers of fabric.** Bring the needle from the bottom to the top and then a ways farther from top to bottom through all layers. Do not pull the thread taut, but rather **leave ½"–1" (1.5–2.5cm) loops standing on the top.** Make normal-size stitches along the straight lines and shorter stitches around curves. **Snip the tops of the loops** and carefully lift away the paper.

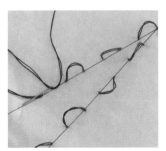

2 Pull the fabric layers carefully apart and cut through the threads in between, so that **thread pieces remain hanging** in every layer. Now all sides are marked. After basting the pieces you may want to use tweezers to help remove the thread markers.

THREAD CHAIN

A thread chain is used to hold **two fabric layers together with a certain amount of leeway**; for example, on a coat where the lining is loosely bound to the outer fabric. Thread chains can be made to any desired length and can also be employed as **eyes for hooks or as button shanks.**

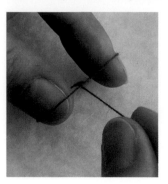
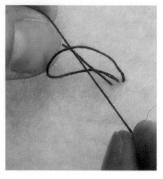

1 Knot the end of your thread and work a small *backstitch (see page 74)*, but do not pull the thread all the way through; instead, **leave a large loop.** Insert two fingers into the loop.

2 Pull the thread through so that another loop is created, **similar to making a crochet chain stitch.**

3 Pull the first loop tight against the fabric, **holding on to the second loop.**

4 Work further loops until the chain is the desired length. **Pull the thread through the last loop,** pull taut, and sew the thread chain down at the desired point.

BUTTONHOLE STITCH

Handsewn buttonholes add an attractive accent to items such as thick coats or boiled wool fabrics and should be made using especially sturdy buttonhole, silk, or cotton thread.

1 To begin, bring the needle up from the back of the fabric, ¹⁄₁₆"–¹⁄₈" (1.5–3mm) from the edge, and work stitches horizontally toward the edge. On the next stitch, bring the needle up from below again **very close to the previous exit point, leaving a small loop** as you pull it through.

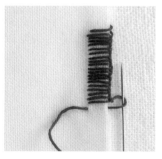

2 Guide the needle **through the loop from below.** Tug on the thread so that the tiny **knot that is formed lies directly on the cut edge.**

! IF YOU ARE MAKING A BUTTONHOLE with heavy thread, such as buttonhole silk, use a single strand. If you would rather use normal sewing thread, use a double strand and pull evenly on both strands after every stitch.

! IN ORDER TO BETTER SHOW THE INDIVIDUAL BUTTONHOLE STITCHES, they are shown here as longer than usual and slightly separated, using contrast thread. When actually sewing buttonholes, be sure that the STITCHES LIE CLOSE TOGETHER.

BEADED EMBROIDERY

Beaded and sequin embellishments can give clothing and home décor pieces a glamorous touch. They may be sewn on **individually or in clusters,** or already strung together, preferably using matching or transparent thread. For beads with very small openings it is best to use a thin *beading needle (see page 34, number 5).* **Depending on their purpose and on your preferred look,** there are **various ways to apply them** to your fabric.

! DEPENDING ON THE INTENDED USE OF YOUR ITEM, pay attention to whether BEADS ARE WASHABLE. Many types of beads and, especially, sequins are also heat-sensitive and can easily fade or melt upon encountering a hot iron.

SEQUINS

Bring the needle from the **bottom to the top** through the fabric and stick it through the sequin, then insert the needle into the fabric **close to the left edge of the sequin.** Come up through the hole again and insert the needle at a different point along the sequin edge. **The number of repeats is up to you.**

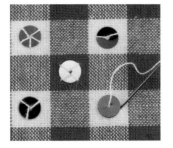

SEQUINS COMBINED WITH BEADS

Bring the needle from the **bottom to the top** through the fabric and stick it through the sequin, then thread a **small round or seed bead** onto it. Insert the needle back through the center of the sequin to the back of the fabric.

BEAD ROWS

Bring the needle from the **bottom to the top** through the fabric and thread the bead onto it; insert the needle back into the fabric behind the bead. Two bead lengths farther ahead, bring the needle back to the top and thread on the next bead. If the beads are of varying sizes, the stitch length must be adjusted accordingly.

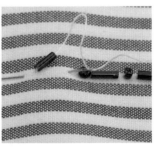

» STRANDED SEQUINS AND BEADS can also be applied with a machine using a zigzag stitch. For this you will need a special *beading foot (see page 25, number 9).*

STRANDED BEADS

Stranded beads may be purchased ready-made or can be **made from scratch to the desired length.** Strand the beads (or sequins, bugle beads, seed beads, et cetera) in the required amount on a strong thread and attach them to your fabric using a *whipstitch (see page 74).*
Bring the **needle** from the bottom to the top and lay the thread **at a right angle** over the string. Insert the needle close to the string and bring it back out one bead away. On a string of sequins, slip the thread between the sequins with every stitch, so that it is hidden. With very small beads such as seed beads, a strand may be **tacked down** at approximately ⅜" (1cm) intervals.

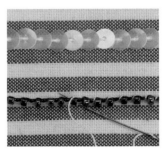

RHINESTONES

Sew-on rhinestones come in some interesting shapes, with and without metal mountings. They have **holes or tunnel-like channels** so that they can be sewn on.
Bring the needle from the bottom to the top through the fabric and through one of the openings in the rhinestone, then insert the needle back into the fabric behind the stone. Sew through the opening three or four times in the same direction, then sew any remaining openings in the same manner.

essential machine stitches

Modern sewing machines offer a number of utility and decorative stitches. With them you can sew and finish clothing, accessories, and home décor items. A large selection of decorative stitches is available to combine with novelty thread, machine embroidery thread, and specialty presser feet to add embellishment and structure to textile surfaces.

UTILITY STITCHES

Machines come with different utility stitches depending on the model and manufacturer. With these stitches you can accomplish all **standard sewing on all types of fabric.** Variations can be created through use of double eye, twin, and triple needles; with the help of these, **even simple straight and zigzag stitches can become eye-catching borders, quilting, and embroidery,** and lend a unique touch to textile surfaces.

>> HEAVIER FABRICS should be sewn with a longer stitch length.

! SECURE THE BEGINNING AND END of a seam with backstitches.

STRAIGHT/RUNNING STITCH

The straight stitch, or running stitch, **consists of straight, regular stitches** and is the standard sewing machine stitch. It is the most frequently used utility stitch. With it you can accomplish all kinds of **basic sewing tasks,** such as seams, hems, pleats, gathers, darts, and much more. The stitch length is adjustable—the longer the stitch, the looser the seam. Straight stitches can be made both forward and backward using a *standard or straight stitch foot with a round opening (see page 20).*

- Three or four backstitches at the start and end of a seam will secure it. **You may also see this referred to as** *locking* the seam.
- With appropriate decorative thread and a *twin, triple, or double eye needle (see page 38),* a **standard utility stitch can become a decorative topstitch or embellishment.**
- With the stitch length set to the longest setting and the top thread tension loosened, a straight stitch may be used to **create gathers on a single fabric layer** or to **baste two pieces of fabric together.**
- All fabrics can be sewn with a straight stitch. It is also used for **freehand embroidery** *(see page 132)* or for **staystitching** *(see page 202).*

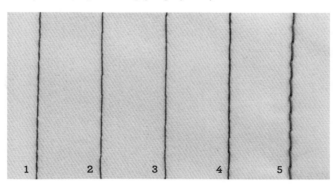

Seams 1–5: Straight stitch
Seams 1–3: Standard thread, stitch length 11 spi* (2.5mm), 5.5 spi (4.5mm), 4 spi (6mm)
Seam 4: Cotton embroidery thread, 30 weight, stitch length 7.5 spi (3.5mm)
Seam 5: Decorative/topstitching thread, stitch length 6 spi (4mm)
* = stitches per inch

ZIGZAG STITCH

Like the straight stitch, the zigzag stitch is among the **standard stitches of a modern sewing machine**. This **stitch is adjustable**, in that its length and width may be changed, and it may be used on all types of fabrics. It requires a *zigzag foot (see page 20)* and can be sewn forward and backward.

- The zigzag stitch can be used to **finish fabric edges**; a stitch length and width setting of 6 spi (4mm) is recommended.
- A tight zigzag stitch with a stitch length of 18 spi (1.5mm) is **slightly elastic** and can be used to sew jersey and knit fabrics, but also to sew **seams, embroidery, and appliqué**.
- A wide zigzag stitch can be used to sew over elastic thread to **gather** fabric.
- Multiple rows of zigzag stitching in various colors will create pretty **embroidery borders**.
- With an appropriate specialty presser foot, such as a cording foot, open toe foot, or darning foot, the zigzag stitch can be used to **apply and additionally embellish ribbon, cording, and yarn**.

Seams 1-5: Zigzag stitch
Seam 1: Standard thread, stitch length 6 spi (4mm), stitch width 6 spi (4mm)
Seam 2: Standard thread, stitch length 18 spi (1.5mm), stitch width 18 spi (1.5mm)
Seams 3 + 4: Embroidery cotton, 30 weight, stitch length 7.5 spi (3.5mm), stitch width 5.5 spi (4.5mm)
Seam 5 (fabric edge): Embroidery/topstitching thread, stitch length 6 spi (4mm), stitch width 6 spi (4mm)

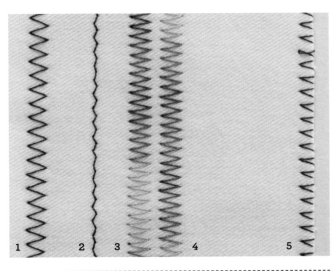

! WHEN OVERCASTING FABRIC EDGES, make sure that the needle ALTERNATES BETWEEN STITCHING INTO THE VOID AND STITCHING INTO THE FABRIC.

ELASTIC ZIGZAG STITCH

The elastic zigzag stitch is a three-part stitch and is appropriate for **sewing together stretch fabrics** and for **applying elastic bands or sewing them together**. Because of its three-part composition, the stitch does not pull together fabric as much as a standard zigzag stitch and is therefore popular for **finishing the edges of thick fabric**.

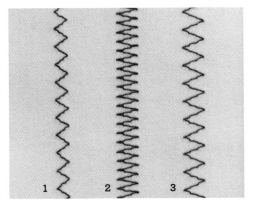

Seam 1: Stitch length 5 spi (5mm), stitch width 6 spi (4mm)
Seam 2: Stitch length 13 spi (2mm), stitch width 4 spi (6mm)
Seam 3: Stitch length 4 spi (6mm), stitch width 4 spi (6mm)

! ELASTIC THREAD is lightly stretched during sewing, so an ELASTIC STITCH looks SHORTER after sewing as the elastic pulls back into shape.

» WITH STRETCH FABRIC, use a ball point needle *(see page 37)*.

STRETCH STITCH

The stretch stitch is a three-part stitch that is **slightly elastic and extremely durable.** It is ideal for all textiles with elastic or spandex content, as well as for pant hems and work clothes that must endure high stress at the seams.

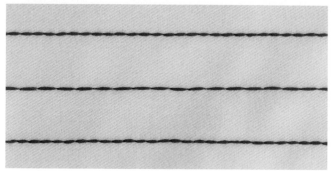

Top: Stitch length 9 spi (3mm)
Middle: Stitch length 5 spi (5mm)
Bottom: Stitch length 11 spi (2.5mm)

» FOR A MINIMALLY VISIBLE HEM, the thread color must match exactly that of the fabric.

! REINFORCE SEAMS IN LOOSELY WOVEN FABRICS with lightweight stabilizer, so that they do not stretch during sewing.

BLIND STITCH

The blind stitch is appropriately named: with it you can create **practically invisible hems,** as is desirable on most garments. This stitch consists of a number of straight stitches followed by a zigzag stitch that grabs a thread of fabric, thus securing the hem. A *blind stitch foot (see page 20)* is required with this stitch.

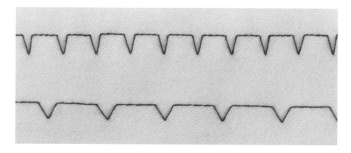

Top: Stitch width 5.5 spi (4.5mm), stitch length 11 spi (2.5mm) (standard setting)
Bottom: Stitch width 11 spi (2.5mm), stitch length 9 spi (3mm)

OVERLOCK STITCH

High-end sewing machines are equipped with overlock stitches for **sewing together elastic** fabrics while simultaneously **finishing** and **reinforcing fabric edges.** Overlock stitches are made with the blind stitch foot and are especially elastic.

» OVERLOCK STITCHES can also be used as decorative stitches.

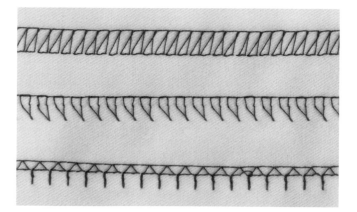

Top: Closed overlock stitch
Middle: Closed overlock stitch with reinforced edge
Bottom: Open overlock stitch

DARNING STITCH

The darning stitch repairs **holes, tears, and worn spots** in textiles. It requires the use of a **darning foot**, and the **feed dogs must be lowered** or covered (see your machine's user manual for instructions) so that the fabric is not fed through the machine but rather can be **moved freely.** Embroidery and darning thread (*see page 42*) is used for both the top and bottom thread. The darning stitch, which is preprogrammed on many machines, can be a **straight** stitch, a **zigzag** stitch, or an **elastic zigzag** stitch.

» CHOOSE AN EMBROIDERY FRAME LARGE ENOUGH so that the presser foot will not run into it.

FREEHAND DARNING

Install the darning foot, lower the feed dogs, and thread the top and bottom threads. Select a straight stitch and set the machine to darning mode (see your machine's user manual for instructions). Reinforce the damaged area from the back with fusible stabilizer or with additional fabric and **pull the working area taut in an embroidery hoop.** Guide the embroidery hoop evenly backward and forward while maintaining a medium sewing speed, until the damaged area is completely sewn over. The stitch length will be determined by the movement of the hoop. **The faster you sew, the more even the stitching will be.** Sew over the damaged area from left to right and then from top to bottom. Alternatively, you may rotate the work 90 degrees and sew from left to right (or right to left) again. **Important guidelines for machine darning will be found in your machine's user manual.**

! **FREEHAND DARNING** and freehand machine embroidery are identical as far as technique.

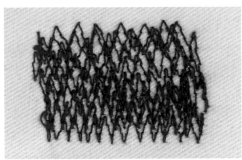

Top: Programmed darning stitch
Middle: Freehand darning with straight stitch
Bottom left and right: Freehand darning with zigzag stitch

BUTTONHOLES

With the help of a modern sewing machine, you can sew all kinds of different buttonholes *(see pages 228–232)* that harmonize with different fabric types and clothing styles. Machine-sewn buttonholes generally require a *buttonhole foot (see page 21)*. There are **automatic buttonholes** that are created in one step, and buttonholes that are worked in two to four steps (see your machine's user manual for instructions). In addition to standard programmed buttonholes, some machines will have **eyelet and stretch buttonholes.**

Buttonholes are made up of two long rows of stitching (called the *legs*) that are made with narrow zigzag stitches and of two *crossbars* that are made with wide, overlapping zigzag stitches. **The crossbars delineate and secure the buttonhole.** After sewing, buttonholes are opened with a *seam ripper (see page 31, number 4).*

Buttonholes can also be made incorporating **lightweight cording or pearl cotton.** Corded buttonholes are **slightly raised and more clearly defined.** The cording is covered by the buttonhole leg stitches. Some buttonhole feet are designed to hold cording taut during sewing.

! BUTTONHOLES IN LINENS will come out especially even when they are made with EMBROIDERY AND DARNING THREAD OR 80-WEIGHT SEWING THREAD.

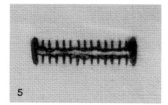
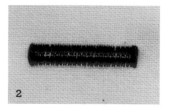

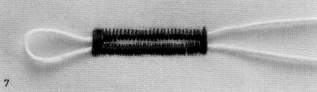
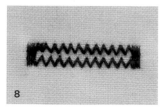

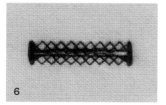
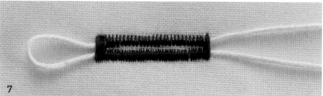

>> To avoid inadvertently damaging the crossbar WHEN RIPPING OPEN A BUTTONHOLE, stick PINS HORIZONTALLY IN FRONT OF THE CROSSBARS to stop the seam ripper (as shown at bottom). Buttonholes in lightweight fabrics should be reinforced with stabilizer.

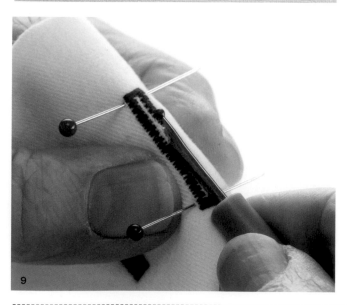

1 Rounded buttonhole
2 Wide linen buttonhole
3 Narrow linen buttonhole
4 Eyelet buttonhole
5 Blanket stitch buttonhole
6 Stretch buttonhole
7 Corded buttonhole
8 Stretch buttonhole
9 Cutting open a buttonhole with a seam ripper

ATTACHING BUTTONS

Not having to sew on buttons by hand is a great time saver, especially when multiple buttons need to be attached. With a sewing machine and a *button attachment foot (see page 21)*, the work is quick and easy. The first step is to mark the button placement points *(see page 236)*.

BUTTONS WITHOUT SHANKS

Buttons without shanks, or **sew-through buttons**, can be quickly attached using a sewing machine.

Remove the presser foot from the machine and lower the feed dogs. Place the fabric and the button under the presser foot holder. Lower the presser foot lever and select a **zigzag stitch** (stitch length 0, stitch width = distance between holes). Sew back and forth through the holes about 5 to 7 times, then **pull the thread ends to the back of the fabric and tie them off.**

BUTTONS WITH SHANKS

A shank prevents the button from **compressing the lapped edges of a garment when it is closed.**

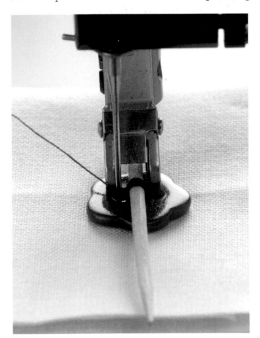

A toothpick or matchstick is used to maintain a separation between the button and the presser foot holder and is sewn over with a zigzag stitch. Pull the thread ends up between the button and the fabric using a sewing needle, remove the toothpick, and **wrap the shank section multiple times with the thread ends**; tie off the thread ends on the back.

» USING CONTRASTING THREAD TO ATTACH BUTTONS can lend a decorative, whimsical element to children's garments.

! A BUTTON ATTACHMENT FOOT *(see page 21)* is available as a supplemental presser foot. However, it is not strictly necessary *(see page 237)*.

» INSTEAD OF A MATCHSTICK you can also use a universal tool and height equalizer *(see page 18, number 8)*.

DECORATIVE STITCHES

Many sewing machine models come equipped with a number of decorative stitches that let your creativity run wild. They are adjustable in height, width, and thickness; may be combined; and can change in appearance depending on the chosen thread, needle, and fabric. They are used for **quilting and embellishing textiles, and for home décor items.** A few ground rules must be followed to achieve good results.

STABILIZERS

All fabrics are easier to embroider when they are **reinforced with a stabilizer** (*see page 56*), since densely spaced and wide embroidery stitches tend to pucker fabric.

THREAD TENSION

A looser thread tension (–2) than that for regular sewing is generally used when working decorative stitches. The bobbin tension may also be slightly increased.

THREAD WEIGHT

Perfect machine embroidery can be achieved with 40-weight rayon machine embroidery thread (*see page 43*). If the density of the embroidery is insufficient to cover the background fabric, and there is no way to further adjust the density, changing to 30-weight thread will quickly solve the problem.

STITCH BALANCE

Decorative stitches are programmed into the machine with the **optimal stitch and width values preset.** Depending on your working fabric, these presets may need to be adjusted, **which is done via the stitch balance control.**

NEEDLES

Machine embroidery threads are thicker than standard sewing thread and therefore require a bigger needle eye. Use machine **embroidery or topstitching needles.**

>> ALWAYS DO A TEST RUN on a scrap of your actual fabric, using machine embroidery thread and INCLUDING AN APPROPRIATE STABILIZER.

1 Border
2 Motif stitch
3 Floral motif stitch
4 Quilting stitch
5 Cross stitch
6 Satin stitch

SCRIPTS AND MOTIFS

Modern sewing machines are often equipped with alphabets, monogram letters, and small motifs. These are lovely design elements to embellish and personalize clothing, linens, home textiles, and accessories.

>> PURCHASED CLOTHING can be PERSONALIZED to your own taste through embroidery of small MOTIFS or LETTERING.

! EMBROIDERY WORK should always be reinforced underneath with STABILIZER, which may be applied using a temporary SPRAY ADHESIVE.

PROGRAMMED LETTERS AND MOTIFS

Reinforce the working fabric on the back and possibly also the front with stabilizer, and pull the drum tight in a sufficiently large embroidery hoop. If the fabric is smaller than the hoop, place *self-adhesive, tear-away stabilizer (see page 57)*, with the paper backing facing up, into the hoop. Pull off the backing and press the back of the fabric onto the adhesive surface.

MACHINE SETTINGS
Stitch: Motif chosen from machine
Presser foot: Standard or specialty embroidery foot
Needle: Machine embroidery or topstitching needle
Thread: Machine embroidery thread, both upper and lower

! FOR EMBROIDERY WORK, 30- OR 40-WEIGHT RAYON MACHINE EMBROIDERY THREAD and a machine embroidery needle are recommended.

fundamental machine seams

Seams give textiles structure, add fashionable accents, and create focal points. The seam you choose, from a multitude of seaming styles, is guided by the type of fabric and its intended use. Seams can be made visible or invisible depending on the technique employed. Whether a garment has a sporty or an elegant feel is dependent on the fabric itself in combination with the chosen seaming style and its execution. As a rule, polyester, silk, or cotton thread is used for seaming.

SIMPLE SEAM

The so-called simple, or straight, seam is the simplest and most frequently used seaming technique to sew together two or more pieces. It is sewn using a **straight stitch**.

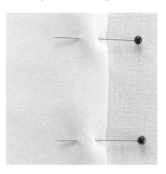  

>> Sew **LIGHTWEIGHT FABRICS** with a stitch length of 11 spi (2.5mm) and needle size 11 (75 European).

Sew **MEDIUM-WEIGHT FABRICS** with a stitch length of 9 spi (3mm) and needle size 12 (80 European).

Sew **HEAVYWEIGHT FABRICS** with a stitch length of 7.5–6 spi (3.5–4mm) and needle size 14–16 (90–100 European).

! **LOOSELY WOVEN AND KNIT FABRICS** tend to stretch out. Seams can be **STABILIZED** by sewing **COTTON TAPE** onto the seam allowances close to the stitching line. An alternative is to use iron-on **STAY TAPE**, which comes in black or white and is applied directly next to the seam line on the wrong side of the seam allowances.

Place two fabric pieces together with right sides facing and pin along the edges with straight pins. Mark the sewing line and sew along it with a straight stitch, removing pins as you go. **At the start and end of the seam, work a couple of backstitches (using the reverse button), or knot the ends.** Press the seam allowances apart and *finish (see page 102)* the edges of the seam allowances with a zigzag stitch or pinking shears.

MACHINE SETTINGS
Stitch: Straight stitch, stitch length 11 spi (2.5mm)
Presser foot: Standard or straight stitch foot with round opening
Needle: Standard needle
Thread: All-purpose thread on top and bottom, in color matching fabric

SIMPLE SADDLE STITCH SEAM

The simple saddle stitch seam consists of a simple seam with an additional line of stitching on the right side of the fabric. This creates a decorative seam and eliminates the need to finish the seam allowances.

 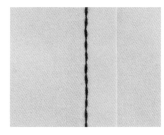

MACHINE SETTINGS
Stitch: Straight stitch
Presser foot: Standard or edging foot
Needle: Standard needle
Thread: All-purpose thread on top and bottom, in color matching fabric

Sew a simple seam, press the seam allowances to one side, and then sew down the seam allowances from the right side using a straight stitch. Use the presser foot as a guide to maintain an even distance from the seam.

» SEAM ALLOWANCES can be sewn down on the right side of the fabric with decorative thread using a straight stitch, or try a ZIGZAG OR EMBROIDERY STITCH.

DOUBLE SADDLE STITCH SEAM

The double saddle stitch seam consists of a simple seam whose seam allowances are sewn down on either side.

As with the simple saddle stitch seam, first sew a simple seam, but press the seam allowances apart. From the right side, sew down the seam allowances with a straight or zigzag stitch on both sides of the seam, using the presser foot as a guide to maintain an even distance.

MACHINE SETTINGS
Stitch: Straight or zigzag stitch
Presser foot: Standard or edging foot
Needle: Standard needle
Thread: All-purpose thread on top and bottom, in color matching fabric

RAW SEAMS

Raw seams are sometimes used as a modish detail on contemporary clothes. In this case, the seam allowances lie on the right side of the garment and can be frayed, embroidered, or beaded.

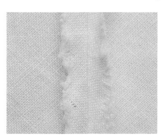

Place two fabric pieces together with wrong sides facing, pin, and sew with a straight stitch ⅝" (1.5cm) from the edge. Work the fabric edges with a stiff brush, so that they fray slightly.

» ROLL UP THE FABRIC and then brush the raw edges.

! LOOSELY WOVEN OR BIAS CUT FABRICS are best suited for this technique.

FRENCH SEAM

This seam is used to sew two fabric pieces together and finish the seam simultaneously. It is appropriate **only on straight seams** and is frequently used for delicate fabrics, lingerie, bed linens, and unlined clothing.

⚠ A SLIGHTLY MODIFIED, NARROWER VERSION of this seam, called a chiffon seam or chiffon hem, is used for sewing together very thin and sheer fabrics, such as chiffon, georgette, voile, and satin crêpe. Place TWO FABRIC PIECES WRONG SIDES TOGETHER, pin the edges, and sew using a straight stitch with a 1/16" (1.5mm) seam allowance. Sew A SECOND SEAM PARALLEL TO THE FIRST, a little more than 1/16" (2mm) away. Trim the seam allowances close to the seam and FOLD THE FABRIC RIGHT SIDES TOGETHER, so that the seam lies within the folded edge and the raw edges are enclosed. SEW OVER THE SEAM EDGE USING A ZIGZAG STITCH. Thin, water-soluble stabilizer will prevent the fabric from being pulled into the feed dogs.

Cross section

Place two fabric pieces wrong sides together, pin edges, and sew together using a straight stitch with a 1/4" (6mm) seam allowance. Trim seam allowances to 1/8" (3mm) and press apart. Fold fabric **right sides together** so that the seam lies within the folded edge and the raw edges are enclosed. Stitch again approximately 3/8" (1cm) away from the fold.

MACHINE SETTINGS
Stitch: Straight stitch
Presser foot: Standard, straight stitch foot, or edge stitch foot
Needle: Standard needle
Thread: All-purpose thread on top and bottom, in color matching fabric

FELLED/FLAT FELLED/DENIM SEAM

Felled seams are double-sewn seams. They are very sturdy, and the second topstitching eliminates the need to finish the seam. Felled seams are most often used on **unlined garments** where the inner seams are partially visible and must look tidy. Jeans are sewn in part using felled seams with a contrasting topstitching thread.

 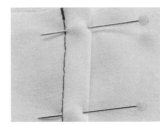

MACHINE SETTINGS
Stitch: Straight stitch
Presser foot: Standard, edge stitch foot, or felling foot
Needle: Standard needle
Thread: All-purpose thread on top and bottom, in color matching fabric

Place two fabric pieces right sides together, pin, and sew together with a 5/8" (1.5cm) seam allowance. Press the seam allowances to one side and **trim the bottommost seam allowance by 1/4" (5–6mm).**
Fold the wider seam allowance over the trimmed allowance so that the trimmed allowance is enclosed. Press and pin the seam.
Topstitch the folded seam from the right side, **parallel to the first seam, at a 1/4" (5mm) distance.**

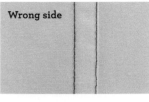

Wrong side

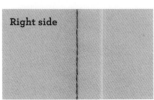

Right side

MOCK FELLED SEAM

For time and cost considerations, the garment industry uses mock felled seams in some unlined outerwear and on almost all jeans.

 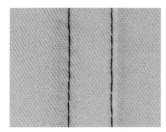

MACHINE SETTINGS
Stitch: Straight stitch
Presser foot: Standard or edge stitch foot
Needle: Standard needle
Thread: All-purpose thread on top and bottom, in color matching fabric

Place two fabric pieces right sides together, pin, and sew using a straight stitch with ⅝" (1.5cm) seam allowance. Press the seam allowances to one side and finish with a zigzag or overcast stitch. Topstitch from the right side.

! THE MOCK FELLED SEAM is an especially durable seam.

» USE BUTTONHOLE THREAD for topstitching on sturdy fabrics. Stitch length 9–6 spi (3–4 mm), needle size 16 (100 European).

OVERLAP SEAM

The overlap seam is appropriate for **textiles that fray either very little or not at all**—for example, flannel, boiled wool, loden, sweatshirt material, leather, suede, vinyl, and oilcloth. The seam is flat and has minimal bulk.

 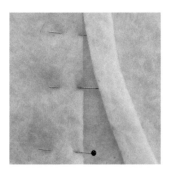 

» OVERLAP SEAMS are especially attractive when a DECORATIVE STITCH is used to sew them.

LIGHTLY FRAYING FABRICS

Place two fabric pieces next to each other, right sides up. Fold the seam allowance on one piece to the wrong side and lay this piece over the unfolded piece to the desired seam width. Pin and topstitch from the right side close to the folded edge and, if desired, again about ¼" (5mm) away.

NON-FRAYING FABRICS

For boiled wool, leather, vinyl, et cetera, place two fabric pieces next to each other and **trim the seam allowance from one piece** (rather than folding it under). Lay this piece over the untrimmed piece to the desired seam width; secure the overlap with fabric glue or water-soluble double-sided *basting tape (see page 55)*. Pin and topstitch from the right side close to the edge and, if desired, again about ¼" (5mm) away.

MACHINE SETTINGS
Stitch: Straight stitch
Presser foot: Standard or edge stitch foot, or a roller or non-stick foot for leather or vinyl *(see page 22, number 4 and page 24, number 6)*
Needle: Leather needle
Thread: All-purpose thread on top and bottom, in color matching fabric

MOCK COVERSTITCH SEAM

A mock coverstitch seam can be made on any sewing machine. The **seam is elastic** and is well suited for **sewing stretch fabrics together.** It resembles the coverstitch seam made by a coverlock machine. On the front are two parallel stitching lines, and on the back a slightly shifted zigzag stitch. The seam is appropriate for hems and interior seams. Work the seam like an **overlap seam** (*see page 91*), but using a **twin needle and two spools of thread,** mounting the spools so that they feed in *opposite* directions.

! WHEN WORKING WITH A TWIN NEEDLE and two spools of thread, the spools should be attached so they feed off in *mirror image* (opposite) to each other. They can then be FED THROUGH THE TENSIONER AND THE THREAD TAKE-UP LEVER AS IF THEY WERE A SINGLE THREAD.

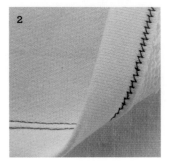
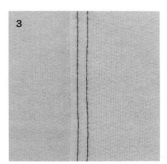

MACHINE SETTINGS
Stitch: Straight stitch, stitch length 9–7½ spi (3–3.5mm)
Presser foot: Standard foot
Needle: Twin stretch needle, needle distance 2.5mm (about ³⁄₃₂")
Thread: All-purpose thread on top and bottom, in color matching fabric; mount the second spool so that the two threads feed in opposite directions
Tension: Loosen upper tension slightly

In order to generate even stitching, apply a thin, water-soluble adhesive stabilizer film to the fabric. After sewing, either tear away the film or rinse it out. Mock coverstitch is appropriate for both hems (2) and seams (3).

OVERLOCK SEAM

Modern sewing machines are outfitted with an overlock stitch, which is used to **sew seams and edgings on elastic fabrics** so that the seams will not stretch out. A *blind stitch foot (see page 20)* may be used to achieve additional elasticity.

! OVERLOCK STITCHES can be made using either a standard or a blind stitch foot.

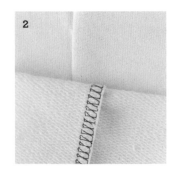
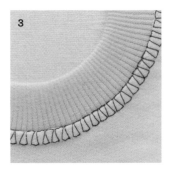

Place the fabric right sides together; **loosen upper thread tension slightly,** mark the sewing line, and stitch. Trim any excess seam allowances to the overlock stitching (1). Overlock stitch as it appears on both front and back (2). Overlock stitch on a curve (3).

MACHINE SETTINGS
Stitch: Overlock stitch
Presser foot: Blind stitch foot
Needle: Ball point needle
Thread: All-purpose thread on top and bottom, in color matching fabric

sewing with specialty fabrics

Materials such as stretch fabrics, velvet, leather, faux fur, sequined fabrics, and PVC are popular and available by the yard. Working with them takes extra care and the use of special needles, tools, threads, and/or techniques.

ELASTIC MATERIALS

These fabrics get their elasticity from the way they are manufactured and the incorporation of elastic threads. **Warp knit fabrics** are not created on a weaving loom with warp and weft threads, but rather are **made up of stitches** created on knitting machines *(see page 139)*. Stretch and knit fabrics are stretchy because of their construction and require **special cutting and sewing techniques** to preserve their elasticity and corresponding comfort when wearing. The elasticity of the seams should match the fabric, so a **short stitch length** should be used—at most 13 spi (2mm)—so that the seams contain enough thread to remain elastic.

STRETCH FABRICS

Stretch fabrics contain elastic fibers such as spandex (also called elastane) and may be **woven or warp knit**. *Stretch needles (see page 37, number 2)* are used for sewing these fabrics, since their lightly rounded tips cannot split the spandex fibers. **All-purpose polyester thread, with its slight elasticity** *(see page 41)*, is ideal for creating seams in *stretch fabrics*. Stretch fabrics are optimally sewn with an overlock machine, but modern sewing machines are typically outfitted with stretch and overlock stitch capabilities; many also have integrated walking feet to **feed the fabric evenly from both top and bottom,** which allows for the creation of elastic seams without any waviness.

It is possible to create a seam that closely simulates an elastic seam on a basic sewing machine by using a **narrow zigzag stitch with a width of 70 spi (0.3mm) and a length of 6 spi (4mm).** Seams may also be sewn with a **twin stretch needle (2.5mm needle spacing);** such seams will be elastic but cannot be pressed apart. The top thread tension should be reduced when using this method. Seams also will remain elastic if sewn with a *mock coverstitch (see page 92)*. Use a twin stretch needle (4.0mm needle spacing), loosen the top tension slightly, and decrease the pressure on the presser foot.

Some machines are programmed to make stretch buttonholes. Buttonholes in stretch and knit fabrics can also be made with the help of **fusible, tear-away stabilizer or water-soluble stabilizer.** Fusible stabilizer is ironed onto the back of the fabric and torn away after the buttonhole is completed. The stabilizer prevents the fabric from stretching during sewing. Another option is to use a heavy, water-soluble stabilizer under the fabric; it can be washed out after use. A supplementary layer of thin, water-soluble stabilizer may be used on top of the fabric to make the buttonholes appear more even.

>> **SEW ELASTIC FABRICS** with programmed overcast stitches to simultaneously stitch and finish the seams. Using a **BLIND STITCH FOOT** will prevent the fabric from puckering when sewn with wide stitches.

1 Narrow zigzag stitch
2 Programmed stretch stitch
3 Seam with twin needle/programmed overlock stitch
4 Mock coverstitch/twin needle seam

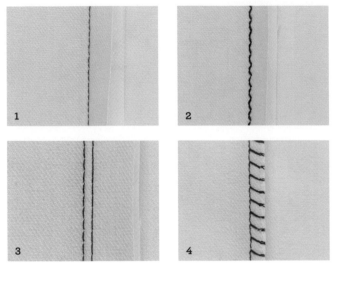

MACHINE SETTINGS

Stitch: Zigzag stitch, stitch length 6 spi (4mm), stitch width 70 spi (0.3mm); stretch or overlock stitch

Presser foot: Standard foot; blind stitch foot for overlock stitch

Needle: Ball point needle, twin stretch needle Engage integrated walking foot or install walking foot

Thread: All-purpose thread on top and bottom, in color matching fabric; for a coverstitch seam set the second spool of thread on a separate spool pin

>> THE SEAMS AND CUT EDGES of lightweight jersey/knit fabrics should be reinforced before sewing with iron-on, tear-away stabilizer (see page 58) to prevent seams from pulling together. Remove stabilizer carefully after sewing.
BUTTONHOLES SHOULD LIKEWISE BE STABILIZED FROM THE BACK BEFORE SEWING.

>> TO PREVENT SHOULDER, neckline, and arm opening edges from stretching out of shape, apply fusible bias tape along the stitching line.

>> HEMS MAY BE SEWN WITH A MOCK COVERSTITCH (see page 92); loosen the upper tension somewhat, decrease the presser foot pressure, and use a stabilizer underneath the fabric.

! CURVED EDGES in lightweight jersey and other knit fabrics are EASIER TO CUT PRECISELY if they are first reinforced with iron-on, tear-away stabilizer.

KNIT FABRICS

Jersey and other knit fabrics are warp knit, and are soft and stretchy. A *ball point needle (see page 37, number 4)* must be used with these fabrics, as the rounded tip slips through the spaces between the stitches without damaging them. Use all-purpose polyester thread *(see page 41).* Like stretch fabrics, warp knit fabrics are optimally sewn with an overlock machine, but they may be equally well sewn using the stretch and overlock stitch capabilities on a modern machine combined with a walking foot (whether integrated or separate) to create elastic seams without any waviness.

Seam allowances on **lightweight knits** do not need finishing, while seam allowances on **heavier knits** may be finished using a large zigzag or overlock stitch. Adding in a heavier thread (such as thin crochet thread) will help prevent fabric edges from stretching out of shape.

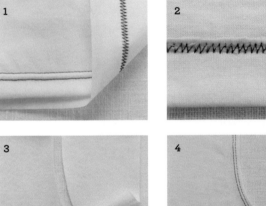

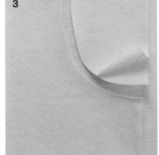

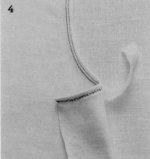

Stitch: Zigzag stitch, stitch length 6 spi (4mm), stitch width 70 spi (0.3mm); stretch or overlock stitch

Presser foot: Standard or blind stitch foot

Needle: Ball point needle, twin stretch needle Engage integrated walking foot or install walking foot

Thread: All-purpose thread on top and bottom, in color matching fabric; for a coverstitch seam set the second spool of thread on a separate spool pin (thread must feed off spools in opposite directions)

1 Hem without stabilizer
2 Hem with stabilizer
3 Precise cutting with adhesive stabilizer
4 Seam with bias tape

CHIFFON

Delicate, soft, sheer fabrics such as chiffon, georgette, crêpe, or voile are ultrathin, **very slippery,** and difficult to work with. They are made primarily from synthetic fibers, though chiffon and georgette may also be made from silk. Before cutting, iron the fabrics **on a low heat setting with no steam.** Sheer fabric pieces **cannot be reinforced with normal interfacings,** as these would show through. Instead, these pieces are cut in double layers or, more economically, can be interfaced with organza in as close to the same color as possible.

For sewing, choose polyester serger thread, embroidery thread, or transparent thread *(see pages 41-42)*; a microtex needle, size 8–9 (60–65 European) *(see page 37, number 6)*; and a straight stitch setting no longer than 13 spi (2mm). If available, use a straight stitch needle plate and a straight stitch presser foot, to prevent fabric from being pulled down through the needle plate.

A French seam *(see page 90)* is standard on thin and sheer fabrics, as it encompasses the raw edges. A felled seam *(see page 90)* is also appropriate but can be hard to work on these types of fabrics.

MACHINE SETTINGS

Stitch: Straight stitch, stitch length 13 spi (2mm)
Presser foot: Standard foot
Needle: Ball point needle or twin stretch needle
Thread: All-purpose, embroidery, or serger thread on top and bottom, in color matching fabric

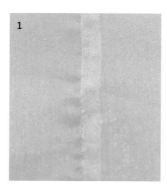

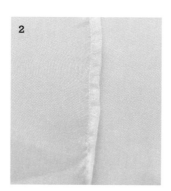

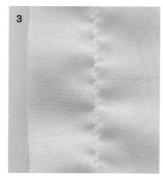

Organza felled seam
Front (1)
Back (2)

Chiffon simple seam
Without stabilizer (3)
With stabilizer (4)

Chiffon French seam (5)

>> Cover your CUTTING SURFACE with a cloth so that the fabric cannot SLIDE AWAY during cutting.

>> IF SEAMS ARE WAVY or pull together, use a strip of HEAVY, WATER-SOLUBLE STABILIZER TO REINFORCE the seam (make sure your fabric is washable).

>> Hold on to the thread ends WHEN STARTING TO SEW.

! CHIFFON, GEORGETTE, AND VOILE are more easily sewn with a serger/overlock machine.

VELVET AND MINKY FABRICS

These fabrics, as well as chenille, are characterized by their **soft and plush surfaces.** Velvet and minky fabrics are available in both **woven and warp knit varieties.**
Velour is the warp knit version of velvet; it is shinier and has a softer hand.
Fabrics of this type with low pile—the fibers that constitute the plush surface—must be **sewn with the grain,** while those with **high pile should be stitched against the grain.** For basting, use thread that will not damage the pile, and do not use heavy basting needles.
If the fabric does not feed well and seams have uneven stitches and tend to shift, a **thin, water-soluble stabilizer film** laid on top of the fabric will help. The seam stitching perforates the film so that it may easily be pulled away; **it does not need to be rinsed out.**

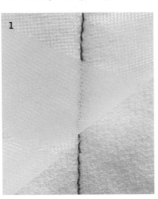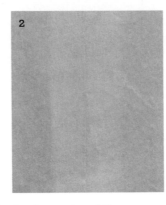

MACHINE SETTINGS
Stitch: Straight stitch, stitch length 9 spi (3mm)
Presser foot: Standard foot
Needle: Ball point needle, size 10–14 (70–90 European)
Thread: All-purpose thread on top and bottom, in color matching fabric
Engage integrated walking foot or install walking foot
Loosen presser foot pressure

1 Simple seam on panné (crushed) velvet with stabilizer
2 Simple seam viewed from front

MAKING BUTTONHOLES

Buttonholes are made with the help of heavy, water-soluble stabilizer film inserted between the fabric layers. To prevent the buttonhole from sinking into the pile, thin, water-soluble film may be placed on top of the fabric. The thin film may be carefully removed once the buttonhole is completed; the heavier film between the fabric layers will dissolve upon washing. This method is appropriate only for washable fabrics. Embroidery and darning thread are recommended for buttonholes. On non-washable fabrics, use iron-on, tear-away stabilizer.

LEATHER

Depending on type, both leather and imitation (faux) leather can be used to make garments, bags, and accessories on conventional sewing machines. Thin leather and thin faux leather may be sewn just like fabric. **Every needle or pinprick in leather will remain visible, so** *quilt clips (see page 35, number 6)*, or alternatively clothespins or bulldog clips, are used instead of pins to hold leather pieces together. Adhesive tape, glue stick, or double-sided, water-soluble wonder tape *(see page 33, number 6)* can be used in place of basting stitches. If pins are used at all, it is always within the seam allowances.

For soft leather a size 80 (US 14) standard machine needle is appropriate; otherwise a leather needle *(see page 37)* can be used. These have a honed tip and can easily pierce leather. Embroidery, buttonhole, or 30-weight cotton thread is best to use here. The stitch length on straight stitching should be set at a minimum of 9 dpi (3mm). A roller or non-stick foot *(see page 24)* will ensure an even transport of the leather during sewing; also engage or install a walking foot for best results.

>> Using a *hobby knife (see page 31, number 12)* or *rotary cutter (see page 31, number 10)* to cut leather will result in **CLEAN EDGES.**

WORKING WITH THIN LEATHER

- Pieces of thin leather and faux leather are sewn together with a *simple seam (see page 88)*; seam allowances may be held down with adhesive or topstitched from the right side to make them lie flat.
- Edges on cuffs, collars, or facings are sewn with an *overlap seam (see page 91)*. Fold under and glue down the seam allowance on the top piece; cut away the seam allowance on the bottom piece and glue the folded edge on top of the trimmed edge.

WORKING WITH THICK LEATHER

- Thick leather pieces are sewn together using an *overlap seam (see page 91)*.
- Cuffs, collars, and facings are glued wrong sides together and topstitched on the right side.
- Buttonholes can simply be stitched all around. Mark the buttonhole size and sew once or twice around using a straight stitch; cut the buttonhole. Preprogrammed buttonholes can also be made in leather, as well as corded buttonholes.
- For a bound buttonhole *(see page 232)*, the facing is not folded under and sewn; rather, the buttonhole is sewn from the right side in the ditch of the seam and the facing is trimmed away on the reverse side in between the seams.
- Buttons should always be sewn on with a backing button to prevent them from tearing out. An additional scrap of leather can also be used to reinforce the attachment point; this is also true for snaps and rivets.

! A BACKING BUTTON is a second, approximately ⅓ smaller button that is ATTACHED SIMULTANEOUSLY WITH THE MAIN BUTTON, but on the reverse side.

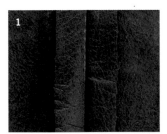
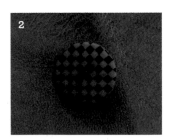
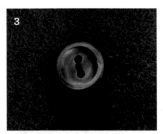
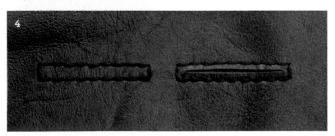

1 Simple seam
2 Button, front
3 Backing button, back
4 Buttonhole

MACHINE SETTINGS

Stitch: Straight stitch, stitch length 9 spi (3mm)
Presser foot: Roller or non-stick foot
Needle: Leather needle
Engage integrated walking foot or install walking foot
Thread: For top and bottom thread use either all-purpose thread, decorative thread, or 30-weight cotton thread, in color matching fabric

FAUX LEATHER, COATED MATERIALS, AND VINYL

Materials of this type are best sewn with a **microtex needle size 12 or 14 (80 or 90 European)** and all-purpose polyester thread. A **roller foot or non-stick foot** will allow the fabric to feed evenly during sewing and not stick to the presser foot. **Seam allowances must be glued down with fabric glue** or topstitched in place so that they will lie flat.

>> FOR TOPSTITCHING use 30-weight decorative thread or cotton machine embroidery thread with a straight stitch length of 5 spi (5mm); WORK SLOWLY.

! DO NOT GLUE DOWN THE SEAM ALLOWANCES ON CLEAR VINYL; it will show through.

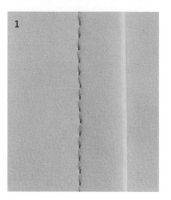 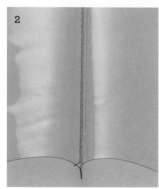

1 Overlap seam, faux leather
2 Simple seam, vinyl

MACHINE SETTINGS
Stitch: Straight stitch, stitch length 9–6 spi (3–4mm)
Presser foot: Roller or non-stick foot
Needle: Microtex needle
Thread: For top and bottom thread use either all-purpose thread, decorative thread, or 30-weight cotton machine embroidery thread, in color matching fabric

MULTILAYERED DENIM

On hems one frequently must sew **over multiple layers of fabric**; hems can have spots with as many as four to six layers. This is especially likely to become a problem with heavy and densely woven fabrics—the machine refuses to feed, the presser foot gets hung up, the needle breaks, or badly formed stitches ensue. Here a **bi-level foot** can be of assistance *(see page 24, number 5)*, as it helps the presser foot to sew over even the thickest seams. There are different types of bi-level feet that vary by manufacturer. Depending on the thickness of the seam you may position the bi-level foot to the side of, behind, or in front of the presser foot so that it can be on the same level as the seam and thus sew easily over it.

>> INSTEAD OF USING A BI-LEVEL FOOT, you can also fold up a scrap of fabric and place it behind the hem under the presser foot. ALWAYS WORK SLOWLY OVER THICK FABRIC LAYERS.

! Reduce the presser foot pressure when sewing THICK FABRIC LAYERS.

1 With bi-level foot
2 With folded fabric scrap

MACHINE SETTINGS
Stitch: Straight stitch, stitch length 9–7½ spi (3–3.5mm)
Presser foot: Standard or edging foot, bi-level foot
Needle: Denim needle size 14–18 (90–100 European) Engage integrated walking foot or install walking foot
Thread: For top and bottom thread use either all-purpose thread, denim thread, or 30-weight cotton machine embroidery thread, in color matching fabric

FAUX FUR/IMITATION FUR

Faux fur with long hair (or pile) may also be called **imitation fur**, while fur with shorter pile may be referred to as **teddy fur**. These materials come in various styles—in bright colors or animal prints and with short, long, straight, or curly hair, to name just a few variations. Pieces should always be cut along the nap so that the hair will lie facing downward on the finished piece. You can determine the nap direction by stroking the pile with your hand; be sure to orient all pieces so that the pile will lie in that direction. Cut these fabrics from the back **using a rotary cutter or razor blade, being careful to cut only the woven backing and not damage the fur itself!** Tug the pieces apart after cutting.

IMITATION FUR

- Pin imitation fur right sides together with extra-long pins and sew a simple seam in the direction of the nap, using a chopstick or closed pair of scissors to push any stray hairs back in between the fabric layers.
- Any hairs caught in the seam should be carefully pulled out using a pin.
- Seams that will not be highly stressed, such as those on **collars and cuffs**, may be sewn **edge to edge** using a zigzag stitch. Trim the seam allowances to ⅛" (3mm), abut the edges, and sew over with a zigzag stitch, using a long pin to push hairs out of the way. Afterward, use a pin from the right side to carefully and thoroughly pull out any hairs caught in the seam. This type of seam is very flat and is quite apparent on the right side.
- Buttonholes are not suited for use on long-haired imitation furs. Instead, fur hooks or fur clips are used; large snaps can also work well.

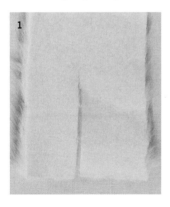

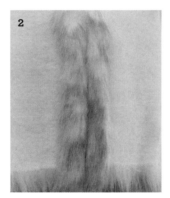

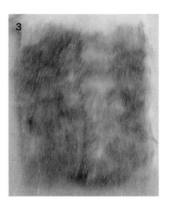

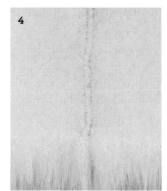

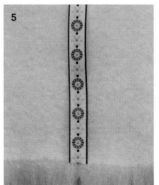

MACHINE SETTINGS
Stitch: Straight stitch, stitch length 7.5 spi (3.5mm)
Presser foot: Standard foot
Needle: Standard needle size 12–14 (80–90 European) Engage integrated walking foot or install walking foot Decrease pressure on presser foot
Thread: All-purpose thread on top and bottom, in color matching fur

>> Cut or shave away FUR FIBERS from seam allowances to make seams less bulky.

>> ON UNLINED FAUX FUR GARMENTS, finish the seams using a Hong Kong seam (see page 105).

! AFTER SEWING with fur and other high pile fabrics, clean your machine thoroughly.

>> Always immediately vacuum dust and hairs from your work surface with a HAND VACUUM.

>> ABUTTED SEAMS in unlined fur pieces can be covered with glued-on woven ribbons.

1 Cutting in the direction of the nap
2 Simple seam, back view
3 Simple seam, front view
4 Zigzag abutted seam
5 Seam with ribbon glued on to cover it

TEDDY FUR

- **Pin teddy fur with extra-long pins** and sew it, right sides together, with a **simple seam** in the direction of the nap. You may wish to glue down the seam allowances so that they lie flat. Cut edges may also be finished using a zigzag or decorative stitch. The fur on the seam allowances should be trimmed away.
- To create **attractive, raised buttonholes**, lay thin, water-soluble stabilizer on the plush side of the fabric. The stabilizer is removed after the buttonhole is cut open.

>> Bind SEAM EDGES with contrasting BIAS TAPE.

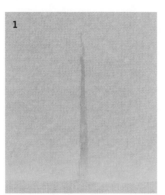 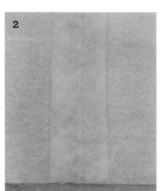 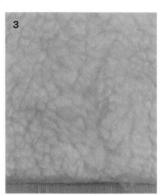

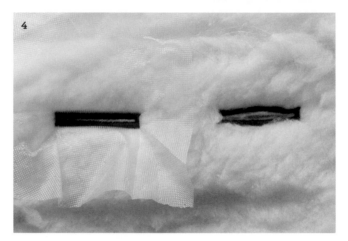

1 Cutting in the direction of the nap
2 Simple, shaved seam; back view
3 Simple, shaved seam; front view
4 Buttonhole with stabilizer (left) and without stabilizer (right)

MACHINE SETTINGS

Stitch: Straight stitch, stitch length 7½ spi (3.5mm); Zigzag stitch, stitch length 3 spi (7mm), stitch width 3 spi (7mm)

Presser foot: Standard foot or roller foot

Needle: Standard needle size 12–14 (80–90 European) Engage integrated walking foot or install walking foot Decrease pressure on presser foot

Thread: All-purpose thread on top and bottom, in color matching fur

BEADED AND SEQUINED FABRICS

Beaded and sequined fabrics are used for evening and bridal gowns, jackets, wraps, corsets, and purses. They are difficult to sew and **require careful advance preparation.** The simplest solution would be to always sew these fabrics by hand—a task that is often not feasible time-wise when it comes to elaborate jackets or evening gowns. Of course, these fabrics may also be sewn by machine, and the approach is the same whether the fabric is beaded or sequined. It is inevitable that a needle or two will be broken during the process, as occasionally a bead, sequin, or rhinestone will get sewn over.

Spread the fabric wrong side up on a table, lay down the pattern pieces, and determine approximately where the seam lines and seam allowances will be. Use a *seam ripper (see page 31, number 4)* to **remove all beads within a good presser-foot's breadth from the seam lines** by breaking the attachment threads on the back of the fabric. Set removed beads aside. **Glued-on beads should be shattered with a small hammer** and pulled off the fabric.

Once the seam allowances and stitching lines are free of beads, the fabric may be cut and the seams pinned and sewn together. Reduce your sewing speed so that any lingering beads in the sewing area can be removed before causing a broken needle. **When all seams are completed, sew the reserved beads back onto the fabric along the seam lines by hand,** filling in any "bald" spots. A beading needle is recommended for this task. Use fusible *hemming tape (see page 109)* to finish hems.

» DARTS, HEMS, COLLARS, AND CUFFS out of beaded and sequined fabric are more quickly and easily worked by hand.

» KEEP PLENTY OF EXTRA NEEDLES at hand so that there will be no forced interruptions in your progress while you go out to buy more.

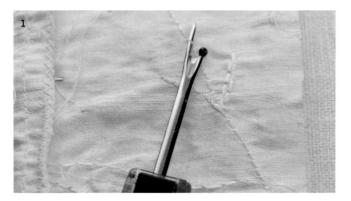

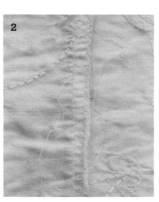

MACHINE SETTINGS
Stitch: Straight stitch, stitch length 7.5 spi (3.5mm)
Presser foot: Standard foot
Needle: Microtex needle size 11–12 (75–80 European)
Engage integrated walking foot or install walking foot
Decrease pressure on presser foot
Thread: All-purpose thread on top and bottom, in color matching fabric

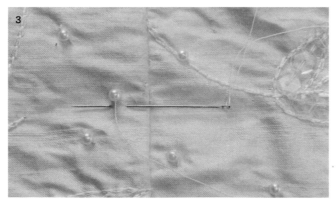

1 Removing beads from sewing area
2 Seam, back view
3 Reattaching beads by hand, front view

finishing seams

SEAM FINISHING done with a serger/overlock machine (*see page 16*) looks professional, and the fabric edges are stitched, finished, and trimmed all in one pass.

On any sewing project there will be cut fabric edges, which on woven fabrics will fray and therefore must be finished. There are several techniques to choose from: finishing by hand, with an overlock or standard machine, or with pinking shears or a rotary cutter with a pinking or wave blade.

FINISHING WITH PINKING SHEARS

A quick and simple method for finishing seam allowances is to cut the fabric with pinking shears. This technique is especially good for thin, soft fabrics such as linings or silk, as these fabrics tend to roll in and pull together when finished with a zigzag stitch.

CUT FABRIC with pinking shears or a rotary pinking cutter **BEFORE SEWING TOGETHER.**

! **THIS METHOD** works well on **OVERLAPPED SEAMS** (*see page 91*).

After sewing the seam, the allowances are either pressed apart or pressed to one side; afterward, trim the allowances either with pinking shears (1) or using a rotary cutter with a pinking blade (2).

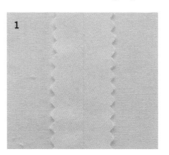

FINISHING WITH ZIGZAG STITCH

The most common and quickest method of finishing seams with a machine is to use a zigzag stitch. When sewing the fabric edges, make sure that the needle is alternating between sewing through the fabric edge and sewing "into the void." The stitch length and width will depend on the fabric: wide zigzags for heavily fraying fabrics, narrow zigzags with a longer stitch length for fabrics less prone to fraying.

USE A BLIND STITCH FOOT and set the zigzag stitch width to 5 spi (5mm) to **KEEP THE NEEDLE FROM HITTING THE PRESSER FOOT.** Finishing done with a blind stitch foot is more even and less likely to roll inward.

Sew the seam, then finish the seam allowance edges either separately or, with lighter-weight fabrics, together, using a zigzag stitch.

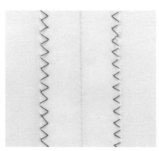

MACHINE SETTINGS
Stitch: Zigzag stitch, stitch width 11–5 spi (2.5–5mm), stitch length 18–7.5 spi (1.5–3.5mm)
Presser foot: Standard foot
Needle position: Center
Thread: All-purpose thread on top and bottom, in color matching fabric

FINISHING WITH STRAIGHT TOPSTITCHING

The straight topstitch finish is a technique left over from the time when sewing machines did not come with zigzag or other edge-stitching capabilities. Today it is used only to **add a stylish touch,** for example when seams are exposed on the right side of a garment or the edges of the seam allowances are intended to be a focal point. That said, this technique is actually quite well suited for **very lightweight fabrics that fray easily.**

Work a simple seam with ⅝" (1.5cm) seam allowances; press the allowances apart, **fold under ⅛" (3mm) on the allowance edges,** and topstitch near the folded edges using a **straight stitch.**

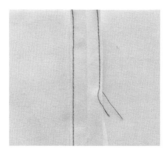

MACHINE SETTINGS
Stitch: Straight stitch, stitch width 11 spi (2.5mm)
Presser foot: Standard foot
Thread: All-purpose thread on top and bottom, in color matching fabric

>> TOPSTITCH fabric edges with novelty thread.

FINISHING WITH ZIGZAG TOPSTITCHING

This technique follows the same steps as straight stitch finishing (see above). Zigzag topstitch finishing is suited for **unlined garments and mid- to heavyweight fabrics.** Use the notch on the presser foot opening as a guide to keep the foot traveling along the seam allowance so that the needle alternates between stitching into the fabric and stitching "into the void."

Work a simple seam with ⅝" (1.5cm) seam allowances; press the allowances apart, **fold under ⅛" (3mm) on the allowance edges,** and topstitch near the folded edges using a **zigzag stitch.**

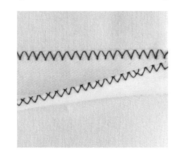

MACHINE SETTINGS
Stitch: Zigzag stitch, stitch width 9–6 spi (3–4mm), stitch length 9–6 spi (3–4mm)
Presser foot: Standard foot
Needle position: Center
Thread: All-purpose thread on top and bottom, in color matching fabric; or novelty yarn as top thread

>> Use NOVELTY THREAD such as 30-weight cotton multicolor for zigzag topstitching.

FINISHING WITH BIAS TAPE

Bias strips are cut diagonal to the fabric grain and therefore are **very flexible** and suited for finishing (or binding) curved edges. They can be made from scratch *(see page 258),* but flat and pre-folded bias tape are also available for purchase in many colors. Bias tape finishing is used on **unlined garments** or on any textile items where the **seam allowances will be visible.** Both *concave and convex curves (see pages 105–106)* may be finished with bias tape. Seam allowances finished with this technique look very elegant and increase the general sophistication of a sewn item, but the technique does take some time to execute. The finishing may be done with identical fabric (or the same fabric in a different tone), or with contrasting fabric. **Bias finishing on heavy fabrics is done using lining fabric or satin.**

>> BIAS TAPE can be made from scratch with the help of a BIAS TAPE MAKER *(see page 259).*

! Once sewn, the BIAS TAPE FINISH will be one-quarter the width of the starting strip of bias fabric.

BINDING CURVED EDGES

To bind curved edges, flip open the folded bias strip and pin it, right sides facing and raw edges aligned, along the edge to be finished. Stretch or pull in the tape to fit smoothly, and stitch along the fold. Flip the strip to the reverse side of the fabric, covering the first stitching line. Sew down the inner folded edge of the strip by hand with small hem stitches, or stitch it down from the right side using the machine.

>> A RIBBON FOOT can help to bind straight edges quickly and evenly. Cut a 1⅛" (3cm)-wide cotton bias strip and **INSERT ABOUT 1" (2.5CM) INTO THE FEEDER CHANNEL.** Position the needle to sew the strip close to its edge.

BINDING STRAIGHT EDGES

To bind straight edges, fold pre-folded bias tape in half, wrong sides together; then place it so that it evenly encompasses the seam allowance edges and pin. Stitch the bias tape down from the right side, close to the edge of the tape. **Binding strips for straight edges** can also be cut along the fabric grain instead of on the bias.

BINDING CORNERS

The binding of straight edges and corners comes up when working with flat textile pieces such as patchwork blankets, pot holders, place mats, tablecloths, and wall hangings. This style of corner binding can also be used in place of a *mitered corner (see page 281).*

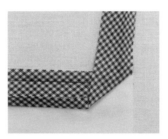  

! DEPENDING ON THE FABRIC, these edge finishings may become bulky, given that up to five layers may end up on top of one another.

>> WITH THIS METHOD you can easily bind quilt edges.

>> WITH A RIBBON FOOT and a bit of practice you can learn to quickly and evenly bind straight edges.

1 **Unfold the binding strip;** place it, with right side edges together, along the front of the piece; and pin the strip up to the first corner, starting at the middle of one edge. Skipping the first ¾" (2cm), stitch the binding down at presser foot width, or approximately ⅜" (7.5mm); stop a presser foot's width away from the corner and secure the stitching.

2 **Turn the piece 90 degrees to the left** and fold the binding strip upward, thereby creating a fold at a 45-degree angle. Fold the strip back down, so that the fold is even with the top edge of the fabric.

3 **Sew the binding along the edge,** starting at the top and securing the beginning of the seam. Continue to sew the strip all around the remaining three corners in the same fashion.

4 **To finish, trim the binding,** fold it under ⅝"–¾" (1–2cm), and tuck the end underneath the starting point of the binding. Stitch down the end and start of the binding.

5 **Fold the binding to the inside all around the edge** and pin, making sure the attachment seam line is covered. Form diagonal folds at the corners.

MACHINE SETTINGS
Stitch: Straight stitch, stitch length 11 spi (2.5mm)
Presser foot: Standard or edging foot
Thread: All-purpose thread on top and bottom, in color matching binding

6 **Sew down the binding** by hand on the inside fold using small hem stitches, or stitch by machine from the right side.

 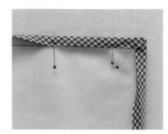 

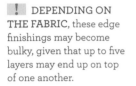

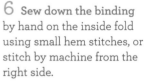

HONG KONG SEAM FINISH

The Hong Kong finish resembles a bias tape finish. It is popular for finishing edges on unlined garments, for hemming, for jacket and coat pockets, on neck and arm openings, and for attractive inner seams.

! THE ADVANTAGE of this method over bias tape finishing is that the **HONG KONG SEAM FINISH IS ONLY FOUR LAYERS** (as opposed to five), making it flatter and less bulky, since the inner edge is not finished.

>> USE PATTERNED bias strips to give additional pep to solid-color garments.

 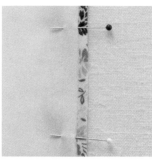 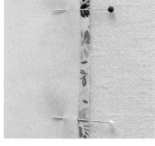

1 Cut a bias strip about 1⅛" (3cm) wide, pin it along the fabric with right side edges together, and sew about ¼" (0.6cm) away from the edge.

2 Trim seam allowances to ⅛" (0.3cm), fold the bias strip to the back around the cut edge, pin, and sew from the right side.

3 Trim the remaining raw edge of the bias strip close to the stitching.

FINISHING CURVED EDGES

Rounded edges are found on both garments and home décor items. They can be finished with a simple hem, but this tends to end up with small wrinkles. Finishing with a bias strip or other trim is more attractive and professional-looking.

FINISHING A CONCAVE EDGE

Concave edges are found on **neck and arm openings as well as hems.**

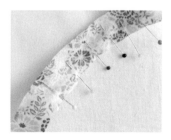  

1 Cut a bias strip about 1⅛" (3cm) wide and pin along the fabric with right side edges together, **pulling to stretch the bias strip so that it fits smoothly along the curve.**

2 Sew with a seam allowance of about ¼" (0.6cm); **trim allowances to ⅛" (0.3cm). Fold the strip to the wrong side all around and sew it from the right side.**

3 Trim the remaining raw edge of the bias strip close to the stitching (Hong Kong seam finish); **press.**

MACHINE SETTINGS
Stitch: Straight stitch
Presser foot: Standard or edging foot
Thread: All-purpose thread on top and bottom, in color matching bias strip

! The Hong Kong finish saves time when **FINISHING CURVED EDGES**, since it eliminates the need to stitch down the binding from the wrong side.

FINISHING A CONVEX EDGE

Convex edges are found on patch pockets, collars, and hems.

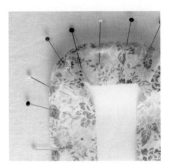  

1 Cut a bias strip about 1⅛" (3cm) wide and pin it along the fabric with right side edges together, pulling in the bias strip slightly so that it fits smoothly along the curve.

2 Sew with a seam allowance of about ¼" (0.6cm); trim allowances to ⅛" (0.3cm). Fold the strip to the wrong side all around.

3 Sew from the right side.

4 Trim the remaining raw edge of the bias strip close to the stitching (Hong Kong seam finish); press.

handsewn hems

Hems are usually sewn by machine, but you may wish to sew a hem by hand so that no stitching is visible on the right side. A hem may be a single hem (fabric is folded once) or a double hem (fabric is folded twice). Which one is best depends on the type of fabric, the way it will be sewn, and the desired finished look. Choose thread that matches your fabric.

PICK STITCH

This is a sturdy stitch for tacking down a folded hem edge. Since the thread is mostly covered by the fabric, it is unlikely to catch or tear.
Pull the needle through close to the top inner folded edge of the hem. Use the needle to catch just a couple of threads from the single lower (outside) layer of fabric. Guide the needle diagonally through the hem edge, working right to left, and pull the needle back out about ¼"–⅜" (6–10mm) farther along the edge.

>> TRIM SEAM ALLOWANCES on vertical seams in the HEM AREA to prevent bulkiness.

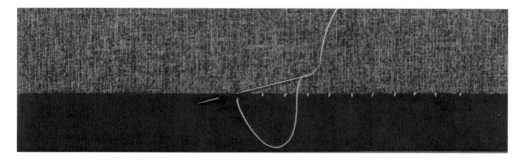

HERRINGBONE STITCH

The herringbone stitch is a strong and elastic stitch that may be used to quickly secure single or double hems, especially on lined garments and those made from thick or stretchy fabrics. Abutted edges, such as on patchwork items, can also be sewn together decoratively with this stitch.
Work from left to right along the edge, with the needle pointing toward the left. Make the short stitches parallel to the edge and against the direction of the sewing, catching just two or three threads from the topmost layer of the hem allowance. The next stitch is made diagonally rightward and directly above the upper folded edge; here catch only one or two of the threads from the weave of the outer fabric. Do not pull the thread too tight.

! On a SINGLE HEM, the edge should be FINISHED beforehand if the FABRIC TENDS TO FRAY.

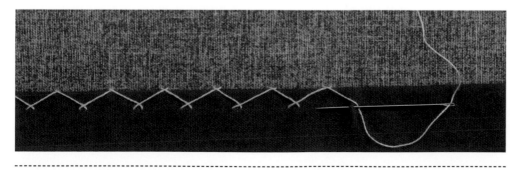

BLIND STITCH

This stitch is practically invisible not just on the right side but on both sides of the fabric, provided the thread matches the fabric color. It is used frequently on thin or delicate fabrics.

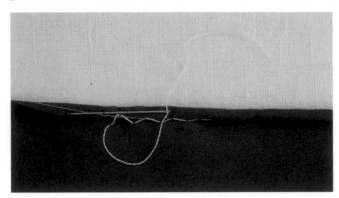

Fold in the hem allowance and work in **short stitches** along the folded edge. On the topmost layer of the hem allowance, catch only two to four threads. Make the next stitch slightly to the left next to the edge, now catching one or two threads. Do not pull the thread too tight.

ROLLED HEM

This very narrow hem is **especially well suited to delicate and sheer fabrics** such as silk and chiffon. It is sewn with tiny blind stitches (see above) that catch only one or two threads of the fabric; stitches along the inner fold may be somewhat longer. It is best to use a thin, short needle and lightweight thread matching the fabric. Rolled seams can be made with or without a supporting line of machine stitching.

ROLLED HEM WITH SUPPORT SEAM

With delicate fabrics that are cut on the bias, a supporting seam should be used to **prevent the hem from stretching out of shape.**

1 Mark the hem/fold line and work a line of stitching about ¼" (6mm) away. Trim the fabric alongside the stitching line to ⅛" (3mm).

 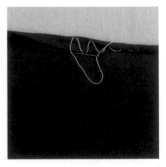

2 Roll the fabric to the inside so that the support seam is still visible, and sew with blind stitching. Alternate between making stitches next to the cut edge through the single layer of fabric and making stitches just beyond the supporting seam stitches. **Gently pull on the sewing thread every few stitches to encourage the hem to roll inward.**

ROLLED HEM WITHOUT SUPPORT SEAM

If a hem follows the grain of a fabric, **you may forego a support seam.**

Fold under a hem allowance of about ⅜" (1cm) and sew with blind stitching, alternating between making stitches into the folded edge and making stitches next to the cut edge. **Pull gently on the sewing thread every few stitches to encourage the hem to roll inward.**

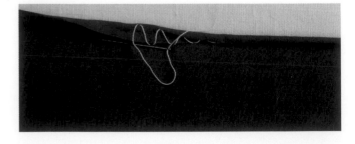

glued hems

On fabrics that are difficult to work with, on items that are primarily decorative, or on textiles that are unlikely to be washed frequently, such as drapes, hems may be glued instead of sewn. This simple method of creating hems may be accomplished with special glues or with adhesive stabilizers, depending on the fabric used.

USING HEMMING TAPE

Double-sided adhesive hemming tape binds fabric layers together through the application of heat and pressure. Especially on fabrics where needle marks remain visible after sewing, it may be a better idea to make an adhesive hem. Test the iron first on a scrap of fabric.

1 Mark the hem depth. Cut the hemming tape about ¼" (5mm) narrower than the hem allowance and place it, coated side down, on the allowance at a small distance from the edge. For curved hems, first snip the hemming tape at regular intervals, so that it can better follow the contours of the hem. With the iron set at a medium temperature, iron on the hemming tape. Allow to cool, then peel off the paper backing.

2 Fold up the hem allowance and steam press in sections, ideally using a pressing cloth. Do not allow the iron to shift while pressing.

USING GLUE

For heat-sensitive materials such as leather, fur, and vinyl that cannot be ironed, special glues may be used; for example, PVA (polyvinyl acetate) adhesive for leather, or rubber-based textile adhesives. This method should not be used on woven or knit fabrics or other materials where the glue could soak through to the front. Always test glues first on a scrap of fabric, following manufacturer's instructions.

1 Mark the hem depth. Spread the glue evenly on the wrong side of the hem allowance.

2 Fold up the hem allowance and apply weights to maintain pressure; allow to dry.

! Glue should be used with **PLASTIC-COATED FABRICS**, since otherwise the needle holes created during sewing will nullify the waterproof properties of the item.

ON WOVEN FABRICS the cut edges must be finished with a zigzag stitch or with pinking shears before gluing, to discourage fraying.

» **HEMMING TAPE CAN BE USED FOR QUICK REPAIR JOBS** when a sewing kit is not available.

» You can **SHORTEN LEATHER GARMENTS** especially quickly if you use special **DOUBLE-SIDED LEATHER ADHESIVE TAPE.**

machine-sewn hems

A hem completes a sewing project and keeps edges from fraying. Hems may be single (also called *flat*) with one turned-up fold, or they may be double folded. On single hems the edge of the hem allowance must be finished before sewing. Once the hem is marked, the amount of hem allowance is determined. Hem allowances are usually provided on patterns, but the general rule is that hems on children's garments, skirts, and coats are 2"–3" (5–8cm); jackets 1½"–2" (4–5cm); pants 1⅛"–1½" (3–4cm); and shirts and blouses ⅝"–1⅛" (1.5–3cm). The hem allowances on home décor items vary depending on fabric type and type of item.

SINGLE HEM

Single hems are suited to **midweight to heavyweight thick, low-fraying fabrics**. They are flat and do not add bulk. Single hems are commonly used on coats and jackets.

>> INSTEAD OF FINISHING THE HEM with a zigzag stitch, pinking shears, or bias tape, SEW A WOVEN RIBBON OVER THE EDGE.

! WHEN SEWING WITH A STRAIGHT STITCH, use a hem-measuring tool (*see page 32, number 3*) to ensure an even distance between the stitching and the lower hem edge.

Finish the hem allowance edge with a zigzag stitch, pinking shears, a rotary cutter with a pinking or wave blade, or *bias tape (see pages 103–104)*. Fold the hem allowance to the inside, press, pin, and stitch from the right side using a straight stitch or *blind stitch (see page 111)*; press again to finish.

MACHINE SETTINGS
Stitch: Straight stitch, blind stitch
Presser foot: Standard or blind stitch foot
Thread: All-purpose thread on top and bottom, in color matching fabric

SHALLOW FOLDED HEM

This hem is suitable for **light- to midweight woven fabrics with a tendency to fray**. It is used for home décor items and garments.

 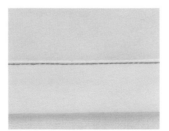

MACHINE SETTINGS
Stitch: Straight stitch, stitch length 1"–1⅛" (2.5–3cm)
Presser foot: Standard or edging foot
Thread: All-purpose thread on top and bottom, in color matching fabric

Fold up ⅝" (1.5cm) along the hem edge and press. Fold again along the desired hemline; press, pin, and edge stitch from the inside close to the top folded edge.

DEEP FOLDED HEM

A deep folded hem is suitable for light- to midweight woven fabrics. It is used on garments such as dresses, blouses, shirts, and pants. Drapes hang especially well when finished with a deep folded hem.

 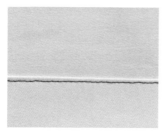

MACHINE SETTINGS
Stitch: Straight stitch, stitch length 11–9 spi (2.5–3mm)
Presser foot: Standard or edging foot
Thread: All-purpose thread on top and bottom, in color matching fabric

Fold up half the desired hem allowance to the wrong side of the fabric, press, and then fold up again along the raw edge and press. Pin and edge stitch the hem close to the upper fold from the inside.

>> A FOLDING TEMPLATE saves time. It is laid on the wrong side of the fabric at the desired hemline, and the fabric is ironed along the edge of the template. EXTENSIVE MEASURING AND PINNING BECOME UNNECESSARY.

! A DOUBLE FOLDED HEM is INAPPROPRIATE FOR CURVED HEMS, as it will develop small wrinkles during sewing. In these cases opt instead for a CURVED HEM WITH FACING (see page 112).

BLIND STITCH HEM

Practically invisible machine-sewn hems can be accomplished with a programmed blind stitch and a *blind stitch foot (see page 20, number 3)*. Blind stitches will disappear into the weave of mid- to heavyweight fabrics; on lighter-weight fabrics, tiny stitches will be visible on the right side.

 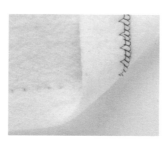

MACHINE SETTINGS
Stitch: Blind stitch
Presser foot: Blind stitch foot
Thread: All-purpose thread on top and bottom, in color matching fabric

Begin by finishing the hem edge as you would for a single hem. Fold the hem allowance wrong sides together, pin, and press. Turn up the folded edge of the hem to the right side, so that the fabric sticks out about ⅜" (1cm) beyond the folded portion. Install the blind stitch foot on the machine and select blind stitching. Place the fabric under the presser foot so that the fabric edge lines up with the blade on the foot. Begin sewing, making sure that the needle catches only a thread or two each time as it pierces the fold. Fold the hem back down and press. If the stitching is visible on the right side, the blade on the blind stitch foot may need adjustment.

>> MATCH YOUR THREAD EXACTLY to your FABRIC COLOR to ensure that hems will be invisible.

ROLLED HEM

A rolled hem is an especially narrow hem ¹⁄₁₆"–¼" (2–6mm). It is commonly used with delicate fabrics on scarves, shawls, chiffon or plissé skirts, lingerie, curved hems, and napkins. It can be made using **several types of stitches**, including straight, zigzag, overlock, or elastic stitch. A *rolled hem foot (see page 20, number 4)* simplifies the task, as it folds the hem double and sews it all in one pass.

》 SEW A ROLLED HEM USING A ZIGZAG STITCH and novelty thread. To prevent the fabric from slipping out of the spiral channel, **HOLD IT GENTLY TO THE LEFT.**

! ROLLED HEM FEET are available for hems with a width of ¹⁄₁₆", ⅛", and ¼" (2, 4, and 6mm). **ZIGZAG** and other **DECORATIVE STITCHES** require a rolled hem foot with a **WIDE STITCH OPENING.**

MACHINE SETTINGS
Stitch: Straight stitch (or other stitch as desired), stitch length 13–11 spi (2–2.5mm)
Presser foot: Standard or rolled hem foot
Thread: All-purpose thread on top and bottom, in color matching fabric

If you are using a rolled hem foot, the groove on the bottom of the foot will be the width of your finished hem. Install the rolled hem foot on the machine and place the fabric wrong side up under the foot; the fabric edge should be flush with the outer edge of the foot. Begin by sewing four to five straight stitches, then lift the foot and pull back about 2" (5cm) of fabric without breaking the thread. Using the thread to assist you, guide the fabric into the spiral channel on the foot. Choose your desired stitch and complete the hem.

CURVED HEM WITH FACING

Full skirts and dresses as well as evening and bridal gowns often have curved or shaped hems. These hems are also found on home décor items such as tablecloths, drapes, and pillows. Curved and shaped hems should not be finished using a standard folded hem technique, as the hem will develop wrinkles during sewing. Curved hems are sewn using a **hem facing** or are *finished using bias tape (see pages 103, 105–106).* Hem facings might be marked on **pattern pieces** themselves or provided as separate pieces to cut out.

! TO HELP SEAM ALLOWANCES lie flat between the fabric and the facing, cut **TRIANGULAR NOTCHES** into the allowances on **CONVEX CURVES**, almost to the seam stitching. On concave curves, only **SNIP** into the **ALLOWANCES.**

》 INSTEAD OF NOTCHING the seam allowance, trim it with pinking shears.

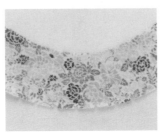 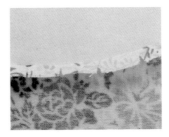 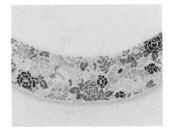

1 Cut the facing fabric in the **shape of the hem**; it should be the desired **hem depth plus seam allowances.** Pin the facing to the hem, right sides together, and sew with a ⅝" (1.5cm) seam. Notch the allowances almost to the stitching line, fold the **facing to the inside**, and press.

2 Snip along the raw edge of the facing about ⅜" (1cm) deep at regular intervals of 1" (2.5cm), then fold ⅝" (1.5cm) to the inside.

3 Pin, then stitch the facing close to the top edge from the wrong side.

MACHINE SETTINGS
Stitch: Straight stitch
Presser foot: Standard or edging foot
Thread: All-purpose thread on top and bottom, in color matching fabric

DECORATIVE HEMS

There are many ways to create decorative hems. Linens, dresses, and blouses are especially popular candidates for this treatment. Lace borders, rickrack, ribbon, ruffles, tulle, organza, and voile are just a few materials that can be used to embellish hemlines. Depending on the shape of the trim, these may be applied edge to edge or overlapping, may be gathered or flat, and may use either a straight stitch or a decorative stitch for attachment. For specialized sewing techniques there are a variety of *specialized presser feet (see pages 22-23)* available.

Finish the hem edge with a zigzag stitch. Fold ¼" (6mm) of the fabric to the wrong side and press. Tuck lace, a ruffled tulle strip, folded bias tape, et cetera ¼" (6mm) underneath the folded hem edge and sew from the right side close to the folded edge using a straight stitch or decorative stitch. Rickrack or ribbon may be applied simultaneously.

 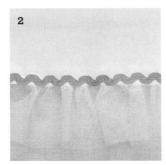 

MACHINE SETTINGS

Stitch: Straight, zigzag, or decorative stitch
Presser foot: Standard, edging, or border guide foot
Thread: All-purpose thread on top and bottom, in color matching fabric

1 Lace sewn on with straight stitching
2 Gathered tulle with rickrack
3 Bias strip sewn on with decorative stitching
4 Lace sewn on edge to edge

>> Pin the **FABRIC AND LACE** edge to edge atop **ADHESIVE STABILIZER** and sew together using a **ZIGZAG STITCH**, with stitch width 6 spi (4mm), stitch length 11 spi (2.5mm). Carefully remove the stabilizer.

>> **REMOVE LACE EDGINGS** from antique linens and use them to lend vintage style to new hand towels.

specialized
sewing techniques

Specialized sewing techniques to create pintucks, pleats, ruffles, and gathers help you add interesting accents to both home decor items and garments. An off-the-rack dress or blouse can be upgraded to a unique and individualized piece through a few small sewn details. A ruffled child's skirt becomes a favorite garment; pillows get a lovely vintage look with a few gathered extras like pleats or ruffles. The techniques in this section can help you turn everyday pieces into heirlooms.

PINTUCKING

Pintucks give structure and depth to textile surfaces. They are used to embellish dresses, blouses, purses, and home decor items. Pintucks are narrow **ridges sewn between two lines of stitching**; about ⅟₁₆" (2mm) wide, they are worked **prior to cutting out fabric.** Narrow pintucks may be as fine as ⅟₃₂" (1mm) wide (the German term for these translates as "hair pintucks"!). Pintucks are sewn in rows at precise intervals; a straightedge will help in guaranteeing the latter. Pintucks may be created more quickly with a *pintuck foot (see page 26, number 18)* together with a twin needle, as **the specialized foot creates evenly spaced tucks** and eliminates the need for folding and pressing each one individually. Pintucks may be formed **over a heavier thread** (such as buttonhole twist) or using a *cording tongue (see page 26, number 17)* to make them more pronounced. You may need to tighten the upper thread tension slightly.

>> Many kinds of **SPECIALIZED PRESSER FEET** are available to help with **SPECIFIC SEWING TECHNIQUES.**

>> Specialized techniques can also be worked using **BASIC PRESSER FEET.**

>> A mix of specialty techniques and decorative stitches can turn **SHAWLS** and **SCARVES** into conversation pieces.

>> **PINTUCKS** may also be sewn using a **ZIPPER FOOT.**

MAKING PINTUCKS WITH A STANDARD FOOT OR EDGE STITCH FOOT

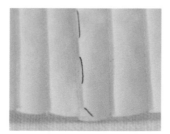
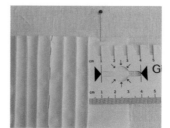

1 Mark the fold line of the first pintuck on the right side of the fabric using basting thread and fold the fabric wrong sides together along this line. Press, then stitch ⅟₃₂" (1mm) away from the fold.

2 Mark the next fold line. It should be at a distance of the desired pintuck spacing **plus half a pintuck's width.**

3 Fold fabric wrong sides together, press, then stitch ⅟₃₂" (1mm) away from the fold. Make remaining pintucks in the same fashion. To finish, iron pintucks from the wrong side, then cut the fabric as needed and continue.

MACHINE SETTINGS
Stitch: Straight stitch
Presser foot: Standard or edging foot
Needle: Standard needle
Thread: All-purpose thread on top and bottom, in color matching fabric

MAKING PINTUCKS WITH A PINTUCK FOOT AND TWIN NEEDLE

1 Install the pintuck foot and twin needle on the machine. Attach a **cording tongue** to the needle plate and add a **second spool of thread.** The thread spools should feed in opposite directions.

2 Mark the line for the first pintuck on the right side of the fabric using a disappearing-ink marker, and sew along this line. To make the second pintuck, **place the first one in the side groove on the pintuck foot.** Continue in this manner so that every following pintuck is created at an equal distance from the previous one. Sew pintucks all in the same direction.

3 Iron pintucks from the wrong side, **then cut the fabric as needed and continue.**

MACHINE SETTINGS
Stitch: Straight stitch, stitch length 11 spi (2.5mm)
Presser foot: Pintuck foot, cording tongue
Needle: Twin needle, needle spacing 1.6mm or 2.0mm (about ⅟₁₆")
Thread: All-purpose thread on top and bottom, in color matching fabric

» USE DECORATIVE STITCHES ON PINTUCKS, but choose only stitches that are narrower than the pintucks themselves.

» SEW PINTUCKS IN DIFFERENT DIRECTIONS to create grid or diamond patterns.

» DECORATIVE STITCHES may be sewn in between rows of pintucks.

! IN LIGHTWEIGHT, THIN FABRICS, sew pintucks with a twin needle with up to 2mm (⅟₁₆") spacing; on heavier fabrics, use a twin needle with 3–4mm (⅛") spacing. Before beginning to sew with a twin needle, BRING THE BOBBIN THREAD UP and position it together with the upper threads behind the presser foot.

TUCKS

In sewing terms, one differentiates between pleats and tucks. In tailoring, pleats are used as a shaping element and can either rein in or add to a garment's fullness. Tucks are **narrow, regularly spaced, stitched-down folds** that may appear singly, in groups, or completely across a piece of fabric to shorten it or reduce its width; they may also be purely decorative. Very narrow tucks are **pintucks** (see above).
Tucks may be **oriented either horizontally or vertically** and tend to work best in midweight cotton and linen fabrics. They are found on children's and adult garments, undergarments, bed linens, home textiles, and accessories.

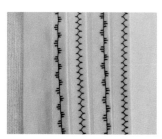

1 Transfer tuck markings from the pattern onto your fabric, or, if creating tucks freehand, use a *ruler or measuring tool (see page 32, numbers 2 and 3)* to **mark the tuck widths.** Fold fabric **wrong sides together at the marking lines and press.**

2 Tucks may be sewn down along their entire length or only partially, with the remainder hanging open. **Stitch tucks along the fold line. Press all tucks in one direction.**

3 Tucks may be embellished with **decorative stitches.**

MACHINE SETTINGS
Stitch: Straight stitch, stitch length 11 spi (2.5mm)
Presser foot: Standard or edging foot
Needle: Standard needle
Thread: All-purpose thread on top and bottom, in color matching fabric

! WHEN IRONING PINTUCKS, place a heavy layer of flannel or similar underneath so that they do not get pressed completely flat.

GATHERS

Gathering pulls in fabric width. Gathers and ruffles are frequently found on children's garments, traditional costumes and aprons, cuffs, sleeves, yokes, tiered skirts, and home décor items; gathering is also used to imitate smocking. There are several ways to gather fabric: the easiest and most familiar method is gathering using straight stitches on light- to midweight fabrics. For this, select the longest stitch length and reduce the upper thread tension. Ease stitching is a type of gathering, but the fabric is gathered so minimally that no wrinkles appear. This technique is used on sleeve caps, necklines, and arm openings or when attaching fabric pieces with splayed edges.

GATHERING USING STRAIGHT STITCHES

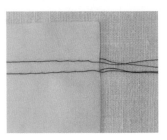 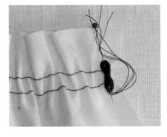 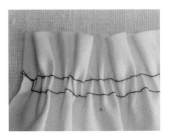

1 On the piece to be gathered, sew two or three parallel lines of stitching about ⅛" (3mm) to each side of the seam line. Do not secure the stitching at the start or end; instead, leave a thread tail that can be pulled of about 2¼" (6cm) at each end.

2 Gather the fabric to the desired width by **pulling on the bobbin thread ends at both right and left**; knot ends or wrap in a figure eight around a pin.

3 Spread the gathers evenly across the width of the fabric. Attach the gathered fabric piece where appropriate and then remove the gathering stitches.

MACHINE SETTINGS
Stitch: Straight stitch, stitch length 5–4 spi (5–6mm)
Presser foot: Standard foot
Needle: Standard needle
Thread: All-purpose thread on top and bottom, in color matching fabric

>> GATHER WIDE PIECES OF FABRIC in two or more SECTIONS to avoid broken thread when pulling the fabric together.

GATHERING USING COUCHED THREAD

 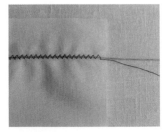 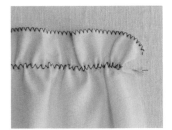

1 With fabric wrong side up, use a wide zigzag stitch to sew over (or "couch") a length of crochet thread or pearl cotton within the seam allowance. The couched thread should be centered under the presser foot, and the zigzag stitching must not pierce it, since that would prevent its ability later to gather the fabric. A ribbon foot may be used for this step, if available.

2 Leave tails of about 2¼" (6cm) at each end of both the couched thread and the sewing threads. On one side, tie all the threads together; from the other side, **pull on the couched thread** until the fabric is gathered to the desired width and then knot those threads as well. The fabric edge near the gathering is best finished beforehand with a zigzag stitch.

MACHINE SETTINGS
Stitch: Zigzag stitch, stitch length 6 spi (4mm), stitch width 6 spi (4mm)
Presser foot: Standard or ribbon foot
Needle: Standard needle
Thread: All-purpose thread on top and bottom, in color matching fabric

! THIS GATHERING TECHNIQUE works well on HEAVY FABRICS.

GATHERING WITH ELASTIC THREAD

This type of gathering is suitable for making narrow, visible gathered elastic seams.

MACHINE SETTINGS
Stitch: Zigzag stitch, stitch length 9 spi (3mm), stitch width 5½ spi (4.5mm); or honeycomb stitch
Presser foot: Standard or ribbon foot
Needle: Standard needle
Thread: All-purpose thread on top and bottom, in color matching fabric

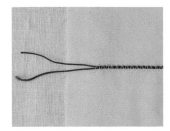 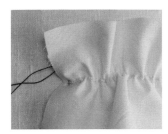

1   Mark the gathering line on the wrong side of the fabric with a disappearing marker. Place elastic thread doubled underneath the presser foot and lower the foot. When sewing over the elastic thread, be careful that the thread does not stretch and that the stitching does not catch it.

2   Pull both ends of the elastic thread until fabric is the desired width; knot to secure.

GATHERING WITH FLAT ELASTIC

This technique creates wide, visible elastic gathering seams.

MACHINE SETTINGS
Stitch: Elastic zigzag stitch, stitch length 9 spi (3mm), stitch width 5½ spi (4.5mm)
Presser foot: Standard or elastic foot
Needle: Microtex needle
Thread: All-purpose thread on top and bottom, in color matching fabric

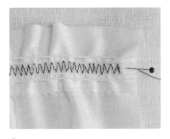 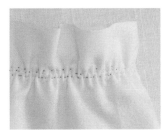

1   Finish the fabric edge and fold it over an amount equaling three times the height of the elastic band. Pin the elastic, lightly stretched, along the bottom third of the folded fabric and sew using an elastic zigzag stitch; alternatively, use an *elastic foot (see page 23, number 9).*

2   Gathers will form evenly.

GATHERING WITH A SHIRRING FOOT

Gathering with a shirring foot is the quickest way of gathering a piece of fabric.

MACHINE SETTINGS
Stitch: Straight stitch, stitch length 7½ spi (3.5mm)
Presser foot: Shirring foot
Needle: Standard needle
Thread: All-purpose thread on top and bottom, in color matching fabric

 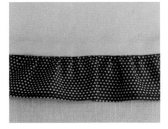

1   The foot creates gathers through uneven feeding of the fabric, and can simultaneously gather a strip of fabric while attaching it onto another.

2   Finish the strip of fabric to be gathered with a **narrow hem** beforehand.

» To PREVENT FABRIC FROM PUCKERING when sewing gathering or elastic stitches, apply WATER-SOLUBLE STABILIZER along the gathering line.

» Using a HONEYCOMB STITCH FOR GATHERING creates an attractive effect. With fabric wrong side up, sew a couple of stitches and leave the needle inserted in the center position. Raise the presser foot and wrap elastic thread around the needle so that two threads emerge in parallel toward the front. Lower the presser foot and SEW OVER THE ELASTIC THREAD, lightly stretching it to increase the gathering effect.

! GATHERING MADE WITH ELASTIC THREAD results in a STRETCHY GATHERED SEAM; multiple rows of elastic gathering resemble smocking *(see page 130).*

! ON SHEER, WHITE fabrics use CLEAR ELASTIC.

» Guide the FABRIC TO BE GATHERED with your left hand, the top fabric with your right hand. WORK SLOWLY.

RUFFLES

Ruffles are gathered or pleated straight strips of fabric, ribbon, or lace that may be inserted between two layers of fabric or applied decoratively on top. Ruffles add a romantic and playful note to garments and home décor pieces. Because ruffles can be seen from both sides, they are usually made from doubled fabric, but in the case of true weave (reversible) fabrics, a ruffle may be made from a single layer with a rolled hem.

It is easy to fold fabric strips evenly using a **ruffler** *(see page 23, number 8)*. With a ruffler you can program the number of pleats according to the number of stitches, pleat distance, and pleat width, which can save significant time when working with long strips of fabric.

TRUE WEAVE FABRIC WITH IDENTICAL RIGHT AND WRONG SIDES

Cut fabric strips double the length of the intended finished ruffle length. Usually this will require that multiple strips be sewn together; in that case, include ¾" (2cm) seam allowance per strip. The height should be the ruffle height plus ⅝" (1.5cm) seam allowance.

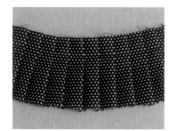

1 Finish the lower edge with pinking shears or a rolled hem. In the case of a rolled hem, be sure to add an additional ⅜"–½" (1cm) to the height of your starting piece. On both short ends, fold under ⅜"–½" (1cm) twice and topstitch close to the edge. Insert the remaining long edge with right side facing up into the guide opening and between the separator plates (consult manufacturer's instructions). **Set the desired pleat number per stitch, pleat distance, and pleat width on the foot; work slowly.** The foot will gather the fabric into even pleats as you sew.

2 Like a shirring foot, a ruffler can pleat and attach a strip of fabric onto another in one pass.

FABRIC WITH DIFFERENT RIGHT AND WRONG SIDES

Cut a fabric strip double the length and height of the intended finished ruffle plus a 1⅛" (3cm) allowance in each direction. Fold the strip lengthwise, wrong sides together, press, and topstitch together ¼" (0.5cm) from the raw edges. Install the ruffler foot and **insert the long edge of the fabric strip** into the guide opening and between the separator plates (consult manufacturer's instructions). **Set the desired pleat number per stitch, pleat distance, and pleat width on the foot; work slowly.** The foot will gather the fabric into even pleats as you sew.

RUFFLES FOR APPLICATION

Ruffles intended for sewn application onto fabric surfaces may be made in **single or double layers**. They are found, for example, **on whimsical dresses and blouses to accent** button plackets, yokes, and sleeves, as well as on skirt hems and folkloric garments.

 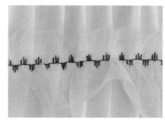

1 For **single-layer ruffles** a rolled hem is sewn along both long edges; for **double-layer ruffles** a fabric strip is folded in half, wrong sides together, and sewn with a ¼" (0.5cm) seam allowance. The seam is positioned in the center back of the ruffle. Press the strips and **use a ruffler to create pleats; use a standard presser foot and straight stitch to apply the finished ruffle to the primary fabric.**

2 One **variation** is to apply the ruffle using an additional **tulle strip and decorative stitching.**

RUFFLES WITH HEADERS

This applied ruffle has a *header* that lends **additional volume** through its construction as a deep folded hem; the ruffle is **applied from the right side.**

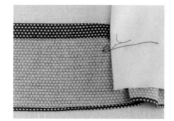 

1 Cut the ruffle strip as follows: **twice the desired finished length and the desired height plus the folded hem allowance for the header and a rolled hem allowance for the bottom edge.** Sew a *rolled hem (see page 112)* along one long edge, and on the other edge sew a *deep folded hem (see page 111)*; press.

2 Sew two parallel rows of 4 spi (6mm) straight stitches, spaced ¼" (0.5cm) apart, just beneath the folded hem. **Pull the bobbin threads until the ruffle is the desired length.** Place the ruffle **wrong side down onto the right side of the primary fabric** and sew between the parallel rows of gathering stitches. Remove the gathering stitches.

RUFFLES INSERTED BETWEEN TWO LAYERS OF FABRIC

 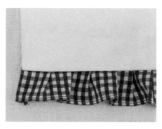

1 Sew ruffles in the desired length and width. Place the top ruffle edge flush along **the edge of the primary fabric piece,** both right side up; stitch with a ⅜" (1cm) seam. Place the second fabric piece right side down on top of the attached ruffle, raw edges flush. Pin and sew with a ⅝" (1.5cm) seam.

2 Pillowcases and bedspreads are often finished with ruffles; the ruffles are attached first and then **caught in as part of the** side seams.

----

decorative
sewing techniques

All sewing machines come outfitted with a variety of standard presser feet and decorative stitches, with the breadth and variety of these depending on the manufacturer and the price point. Supplemental, specialized presser feet may be purchased beyond these basics. With these specially designed feet you can work with more challenging textiles such as leather, PVC, chiffon, fleece, et cetera, but also employ interesting techniques, including making chenille, fringe, freehand embroidery, quilting, couching, hemstitching, and much more.

PIPING AND CORDING

Piping is a thin, narrow fabric roll worked in along edges or incorporated into seams. It adds a **three-dimensional accent in the form of small, firm edges** on garments, such as on cuffs, pockets, and lapels, or on folkloric clothing and children's garments. Cording is found primarily on home décor items such as throw pillows, table linens, upholstery, seat cushions, mattresses, and floor mats. **Piping is narrow and lightweight, while cording is thick and round.** Piping and cording consist of straight or bias-cut fabric strips folded lengthwise, inside of which is fill cord consisting of embroidery thread, cording, string, or rolled fabric. They are **often sewn using contrasting fabric** to emphasize contours, edges, or the shaping of a seam. Piping and cording are applied within seams so that they end up showing on the right side either as small, about ⅛" (3mm)-wide fabric tubes or as wide, thick welts. **Piping and cording** may be purchased ready-made in a variety of colors. They can also be made from scratch, in which case they can be matched perfectly in color and pattern to a given project. Depending on the size of the piping or cording, you will need **fabric, cording or string, crochet thread or embroidery yarn**, and a *cording or piping foot (see page 23, numbers 10 and 11)*; alternatively you may use a **zipper foot**.

MAKING PIPING AND CORDING

Install a zipper foot or piping/cording foot in the machine and cut a straight or bias fabric strip and cord to the desired length.

! The WIDTH OF THE FABRIC STRIP can be calculated as follows: CORD CIRCUMFERENCE PLUS 1⅛" (3CM) SEAM ALLOWANCE. Cut length of cord and fabric strip as needed.

1 Fold the fabric strip in half lengthwise, **wrong sides together,** enveloping the cording with fabric; the **cord should be positioned in the center of the fabric, nestled in the fold line.**

3 Completed piping/cording.

2 Pin the strip closed and sew **closely along the cording** using a straight stitch.

SEWING PIPING OR CORDING INTO A SEAM OR EDGE

 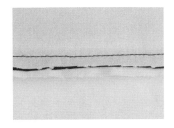 

1 Place the piping/cording onto the main fabric, right sides together, with raw edges aligned; **sew closely along the piping.** Lay the second piece of fabric **right side down on top of the first piece, again with raw edges aligned. Pin through all layers, with pins inserted perpendicular to the piping. Flip the piece over so that the original sewing line is visible.**

2 Sew **a second time directly over the first sewing line and grade seam allowances.**

3 Press allowances to one side and fold fabric up. If desired, **topstitch in the ditch of the seam from the right side** or closely along the piping/cording.

MACHINE SETTINGS
Stitch: Straight stitch, stitch length 11 spi (2.5mm)
Presser foot: Zipper foot or piping/cording foot
Needle: Standard needle
Thread: All-purpose thread on top and bottom, in color matching fabric

---

MAKING DOUBLE PIPING AND CORDING
Cut a straight or bias fabric strip and two pieces of cording to the desired length. **The width of the fabric strip is two times the cord circumference plus 1⅛" (3cm) seam allowance.**

1 Fold the fabric strip in half lengthwise, wrong sides together, enveloping the cording with fabric so it lies nestled inside the fold. **Install a double cording foot or zipper foot and position the fabric strip so that the cord is either underneath the rightward groove in the double cording foot or so that the right edge of the zipper foot pushes up against the cord; the fabric strip sticks out to the left of the presser foot.** Select a straight stitch with stitch length of 9 spi (3mm) and sew closely along the cord, **keeping the cord pressed into the fold** of the fabric. Insert the **second cord into the fabric strip.**

2 Both cords lie under the grooves in the double cording foot, or the right side of the zipper foot presses up against the second cord. **Sew closely along the second cord.**

MACHINE SETTINGS
Stitch: Straight stitch, stitch length 9 spi (3mm)
Presser foot: Zipper or double cording foot
Needle: Standard needle
Thread: All-purpose thread on top and bottom, in color matching fabric

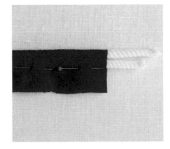 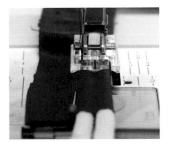

❗ DOUBLE PIPING is attached (as described for single piping) within seams or edges.

DOUBLE PIPING OR CORDING WITH CONTRASTING FABRICS

1 Cut two straight or bias fabric strips and **two pieces of cord** to the desired length. Use one strip to sew a length of single *piping/cording (see page 120)*. Place the piping/cording onto the main fabric, **right sides together**, with raw edges aligned; **sew closely along the piping.** Place the second fabric strip right side down on top of the attached piping, raw edges aligned, pin, and sew close to the piping. **Lay down the second piece of cord,** fold the second fabric strip over it, pin through all layers, and **sew close to the second cord.**

2 Finished double piping/double cording.

> **PIPING MADE WITH THIN, SHEER** fabric should be made using a second layer as lining, so that the fill cord does not show through.

> In situations where cording will be used around rectangular edges, **LIGHTLY ROUND OFF THE CORNERS;** the cording will lie more smoothly and be easier to sew.

! **A PIPING FOOT** has a small groove on the bottom and therefore can also be used to apply **THICKER DECORATIVE** threads or yarn.

! **A CORDING FOOT** may be used to sew together handknit pieces.

ATTACHING CORDING AROUND CORNERS

Lightly rounded corners are easier to finish, since cording lies better around a curved edge. Lightly round off the corners and prepare a strip of cording in the required length.

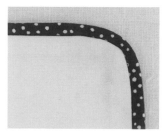

1 Pin the cording onto the main fabric, **right sides together,** with raw edges aligned, and sew through all layers, **leaving 1½" (4cm) of cording loose at the beginning.** Begin sewing along a straight edge, not in a corner. Shortly before reaching the first corner, stop the machine with the needle positioned down in the fabric. **Snip the seam allowance of the cording almost to the seam line,** then sew around the corner in a slight curve. Complete any remaining corners in the same fashion.

2 Place the second piece of fabric, right side down, over the applied cording **with raw edges aligned.** Pin through all layers, with pins inserted perpendicular to the piping, and sew. Flip the fabric so that the cording now is at the bottom; **sew again** directly along the sewing line.

SEWING CORDING TOGETHER

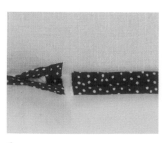 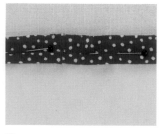 

1 Fold in the fabric strip by ⅜" (1cm) at the beginning of the cording and **trim the fill cord slightly.**

2 Insert the end of the cording into the beginning where you trimmed the cording, so that the **fill cord ends abut.**

3 Sew on the finished cording.

APPLIQUÉ

Appliqués are decorative motifs, made from fabric, lace, leather, or other material, that are applied to a primary fabric piece. Appliqués are found on clothing, bags, home textiles, and accessories. Usually they are made from fabric scraps, ideally ones that are low-fraying. Appliqué can be done by hand or by machine. Helpful aids such as spray adhesives, fabric glue, and *double-sided fusible stabilizer (see page 55)* make the work easier. Appliqués can be given an attractive, sculptural look when they are sewn on **using machine embroidery thread** and are backed with **lightweight fusible fleece** interfacing. An appliqué foot and stabilizer for the primary fabric *(see page 57)* are also helpful.

SEWING ON APPLIQUÉS

1 Trace the design onto the backing paper of fusible stabilizer and cut out generously around it. **Fuse the stabilizer to the wrong side of the appliqué fabric** and carefully cut out the design. **Remove the backing paper and iron the appliqué onto the primary fabric** (following manufacturer's instructions).

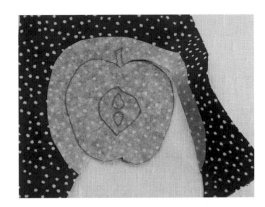

2 Install the appliqué foot on the machine, set up **machine embroidery thread as both upper and bobbin threads**, select a satin stitch (a dense zigzag stitch), and **place stabilizer underneath the working area** (possibly using spray adhesive to secure it). Sew along the edges of the appliqué, making sure that the satin stitch is going **into the appliqué with the left needle strike and into the primary fabric with the right needle strike.**

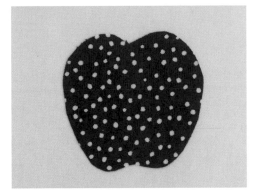

MACHINE SETTINGS

Stitch: Zigzag stitch, stitch length 24 spi (1mm), stitch width 9–7½ spi (3–3.5mm)
Presser foot: Appliqué foot
Needle: Machine embroidery needle
Thread: 40-weight rayon machine embroidery thread on top and bottom, in color matching fabric

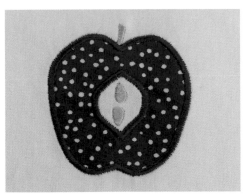

>> WHEN SEWING ON APPLIQUÉS, work stitches on top of a thin length of pearl cotton or other heavy thread; the application stitching will appear MORE SCULPTURAL.

! A SLIGHT 3-D EFFECT can be achieved by applying DOUBLE-SIDED FUSIBLE FLEECE INTERFACING to the back of the appliqué instead of regular fusible interfacing.

>> ADD DETAILS such as stems and seeds to appliqués USING ZIGZAG STITCHES.

FREEHAND APPLIQUÉ

Appliqués can also be applied using a freehand sewing technique. They are **much less polished-looking**, and it is precisely this that lends them a special charm. The design's edges can be smooth or slightly frayed, depending on which type of stabilizer is used (fusible or spray adhesive). The **upper and lower threads may be in different colors**, with the main color used as the upper thread. If the upper tension is then loosened somewhat, the lower thread will appear as tiny points on the right side of the fabric. The freehand technique is worked using an **embroidery/darning foot, lowered feed dogs, and an embroidery hoop**. Experienced sewers can also work without a presser foot and instead use a *spring needle* (*see page 38, number 8*).

>> SIMPLE AND APPEALING APPLIQUÉ MOTIFS can be found in children's books, advertisements, and pamphlets, and on calendars.

! APPLIQUÉ MOTIFS such as letters and numbers must be traced in mirror image onto the fusible stabilizer backing paper.

! ON MODERN SEWING MACHINES a freehand embroidery function is built in; in combination with an appliqué foot it allows for effortless FREEHAND APPLIQUÉ WORK.

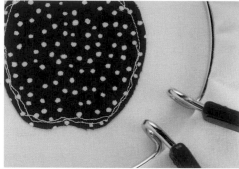

1 If lightly frayed edges are desired, attach the appliqué to the primary fabric using spray adhesive rather than fusible stabilizer; insert the fabric in an embroidery hoop along with a layer of stabilizer underneath.

2 Sew freehand around the design multiple times using a straight stitch.

3 Details on the design, in this example a stem and seeds, are added using zigzag stitching.

MACHINE SETTINGS
Stitch: Straight stitch (outline) and zigzag stitch (details)
Presser foot: Embroidery/darning foot
Needle: Standard needle
Thread: All-purpose thread on top and bottom, in color matching fabric

CHENILLE

Creating chenille involves the stitching together of **multiple layers of fabric** that are then sliced in strips, washed, dried, and brushed to result in a fabric surface with a soft, plush texture and structure.

- -

SEWN AND CUT CHENILLE

Multiple layers of fabric are sewn together at regular intervals with a straight stitch; then the fabric is cut open between the stitching lines.

1 Stack four to six layers of color-coordinated fabrics, all with right sides up. Pin or baste the layers together. Use a disappearing-ink marker to draw a line at a 45-degree angle to the fabric grain across the top piece of fabric; sew the first line of stitching along this marking. Continue to sew lines parallel to the first, at intervals of ⅝" (1.5cm), until the entire piece of fabric is sewn in this way. Use a quilting seam guide or a seam guide foot to maintain even spacing between stitching lines.

2 With scissors or a *chenille cutter (see page 31, number 9),* cut between the stitching lines through all fabric layers *except* the bottommost one.

3 Wash fabric and dry in the dryer. The raw edges will fray to various degrees, depending on the fabric types used, and create a chenille effect.

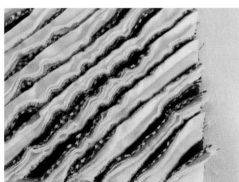

MACHINE SETTINGS

Stitch: Straight stitch, stitch length 11 spi (2.5mm)
Presser foot: Standard foot or seam guide foot; quilting seam guide
Needle: Standard needle
Thread: All-purpose cotton or polyester thread, matching to bottommost fabric layer

>> EVEN SEAM SPACING can be achieved with the help of a quilting seam guide or a seam guide foot.

! THE BOTTOMMOST LAYER OF FABRIC must not be cut, as it is the foundation fabric for the cut layers above.

! Light- to midweight, colorfast woven fabrics made of cotton, linen, viscose, silk, and wool WORK BEST FOR CHENILLE.

>> TO ENHANCE THE CHENILLE EFFECT, ROUGH UP the raw edges with a chenille brush or any other STIFF BRUSH.

≫ WHEN INDIVIDUALLY CUT fabric strips are stacked and sewn together, they require a strong, water-soluble **ADHESIVE STABILIZER TO BE PLACED UNDERNEATH FOR REINFORCEMENT.**

! CHENILLE STRIPS can be used for creative accents on collars, cuffs, pocket openings, shawls, or accessories.

CHENILLE STRIPS

A chenille foot stitches **multiple layers of pre-cut chenille tape or bias strips** onto a piece of foundation fabric, using straight or zigzag stitching. This method **eliminates the cutting step** of sewn and cut chenille.

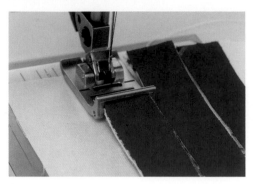

1 Stack three or four bias fabric strips, ⅝" (1.5cm) wide, or strips of ready-made chenille tape and **feed into a chenille foot**; attach the foot to the machine.

2 Depending on the intended use, sew just the strips together using a straight or zigzag stitch, or sew them directly onto a piece of background fabric. **Work slowly,** so that the strips are fed evenly and the **stitching remains centered.** Afterward, rough up the edges with a stiff brush.

MACHINE SETTINGS
Stitch: Straight stitch, stitch length 11 spi (2.5mm), or zigzag, stitch width 11 spi (2.5mm), stitch length 18 spi (1.5mm)
Presser foot: Chenille foot
Needle: Standard needle
Upper thread: All-purpose cotton or polyester thread, matching uppermost fabric layer
Lower thread: All-purpose cotton or polyester thread, matching bottommost fabric layer

FRINGE

Fringe and loops are small, decorative edging details and surface embellishments found on sleeves, hems, patch pockets, home textiles, and accessories such as scarves and purses. They are especially appealing as an addition to appliqués or embroidered pictures and quilts, since tiny loops and short fringe can suggest fur and hair.

Fringe and loops are made with a **fringe/looping foot,** often using contrasting and multicolored rayon, cotton, or novelty thread. **Loosen the upper thread tension enough** that the bobbin stitches do not get pulled up to the top of the fabric. Select a zigzag stitch with a **stitch length of 60–24 spi (0.5–1mm),** depending on the thickness of the thread.

SEWING FRINGE

1 Reinforce fabric with tear-away stabilizer. If you are sewing a motif, first **draw the design outlines** on the fabric surface using a disappearing-ink marker. Install the fringe foot and use machine embroidery thread on both the top and the bottom; **sew slowly along the design outlines and secure the ends of the stitching.** Pull the work carefully out from under the foot, so that the loops do not get caught.

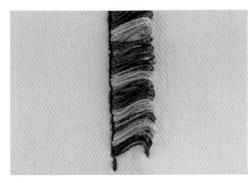

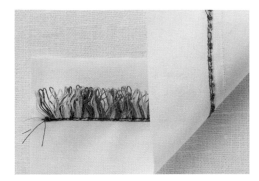

2 Press loops to one side. Install a standard, edging, or open freehand foot, change to all-purpose polyester thread as the top thread, and select a straight stitch with stitch length 13 spi (2mm) or a zigzag stitch with stitch width 24 spi (1mm) and stitch length 55 spi (0.6mm). **Stitch exactly along the edge of the loops, thereby securing them to the fabric.**

3 On the back of the fabric, **remove the bobbin thread** and then carefully pull the loops to the **right side** of the fabric. Snip open the loops, if desired.

MACHINE SETTINGS
Stitch: Zigzag stitch, stitch length 60–24 spi (0.5–1mm), stitch width 4 spi (6mm)
Presser foot: Fringe/looping foot, standard or edging foot
Needle: Machine embroidery needle
Thread: 40-weight rayon machine embroidery thread on top and bottom, in color matching fabric; alternatively, 30-weight rayon or 30- or 12-weight cotton for upper thread, all-purpose polyester thread for bottom thread, matching upper thread in color
Upper thread tension: 2, or as needed considering thread, fabric, and stabilizer weights

>> Use multicolored 30-weight COTTON EMBROIDERY THREAD to create dense, colorful fringe.

>> SEW A TEST ROW on a reinforced scrap of the fabric you will be using.

! THE LOOP-FORMING MECHANISM of the foot can also be used to transfer marking lines from patterns onto fabric or to ATTACH SHANK BUTTONS.

FRINGE AS EDGE FINISHING

1 Finish the fabric edge with a zigzag stitch, fold back ¼" (0.5cm), and press. Slip a 2" (5cm) strip of **heavyweight, water-soluble stabilizer ¾" (2cm) under the edge of the fabric,** so that about 1⅛" (3cm) of stabilizer remains sticking out to the right of the edge. Place the fabric right side up under the fringe foot, so that the **folded edge of the fabric lies directly under the metal bar on the foot.** Sew fringe; the needle will enter the fabric on the left strike and the stabilizer on the right strike.

2 In this step the fringe is secured onto the fabric. Press the fringe to the side, install an open freehand foot or a standard foot, and **sew down the fringe with a narrow satin stitch.** Wash out the stabilizer.

MACHINE SETTINGS
Stitch: Zigzag stitch (for fringe), stitch length 24 spi (1mm), stitch width 4 spi (6mm); satin stitch (for securing fringe), stitch length 24 spi (1mm), stitch width 11 spi (1.5mm)
Presser foot: Fringe/looping foot; standard, edging, or open freehand foot
Needle: Machine embroidery needle
Thread: 40-weight rayon machine embroidery thread on top and bottom, in color matching fabric
Upper thread tension: 2

>> WHEN SEWING DOWN fringe, lay thin, water-soluble stabilizer on top of the fringe so that the presser foot DOES NOT GET CAUGHT IN IT DURING SEWING.

! AN OPEN FREEHAND FOOT is best suited for attaching fringe, since it provides a good view of the sewing area.

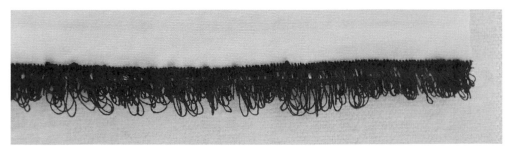

HEMSTITCHING

Hemstitching, also known as **drawn thread work** or **pulled thread work**, is used to embellish **woven cotton and linen fabrics**. The perforations result from the **removal of threads** and the use of specialized needles. Worked by hand or machine, this nostalgic trim is found on **hems and borders, and as insert panels** on garments, undergarments, and home textiles such as table and bed linens.

MACHINE HEMSTITCHING

On **hand-sewn hemstitching**, after about two to eight threads are pulled from the fabric, the resulting thread bars are bundled and sewn with hemstitches. Depending on the bundling and the choice of stitch, various patterns may be created. **Modern sewing machines** take over this work using **programmed hemstitches together with a wing needle**. These needles come as single or *twin needles (see page 38, number 10)*. If a machine does not have programmed hemstitches, a hemstitching effect may be achieved using **zigzag, blind, blanket, or other decorative stitches**. However, it is crucial to use a wing needle.

Machine hemstitching looks particularly elegant when it is worked on a **single layer of lightweight, woven cotton or linen fabric**, where a wing needle will create holes reminiscent of those in traditional hemstitching. The **upper thread tension** should be increased slightly, depending on the fabric. **Reinforce the fabric with strong, water-soluble stabilizer.**

MACHINE SETTINGS
Stitch: Cross stitch (1), zigzag stitch (2), hemstitch (3), or decorative stitch (4)
Presser foot: Standard foot
Needle: Wing needle
Thread: All-purpose thread on top and bottom, in color matching fabric
Possibly increase upper thread tension slightly

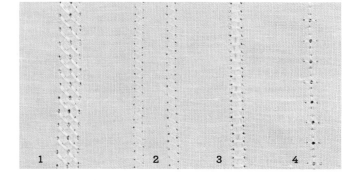

ENTREDEUX

This hemstitching technique is found on elegant linens and undergarments, and also on lightweight blouses and corsets. It creates the **appearance of an inserted border or lace strip**.

1 Install a *ribbon foot (see page 25, number 7)* and a wing needle and select a **double hemstitch**. Thread **thin white cotton crochet thread or pearl cotton** into the two frontmost holes of the ribbon foot. **The stitch will sew over the crochet thread and create an entredeux effect** (as if the stitching had been inserted between two pieces of fabric).

2 Weave a narrow satin or silk ribbon **through the center row of holes** using a blunt tapestry needle.

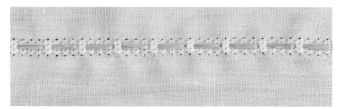

MACHINE SETTINGS
Stitch: Double hemstitch
Presser foot: Ribbon foot with 5 or 9 holes
Needle: Wing needle
Thread: Machine embroidery thread on top and bottom, in color matching fabric

>> Reinforce DELICATE LINEN OR BATISTE with a strong, water-soluble STABILIZER.

>> Additional DECORATIVE EFFECTS can be added by weaving in NOVELTY YARN or NARROW SATIN RIBBONS.

HEMSTITCHING EFFECT USING A FAGOTING GUIDE

With the help of a fagoting guide, two fabric pieces may be sewn together with a hemstitching seam. The fagoting guide is installed onto the machine's needle plate and holds the two fabric edges evenly apart during sewing so that a hemstitching effect is created. Flat fagoted seams are found on blouses, linens, lingerie, home textiles, and accessories. It is crucial to select a stitch that will catch in both fabric edges.

 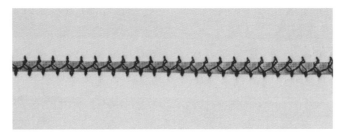

1 Reinforce the back of the fabric with tear-away stabilizer, fold under seam allowances, and press to secure. Install the fagoting guide on the needle plate; place the fabric pieces right sides up with the **pressed edges to the right and left of the guide**. Sew the edges together using a fagot stitch or other appropriate stitch.

2 Finished the fagoted seam.

MACHINE SETTINGS
Stitch: Fagot stitch
Presser foot: Standard foot and fagoting guide
Needle: Standard needle
Thread: All-purpose polyester thread on top and bottom, in color matching fabric

≫ Use 40-weight rayon MACHINE EMBROIDERY THREAD.

! If a FAGOTING GUIDE IS NOT AVAILABLE, a strong, water-soluble stabilizer may be used instead. With water-soluble ink, draw a line along the stabilizer; then set the folded fabric edges to the right and left of this line at a distance of about ³⁄₁₆"–¼" (5mm) and secure with SPRAY ADHESIVE. Sew edges together with fagot stitch or another appropriate stitch; wash out stabilizer.

EYELET STITCHING

Eyelet stitching is handiwork with a long tradition. You can find it today on table and bed linens, dresses, blouses, and tops. Eyelet lace is also popular and can be purchased by the yard. Eyelet stitching is typically done in **monochrome, especially white on white**, and is often classified as whitework embroidery. It can be done on the machine with the help of eyelet plates, which come in various sizes.

≫ DELICATE EYELET EMBROIDERY added to purchased items such as blouses, dresses, or tops lends an individual accent to off-the-rack clothing.

1 Remove the presser foot to install the **eyelet plate**. Mark the eyelet pattern on the fabric using a disappearing-ink marker. Stretch the fabric (optionally along with stabilizer) in an embroidery hoop. In the center of the marked eyelets, snip one of the fabric threads, or carefully puncture the eyelet with an awl, knitting needle, or similar device.

2 Place the punctured area over the pin on the eyelet plate (the fabric must fit snugly over the pin). Set the machine to darning stitch, lower the feed dogs, select a zigzag stitch at 6 spi (4mm) width, lower the presser foot lever, and begin sewing. Turn the embroidery hoop slowly and evenly as you work around the opening. The stitches should form a dense border all around the hole.

3 Cut threads with enough of a tail that they can be pulled to the wrong side of the fabric and tied off.

SMOCKING

Smocking is a decorative technique in which fabric is gathered into the tiniest of folds. It is especially popular for use on babies' and young girls' clothing, where it is used as a shaping element. But smocking is also found on folkloric clothing, yokes, wristbands, waistbands, and wide necklines. Smocking is very **time-consuming to do by hand**, with preliminary stitching done in multiple rows to gather up the tiny folds and then embroidery work done on top of that. Machine smocking, both elastic and nonelastic, can be done instead. Elastic smocking requires elastic thread and a ribbon or cording foot. Smocking that is embellished with decorative stitching is not stretchy; it is first *gathered (see page 116)* to the desired width and then embroidered. **Lightweight linen and cotton fabrics yield the best results.**

! FOR SMOCKED
FABRIC, start with
approximately double
the width of the desired
finish piece.

» Use ALL-PURPOSE
THREAD in pastel
colors, or use machine
embroidery thread.

ELASTIC SMOCKING

Elastic smocking is **stretchy** and suited for sleeve openings on blouses and dresses, as well as for children's and infants' clothing.

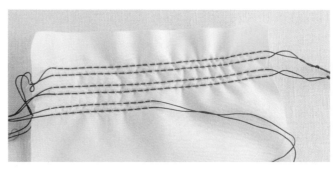
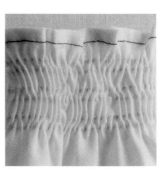

! A needle threader is
good for pulling ELASTIC
THREAD through the
holes in a ribbon foot.

! A BUTTONHOLE
FOOT may also be used
for smocking.

1 With the help of a threader, pull elastic thread through the **two outer holes of the fourth row of a ribbon foot, knot the threads behind the foot, and install the foot on the machine.** Mark the first sewing line on the fabric with a disappearing-ink marker. Sew over the elastic threads along the marked line **with an elastic zigzag stitch, without pulling on the elastic.** At the end of the row, cut the elastic, leaving tails of approximately 2½" (6cm). Sew a second row ⅝" (1.5cm) from the first, paying careful attention **that the elastic thread does not get caught in the zigzag stitching,** since it would then not be able to gather in the fabric. Sew additional rows until the desired width of smocking is complete.

2 Hold the elastic threads on both ends, **pull together, and tie off.**

MACHINE SETTINGS
Stitch: Elastic zigzag stitch
Presser foot: Ribbon foot
Needle: Standard needle
Thread: All-purpose polyester thread on top and bottom, in color matching fabric

EMBROIDERED SMOCKING

This type of traditional embroidered smocking is **nonelastic** and is popular for use on children's and infants' clothing, primarily on yokes and sleeve openings. Folkloric clothing and tunics also often incorporate embroidered smocking details. Smocking work is done **before pattern pieces are cut.**

1 To begin, **finish one edge of the fabric with a narrow hem,** then gather the fabric evenly to the desired smocking height and width; use either the **simple gathering technique** *(see page 116)* or a **shirring foot.**

MACHINE SETTINGS
Stitch: Various decorative stitches
Presser foot: Open freehand foot or standard foot
Needle: Size 14 (90 European) embroidery needle
Upper thread: 40-weight rayon machine embroidery thread, in color matching fabric
Lower thread: All-purpose polyester thread, in color matching fabric

2 Reinforce the gathered fabric from behind with a **heavy water-soluble stabilizer**; lay thin water-soluble stabilizer across the top of the gathers. This way, the embroidery stitches will form evenly on top of the gathering.

3 Install an open freehand foot or a standard foot, a machine embroidery needle, and 40-weight rayon machine embroidery thread; this will make the embroidery more prominent and lend it an elegant sheen. **Choose embroidery stitches and sew them in parallel rows with even spacing.** Wash out the stabilizer. If the gathering threads are still apparent and bothersome, they may be removed.

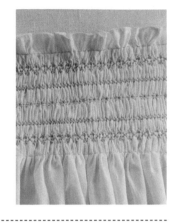

>> SEW EMBROIDERY STITCHES directly over the GATHERING LINE to eliminate the need to remove gathering stitches.

>> To maintain EVEN DISTANCES between lines of embroidery stitches, use a SMALL RULER or an ADJUSTABLE SEAM GUIDE FOOT.

COUCHING

Couching is a technique for embroidering over ribbons, string, cord, flat braids, fabric strips, or bead strings while simultaneously applying them to fabric, leather, faux leather, or other material. Couching **does not require a large time investment or a great deal of previous sewing experience,** and is a great way to embellish and add dimension to textile surfaces by simply using a straight or zigzag stitch to sew over ribbons, yarn, et cetera. The technique is also used to add sculptural elements or to accent seam lines. **Freehand couching** can give structure to large fabric pieces and create outlines around designs such as appliqués, and works both with pre-drawn guidelines or truly freehand. **Various specialized presser feet** are available for this type of work. The feet are designed to be able to thread in cords, ribbons, yarns, et cetera and have wide stitch openings to accommodate embroidery stitches.

! CUT OUT FABRIC LARGER than the desired finished size, as couching will pull in fabric slightly.

>> Reinforce FABRIC FOR COUCHING with ADHESIVE STABILIZER to prevent puckering.

>> String, yarn, and cord can also be sewn on with a ROLLED HEM, cording, or beading foot.

>> A NEEDLE THREADER is useful for quickly pulling decorative threads through a ribbon foot.

MACHINE SETTINGS
Stitch: Straight, zigzag, honeycomb, or other wide decorative stitches
Presser foot: Various ribbon and couching feet
Needle: Standard needle
Thread: All-purpose polyester thread, in color matching fabric, or invisible thread as upper thread
Reduce machine speed

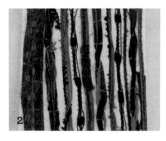
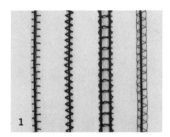
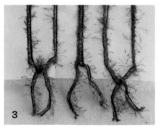

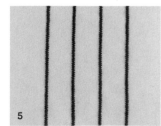

1 Ribbon foot
2 Ribbon foot and elastic foot
3 Braid foot
4 Freehand couching foot
5 Cording foot

! RAISED "CATERPILLAR" SEAMS can be formed by sewing with a zigzag stitch over thin PEARL COTTON. Zigzag setting: stitch length 17 spi (1.3mm), stitch width 15 spi (1.8mm).

» REINFORCE FABRIC WITH STABILIZER and work slowly.

» CORDS can also be sewn on using a beading foot.

! Sew A SHORT LENGTH OF BEADING on a scrap of fabric to determine the correct stitch settings.

! BEADS MUST BE STRUNG before application.

» Use a disappearing-ink marker to draw APPLICATION LINES.

SEWING ON BEADS

Strings of beads and sequined tapes lend fabric and clothing an elegant, festive quality. They may be quickly applied by machine. You will need a *beading foot (see page 25, number 9)*, which has a groove on the bottom to allow the beaded strip to pass through. Sew with a **zigzag or blind stitch and invisible thread.** The stitch settings will depend on the size of the beads.

MACHINE SETTINGS
Stitch: Zigzag
for 2–3mm beads: stitch length 11 spi (3.5mm), stitch width 9 spi (3mm); for 4mm beads: stitch length 11 spi (3.5mm), stitch width 6 spi (4mm); for 6mm beads: stitch length 4 spi (6mm), stitch width 4 spi (6mm)
Presser foot: Beading foot, depending on bead size, either 2–3, 4, or 6mm
Needle: Standard needle
Upper thread: Invisible thread
Lower thread: Bobbin thread
Reduce upper thread tension

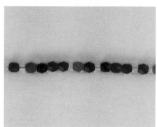

BATTING/WADDING

Two fabrics can gain loft and warmth when they are **quilted, or stitched together with a layer of batting between them.** Batting, which is known as wadding in the UK, can be made from **polyester, flannel, or wool.** The layers of the quilt "sandwich" are sewn with **straight stitching lines in the shape of diamonds, squares, or other patterns.**
Premade quilted fabric (known as pre-quilted, double-faced quilted, or double quilted fabric) may be purchased by the yard, but when you want to use a specific fabric it is very easy to create your own with a sewing machine. You will need an appropriate lining material, most commonly batting (some are pre-quilted), **fleece interfacing, a fusible gridded interfacing (quilter's grid),** or a **quilted interlining.** These are available in different weights, and may be fusible or sewn in (with all-purpose thread). A **ruler grid** or a presser foot with a seam guide will help keep sewing (quilting) lines at a regular spacing. Quilter's grid interfacing and **quilted interlining** already have a diamond pattern, which is apparent in the main fabric after it is ironed on. With these linings, no ruler grid is required.

1 Iron fusible interlining onto the **back of the fabric.** If the lining is not quilted, use tailor's chalk or a marker on the lining side to **mark a stitching line in one corner;** this will become the first stitching line, and **further stitching lines will be created either parallel or at a right angle to this one.** Sew along the marking using a straight stitch. Install the ruler grid and continue to sew **evenly separated lines with about 2"–2½" (5–6cm) spacing** until the entire piece is sewn.

2 Sew **further parallel lines at right angles to the first batch,** so that a grid pattern is created.

MACHINE SETTINGS
Stitch length: 9–6 spi (3–4mm), depending on fabric and lining weight
Presser foot: Roller, non-stick, or standard foot
Needle: Standard needle size 12–16 (80–100 European), depending on fabric and lining weight
Thread: All-purpose thread on top and bottom, in color matching material

QUILTING AND PATCHWORK

Quilting is practiced worldwide and is a beloved sewing technique in which multiple fabric layers are artfully bound together. Patchwork is a technique where various fabrics and fabric scraps—usually cotton or linen, but also sometimes leather or wool—are sewn together to create a single piece of fabric. The fabric pieces are often pieced together in complex patterns. Quilts used as blankets, wall hangings, rugs, or fabric, or in accessories, are usually made in three layers, where the **quilt top** is often done in patchwork and the **quilt backing** is done in a single color. In between is a warm interlining, the **batting** (or wadding), made of polyester, cotton, or wool. To prevent the lining from shifting, all **three layers are bound together** by hand or machine topstitching. This **sewing together of batting and fabric** is the quilting itself, which gives the quilt its **sculpted surface.** Numerous hand and machine stitches, specialized quilting and patchwork feet, freehand quilting frames, quilting needles, and quilting thread are available for use.

1 Sew together fabric pieces to create a patchwork layer of the desired dimensions.

2 Baste together the quilt top and quilt backing with a middle layer of batting.

3 Stitch through all three layers using straight stitches or special quilting stitches; stitch in the ditches of the patchwork stitching lines. Apply a binding *(see pages 103–106)* to finish the edges.

» ONCE SEWN TOGETHER, quilts can be further embellished with appliqués and/or embroidery motifs.

! WAXED QUILTING THREAD must NOT BE USED WITH A SEWING MACHINE.

» 30-WEIGHT COTTON MACHINE EMBROIDERY THREAD is especially good for machine quilting.

» IDEAS, DESIGNS, AND INSTRUCTIONS for quilting may be found in myriad books and special-interest magazines, and on the Internet.

textiles
101

MAKING THE RIGHT FABRIC CHOICES IS EXTREMELY IMPORTANT. IN THIS CHAPTER YOU'LL LEARN EVERYTHING YOU NEED TO KNOW ABOUT STANDARD TEXTILE MANUFACTURING AND FINISHING PROCESSES, WHICH FABRICS ARE BEST SUITED TO WHICH PROJECTS, AND THE CORRECT INTERPRETATION OF CARE SYMBOLS.

textile manufacturing processes

The raw materials for textiles may be either natural or synthetic, and are spun into thread in various ways, depending on the fiber's characteristics. The resulting thread can then be woven, knitted, or warp knitted to create a wide variety of fabric types. For felt and other nonwovens, the fibers are not spun, but rather compacted into sheets.

WOVENS

Woven materials are created through the **interlacing of two sets of thread.** The threads that run lengthwise in the loom are called warp threads, and the threads that are pulled back and forth crosswise are the **weft** threads. On the two long sides of a woven piece there will be **slightly thickened edges,** to which the weft threads will be positioned at a right angle. Depending on the way the warp and weft threads are interlaced, the threads end up bound together in different ways. This determines the woven pattern and also influences the structure, elasticity, strength, and hand (drape) of the resulting weave.

The **three fundamental types of weave** are **plain weave** (also called **linen weave**), **twill weave, and satin weave;** various other weaves are based on these types. Varied and imaginative woven structures, such as embossed surfaces, for example, can be created with special loom accessories. The jacquard loom's elaborate mechanism can generate large-scale patterns with incredible complexity.

» IF A FABRIC IS MADE FROM DIFFERENT STRENGTHS OF THREAD, the warp threads will always be the strongest ones. Therefore you should MAKE SURE, WHILE CUTTING OUT PATTERN PIECES, that the warp threads lie in the direction that will be the most stressed when the garment is being worn.

PLAIN/LINEN WEAVE

In this, the most straightforward and **versatile weave,** the weft thread alternates going over and under the warp threads; the resulting fabric is **identical on the front and back** and is very stable. Examples of plain weave include batiste, taffeta, voile, poplin, and muslin.

One variation on plain weave is **basketweave,** sometimes called Panama weave, in which the warp and weft threads are always worked in sets of two (or more) and **end up looking like little squares.** This weave is more open than plain weave and feels softer. Some home decor, suit, and shirt fabrics are made with this weave.

Warp thread (pink)
Weft thread (gray)

TWILL WEAVE

The weft thread alternates between going under one and over two warp threads. Because the pattern is offset by one thread in every row, visible **diagonal lines are formed** (depending on the style of fabric these may be more or less obvious). Examples of twill weave are denim and gabardine.

SATIN WEAVE

Here the weft thread alternates between going over one and then under four (or several) warp threads; the pattern is offset by one thread in every row, which produces a supple fabric with a soft drape that is smooth and hard-wearing. The **right side of the fabric is smoother and shinier than the wrong side.** Examples of satin weave include satin and brocade fabrics.

KNITTED TEXTILES

Stretchy knit fabrics are made by **looping thread together.** Knits are pliable and do not wrinkle as much as wovens. A knitted fabric's elasticity in lengthwise, crosswise, and diagonal directions depends on the thread type used and the style of knitting involved. Loosely spun thread imparts thermal capacity. Two basic types of knitting are used in fabric manufacturing: **standard knitting and warp knitting.** From these—or by combining these—many variants can be created, ranging from sheer to heavyweight.

KNITS

Standard knits are **derived from hand-knitting methods,** where a continuous thread is worked into the loops of the row below, proceeding back and forth crosswise. **Elasticity is greater widthwise than lengthwise.**

Knits come in single and double knit versions. On **single knit** fabrics the outer edges have a tendency to roll inward. On **double knits,** two needles and threads work simultaneously while creating the fabric; it is less stretchy than single knit and thus maintains its shape better. A common double knit pattern is ribbing, which looks the same on both sides and is often used for sleeve cuffs.

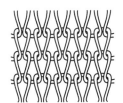

WARP KNITS

Multiple threads and needles work in concert to generate warp knitted fabric, which can only be created by machine. The stitches are created through the **looping together of parallel vertical threads.** The fabric is stretchy widthwise and is often less elastic than standard knit; it stays truer to form and will not develop runs. The outer edges tend to roll inward.

The most common warp knits include minky, tricot, and jersey fabrics; some laces and faux furs are also warp knit.

OTHER TEXTILES

In addition to woven, knitted, and warp knitted fabrics there are some textiles that are manufactured differently: they have no fabric grain, and their edges do not fray. Familiar examples are felt, nonwoven interfacings, and some types of tulle. These fabrics can be referred to simply as "nonwoven."

! IT IS NOT ALWAYS OBVIOUS whether a fabric is woven or knit. WHEN IN DOUBT, PULL OUT A THREAD ALONG A FABRIC'S CUT EDGE. On knits you will see loops; on wovens the edge will fray.

! LEATHER is often mistakenly lumped together with textiles, but of course leather is ANIMAL SKIN THAT HAS BEEN TANNED with either a chemical or a vegetable treatment. Leather has a characteristic grain that is largely preserved during the manufacturing process.

fabric treatments and finishes

Fabrics need to be able to accommodate all kinds of uses and stand up to various demands. They get their specific qualities from specialized techniques. Chemical processing and finishing treatments can change the properties of a thread or weave, and mechanical treatments can create effects such as brushed surfaces. These treatments are mostly done for practical reasons or to make a fabric more versatile. Purely decorative treatments tend to involve dyeing and printing.

INDUSTRIAL TREATMENTS

Various industrial fabric treatments are done before, during, or after the creation of the fabric, and many more are achieved using a combination of methods. The following section covers the most common treatments and explains their most important characteristics.

ACRYLIC-COATED
Cotton weave is sealed with an acrylic coating and thus becomes water repellant. Despite the coating, the look of the fabric remains unchanged and the weave stays flexible.

ANTIMICROBIAL
A chemical treatment makes these fabrics resistant to various bacteria and fungi. The fabric is moisture-wicking and discourages the buildup of odors.

ANTI-PILLING
A chemical treatment introduces a binding agent to reduce the formation of pills.

ANTI-STATIC
Because of their low moisture content, synthetic fabrics tend to build up static electricity in dry conditions and will then cling. This chemical treatment largely prevents this static buildup.

BLEACH

When a **white fabric** is desired, natural colors and stains are removed with a chemical bleaching agent.

BOILED

Boiled wool gets its **characteristic plush texture** from a fulling process involving moisture, heat, pressure, and friction. The fabric weave becomes thick and dense as it shrinks.

BRUSHED

Depending on the brush and the type of fabric used, this can create a **delicate to heavy surface pile** and increase the warmth of a fabric. The fibers are pulled to the surface of the fabric to varying degrees; this is a familiar texture on flannel and velour.

CRUSH, CRINKLE, PLISSÉ

A **crinkled effect** is usually fixed permanently through a chemical treatment. To **maintain this look** on fabric that is not permanently treated, the fabric should be stored, washed, and dried while twisted and folded up like a hank of yarn. It may also be dry-cleaned.

EASY CARE

With this treatment fibers become more elastic and resist wrinkling; any creases that do occur smooth out again upon hanging. The fabrics are machine washable, quick drying, and require **little to no ironing.**

FLOCKING

Fine textile fibers are applied to the fabric surface with adhesive, creating a **velvet-like, slightly raised pattern.**

MERCERIZED

Cotton and other natural fibers are made stronger and thus **tougher wearing** through a treatment with sodium hydroxide (lye). They gain an added sheen and increased break resistance, and their texture becomes pleasantly soft.

SHRINK RESISTANT

Fabric is treated to **prevent any later changes in form or size.** The fabric becomes denser and either **does not shrink further at all with additional washings,** or will not shrink beyond a certain stated amount. A patented anti-shrink treatment is Sanforization, which guarantees that a textile will not shrink by more than 1 percent.

SIZING

In the case of **permanent sizing** treatments, a mixture of chemicals ensures that the fabric maintains its **sheen or strength,** for example, even through regular washings. In contrast, **temporary sizing** will wash out over time (but can be reapplied).

SOIL RESISTANT

Typically these fabrics have a **waterproof finish** and are not vulnerable to dirt or oils.

STAIN RESISTANT

With this treatment, water-, alcohol-, and oil-based **staining** is **inhibited,** and the removal of any stains that do occur is made easier. Fabric care instructions should provide information about treating different stain types.

TEFLON COATED

This chemical treatment makes textiles easy care and wrinkle resistant, as well as water repellant (moisture will bead on the surface). They are especially well suited for **outdoor uses.**

WATER RESISTANT

The fabric surface is treated with water-repellant chemicals to **prevent immediate absorption of moisture;** moisture beads up on the surface, but the fabric remains breathable.

WATERPROOF

The open weave of the textile is sealed, creating a waterproof, **non-breathable** fabric.

WRINKLE RESISTANT

This treatment gives more elasticity to a fabric's fibers, which **prevents most wrinkling** and allows any creases that do occur to smooth out again upon hanging. Cotton, linen, and viscose wrinkle especially heavily and thus are often given this treatment.

➤➤ **ONLY PERMANENT FINISHES** are washable; temporary finishes are not. Some treatments are not obvious or visible, so pay attention to the **INFORMATION LABEL** on the fabric bolt before making a purchase. If no label is attached, inquire further with the fabric seller, as treatments can affect the appropriate uses for a fabric.

⚠ **MECHANICALLY TREATED FABRICS** that have NO CHEMICAL SIZING COMPONENT must be PULLED GENTLY INTO SHAPE WHILE STILL DAMP after washing. Avoid dryers to prevent shrinking.

fibers *and their* properties

! Fibers will often be combined or refined (e.g., mercerized, *see page 141*) to **CREATE THREAD** with superior qualities and/or easier care requirements.

The fundamental component of all textiles is fiber. Due to technical advancements in modern textile manufacturing, it is not always possible to determine with certainty what fibers are in a fabric. Fortunately, this information must be provided on the fabric bolt. In this section, we'll describe the properties of commonly used fibers to give you a better idea of what to expect from various fabrics. We also suggest possible uses for specific fabric types, although the quality and strength of a fabric should be considered on a case-by-case basis.

PLANT FIBERS

These natural fibers are made from plant sources, such as cotton, flax, or hemp, and **consist primarily of cellulose.** Despite an ever-increasing number of synthetic fibers, cotton retains a leadership position in the world of fabric production.

COTTON

Cotton is one of the **most important raw textile fibers in the world**; it is obtained from the fibrous seed boll (pod or capsule) of the cotton plant. It is often blended with viscose or linen. Examples of cotton fabrics include **terry, denim, fine rib, corduroy, and muslin.** Cotton is popular in part because of its great versatility. It is easy to work with and comfortable to wear.

Ripe, open cotton boll

Properties: Cotton is soft, breathable, and can absorb large amounts of moisture. It is strong and durable, but has little elasticity and **tends to wrinkle.** It takes dye easily.

Care: Cotton can withstand frequent washings but may shrink. The appropriate water temperature will depend on the fabric finishing. It irons well, preferably dampened slightly or using steam.
Uses: T-shirts, shirts, blouses, dresses, jeans, bed and table linens, and home textiles and décor items of many types.

LINEN

These fibers come from the stalks of **flax or linen plants,** one of the oldest agricultural crops in the world. Pure linen **encourages the body's natural temperature regulation** and feels cool and comfortable to wear. Linen is often blended with other fibers. Popular linen fabrics are crushed linen, handkerchief linen, and linen suiting.

Properties: The fabric has a matte sheen and is unusually durable and wear resistant. Some types of linen have **small, irregular slubs** as part of the fabric. Linen is minimally elastic, making it prone to wrinkling. Linen feels smooth, slightly stiff and cool to the touch, is stain resistant, and will not develop fuzz. It is also very breathable, absorbent, and tough.

Care: Linen can tolerate high water temperatures (it can be boiled) but, depending on its finishing, may require a lower wash temperature. It is **best to use liquid detergents with linen.** Linen can withstand a hot iron; preferably iron with the fabric damp, or use steam.

Uses: Ideal for sophisticated **summer clothing.** Heavier, more rustic linen makes excellent dish towels, tablecloths, napkins, and bed linens; delicate linens such as **batiste** can be used for sheer curtains.

➤➤ For SEWING LINEN, USE PREMIUM COTTON OR POLYESTER THREAD. Press finished seams flat with a steam iron.

❗ A BLEND OF LINEN AND SILK creates an ATTRACTIVE, STRONG FABRIC with a fine sheen. It works especially well for dresses, pants, and suits.

HEMP

Specific, very productive varieties of hemp are cultivated to generate **raw textile fibers.** Hemp is a **more environmentally friendly crop than cotton,** as it does not require treatment with pesticides. Hemp fabrics have characteristics similar to linen.

Properties: Hemp has especially robust fibers; it is tougher and more durable than cotton and very hard-wearing. It tends to wrinkle, is very absorbent, and is gentle on the skin. Textiles made from hemp get **softer and more supple with use.**

Care: Hemp can tolerate high water temperatures (it can be boiled) and should be washed only with liquid detergents. Iron it damp at a **high temperature.**

Uses: Good for outerwear, dresses, pants, bags, and slipcovers.

ANIMAL FIBERS

This category of fiber includes those made from the hairs of specific animals or from the cocoons of silkworms. Silk is among the most elegant and highly valued natural fibers.

WOOL

In addition to sheep's wool, the fine, **spinnable hairs of angora rabbits, cashmere and mohair goats, alpacas, llamas, and camels** are all considered wool. "Lambswool" refers to the soft, delicate wool from the first shearing of a lamb at approximately six months of age. Wool is versatile and can be blended with many natural and synthetic fibers, and can be turned into anything from a lightweight woven fabric to a heavy knit or a boiled wool. Typical examples of wool fabrics include **bouclé, tweed, worsted, gabardine, and wool felt.**

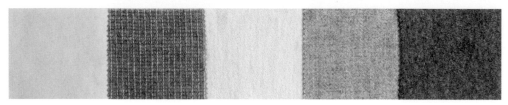

Properties: Wool is **breathable, elastic, wrinkle resistant,** and very absorbent as well as relatively soil resistant. Wrinkles will smooth out overnight if the textile is hung out on a balcony or in a steamy bathroom.
Care: Wool should be washed as **infrequently and as carefully as possible.** Usually airing out wool is sufficient; boiled wool may be brushed. Avoid overly warm water—above 85°F (30°C)—too much or the wrong type of detergent, friction, and wringing: these can all lead to felting. Wool dries slowly. If needed, iron gently at medium temperature under a damp cloth or using steam.
Uses: Very fine merino wool will create elegant garments, while more rustic Shetland wool is better suited to sporty clothing. Mid- and heavyweight wools are good for pullovers, hats, and winter garments, as they have **excellent warming properties.** Wool is also popular for home textile items such as blankets and pillows.

SILK

Depending on the production technique, one differentiates between **pure silk (mulberry silk) and raw silk (Tussah silk).** Because of the latter's characteristic slubby texture, raw silk fabrics tend to have a slightly nubby, uneven surface. Depending on the manner of production, silk may be sheer, light, and supple or heavy and stiff. Examples of silk fabrics are **chiffon, crêpe de chine, organza, satin, and taffeta.**

Properties: Silk has an elegant sheen, is **comfortable on the skin, is tear resistant,** and takes dye easily. Some types tend to wrinkle. Silk is very absorbent and moisture-wicking. Silk is **sensitive to perspiration, deodorants, and harsh light.** The latter can cause fading and eventually lead to a breakdown of fibers.
Care: It is best to have silk **professionally dry cleaned.** If you opt to hand wash silk, do so very carefully. Iron it from the wrong side at a medium temperature, without steam. Silk is susceptible to water spotting.
Uses: Depending on the type, silk is used **for elegant blouses,** lingerie, blazers, scarves, and shawls. Dress shields are advisable with blouses to help protect the delicate fabric.

Washed, combed,
long-staple raw wool

❗ ABBREVIATIONS FOR TEXTILE FIBERS

The following are the abbreviations for the most common and a few less common natural fibers:

CO: cotton
HA: hemp
JU: jute
LI: linen, flax
RA: ramie
SE: silk (mulberry silk)
WA: angora
WM: mohair
WO: wool (lambswool)
WP: alpaca
WS: cashmere
WV: virgin/fleece wool (new wool)

SYNTHETIC FIBERS

Synthetic fibers are categorized into **cellulose fibers from vegetable sources** and **chemical fibers** produced from petroleum and coal. Compared with natural fibers they are **stronger and more durable,** and are wrinkle resistant. Because of their light weight and typically high elasticity they are irreplaceable in the fashion industry, since many designs can only be realized using fabrics made from these fibers.

Granules for production of synthetic fibers

VISCOSE/RAYON

These delicate cellulose fibers can be made shiny or matte and in various styles, and they **resemble natural fibers.** These inexpensive fibers, sometimes called **artificial silk,** are often blended with other fibers. Chiffon and netting sometimes are made of 100% viscose.

Properties: Has a soft hand, **feels pleasantly cool,** and is comfortable on the skin. The fabric has little elasticity and thus tends to wrinkle. Takes dye well, but tears easily when wet.

Care: Hand wash or use a delicate cycle. Do not wring or spin dry in the machine, but rather hang to **drip dry or roll gently in a dry towel.** Iron at medium temperature using a damp pressing cloth or steam.
Uses: Popular for comfortably **light and flowing garments** such as blouses and summer dresses; also used as **lining.**

ACETATE

These very smooth fibers are made from cellulose acetate and have an elegant, matte shine; they **look similar to silk** and have comparable characteristics to viscose. Acetate is frequently blended with other fibers, but taffeta linings and satin may be made of 100% acetate.

Properties: Acetate drapes wonderfully and has good stability, but tends toward static cling.
It is **elastic, nonabsorbent, dries quickly,** holds dyes well, and seldom wrinkles. The fabric is very heat sensitive and will melt at 340°F (170°C).

Care: Hand wash or wash on delicate cycle at 85°F (30°C); **do not wring.** Articles with a high percentage of acetate content should be dry cleaned, as **regular washing in the machine can cause them to lose their sheen and shape.** Do not tumble dry, but rather hang damp to drip dry. If needed, iron on low from the wrong side, using a damp pressing cloth.
Uses: Delicate undergarments, dresses, blouses, shirts, and **linings.**

>> MANY SYNTHETIC FABRICS are HEAT SENSITIVE and can easily melt under a hot iron. Do an IRONING TEST ON A SCRAP beforehand to make sure your fabric can withstand high temperatures. An IRON SHOE can also be used for protection. It is made of durable silicone and fits on all standard irons.

! FABRICS MADE FROM CHEMICAL FIBERS are classified under the general term "synthetics." The production of the first synthetic fibers began in the 1920s and has been evolving ever since.

POLYESTER

These versatile synthetic fibers are manufactured in a large variety of structures and weights and are often combined with other fibers, such as cotton and wool, to create blends.

Properties: Polyester is very durable and wrinkle free; it maintains its shape and does not shrink or fade. It is soft and supple, fairly nonabsorbent, and dries quickly.

Care: Easy care; may be machine washed in water up to 105°F (40°C). It typically requires no ironing, but if needed, iron using a damp pressing cloth at a medium temperature.

Uses: Sportswear, men's shirts, dresses, suits, swimwear, undergarments, curtains, bed linens, and as quilt batting.

POLYACRYLIC

Fabrics made of polyacrylic are usually lightweight, soft, and fuzzy or with a pile. The fiber is often combined with other fibers, primarily wool. Many faux furs are 100% polyacrylic.

Properties: Polyacrylic is woolier than polyester and polyamide. It tends toward static cling, but is durable, tear-resistant, does not fade or lose its shape, is quick drying, and has limited absorbency.

Care: Easy care; machine washable at 85°F (30°C). Do not tumble dry. Iron at a low temperature, if needed.

Uses: Sweaters, rainwear and sportswear, curtains.

POLYAMIDE

This stable, premium synthetic fiber is often combined with cotton or wool fibers to give them greater durability.

Properties: Polyamide is very elastic and tear resistant and has similar qualities to polyester; however, it is not fade resistant.

Care: Heat sensitive. Wash on delicate cycle at 105°F (40°C). If needed, use a cool iron without steam.

Uses: Swimwear, sportswear, and leisure clothing; lingerie and foundation garments.

ELASTANE

Elastane is almost always combined with other fibers and improves the fit and comfort of body-conscious stretch fashions. The higher the percentage of elastane, the more precisely the garment will fit to the body.

Properties: Elastane is extremely stretchy and shape-retaining, and will pull back to its original size after stretching. It is durable and wrinkle resistant.

Care: Easy care. Recommended washing and ironing temperatures will depend on the fibers it is blended with.

Uses: Foundation garments, lingerie, swimwear.

! ABBREVIATIONS FOR TEXTILE FIBERS

The following are the abbreviations for the most common and a few additional synthetic fibers:

AC: acetate

MD/CMD: modal

CU: cupro

VI: viscose

EA: elastane (polyurethane)

MAC: modacrylic

ME: metallic

PA: nylon/polyamide (perlon)

PAN: acrylic (polyacrylic)

PE: polyethelene

PES: polyester

PP: polypropelene

fiber quality marks

Those who prefer to use only natural fibers should look for fiber quality marks indicating all natural fiber content. For people with sensitive skin or allergies, or for children, textiles made from natural fibers are a good choice. A quality mark guarantees that textiles meet production and content requirements that are regulated.

COTTON MARK

The stylized seed boll identifies **textiles made from pure cotton,** whose fibers come from the cotton plant. The use of the mark is not allowed in the case of cotton blends.

WOOLMARK

Pure new wool or virgin wool is the designation for wool sheared from a live sheep. This logo guarantees certain qualities with respect to color fastness, minimum fiber strength, and stability of shape. Designations such as "100% wool" or "pure wool" may point to **lower-quality material** that may even be made from recycled wool scraps (such as wool shoddy).

WOOLMARK BLEND

This logo indicates a blend of fibers where the **virgin wool content must be at least 60%.**

LINEN MARK

The stylized "L" identifies textiles made from pure linen (100% linen) and linen/cotton blends (containing a minimum of 40% linen, with the rest cotton).

fabrics and fabric selection

Today, natural and synthetic fibers are made into an almost dizzying variety of fabrics, often in multiple weights, and in both solids and prints. The quality and character of a fabric depends primarily on its fiber content and the way it is woven or knitted.

FABRIC SELECTION

Different fabrics all have their own particular qualities, and some may require specialized sewing techniques. Knowledge **about the most common natural and synthetic fibers and their specific properties is essential for achieving flawless sewing results.** When multiple types of fabric are used in the same project, it is crucial to test whether they can all be cared for in a uniform way. Most commercial patterns include suggestions for the fabrics that will work best.

THE ABC'S OF FABRIC

In the following pages we present the most common and popular fabrics with notes about their typical fiber contents and their most important or unusual qualities, and provide examples of some potential uses for each.

! The FIBER OR FIBER BLEND used for a particular style of fabric can VARY GREATLY, and different fabrics that all go by the same name can still have considerable differences.

» BUYING FABRIC ONLINE is convenient and practical. However, when ordering large quantities and/or expensive fabrics, you should first always REQUEST A SWATCH, which will often be sent gratis. This is the only way to be sure that the QUALITY, CHARACTERISTICS, AND COLOR of your chosen fabric will meet your expectations.

BATISTE (shown here with embroidery) is a lightweight, sheer, and **delicate plain weave** made from cotton, linen, wool, or polyester. It is used for fine blouses, dresses, linens, and curtains.

BOILED WOOL is a reversible wool fabric made in plain or twill weave. Its **surface texture is created through fulling,** a process similar to felting, which gives it a grainy, felted look. It is generally **wrinkle free, windproof, and moisture repellant.** Its edges do not fray and thus do not require finishing. It is ideal for warm coats, jackets, vests, blankets, and decorative items. Holes may be cut into this fabric.

BOUCLÉ is a wrinkle-resistant plain weave usually made from wool, polyester, or a blend. Textured threads are incorporated to create **nubs and loops on the surface.** The fabric tends to fray at the edges. It is popular for coats, suits, skirts, and slipcovers.

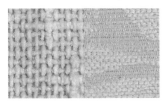

BROCADE is a mid- to heavyweight woven made from natural or artificial silk, usually in plain weave or satin weave, and is characterized by a silky sheen. Its **frequently complex and large-scale patterns** are often accented with metallic threads. The pattern appears in the negative on the wrong side. Brocade frays at the edges and is napped. It is used for festive suits and evening wear.

CHENILLE is a heavy, durable, voluminous woven with a **soft, velvet-like surface.** It typically is made from cotton, silk, or synthetic fibers. Its irregular pile does not have a nap. Chenilles with pile on only one side are very well suited for cushions and upholstery; those with **double-sided pile** are suited for bath towels, bathrobes, scarves, shawls, and drapes.

CHIFFON is a **sheer, very lightweight and flowing fabric,** usually made from fine silk or synthetic and worked in plain weave. It is used for festive dresses, blouses (to wear over camisoles), lingerie, evening and bridal wear, and for scarves and wraps.

>> CHIFFON tends to be slippery. Cover your cutting table with a sheet and use **EXTRA-FINE PINS WHEN SECURING MULTIPLE LAYERS.**

COTTON RIB is an extremely elastic and even knitted cotton fabric with **alternating knit and purl stitches that create lengthwise ribs.** It is identical on both sides, and the edges do not roll. It has a soft hand, is comfortable to wear, and is gentle on the skin. It is often sold in tube form. **Fine rib** alternates single knit and purl stitches, while **double** rib alternates sets of two knit and two purl stitches. Fine rib is used primarily for underwear, T-shirts, and children's clothing, while double knit is used for cuffs.

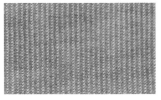

CORDUROY is a cotton or synthetic fabric with **characteristic velvety lengthwise ribs, or wales.** It is durable and soil resistant. The wales may be very thin (baby or pinwale corduroy) to very wide (wide wale corduroy); it may also have irregular wales. **Corduroy is napped,** and depending on its type is used for slipcovers, pants, jackets, and baby and children's clothing.

CRUSHED/CRINKLE is a light woven made from natural or synthetic fibers with a **lengthwise or crosswise wrinkling effect;** the wrinkles may be of varying intensities. Fabrics without a permanent crushed finish must be twisted up and left to dry that way in order to maintain the wrinkled effect. The fabric is **easy care and needs no ironing.** It is used for blouses and light jackets as well as for accessories and decorative items.

CRÊPE DE CHINE is a very delicate, flowing, lightweight plain weave fabric. It has a **characteristic crêpe feel** and is made from silk, wool, or synthetic fibers. It is often **cut on the bias** to create a particularly attractive drape on dresses. In general the fabric is used for lightweight women's garments, blouses, tops, skirts, wraps, and scarves.

149

DAMASK is a dense woven with **subtly shiny patterns on a matte background,** usually made from fine natural fibers or a fiber blend and manufactured as a **satin weave.** Damask is suitable for jackets, pants, and skirts as well as drapes, slipcovers, bed linens, and tablecloths.

DENIM is a **durable cotton fabric** in a twill weave, with contrasting warp and weft threads. Classic denim is indigo blue and has **blue warp threads and white weft threads;** the right side is dark and the reverse side is light. There are many variations in denim washes, however, including stonewashed. Denim is used for jeans, jeans jackets, bags, durable children's clothing, and sturdy work wear.

DOUBLE FACE CLOTH is a two-layered fabric **with no wrong side, and is thus reversible.** Typically it is a doubled weave where the two pieces are held together with threads. It is available in other forms, however, including with glued layers. The **two sides may be identical or contrasting;** often they will have the **negative pattern** on the reverse side. These fabrics work well with specialized techniques such as overlapped seams and bound edges. Depending on the type, double face cloth is used for jackets, pullovers, caps, bags, table runners, pillows, hand towels, and bed linens.

! IF YOU ARE WORKING WITH DOUBLE FACE fabric where the layers are held together with thread, you can work seams as follows: on both fabric pieces, OPEN UP ABOUT ⅝" (1.5CM) ALONG THE EDGE. With right sides together, machine stitch the outside fabrics together, then fold in the inside edges and sew the abutted edges together by hand.

! WHEN SEWING FAUX FUR, the stitch length and thread tension must be set carefully, and usually the presser foot pressure should be reduced. Cut away the hairs on seam allowances *(see page 99)* to minimize bulk.

» OILCLOTH *(page 153)*, FELT, AND BOILED WOOL *(page 148)* can be made quickly into attractive sewn projects. They DO NOT FRAY and therefore do not require edge finishing. The materials are easy to work with and suitable even for BEGINNERS.

FAUX FUR may be woven or knitted, with a short or long pile, and can **very closely imitate the look of real fur.** It may be made from natural or synthetic fibers and **is napped.** Special sewing techniques are called for with faux fur *(see page 99)*. It is primarily used as trim on clothing, bags, hats, and accessories, but also as the main fabric for jackets and coats.

FAUX LEATHER may be made of natural or synthetic fibers and can have a smooth or textured surface; it is not always easy to tell it apart from genuine leather. It has **many of the same properties as real leather** and often provides an **economical alternative** to its use. **Its edges do not fray** and therefore do not need finishing, but it does require certain *specialized sewing techniques (see page 98)*. To clean, either wipe with a cloth or use a brush. Faux leather is used for men's and women's clothing, bags, belts, and upholstery.

FELT is a nonwoven fabric without a grain. It may be cut in any direction, and perforated patterns may be cut into it. Its **edges do not fray** and thus do not require finishing. **Wool felt** (right photo) is made by working fibers into a solid sheet through the application of heat, moisture, and friction. Wool felt is warm, retains its shape, and does not wrinkle. It is often used for hats, bags, slippers, decorative items, and toys. **Plain felt** or "craft" or "hobby" felt (left photo) is usually made from synthetic fibers and is less durable. It is used in craft projects, trims, and decorations, but is **not suitable for clothing.**

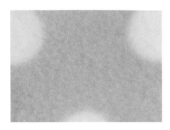

FLANNEL is a classic woven made of cotton, wool, or viscose in plain or twill weave; it has a thick bloom to its surface. It may be **brushed** on one or both sides and is therefore **especially soft, warm, and absorbent.** Cotton flannel is also sometimes called **canton flannel.** Depending on type, flannel is suitable for suits, shirts, costumes, blouses, coats, winter clothing, and sleepwear. Cotton flannel is especially popular for making warm bed linens.

FLEECE may be woven or knitted and is frequently made from polyester. It is heavily brushed on both sides and therefore **especially soft.** It comes in weights light enough for summer wear all the way to heavy and very warm versions for wintertime use. **Microfleece** is a lightweight, breathable version made from delicate fibers. Depending on type, fleece is used for pullovers, jackets, caps, shawls, sportswear, leisure wear, bed linens, and blankets and throws.

GABARDINE is a strong, dense, durable fabric made from cotton, wool, synthetic, or blended fibers worked in twill weave. It has a noticeable **diagonal rib structure.** Depending on the finish, it may be wrinkle free and moisture repellant. It is used for women's garments, suits, pants, coats, bags, and raincoats.

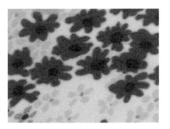

GAUZE is an **airy, sheer, lightweight fabric** made from cotton or polyester in plain weave. It is used mostly for summer blouses, dresses, linings, and curtains.

GEORGETTE is a light, delicate woven made from silk, viscose, or polyester. It is **distinguished by its slightly grainy, crêpe-like surface** and drapes well and is wrinkle resistant. When made from synthetics it tends to be slippery to work with and to fray. The fabric is popular for loosely fitting, elegant blouses as well as for evening wear.

GINGHAM is a **two-colored checkered pattern,** made in plain or twill weave and usually in cotton. It is used for shirts, blouses, skirts, dresses, and home textiles such as curtains and table linens.

GLEN PLAID is a **traditional English twill** that is often made of cotton. It has a pattern of **overlapping small and large squares,** often involving a contrast color. It is used for men's and women's suits, shirts, jackets, and blazers.

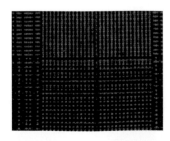

JACQUARD is the **catchall term for large-scale, complex patterns** on wovens and knits, usually made from natural fibers. Typical examples of jacquard are **damask and brocade.** The pattern appears in negative on the wrong side. Jacquards are mainly used for elegant women's suits as well as for pillows and slipcovers.

JERSEY is the **catchall term for stretchy, wrinkle-free, very soft knits with a delicate ribbed structure,** usually made from wool, cotton, silk, or wool blends. The ribbed structure affords a flexible and comfortable fit, especially on close-fitting garments. Types of jersey are distinguished by the knitting technique that creates them: on **single jersey,** stitches look different on the right and wrong side of the fabric, and the **edges roll in strongly.** On **interlock jersey,** the right and wrong sides of the fabric look identical, runs are almost never a problem, and the edges do not roll. Depending on type, jersey is used for T-shirts, tops, dresses, sportswear, children's clothing, sleepwear, and bed linens.

! To make sure that **LACE** motifs or patterns line up as precisely as possible, pay attention when **POSITIONING PATTERN PIECES;** the fabric may need to be handled as if it were napped.

LACE is an airy, **openwork** woven made from silk, cotton, or synthetic fibers; it has **holes and often lightly embossed patterns.** It comes with both straight and scalloped edges. Stretch lace fits well to the body. Lace should be **washed very carefully or professionally dry cleaned.** It is used for decorative detailing, such as borders, and also for lingerie, nightgowns, and evening and bridal wear.

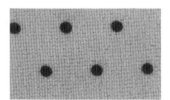

»» **LAMÉ** should be sewn with a fine microtex needle. Heavier needles can pull threads and damage the fabric. Depending on fabric type, it may be advisable to underlay pieces with tear-away stabilizer to make it easier to sew them together.

LAMÉ is a **shiny, opalescent woven** fabric with **metallic** weft threads. The warp threads are usually silk, nylon, or cotton. Lamé has a tendency to fray. It is popular for festive women's tops and evening wear.

MICROFIBER is a very durable, dense weave made from extremely fine polyester, polyamide, or acrylic fibers. It is **silky soft, with a pleasant hand,** and is extremely lightweight but tear resistant. Depending on its finish, it may be **breathable, wrinkle free,** and wind and rain repellant. Depending on its type, it is used for blouses, shirts, skirts, curtains, and easy-care outdoor garments.

MINKY is a **soft and elastic warp knit** made from cotton or synthetic fibers; it has a **velvety surface and is pleasant to wear.** It is used for comfortable leisure and sportswear, children's clothes, toys, and dolls.

MUSLIN is a simple cotton fabric made in plain weave. It is usually **naturally colored or bleached white,** and is available in several weights and widths. **It wrinkles heavily** and takes dye well. A classic use for muslin is to create a muslin **sample** of a garment before sewing the actual garment fabric, so that the garment may be tried on and any adjustments made to the pattern, if needed (see page 181). It is also used for bags, curtains, and home décor.

NONWOVENS come in varying types, usually made from synthetic fibers or a blend. For these fabrics, loose fibers are held together with a binding agent, or pressed together, to create a sheet. The fabric **does not fray, nor does it require ironing.** Some nonwovens are very **economical,** though not durable, and are used as disposable tablecloths or table runners or for decorations and craft projects. **Microfiber nonwoven fabric** is stable, machine washable, and can be worked like regular fabric; it is suitable for making curtain linings, room dividers, and tablecloths. Nonwoven **interfacing** is used to stabilize fabric pieces in sewing projects.

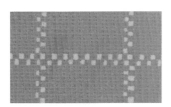

OILCLOTH is a **waterproof woven** made of cotton or sometimes other fibers. Its surface may be shiny or matte, depending on the finish. Its **edges do not fray** and thus do not require finishing. **Pins can leave permanent holes in oilcloth.** Iron it only from the wrong side and at a low temperature. Oilcloth is used for rain jackets, aprons, totes, tablecloths, and a variety of creative sewing projects.

ORGANZA is a **sheer, lightweight, opalescent** fabric made of silk or synthetic fibers in plain weave (shown here with embroidery). It has a **somewhat stiff hand.** It is suitable for lightweight women's garments, elegant blouses, evening wear, curtains, fabric flowers, and as lining.

OXFORD POLYESTER is a midweight woven with a lightly textured surface; it is extremely tear resistant and durable. With special finishing it may be **watertight, weatherproof, and soil resistant,** and is thus ideal for bags, backpacks, seat cushions, rainwear, and outdoor accessories.

» **OILCLOTH** should be stored **ROLLED,** or hanging from a clothes hanger with clips, to prevent creasing.

! **ORGANZA HAS A VARIETY OF USES;** for example, as a pressing cloth to protect delicate fabrics. It is also ideal as an interfacing for sheer fabrics, as it is lightweight but also quite stable.

PILE FABRICS are voluminous woven or knitted materials with a thick pile and soft hand, usually made from cotton, wool, or synthetic fibers. The catchall term for fabrics with brushed, short pile surfaces is **velour.** Starting at around ⅛" (4mm) pile depth, the fabric is called **plush.** Pile fabrics are **napped** and require specialized techniques. They are used for warm coats and jackets, linings, snuggly throws, and stuffed toys.

PINSTRIPES are typically found on woolen weaves; these fabrics are characterized by **very fine lengthwise stripes with regular or irregular spacing.** Classic pinstripes are light against a dark background. This is a popular fabric for suits for both men and women.

POPLIN is an elastic, lightweight, and **especially dense fabric** made in plain weave, usually out of fine cotton but also sometimes of wool or synthetic. Typical for poplin are a fine crosswise ribbed texture and, depending on the fiber content, a **gentle sheen.** It is used for shirts, blouses, women's garments, pants, jackets, coats, and home textiles.

QUILTED FABRIC is usually a three-layer fabric consisting of a top and bottom layer with a **layer of nonwoven batting in between.** The outer fabrics may or may not be identical. The layers are **quilted together, for example in a diamond pattern, but also sometimes in more intricate designs.** Reversible fabrics call for specialized sewing techniques, such as overlapped or bound seams. Quilted fabrics are used for jackets, bedspreads, or as warm linings.

! SHINY FABRICS such as satin should be cut **IN A SINGLE DIRECTION,** as their color can appear different from different angles.

! When cutting **SEERSUCKER** it is important to make sure that the **CRINKLED STRIPES WILL LATER MATCH UP** and all run in the same direction.

» SEQUINED OR BEADED FABRIC should be placed **RIGHT SIDE DOWN** for cutting, so that the fabric may be carefully cut without severing the sequins.

» TERRYCLOTH, WHEN CUT, generates many tiny thread snippets, so it's best to have a vacuum at the ready. Shake out fabric pieces before sewing.

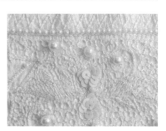

SATIN is a delicate, supple, and dense fabric made in satin weave, usually of silk, viscose, or polyester. It has a **smooth, shiny upper surface and a matte reverse side.** It is used for elegant suits, blouses, pants, dresses, skirts, and lingerie, as well as for lining and bed linens.

SEERSUCKER is usually a light cotton fabric made in plain weave, either with **alternating crinkled and smooth stripes or an overall crinkled texture.** Seersucker is **temperature regulating, easy care, and does not require ironing,** and so is used above all for summer clothing (including suits), shirts, children's wear, tablecloths, and bed linens.

SEQUINED OR BEADED FABRIC may have a woven or warp knit background with **small metal or plastic sequins and/or beads sewn on.** It must be **cut out in a single layer,** and additionally requires *specialized sewing techniques (see page 101).* It is heat sensitive. It is used for elegant bridal and evening fashions, suits, fancy purses, and accessories.

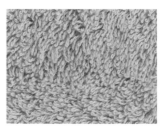

SWEATSHIRT FABRIC is a type of stretch knit, usually jersey or tricot, made of cotton or a cotton blend. The inside surface is brushed and soft, and the fabric is **warm and comfortable to wear.** It is used for sweatshirts, hoodies, caps, leisure wear, and pillow covers.

TAFFETA is a stable, delicate, dense fabric made from silk or synthetic fibers in plain weave. Taffeta (shown here with embroidery) has a smooth surface with a matte shimmer; it makes a **characteristic rustling sound** when it moves. Taffeta is popular for festive evening wear, lightweight jackets, costumes, home decorations, curtains, throws, and pillows.

TERRYCLOTH is a voluminous, soft, absorbent cotton woven; it has a **looped surface on one or both sides** and is **napped.** It is a popular fabric for bathrobes, towels, sportswear, and leisure wear, and is also well suited for stuffed animals and baby toys.

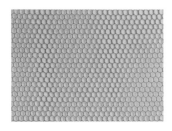

TULLE is a lightweight, sheer, and rough textile with a **net-like structure** made from cotton or synthetic fibers; it may be woven or nonwoven. Tulle requires hand washing and **should not be wrung.** Tulle is used primarily for curtains, costumes, and decorative items, but also for making voluminous, multilayered petticoats for skirts, bridal gowns, and evening wear.

⇥ It can be difficult to transfer pattern markings with tailor's chalk on OPEN WEAVE FABRICS such as lace and tulle. Instead, use a DISAPPEARING INK MARKER, BASTING THREAD, OR SAFETY PINS.

TWEED is the catchall term for a wide array of sturdy woolen fabrics in plain or twill weave. They are made from mid- to coarse-weight wools, such as virgin wool. They have a **roughly textured surface, often with nubs.** The fabric is **elastic when pulled on the diagonal.** One premium, hand-woven Scottish tweed is sold under the brand name Harris Tweed; it comes as a solid or in **classic patterns such as herringbone and houndstooth.** Lighter tweeds can be used for men's and women's suits and vests, while heavier versions are suitable for jackets and coats.

VELOUR is similar to velvet but has a **deeper pile and a softer hand.** Velour is napped. The fabric can be refreshed with regular dampening and brushing in the direction of the nap. It is suited for tops, pants, warm linings, drapes, and slipcovers.

VELVET is a plain or twill weave **with dense, fine pile;** it is made of cotton, wool, silk, or synthetic fibers. The pile depth is usually ⅟₃₂"–⅟₁₆" (1–2mm). One variation is **panne velvet** (right), which gets its unusual look during the manufacturing process when patterns are pressed into the surface. **Stretch velvet** (left) has a knitted foundation and is therefore elastic. Velvet is napped. It is used for elegant blazers, coats, jackets, bags, and home textiles; panne velvet is frequently used for decorations and costumes.

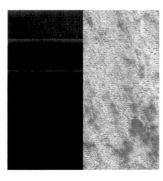

VOILE is an **elastic, sheer, transparent fabric** made in plain weave with very delicate thread, usually out of cotton or polyester. It has a thready feel and soft hand and is used for blouses, shirts, curtains, and home décor items.

← 12 cm →

35 cm

30 cm

all about patterns

THE FOUNDATION FOR A HOME-SEWN GARMENT IS ALMOST ALWAYS A PAPER PATTERN. TO CREATE A SUCCESSFUL PROJECT FROM A PAPER PATTERN, IT IS IMPORTANT TO KNOW AND UNDERSTAND YOUR OWN BODY MEASUREMENTS. THE INSTRUCTIONS IN THIS CHAPTER PROVIDE ESSENTIAL INFORMATION FOR A BEAUTIFULLY FINISHED FINAL PROJECT THAT FITS YOU WELL, WHATEVER PATTERN YOU SELECT.

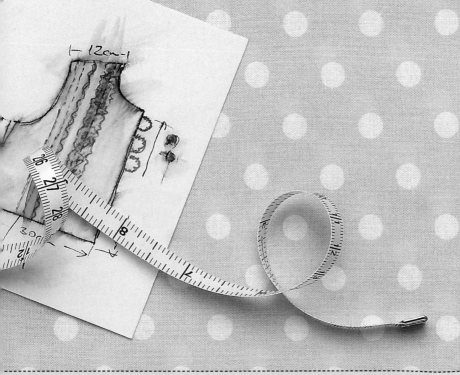

body measurements and figure types

Before taking your body measurements, become familiar with the most important measurement points and the proper way to measure. You will need a tape measure, paper, pencil, and possibly a waistband—an elastic strip about ⅜" (1cm) wide.

>> WHEN DETERMINING YOUR BODY MEASUREMENTS, wear close-fitting garments or just underwear. It is especially helpful to have A SECOND PERSON DO THE MEASURING. It is a good idea to include the date if you save the information.

>> THE SEVENTH VERTEBRA is easy to locate. It is the first prominent vertebra on the spine, working down from the top—at the point where the neck joins the body.

ESSENTIAL BODY MEASUREMENTS

Knowing key measurements such as chest/bust, waist, and hip circumferences, as well as body height, will lead to a proper fit.

BODY HEIGHT (BH) is measured without shoes, preferably with the body backed up straight **against a wall.** A triangular ruler can help here.

CHEST/BUST CIRCUMFERENCE (CC) is measured at the **fullest point of the chest or bust;** hold the tape measure together at the front and lightly pull it upward in back. Women may also want to take a chest measurement by measuring around the body about 2–3" (5–8cm) above the fullest part of the bust.

WAIST CIRCUMFERENCE (WC) should be measured around the **narrowest part of the torso** without pulling the tape too tightly.

HIP CIRCUMFERENCE (HC) is measured around the **widest part of the hips, usually 7–9" (18–13cm)** below the waist. The person measuring should ideally stand to the side, to be able to see whether the tape is level around the body and sitting at the correct position.

SHOULDER WIDTH is the distance from the **base of the neck to the outside edge of the shoulder.**

ARM LENGTH is the length from the **outside edge of the shoulder over a lightly bent elbow to the wrist.**

- -

TAILORED PATTERNS
On tailored patterns the back and front waist lengths often play a role.

BACK WAIST LENGTH is measured by first placing a ⅜" (1cm) elastic strip around the natural waistline. Measure from the **seventh vertebra** down the center of the spine to the **bottom of the waistband elastic.**

FRONT WAIST LENGTH is measured using the elastic waistband. Measure from the **side of the base of the neck,** over the fullest point of the bust, to the **bottom of the waistband.**

OUTSEAM LENGTH is measured, standing up, from the bottom of the waistband to the **desired hem length.** For classic pant length, measure without shoes and ending at the floor.

- -

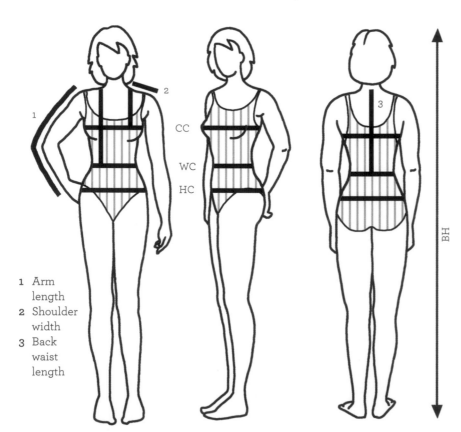

1 Arm length
2 Shoulder width
3 Back waist length

STANDARD SIZE CHARTS

Clothing manufacturers use body measurements to designate standard sizes. You'll use them to determine the size of your sewing pattern. Different companies may size patterns differently, so check your measurements against the charts on the back of your particular pattern. Pattern size is determined by your width/circumference measurements. Below are the standard charts used to size McCall's patterns.

MISSES' SIZES About 5'5" to 5'6" height.　**MISSES' PETITE** About 5'2" to 5'3" height.

SIZES	Bust		Waist		Hip		Back waist length		Petite back waist length	
	in.	cm.	in.	cm.	in.	cm.	in.	cm.	in.	cm.
4	29½	75	22	56	31½	80	15¼	39	14	35.5
6	30½	78	23	58	32½	83	15½	39.5	14¼	36
8	31½	80	24	61	33½	85	15¾	40	14¾	37.5
10	32½	83	25	64	34½	88	16	40.5	15	38
12	34	87	26½	67	36	92	16¼	41.5	15¼	39
14	36	92	28	71	38	97	16½	42	15½	39.5
16	38	97	30	76	40	102	16¾	42.5	15¾	40
18	40	102	32	81	42	107	17	43	16	40.5
20	42	107	34	87	44	112	17¼	44	16¼	41
22	44	112	37	94	46	117	17½	44.5	16½	42
24	46	117	39	99	48	122	17¾	45	16¾	42.5
26	48	122	41½	104	50	127	18	46	17	43

WOMEN'S SIZES About 5'5" to 5'6" height.　**WOMEN'S PETITE** About 5'2" to 5'3" height.

SIZES	Bust		Waist		Hip		Back waist length		Petite back waist length	
	in.	cm.	in.	cm.	in.	cm.	in.	cm.	in.	cm.
18W	40	102	33	84	42	107	17⅛	43	16⅛	41
20W	42	107	35	89	44	112	17¼	44	16¼	41.5
22W	44	112	37	94	46	117	17⅜	44	16⅜	42
24W	46	117	39	99	48	122	17½	44.5	16½	42
26W	48	122	41½	105	50	127	17⅝	45	16⅝	42.5
28W	50	127	44	112	52	132	17¾	45	16¾	42.5
30W	52	132	46½	118	54	137	17⅞	45.5	16⅞	43
32W	54	137	49	124	56	142	18	46	17	43

MEN'S SIZES For men of average build; about 5'10" height.

SIZES	Chest		Waist		Hip (Seat)		Shirt sleeve		Neckband	
	in.	cm.	in.	cm.	in.	cm.	in.	cm.	in.	cm.
34	34	87	28	71	35	89	32	81	14	35.5
36	36	92	30	76	37	94	32	81	14½	37
38	38	97	32	81	39	99	33	84	15	38
40	40	102	34	87	41	104	33	84	15½	39.5
42	42	107	36	92	43	109	34	87	16	40.5
44	44	112	39	99	45	114	34	87	16½	42
46	46	117	42	107	47	119	35	89	17	43
48	48	122	44	112	49	124	35	89	17½	44.5
50	50	127	46	117	51	130	35	89	18	46
52	52	132	48	122	53	135	35	89	18½	47
54	54	137	50	127	55	140	35	89	19	48.5
56	56	142.5	52	132	57	145	35	89	19½	49.5

! FILL IN A SIZE CHART with your personal body measurements.

! TO DETERMINE YOUR OWN SIZE, compare your KEY MEASUREMENTS (BH, CC, WC, HC) WITH THOSE OF THE PATTERN MANUFACTURER'S SIZE CHART and choose the size that is closest to your measurements. This is the first step toward creating a comfortable, well-fitting garment.

INFANTS' SIZES For babies who are not yet walking.

SIZES	Weight		Height		Age
	lbs.	kg.	in.	cm.	months
Newborn	8–12	4–6	18–21	46–61	0–3
Small	13–17	6–8	25–26	64–66	6
Medium	18–21	8–10	27–28	69–71	9
Large	22–25	10–11	29–30	74–76	12
X-Large	26–29	12–13	31–32	79–81	18–24

TODDLERS' SIZES Between a baby and child. Pants have diaper allowance.

SIZES	Chest		Waist		Height	
	in.	cm.	in.	cm.	in.	cm.
½	19	48	19	48	28	71
1	20	51	19½	50	31	79
2	21	53	20	51	34	87
3	22	56	20½	52	37	94
4	23	58	21	53	40	102

CHILDREN'S SIZES Child who is walking and not wearing diapers.

SIZES	Chest		Waist		Hip		Back waist length		Height	
	in.	cm.	in.	cm.	in.	cm.	in.	cm.	in.	cm.
2	21	53	20	51			8½	22	35	89
3	22	56	20½	52			9	23	38	97
4	23	58	21	53	24	61	9½	24	41	104
5	24	61	21½	55	25	64	10	25.5	44	112
6	25	64	22	56	26	66	10½	27	47	119
6x	25½	65	22½	57	26½	67	10¾	27.5	48	122

GIRLS'/BOYS' SIZES For growing girl/boy who has not yet begun to mature.

SIZES	Chest		Waist		Hip		Back waist length		Height	
	in.	cm.	in.	cm.	in.	cm.	in.	cm.	in.	cm.
7	26	66	23	58	27	69	11½	29.5	50	127
8	27	69	23½	60	28	71	12	31	52	132
10	28½	73	24½	62	30	76	12¾	32.5	56	142
12	30	76	25½	65	32	81	13½	34.5	58½	149
14	32	81	26½	67	34	87	14¼	36	61	155
16	34	87	27½	70	36	92	15	38	61½	156
GIRL'S PLUS										
8½	30	76	28	71	33	84	12½	32	52	132
10½	30½	80	29	74	34½	88	13¼	34	56	142
12½	33	84	30	76	36	92	14	35.5	58½	149
14½	34½	88	31	79	37½	96	14¾	37.5	61	155
16½	36	92	32	81	39	99	15½	39.5	63½	161

FIGURE TYPES

People have differing body types that are identified by various attributes. If you understand your body type, it will help you choose garments that either accentuate or downplay features as you wish.

❗ Bear in mind that your garment is not the only thing that creates your silhouette. ACCESSORIES CAN ALSO AFFECT PROPORTIONS. A belt worn at the waist and a belt at the hips divide the body in different ways. A necklace can elongate. Dark, ankle-length leggings can make you look shorter. Pay attention to these styling effects and use them to your advantage.

A-TYPE
Narrow shoulders contrast with **pronounced hips.**

O-TYPE
The overall shape is **rounded,** without a defined waist.

H/I-TYPE
Chest, waist, and hip measurements are approximately equal.

Y-TYPE
Narrow waist and hips contrast with **broad shoulders.**

X-TYPE
A **small waist** contrasts with pronounced hips and bust.

SILHOUETTE

A silhouette is the first impression and general outline one perceives from a garment, without paying attention to smaller details. Like body types, common silhouettes can be characterized with letters of the alphabet—A, O, H, I, Y, and X silhouettes.

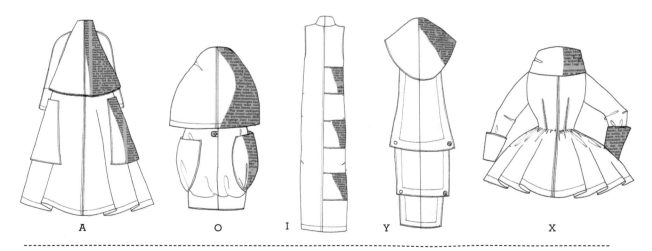

A   O   I   Y   X

what is a pattern?

Geometrically speaking, a pattern represents the flattened surface of a person's body (or an object like an armchair). The 3-dimensional object becomes a set of planes. An appropriate paper pattern is the first step toward your finished product and usually consists of multiple pieces. The paper pattern (or pattern pieces) includes the templates for cutting the fabric. The patterns we can so easily obtain today start out as sketches in a design studio, and are developed using complicated formulas and an abundance of technical skill and attention to detail.

SINGLE- AND MULTI-SIZE PATTERNS

Patterns, especially for apparel, often cover a range of sizes rather than just one.

SINGLE-SIZE PATTERN

If a pattern comes in one size only, it is a single-size pattern. These are often used in **tailor shops,** where a pattern is created for a specific individual. They are also common for **home décor items,** where standard sizing often makes a multi-size pattern unnecessary.

MULTI-SIZE PATTERN

Multi-size patterns are more common for home sewing, and most sewing magazines offer them. Patterns are offered in a **range of sizes** so they can serve a **wide range of customers.** All available sizes in a given pattern appear together, using different outlines (usually the cutting lines) to distinguish them. The multiple outlines are the result of the pattern being graded into various sizes.

! PATTERN GRADING is the process of INCREASING OR DECREASING PATTERN SIZE using standard amounts of deviation between sizes. Thanks to computers, today this complicated process is only rarely done by hand.

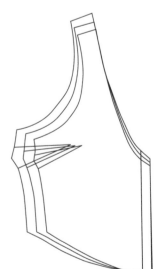

PATTERN SELECTION

First things first: you need to find a pattern you love and want to make. Allow yourself plenty of time to find the right one. Your choice should take into consideration your **personal body type and proportions** as well as your preferences as to color and **style**. Consider also your **experience level and technical abilities** when selecting a pattern.

PATTERN SOURCES

In addition to individual packaged patterns, there are also **sewing magazines, sewing books, and downloadable patterns** on the Internet. From this multitude of sources you will have to filter the best candidates.

LINE ART DRAWINGS/FLATS

Pattern line drawings (also called flats) show **details such as overall shape, cut, seam lines, darts, and topstitching without the distractions** of fabric texture and color. The flat line drawing provides a good basis for deciding whether a pattern matches both your wishes and your sewing abilities, so you need to **learn to read them.**

>> THE CLOSER YOUR PATTERN IS TO YOUR DESIRED RESULT, the less you will have to alter and the happier you will be with the final product.

1 **Simple kimono-style jacket** has front edge facings that extend around the collar, no front panel seams, and a single seam at the center back. The belt is separate and has a loop and pointed end. This garment is **appropriate for beginners with minimal sewing experience.**

2 **Classic blazer** with boxy neckline and visible facing without lapels, princess seaming (shaped panel seams) in front, welted front pockets, single button closure with six buttons, two-piece sleeves with visible seam treatment (diagonal line on sleeve drawing). **This garment is appropriate for intermediate sewers with good general knowledge of technique.**

3 **Waist-length motorcycle-style jacket** with fur collar, front panel seams, front zipper, raglan sleeves with epaulets, a tie belt fed through loops over topstitched waistband panel, sleeves with buttoned cuffs, and zippered pockets at the waistband. All seams are topstitched. **This garment is appropriate for advanced sewers with mastery of challenging techniques.**

>> A SKETCH CAN HELP YOU SOLIDIFY YOUR IDEAS and narrow down the pattern selection process. IF YOU ARE BROWSING PATTERNS WITH NOTHING SPECIFIC IN MIND, think instead about the general style of garment that appeals to you—businesslike, classic, avant-garde, provocative, demure, etc.

INSTRUCTIONS AND FABRIC REQUIREMENTS

Pattern instructions provide valuable information about fabric requirements and the individual steps involved in creating a garment. The instructions function like a **roadmap for the creation process.** They are required all the way through to the final stitch, so be sure to **read them thoroughly and save them!**

1 Front and back view line drawings of the garment, with details clearly marked.

2 All numbered pattern pieces required, including quantity required and details such as fold lines, darts, etc.

3 List of pattern pieces with numbers, including relevant sizes.

4 Size range and instructions for determining key measurement (bust).

5 Suggested layouts for cutting pattern pieces for each size, including fabric amounts required.

6 Key indicating how each required fabric is depicted in the instructions.

7 Guide to measuring and trimming seam allowances.

8 Sewing instructions (partial).

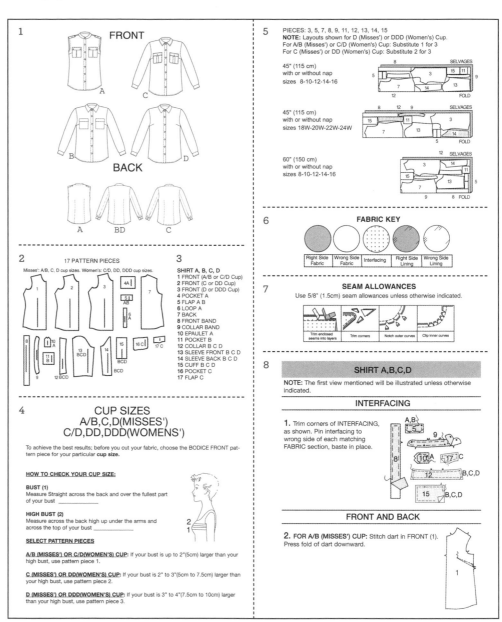

FABRIC REQUIREMENTS

Most patterns tell you the amount of fabric needed for each size and style on the back of the pattern envelope. If you need to calculate the fabric yardage needed yourself, the primary factor is usually the length of the garment. The following rules of thumb will help you quickly calculate yardage. They also help for estimating the overall cost of the project.

Pencil skirt/straight skirt: equal to the length of the skirt

Pants: equal to the length of the pants (however, on wide-legged pants calculate 1.5 times the pant length)

Full skirt: twice the length of the skirt

Blouse: length of the body section plus length of sleeves

Jacket: twice the length of the body section plus length of sleeves

the
paper pattern

To work with a paper pattern you must prepare all the individual pieces for use. There are convenient packaged individual patterns, and some that come on large multi-pattern sheets in sewing magazines or books. The pattern pieces are the basis for cutting out the main fabric, lining, interfacing, and other components of the design. One rarely cuts fabric pieces without a pattern of some kind.

INDIVIDUAL PATTERNS

Individual patterns, frequently sold in envelopes but also sometimes found in pattern booklets or downloadable from the Internet, are very **easy to work with**. All the required pieces are laid out on a large sheet next to, or nested into, one another. For patterns without included seam allowances, the *allowances must be added (see page 186)* before cutting. Most individual garment patterns **come in a range of sizes**. This can be an advantage if you end up wanting to alter any part of the design (*see page 178*).

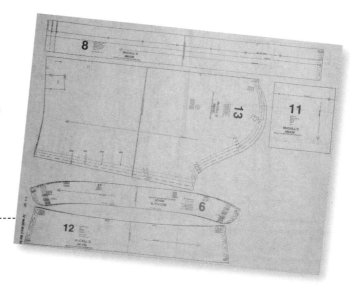

PATTERNS FROM SEWING MAGAZINES

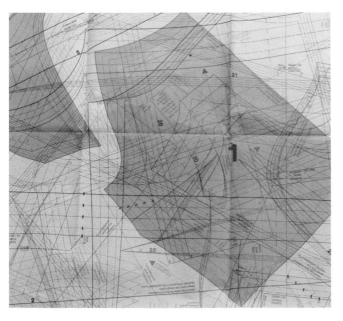

When using patterns from sewing magazines you will first need to locate all the pattern pieces you'll need according to the instructions for the item you intend to make. The pattern pieces come on a sheet in their full size, but with extensive **overlap among the pattern outlines in order to conserve space, so you will need to trace some (or all) of the pieces.** Pattern pieces for a single model will all use **the same distinctive outline, which will also always be the same color or line quality.** *Identification numbers (see page 170)* found at the top and bottom of the pattern sheets will help you to locate the pieces you need to *trace (see page 170).*

! WHEN TRACING WITH A THICK PENCIL, BE CAREFUL that you are really tracing THE CORRECT OUTLINE. Since many lines lie directly adjacent to one another, it can be confusing.

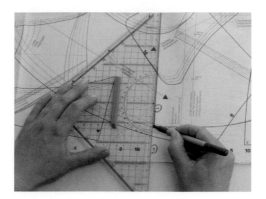

FINDING PATTERN PIECES BY ID NUMBERS

When using patterns from sewing magazines, the tiny renderings of the pattern pieces on the instruction page will have **identification numbers** associated with them. At the **top and bottom edges of the pattern sheet** itself you will find these ID numbers in the color matching the corresponding pattern outline. The number can be found again within the sheet, directly vertical from where it appears on the edge. It will appear **directly adjacent to the outline of the corresponding pattern piece.** It can help to circle the numbers to make them easier to find again.

! PATTERN DETAIL MARKINGS such as fold lines, grain lines, pocket attachment points, front center, back center, zipper end points, etc. will help you later while sewing. THEY SHOULD ALWAYS BE INCLUDED IN THE TRACING AND MARKING.

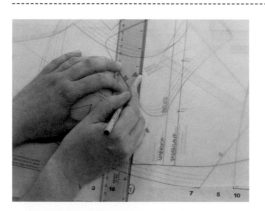

COPYING THE PATTERN PIECES

To copy the pattern in its entirety, every piece must be neatly **traced using a sharp pencil onto transparent tracing paper.** Leave a little space between the pieces (especially if you will need to add seam allowances). The pattern sheet should lie underneath the tracing paper on a large, even surface.

The pieces **must not overlap once traced,** since every piece will need to be cut out separately from your fabric.

Any **measure-and-cut pieces,** that is, those that are not included as separate pattern pieces, **must be created now as well.** These are usually **rectangular pieces** such as belt carriers, cuffs, or ruffles.

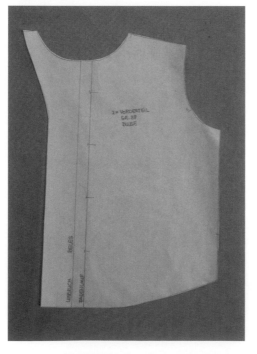

» CUTTING OUT PATTERN PIECES WILL GO ESPECIALLY QUICKLY if you place the sheets to be cut on a large carpeting scrap and use a hobby knife.

! Use different, designated scissors FOR PAPER AND FOR FABRIC. Paper will quickly dull your fabric scissors!

CUTTING OUT THE TRACED PIECES

Once all the required pieces have been traced onto separate copy paper, add seam allowances, if necessary, and any pattern symbols *(see page 171)*. Use **paper-dedicated scissors to cut them out neatly along the outlines (cutting lines).** Set pieces aside until you are ready to cut your fabric.

EXPLANATION OF PATTERN SYMBOLS AND MARKINGS

When tracing pattern pieces (especially from international sewing magazines) you will run across various **pattern detail markings**. These provide helpful information and will make sewing and assembly easier, so you'll need to copy these symbols and marks onto your traced pattern. They are **not entirely standardized** across the industry internationally, but many symbols and markings are well established and recognized worldwide.

1 **LENGTHENING** If pattern pieces do not fit entirely on the pattern sheet they may require **lengthening in a straight line to whatever distance is specified.** Measure starting from the tip of the arrow—in this example, 4" (10cm).

2 **SPLIT PIECES** If a large pattern piece is too complex to be lengthened using a straight extension, it may be split into two pieces on the pattern sheet. Upon copying, it should be **put together as a single piece.** The pieces will be marked (1a and 1b, in this example) to indicate that they belong together; **the double line is the attachment line.** There are markings (here, triangles) to show where the pieces should line up for copying.

3 **SEAM NUMBERS** These numbers indicate which edges will come together later as seams.

4 **NOTCHES/MATCHING LINES** Notches (or matching lines) may be included to **help keep long seam lines aligned** by breaking up long stretches into manageable segments. The markings should meet up when the pieces are sewn together, as shown here on a front and back piece.

5 **DARTS** are shown as triangles if they start at a seam edge or as diamonds if they lie within the pattern piece (as shown).

6 **FOLD/PLEAT LINES** The folds are made in the direction of the arrows. **Make sure to copy these markings onto your pattern pieces.**

7 **SLITS** These mark the beginning and end points of any kind of slit opening, including those for zippers and plackets.

8 **SLEEVE INSERTION MARKS** These are a type of notch or matching line that helps with setting in sleeves. The marking on the sleeve should meet the corresponding marking on the armhole. With plaids, this marking also works as a guide point for a horizontal reference line.

9 **SCISSORS SYMBOL** This symbol appears **where a cut into the fabric will be required.** It might be seen, for example, at the location of a welt pocket.

10 **BUTTONHOLE** Transfer these markings onto your pattern piece and **then transfer the markings to your fabric** when you reach the buttonholing step.

11 **BUTTON** These marks show where buttons should be sewn to match the buttonhole positions. They can also be used for snap placement.

12 **EYELET** Indicates the location of an eyelet.

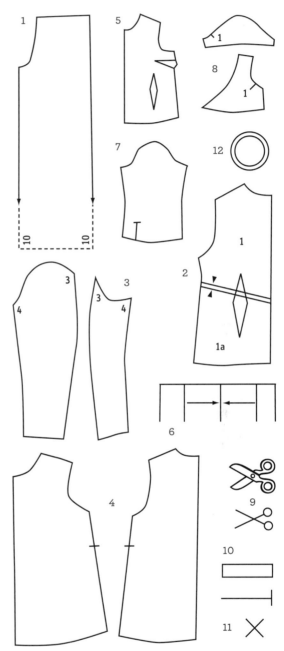

ADDITIONAL SYMBOLS

The following are also sometimes found on pattern pieces and in instructions. **They may also be written out on the pattern** and show starting and ending points.

GATHERS – – – – – – – –

EASE STITCHING ∿∿∿∿∿

STRETCH ·················

DOTTED FOLD LINE A broken line on a pattern indicates that this piece should be placed on a fold for cutting. It will be represented the same way on the pattern-cutting layout diagram.

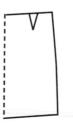

ADDITIONAL IMPORTANT TERMS

There are a few additional specialized terms that you may encounter when tracing patterns that are not necessarily self-evident.

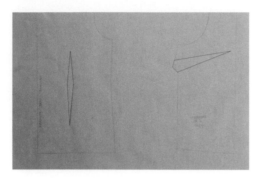

DARTS are marked on a pattern as **triangles if they start at the seam line** and as **diamonds if they are in the interior of a pattern piece.** They must be traced onto the pattern pieces. Darts are a simple and important way to **bring in excess width** without having to make cuts in the fabric.

ATTACHMENT LINES for pockets, belt loops, and similar design details are **often only partially drawn in.** Transfer these onto the traced pattern to guide the placement of these elements during sewing.

A **FACING** is a way of finishing edges, for example, on abutted front openings. The edges may be straight, as on a blouse front, or curved, as on the neckline of a collarless jacket. Unusually shaped hems may also be finished with a **hem facing.** On **complicated edges the facing may be its own pattern piece.** On straight edges the facing may be **built into the main pattern piece as an extended facing.**

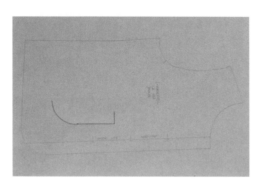

FABRIC GRAIN refers to the direction of the **warp threads (the lengthwise threads that run parallel to the selvage edge, known as the straight grain).** The grain line indicated on a pattern piece must **be lined up along the actual straight grain line** of the fabric when cutting. The grain line, selvages, and some fold lines run parallel to one another. Some pieces may be **deliberately cut diagonal to the grain** line (or on the bias), such as bias strips, pockets, lapels, and skirt panels; some pieces may be cut perpendicular to the straight grain, on the cross grain. Always transfer grain markings onto your pattern pieces and pay attention to them when preparing to cut your fabric.

! When it's necessary to add seam allowances to your pattern pieces, the following exceptions apply to the standard **SEAM ALLOWANCE MEASUREMENTS:**

• Seam allowance at **ZIPPERS:** ¾" (2cm)

• Hems on **STRAIGHT SKIRTS OR PANT LEGS:** 1¼" (3.5cm)

• Hems on wide, **SWINGY SKIRTS:** ½–⅝" (1–1.5cm)

Exceptions to standard seam allowances may be indicated on pattern pieces with a small marking at the seam line.

SEAM ALLOWANCES are essential, since without them a finished item will end up smaller than intended! If you are working with a pattern that does not already include allowances, be sure to add them to all seam lines—a **standard seam allowance is ½–⅝" (1–1.5cm).**

The **FABRIC FOLD** is where the fabric folds in half, lengthwise (on the straight grain) or widthwise (on the cross grain). The lengthwise/straight grain fold (left edge in the artwork) is opposite and parallel to the selvages (right edge in the artwork) and very important! The bodice piece that is placed and cut on the fold will end up twice as wide, without requiring a seam (the fold is in the center of the bodice piece). If the piece is mistakenly placed on the selvage edge, it will end up as two pieces. (If this is necessary due to fabric restraints, be sure to add a seam allowance.)

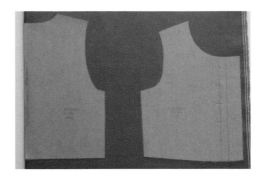

A **SOLID FOLD LINE** on a pattern piece indicates where the piece will eventually be **folded over,** such as at a hem or on a waistband.

OVERLAP AND UNDERLAP refer to the **additional width** required on a **lapped closure.** The flap with a buttonhole on a skirt waistband is an overlap. An underlap is the opposite, and is where the button would be sewn.

FACING an edge refers to a common method of **finishing raw edges;** it may or may not employ an actual facing piece or facing extension *(see pages 172 and 203-204).* It involves sewing on an identical fabric piece (a true facing) or a bias strip, wide ribbon, etc. and folding the ensuing seam wrong sides together to enclose the raw seam allowances *(see page 89).*

CENTER FRONT refers to an **imaginary line dividing the body lengthwise in two equal halves.** The center front line is often shown on pattern pieces to better enable symmetrical work. It is especially important to use as a **guideline when cutting certain patterned fabrics.** The design pattern of the fabric should flow symmetrically to the left and right of the center front. In practice the center front on tops is often a closure of some kind, while on skirts the center front is frequently positioned on the fabric fold line. Pants are likely to have a seam at the center front.

CENTER BACK is the **counterpart to center front.**

SELVAGES are the two **pre-finished edges on a length of fabric.** The straight/lengthwise grain of the fabric runs parallel to the selvages. (The width of a fabric corresponds to the width of the loom it was made on, and the **selvages form at the side borders of the loom.)** For easier handling, fabric is usually folded in half on the lengthwise grain so that the selvages lie on top of each other.

! **ALWAYS COPY PATTERNS** using a sharp pencil, triangular ruler, and straightedge, and **NOTE INFORMATION ON THE PATTERN PIECES** such as the garment type (e.g., blouse), the type of pattern piece (e.g., front), the size, and, if desired, the date made.

! **COPY ALL LINES AND MARKINGS.** They are intended to help with the eventual sewing process and can significantly shorten preparation time when used as intended.

» Light-colored **TISSUE PAPER OR BLUEPRINT PAPER** works very well for pattern tracing.

» **IF PATTERN PIECES BECOME WRINKLED** or bent, simply iron them with a *dry* iron until they are flat again. (Steam or moisture will wrinkle the paper even more.)

pattern alterations

Unfortunately, a pattern won't always fit perfectly—maybe you are shorter or taller than average, for example. Adjustments are usually made on the pattern itself. To make pattern adjustments you will use a tape measure, a sharp pencil, a triangular ruler, a straightedge, and possibly a curved tailor's ruler. Adhesive tape, scissors, and some paper (of similar weight to the pattern paper) should also be near at hand.

! PATTERN ALTERATIONS SHOULD ALWAYS BE MADE in accordance with the manufacturer's size charts. Do not measure pattern pieces and compare directly with your own body measurements; instead, **COMPARE THE VARIOUS SIZE CHART MEASUREMENTS AGAINST YOUR OWN** and then make alterations using that information. After altering the pattern, lay corresponding pieces together and compare them. Errors at this point usually will be immediately noticeable. **AS A FINAL CHECK, HOLD THE PATTERN PIECES UP TO YOUR BODY IN FRONT OF A MIRROR.**

» DO NOT ALTER A PATTERN BY MORE THAN TWO SIZES; it is better to purchase a new pattern in the correct size. **PROPER FIT IS OTHERWISE NOT ENSURED.**

LENGTH ALTERATIONS

There are various alterations that can be made even if you don't have a great deal of previous sewing experience. Among these are length alterations, i.e., shortening and lengthening. To shorten a skirt or lengthen a pair of pants, or to get sleeves to the correct length, is usually as simple as measuring the relevant body lengths, comparing them with the corresponding seam length measurements, and transferring the revised measurements to the pattern piece itself. **When multiple pieces correspond to each other,** as with the front and back of a skirt, be sure to **adjust the length on both pattern pieces!**
Sometimes, though, more significant changes must be made in order to achieve the correct fit.

LENGTHENING OR SHORTENING SINGLE-SIZE PATTERNS

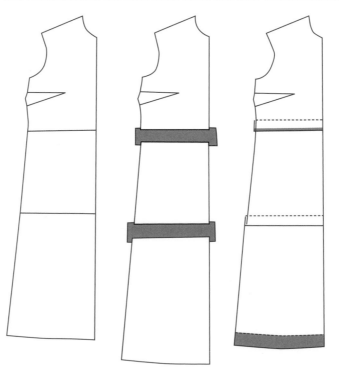

On a dress with bust darts, you can lengthen or shorten the pattern by cutting along **horizontal reference lines at the waist and hip points** (as shown) and separating the pattern pieces by a distance equal to the desired adjusted length. Connect the cut pieces with paper of a similar weight to the pattern paper. You can also alter the length at the hemline.

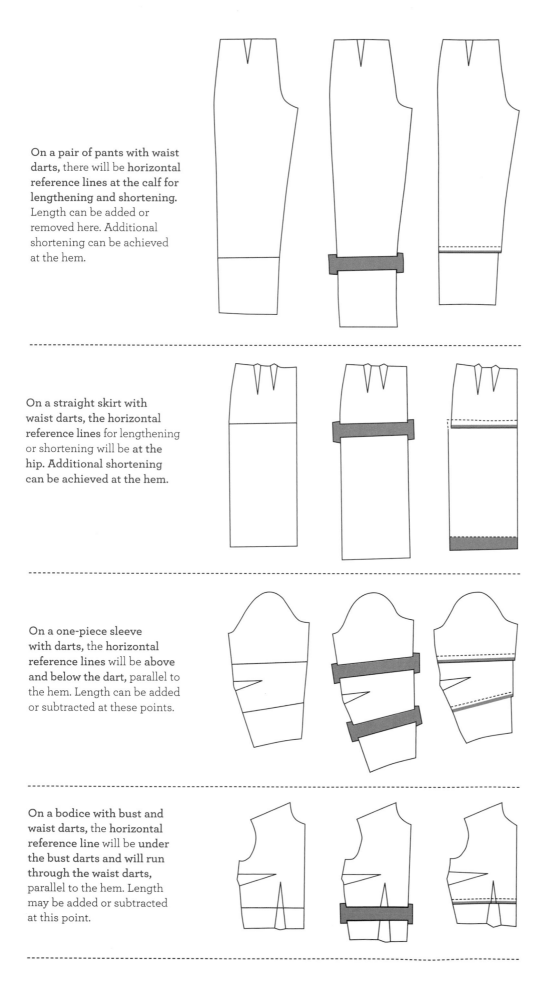

On a pair of pants with waist darts, there will be horizontal reference lines at the calf for lengthening and shortening. Length can be added or removed here. Additional shortening can be achieved at the hem.

On a straight skirt with waist darts, the horizontal reference lines for lengthening or shortening will be at the hip. Additional shortening can be achieved at the hem.

On a one-piece sleeve with darts, the horizontal reference lines will be above and below the dart, parallel to the hem. Length can be added or subtracted at these points.

On a bodice with bust and waist darts, the horizontal reference line will be under the bust darts and will run through the waist darts, parallel to the hem. Length may be added or subtracted at this point.

>> It is best to cut the pattern pieces apart on the lines and tape a piece of paper between them.

! BE SURE to alter all coordinating pieces; e.g., the front and back of a skirt.

! A LONG TAILOR'S SQUARE or ruler is HELPFUL FOR MARKING longer sections. Otherwise markings can become imprecise.

WIDTH ALTERATIONS

Width alterations are not quite as simple as length alterations. It is not always possible to add enough extra width at the side seams. But, **with the help of vertical reference lines,** you can often adjust the width of pattern pieces without a problem. A crucial point to keep in mind is that multiple pattern pieces contribute to a garment's total width. If a shirt is 1" (2.5cm) too wide or small overall, you'd need to alter each of the four seams in the bodice by only ¼" (.6cm).

WIDENING OR NARROWING SINGLE-SIZE PATTERNS

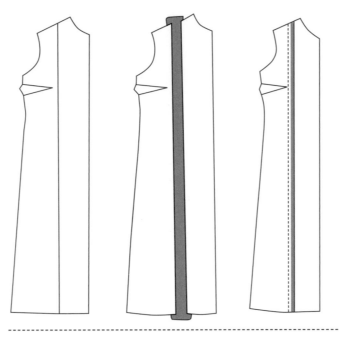

On a dress with bust darts, a **vertical reference line** next to the darts, **parallel to the center front,** can be used to add or remove width.

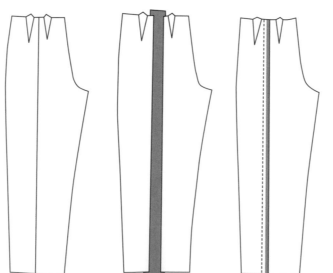

On pants with waist darts, the **vertical reference line will be found between the darts,** parallel to the side seams. It can be used to add or remove width.

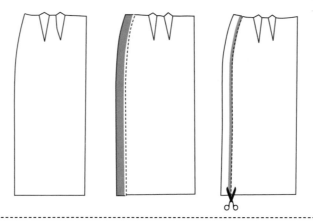

On a pencil skirt with waist darts, width can be added or removed at the sides, parallel to the seam.

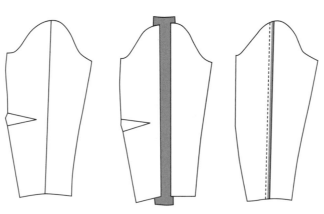

On a single-piece sleeve with darts, the vertical reference line lies parallel to the grain line. Width can be added or removed beyond the dart.

On a top with bust and waist darts, it is not possible to make width adjustment using this method without causing serious changes to the garment's shaping.

>> PATTERN PIECES are best reduced in size or length by FOLDING BACK THE EXCESS at the appropriate point and fastening it with pins. This way the piece can easily be returned to its original size.

! NEVER MAKE ALL OF A WIDTH ADJUSTMENT ON A SINGLE PATTERN PIECE. Distribute the alteration equally among the front and back pieces. This applies whether you are increasing or reducing the width. ALWAYS DISTRIBUTE WIDTH ADJUSTMENTS EVENLY!

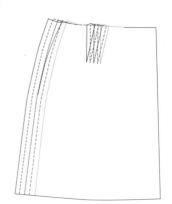

ALTERING MULTI-SIZE PATTERNS

Multi-size patterns have many advantages, among which is their **simplicity in alteration**. The outlines for all the available sizes are nested directly next to one another. It is not only easier to alter a multi-size pattern, but the results will also be more accurate and **true to form** than they would be when working only with reference lines. The following types of alterations can be achieved fairly easily.

GENERATING A MISSING SIZE

Your pattern's sizes are indicated on the pattern pieces by corresponding outlines (usually cutting lines) nested next to one another. If your **desired size** is not among those offered in the pattern's size range, the **remedy is easy**. You just need to draw new cutting lines for your desired size **at a consistent distance** from an existing size's cutting lines.

First draw reference lines at the pattern's corners; draw through and connect all the existing lines (as shown), **paying careful attention to the smallest and largest sizes**. (You can also do the same along longer, straight edges, drawing the reference line at a 90-degree angle to the cutting lines.)

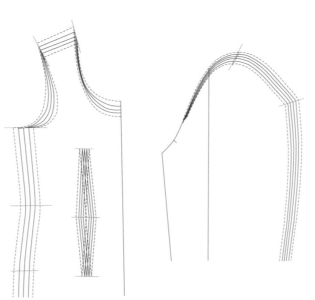

Measure the distance between the cutting lines of two consecutive sizes (for example, between size 8 and 10). This will be the distance between the existing cutting line and the new cutting line you will mark. Mark the new size's cutting lines in or out from the existing size's cutting lines, keeping the distance between the existing and new lines consistent with the measurement you took. Mark to the outside of the existing lines to make a pattern a size bigger, or to the inside to make it a size smaller. Draw cutting lines for **your new size according to these reference points.**

SIZE VARIATION WITHIN PATTERN PIECES

The size range available for a particular pattern can also be used to vary the sizing within a single piece, such as **when a single size does not fit properly in all areas** (for example, if your waist corresponds to one size but your hips correspond to the next larger or smaller size).

First check the pattern manufacturer's size chart to determine the key measurements of the individual sizes. With these as a guide, use a pencil to connect one size's cutting line to another size's corresponding cutting line. Be sure to blend the connecting line with the existing lines so the transition between the cutting lines maintains the overall shape of the piece. In the example shown here, the hip is being made a size larger than the overall garment size.

To finish, simply copy the pattern with the alteration included.

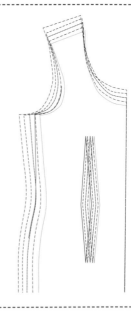

> **!** NO MATTER WHAT THE ALTERATION, do not rely on sight; always MEASURE CAREFULLY. Once you have adjusted all the affected pieces, compare them along their seamlines to verify that the alterations were made consistently. Remember also that PATTERNS SHOULD NEVER BE ADJUSTED BY MORE THAN TWO SIZES.

styling
alterations

When making alterations, always keep in mind that multiple corresponding pieces may need to be altered. For example, if you shorten the length of a skirt front, the same changes must be made to the back. It is best to limit alterations to things that will not interfere with the final shape of the garment in any serious way. Take care, for example, when altering the shape of darts; they are usually best left as designed. Armholes and neck openings should also be altered very carefully, if at all.

SIMPLE CHANGES

If a pattern appeals to you in general and you want to change just a few details, the following can be done quite easily and allow you to **express your creativity** at the same time.

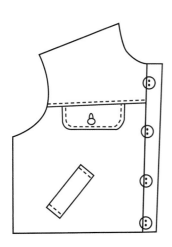 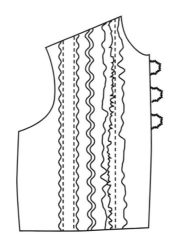 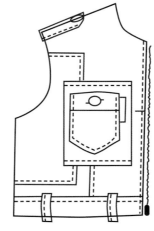

! TEST STYLING ALTERATIONS on a test version (muslin) of the garment.

» THE FOLLOWING ALTERATIONS are examples of the types of changes that are easy to make: leave off the cuffs of a blouse and instead create a casing through which a tie or elastic band can be threaded; leave off the sleeves entirely and bind the armholes with bias strips; finish skirt hems, on the main fabric or the lining, with ruffles rather than a plain hem; etc.

DISCARDING DESIGN ELEMENTS
It is especially easy to simply **discard elements** that do not affect the function of the garment. For example, if a blouse is shaped close to the body with darts and this is not a feature you want, you can just not sew them. Patch pockets, belt loops, epaulets, etc. can also be left off.

EMBELLISHING
In contrast, you may wish to **increase the number of decorative elements**. Ribbons or ruffles may be added, a second belt made to add variety, multiple overlapping pockets applied—none of these embellishments will present great technical challenges.

! KEEP ANY ADDITIONAL EMBELLISHMENT PIECES in mind not only when creating the pattern but also when buying fabric—you may need additional yardage.

ADJUSTING POSITIONING
You can often adjust the positioning of applied elements if their prescribed location does not appeal to you. Belt loops, patch pockets, elbow or knee patches, etc. can all be **repositioned without concern**.

MORE COMPLEX ALTERATIONS

There are some alterations that should be undertaken only once you have some **sewing experience** under your belt. These changes often will require you to **deviate from the pattern instructions.**

CREATING A FACING

If you decide to change a design element of a garment; for example, leaving off the collar of a jacket, you can't leave the raw edge of the neckline as is. A good and fairly straightforward method of finishing this raw edge is to create a facing. In this collarless jacket example, the raw **neck edge would be faced** with a neckline facing.

! FACINGS can be used to finish many types of raw edges.

! Facing is a SIMPLE AND EFFECTIVE EDGE-FINISHING METHOD that even beginners can use to FINISH OPENINGS on a garment. You need only the RAW EDGE of the opening as your guide for creating a facing that covers 1–2" (2.5–5cm) of the main piece. You'll add a a SEAM ALLOWANCE ON THE ATTACHMENT EDGES of the facing and the raw edge of the opening (if it's not included). Your facing is now ready to use.

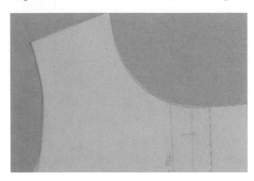

To create a facing, you'll use the existing **pattern pieces that correspond to the altered element,** in this case, the jacket front and jacket back pattern pieces. **Beginning with the jacket front pattern piece, draw** a precise outline of the entire neck opening and the shoulder seam.

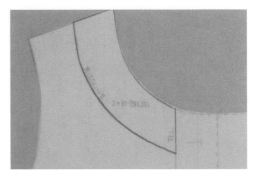

Draw a curved line parallel to the traced neckline edge, about 1¼" (3cm) away from the neckline edge, as shown. Start at the shoulder and end wherever the neckline of the original pattern piece ends. Cut out the facing along the drawn lines. You now have a front neckline facing pattern piece. Repeat for the back neck facing. Create just about any facing pattern using this method.

VARYING PATTERN PIECES

A popular method for altering the style of a garment is to **substitute pattern pieces from a different pattern.** This technique will be familiar if you have purchased prepared patterns that offer styling variations. Perhaps you would like to make a shirt using the front and back from style A, the sleeves from style B, and the collar treatment from style C. On patterns that already **include variations,** this sort of swapping out of elements is usually **no problem.**

If you want to try this with pattern pieces that are not designed to be used together, however, you will need a bit of experience to know **which pieces will be compatible.** It is worth the effort, however, to add some pep and creativity to the mix!

MUSLINS

Making a test garment is an **especially good idea when a pattern has been heavily altered,** is **closely fitted,** or will be made from **expensive fabric.** In those cases we advise that you make a test garment **out of inexpensive material with similar characteristics to your actual fabric; this is known as a muslin.** The payoff for the additional time investment a test garment requires will be a final garment that fits perfectly.

At one time, test garments were almost always made from **muslin, an inexpensive raw cotton fabric.** Since muslin does not always mirror the characteristics of your final garment fabric, however, it is not always the ideal choice. Nonetheless, the name "muslin" has stuck to test garments, regardless of the fabric used. When making a muslin, it is not necessary to include all the details of the final garment; you are mainly looking toward perfecting the fit or construction. You **do not need to finish seam allowances or install zippers** (you can use pins) to determine the correct fit.

Draw any alterations directly on the muslin, or mark them with pins and immediately transfer them to the corresponding pattern pieces.

➤➤ UNUSUAL OR NOVEL FINISHING TECHNIQUES can be TESTED FIRST using simple, inexpensive fabric with similar properties to your actual fabric. Design houses and pattern companies make muslin test versions of their designs; you can use remnants or inexpensive fabrics. Testing will help you AVOID ERRORS ON THE FINAL GARMENT.

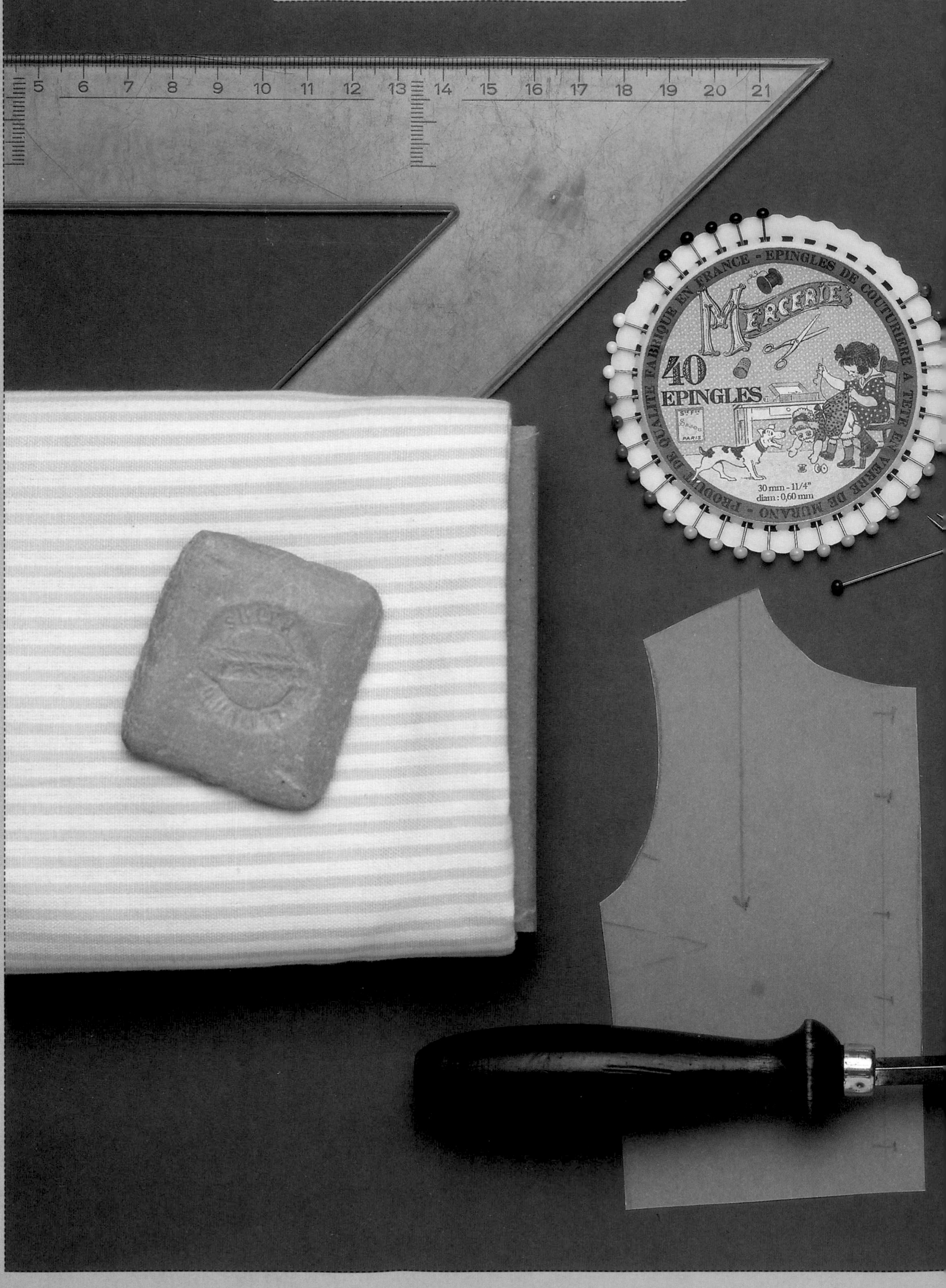

5 6 7 8 9 10 11 12 13 14 15 16 17 18 19 20 21
PRODUIT DE QUALITE FABRIQUE EN FRANCE - EPINGLES DE COUTURIERE A TETE EN VERRE DE MURANO
MERCERIE
40
EPINGLES
PARIS
30 mm - 11/4"
diam : 0,60 mm

preparing
to sew

BEFORE YOU MAKE YOUR FIRST CUT INTO YOUR FABRIC, YOU'LL NEED TO MAKE A FEW ADVANCED PREPARATIONS. IT IS CRITICAL THAT YOU UNDERSTAND FABRIC PROPERTIES AND LAYOUT AND CUTTING TERMINOLOGY, SUCH AS SELVAGES, FOLDS, PATTERN LAYOUT, FABRIC GRAIN, AND SEAM ALLOWANCES.

before cutting

You've chosen a pattern, copied it (if needed), and have your pattern instructions, your primary fabric, and all the other materials and notions at hand in the correct quantities. Before you start to cut, there are a few more preparations to take care of to ensure optimal results.

PREPARING YOUR FABRIC

Many fabrics can be used immediately after purchase, but some require additional preparation.

PRESHRINKING

New fabrics, especially **cottons,** that shrink heavily should be washed according to the manufacturer's care guidelines and then pressed before use. **Lining fabrics** may have an odd, vinegary odor depending on their finishing treatment, which can be washed out before use. But linings usually do not shrink and so don't require prewashing for that reason. **Fusible interfacings** made from synthetic fibers do not require preshrinking. Fabrics that have a protective **finish** *(see page 141)* should be handled so that the finish is not washed out.

STEAM SHRINKING

Steaming with a steam iron can replace prewashing for fabrics that shrink only slightly, but use caution, because some fabrics can be ruined by steaming. Always do a test patch first at a corner of the fabric!

STRAIGHTENING FABRIC EDGES

Spread out the prepared fabric on a sufficiently large, clean surface (this can be a smooth floor or a carpeted area). Use a long ruler to **trim the cut ends to a right (90-degree) angle to the selvage.** On patterned fabrics you can often use the design pattern as a placement guide for the pattern pieces. Before cutting, fold the fabric in half lengthwise (on the straight grain) with the selvage edges together so that the **fold line forms a straight, unwrinkled line parallel to the selvages.**

! **TEARING YOUR FABRIC** will not produce straight edges, especially on the cross grain. It is better to cut on the cross grain at a 90-degree angle to the selvages.

FOLDING THE FABRIC

Usually fabric is folded lengthwise on the straight grain before cutting out pattern pieces. Some pieces will be positioned **directly on the fold,** or pieces that must be **mirror images** (such as shirt fronts) will be **cut as one** on a double layer of fabric.

REFOLDING

Some patterns require the fabric to be folded lengthwise with **both selvages in the middle;** for example, when both the front and back pieces of a garment are cut on a fold line. The selvages meet at the original lengthwise fold line, creating two **new lengthwise fold lines parallel to the original one.**

DIFFERENT SIDES OF FABRIC

Fabric (with a few exceptions) has two different sides: the *right* side, the outside that everyone sees, and the *wrong*, or back, side on the inside of the project. When you cut out a pattern, the fabric is typically **folded right sides together,** so that marking lines can be made on the wrong side. (And the fabric is less likely to get dirty.)

RIGHT SIDE

On **printed fabrics** the right side, which will eventually be on the outside of a garment, is **easy to recognize: the color and pattern** are more intense and obvious, any shine the fabric may have is more noticeable, and textures (such as corduroy wales) are easily seen and felt. On **color-woven** fabrics it can be more difficult to determine the right side, since the fabric is woven and not printed, and the colors appear equally strong from both sides. In this case you can use whichever side has fewer flaws (such as thickened spots in the thread or loose hanging ends) as the right side.

WRONG SIDE

The wrong (or back side) of the fabric may also be referred to as the *reverse* side.

! IF YOU ARE HAVING TROUBLE DETERMINING which is the right side of your fabric, take a closer look at the selvages. You will see tiny needle holes left over from the manufacturing process. THE HOLES WILL FEEL MORE BUMPY AND NOTICEABLE FROM THE RIGHT SIDE OF THE FABRIC. Once you have determined a right side, stick to it consistently. (You may want to mark the right side with tailor's chalk or another erasable or disappearing-ink marker.)

pattern preparation

Most commercial patterns include seam allowances, so you can simply lay them out on the fabric as is and cut along the pre-printed cutting lines. However, patterns in sewing books and magazines, and from certain manufacturers (especially in Europe), often do not include seam allowances and may require that you trace the pieces onto a separate medium and add seam allowances before cutting. This section offers guidelines for using these patterns.

STITCHING LINE METHOD

With the stitching line method, each paper pattern piece is **cut out along the stitching lines (i.e., seam lines),** with no seam allowances added. Seam allowances will be added before the fabric is cut.

>> When ADDING SEAM ALLOWANCES TO SHARP CORNERS ON A PATTERN PIECE (for example, at the underarm of a two-piece sleeve), you can create long and UNNECESSARY TRIANGLE POINTS. You should cut these points back to ⅜" (1cm), which will decrease the amount of excess fabric during sewing and make placement of the pattern pieces more efficient.

! ANYONE CAN LEARN to use our SEAM ALLOWANCE METHOD. It does not require special materials or any additional skills. It OPTIMIZES EACH STEP in the process.

SEAM ALLOWANCE/CUTTING LINE METHOD

Pattern preparation using this method is somewhat different, because either the seam allowances are already included in the pattern pieces (requiring no additional preparation) or you add them to the paper pattern itself before the pattern pieces are cut out. A good rule of thumb is that seam allowances should be ⅝" (1.5cm) all around. There are only a few exceptions:

- **On hems that are relatively straight** (such as on pant legs, narrow skirts, or jackets), 1¼" **(3cm) hem allowances** are typical.

- **On hems where the piece widens** (such as on full or belled skirts), the hem allowance may be **narrower than ⅜" (1cm).**

- **Seam allowances around zippers should be ¾" (2cm).** Beyond the zipper, the allowance tapers back to ⅝" (1.5cm).

Once the seam allowances have been carefully added, you can cut the pattern pieces **along the newly drawn cutting lines.**

cutting

Fabric, lining, and interfacing are cut out using the paper pattern pieces as guides. Be sure to work economically and avoid unnecessary cuts and waste. The pattern layout guide on the instruction sheet will show the optimal pattern layout. Be sure to have sharp fabric shears, pins or pattern weights, a measuring tape, and your pattern pieces ready and close at hand.

» SAVE USED PATTERN PIECES along with project information such as size, date made, and a scrap and description of the fabric, and store them inside CLEAR PLASTIC SHEET PROTECTORS. This will make it easier the next time you use the pattern.

! It is helpful to have a dedicated WORK SPACE where you can leave large pieces of FABRIC SPREAD OUT for the duration of the project.

PATTERN LAYOUT

The pattern layout is a helpful drawing that shows the optimal positioning of your pattern pieces; **pay attention to the location of fold lines, selvages, grain lines, and any directions printed on the pattern pieces.** Unless otherwise indicated, pattern pieces are placed printed side up on the fabric.

CUTTING OUT STITCHING LINE PATTERN PIECES

When paper pattern pieces are cut out on the stitching line, they must be placed on the fabric according to the pattern layout and with **enough distance between them** to accommodate the seam allowances that are still to be added *(see page 189)*. The pieces are aligned with the *fabric grain (see page 172)* and fastened with pins. All stitching and seam lines and pattern markings will be transferred to the fabric in multiple, distinct steps.

! WITH *STITCHING LINE METHOD* PATTERNS, the fabric must be folded right sides together so that marking lines end up on the wrong side of the fabric.

! U.S. AND BRITISH PATTERNS almost always include seam allowances.

ALIGNING PATTERN PIECES WITH THE FABRIC GRAIN

The grain lines marked on the pattern pieces (usually the lengthwise/straight grain) correspond to the fabric's woven grain. Place a pattern piece on the fabric and **measure the distance from one end of the marked lengthwise grain line to the fold or selvage of the fabric,** whichever is closest, as shown. Secure the pattern piece with a weight and repeat the measurement at the bottom end of the marked grain line (as shown) and adjust so that it is the same measurement as the first, making the entire line parallel to the fold or selvage. Now **the pattern piece is aligned with the grain.**

 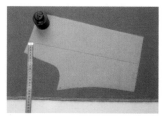 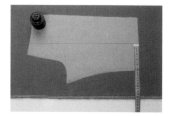

TRANSFERRING PATTERN MARKINGS

Fold the fabric in half lengthwise with right sides together and lay it on a hard, even work surface. You'll use a tracing wheel and tracing paper *(page 33)*, or tailor's chalk *(page 33)* or a disappearing-ink marker *(page 33)*.

Place the tracing paper chalk side up underneath the fabric and chalk side down between the pattern piece and the fabric. Using the tracing wheel, run along all **cutting lines, seam lines, dart markings, and any other indicated sewing or stitching lines.** The tracing will leave fine dotted lines on the fabric. Transfer all markings for all pieces in this manner, moving the tracing paper underneath the fabric rather than shifting the fabric itself.

The traced sewing/stitching lines will be used later as a guide to create **seam allowance** lines using tailor's chalk or a disappearing-ink marker.

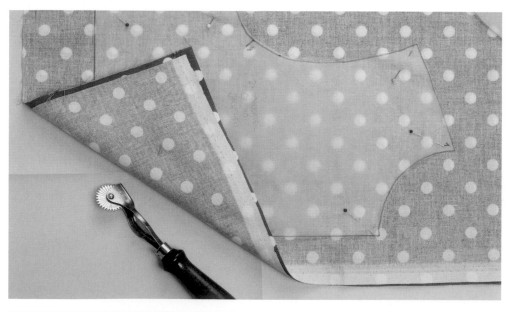

MARKING SEAM ALLOWANCES AND CUTTING LINES

Pattern pieces made with the stitching line method need to have their seam allowances marked onto the fabric using tailor's chalk or an erasable or disappearing-ink pencil or pen and a measuring tape or ruler, in an additional step. **Recommended seam allowances are ⅝" (1.5cm), the same as with the seam allowance/cutting line method** *(see page 186).*

Since the seam allowances are marked directly onto the fabric, they will be **less precise** than they would be with the seam allowance/ professional method—fabric tends to shift, and a chalk line on fabric is not as exact as a pen or pencil line on paper. This is why a separate, marked sewing line is also needed. One way to mark the stitching/seam line is to carefully trace around the cut edges of the pattern pieces directly onto the fabric using tailor's chalk or an erasable or disappearing-ink pencil or pen. To mark stitching/seam lines and other marks on the underside of the fabric, see page 186 and below.

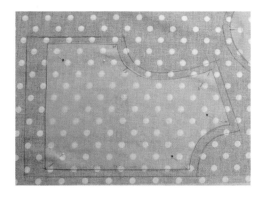

! EXPERIENCED SEWERS can cut directly along the seam allowance cutting lines without having to mark them first, using a TAPE MEASURE as a guide while cutting.

CUTTING

Cut the pattern pieces out **along the seam allowance/cutting lines** using sharp scissors.

» CUTTING GOES EVEN FASTER with electric scissors.

TRANSFERRING LINES ON THE REVERSE SIDES

To mark the stitching/seam lines on the cut-out but as yet unmarked sides (that is, the sides that were facing up during the tracing process and did not receive chalk markings), unpin and remove the paper pattern pieces, setting them aside. **Flip the cut fabric pieces over, being careful not to let them shift and become misaligned, so that the previous chalk markings are facing up. Place the fabric piece on top of the tracing paper again** and trace along all the stitching/seam lines with the tracing wheel. Now the exact stitching lines are marked on both pieces. The **unmarked stitching/seam lines** may also be marked more quickly by tracing around the paper pattern piece before removal, using tailor's chalk or a disappearing-ink marker.

! THE CUTTING OF LINING AND INTERFACING follows the same principles. Details will be provided in your pattern instructions.

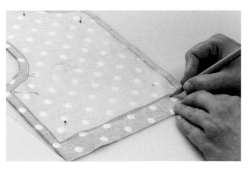

CUTTING OUT SEAM ALLOWANCE/ CUTTING LINE PATTERN PIECES

The advantages of the seam allowance/cutting line method lie in that all stitching, placement, and cutting lines can be exactly drawn on the paper pattern. The separate marking of stitching/ seam lines on the fabric, as well as time-consuming tracing, are unnecessary. **If the pattern is ever used again, all the needed preparations are still intact,** and cutting can begin immediately. The following guidelines apply to any pattern pieces with included seam allowances, including those that come ready to use.

ECONOMICAL POSITIONING OF PATTERN PIECES

All pattern pieces are placed onto the fabric in accordance with the instruction sheet's pattern layout. They may be **positioned very close to one another (as shown),** since the seam allowances are already included. They should be fastened to the fabric in alignment with the *fabric grain (see page 172),* using **small pattern weights (preferable)** or pins. Weights offer the advantage that the **fabric cannot accidentally be damaged by pin pricks,** and they are also faster to remove.

! MARKINGS SITUATED WITHIN the pattern's sewing lines must also be transferred.

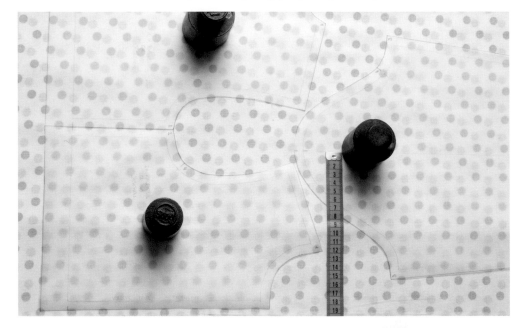

After all the pattern pieces are properly laid out on the fabric, cut out **along the paper pattern edges** using sharp scissors or, even better, electric scissors.

TRANSFERRING DETAIL MARKS

Detail positioning marks, matching points, darts at seam lines, and any deviations from standard seam allowances are marked during cutting with **small snips/notches—about ⅛" (0.3cm) deep—into, or out from, the seam allowances.** On most home sewing patterns from pattern companies, notches are indicated on the pattern piece with a triangle shape on the cutting line. These notches are a great help when sewing pieces together at the machine.

TRANSFERRING MARKINGS WITHIN THE FABRIC PIECES

For **darts or stitching lines** marked internally on a pattern piece, for example, indicating pocket attachment points or belt loop positions, only the **corner and/or end points** are marked. Some sewers prefer to use tracing paper and a tracing wheel to transfer all the positioning and dart lines.

1 Stick pins vertically into the corner points through the paper pattern and both layers of fabric.

2 These positioning points can now easily be marked with a soft pencil or chalk. Afterward, remove the paper piece and set aside.

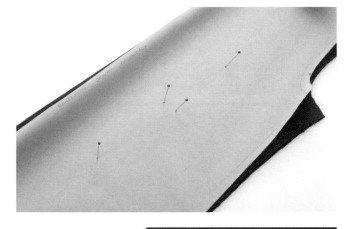

! THE CUTTING OF LINING AND INTERFACING follows the same principles as the cutting of the main fabric. Details can be found in the pattern instructions.

cutting various fabrics

When cutting single-color fabrics, or solids, you only need to worry about positioning pattern pieces economically and correctly on the grain. Cutting out patterned fabrics, however, calls for a little more skill. The pattern instruction sheet will sometimes show you layout options for large design motifs, stripes, and plaids, and the pattern envelope will let you know how much extra fabric yardage may be required (or if the design is not appropriate for stripes, plaids, or large design motifs).

! ADJUSTING FOR large or conspicuous design patterns in your fabric will **REQUIRE ADDITIONAL FABRIC** and increase the amount of fabric wastage.

» FABRIC SCRAPS can be collected and used for craft projects or patchwork.

FABRICS WITH SYMMETRICAL PATTERNS

With fabric patterns that are symmetrical to the left and right and regularly spaced (e.g., stripes, checks, small motifs), **the center front piece of the garment is positioned with the pattern repeat at its center,** and all further pattern pieces are positioned in relation to that; the finished item should (as much as possible) show the pattern flowing uninterrupted.

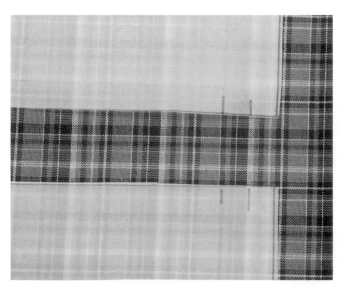

PLAIDS

It can be especially difficult to cut out plaids or fabrics with large and conspicuous patterns. A classic collared blazer made from fabrics such as those is a true challenge. **Plaids seem less busy if they are cut at a consistent seam height** (that is, when a row of plaid always begins at the same spot). Plaid curtains will look much better if they are cut to always begin at the same point in the pattern.

FABRICS WITH OVERALL PATTERNS

Some patterned fabrics can be treated like **solids**, because the pattern either is **especially small, especially large,** or very irregular, or has motifs so far apart that they will not end up interacting.

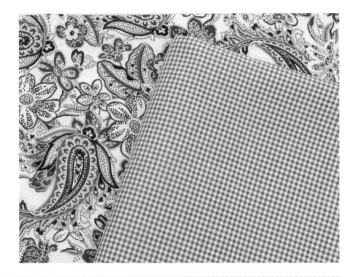

! WITH PATTERNED FABRICS the REPEAT must be considered in the yardage calculations. A good rule of thumb is that it is better to buy too much fabric than too little. Check your pattern envelope to see if it tells you how much extra fabric you may need for a patterned fabric.

DIRECTIONAL FABRIC

With patterns that only go in one direction, such as those with human or animal figures, objects, script, et cetera, **all fabric pieces that will be visible on the finished item must be cut out with the pattern running in the same direction,** so that the design doesn't run in opposite directions on different pieces of the project.

NAPPED FABRIC

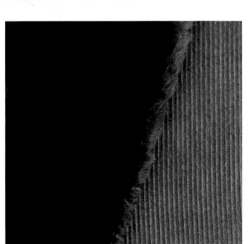

On fabrics with nap (also called pile), all pattern pieces are cut out with the nap running in the same direction, **downward from the point of view of the wearer.** Since napped fabric looks different when viewed from different angles, a single piece placed with the nap in the wrong direction will be distracting. **Nap direction can be determined by stroking the fabric** to see which direction flows more comfortably.

! Fabrics that reflect light differently from different angles should be TREATED AS IF NAPPED.

cutting
interfacings
and linings

Once your fabric is cut, a great deal of your preparation work is taken care of. But there are a few more preparations that will either streamline the actual sewing process or improve on the final results. These include the cutting of interfacing and lining.

INTERFACING

The purpose of interfacing is to **support a fabric's ability to meet various requirements or withstand certain types of stresses.** For example, on a blouse made with sheer, drapey fabric, the collar and cuffs require more stability. This is achieved with interfacing. Even if you have never used it before, please do not be tempted to skip it! **Interfacing is a thin, nonwoven fabric** that is typically ironed onto the wrong side of the main fabric (*see pages 60–61*). It is not expensive, yet it will improve your results tremendously.

CUTTING INTERFACING

The same pattern pieces used to cut the main fabric are also used to cut interfacing pieces. **Interfacing is usually cut with a seam allowance included,** so that it will get caught in the seams during sewing. Interfacing is often shown **shaded gray in pattern layouts.** Many patterns give instructions for cutting and applying interfacing.

! MATCH THE INTERFACING COLOR to that of the main fabric, or the interfacing may shine through—especially on thinner materials.

» IF YOU HAVE NEVER WORKED WITH INTERFACINGS, experiment a bit first using a FABRIC REMNANT.

! DIFFERENT TYPES OF INTERFACINGS ARE AVAILABLE for different types of fabrics and uses: perforated, stretchy interfacing for elastic fabrics, interfacings for leather, pre-cut waistband interfacings for skirts and pants, heavyweight interfacings for belts or valences, lofty interfacings for winter clothing or quilted surfaces, and many more (*see pages 60–61*).

APPLYING FUSIBLE INTERFACING

Fusible interfacing has a right and a wrong side. The wrong side has a coating that makes it fusible. This may consist of tiny, rough raised dots or a slightly shiny, flat, homogenous layer of adhesive. The ideal method to apply a given interfacing will be noted on the interfacing edges themselves or on the product packaging. The instructions will provide details about the product, and the required temperature and duration of pressing for a lasting application. **Do not use steam when pressing. Heat, pressure, and a little time** work best. Do not slide the iron along the interfacing; instead, lift and press straight down on multiple areas in succession.

>> IN CASES, SUCH AS OCCASIONALLY WITH VESTS, where every pattern piece is backed with fusible interfacing, the ENTIRE FABRIC PIECE MAY BE INTERFACED before cutting. Allow the fabric to cool before cutting and working further.

LINING

Lining is a lightweight fabric, usually synthetic, that conceals the inner workings of a garment, offers **additional wearing comfort** (garments slip on more easily), and increases the garment's life (by adding to durability). In winter clothing, linings can also provide additional warmth and may be combined with a nonwoven batting; quilting holds the lining layers together. Lining can be made unobtrusive in **matching tones** or worked in **contrasting colors**.

CUTTING LINING

Lining pieces are usually cut similarly to the main fabric pieces. They will be **identical** when used for **strengthening**, such as on pocket flaps, patch pockets, or collars. Often a **lining piece will need to be a little shorter or longer than the main piece.** In these cases it is enough to fold the pattern piece to shorten it, or to tape in an additional paper strip to lengthen it. See the directions for your specific pattern to determine the best way to cut the lining pieces.

getting connected

There are times throughout the sewing process when multiple layers need to be secured together: paper pattern pieces are attached to fabric with weights or pins; two fabric pieces are basted together; a seam stays in place with a touch of fabric glue.

>> EXPERIENCED SEWERS may require pinning only at the beginning and/or end of a seam.

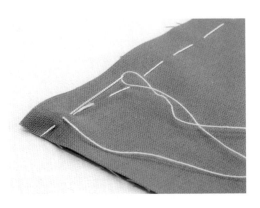

THREAD BASTING

Thread basting is a way to temporarily connect two fabric pieces with somewhat **lengthened hand stitches** (or extra-long machine stitches), using a lightly spun and therefore easily breakable *basting thread (see pages 42, 44)*. Once the machine seam is completed, though, **the basting thread must be removed**—a rather fiddly and lengthy process, especially if the basting thread gets caught in the machine stitching. For this reason, most sewers generally prefer pin basting.

! SLEEVE OR PANTS PATCHES (particularly on pants where the leg seams are already sewn) are especially good candidates for fastening with adhesive, since the patches then cannot shift during sewing. Seams also stay nicely in place when glued. GLUED SEAMS ARE STANDARD ON LEATHER (*see page 109*). Ready-made adhesive patches are ironed on from the reverse side, and need additional topstitching only if desired, or if they will be heavily stressed.

PIN BASTING

Pieces that need to be sewn together are best held together first with pins. The pins are placed at the beginning, end, and middle of the area to be sewn, **either parallel or perpendicular to the seam line,** through both layers of fabric. **Remove pins just before you reach them,** to prevent broken needles and bent pins.

GLUE BASTING

Sometimes glue may be used to **hold fabric pieces together.** There are liquid textile glues in tube or spray form, glue sticks, and special adhesive sheets with backing paper that are applied similarly to interfacing.

recovering from errors

Whenever you sew, there will be some mistakes—whether you're a professional or a hobbyist. Often it is best to set the work aside and return to it later—instead of frantically undoing your work, come back later with a cool head and consider your options.

ERRORS IN THE PATTERN

If you have altered any part of the pattern and the pieces do not seem to line up, re-measure the pieces to troubleshoot. Remember that an **alteration in length,** for example, usually must be mirrored on multiple pieces, such as the front and back of a skirt or dress.

ERRORS IN CUTTING

If pattern pieces are too large but have already been sewn together, some of the excess can often be brought in at the seam lines. Or you may have enough fabric left over to recut a piece that is the wrong size. **The most common cutting error is to fail to place a piece on the fold.** Pay extra attention for this type of layout.

>> One of the most common errors is to **NOT CUT A PIECE ON THE FOLD.** If you have enough fabric left over, cut the piece a second time, this time on the fold. Otherwise plan to make a **SEAM WHERE THE FOLD WOULD HAVE BEEN,** keeping in mind that this will require seam allowances.

ERRORS WHEN SEWING

Snips and notches often cause problems for beginning sewers. For example, sometimes a seam allowance requires snipping—with the presser foot lifted and the needle positioned down in the fabric—almost **to the stitching line, to create sufficient flexibility around a curve or corner.** When such adjustments are not made, for example, on collars and at sharp corners, the corresponding pieces may not fit correctly. It is always a good idea to pay careful attention to the pattern instructions, which may provide suggestions for snipping and notching. A **sewing course** can boost skills and confidence, while **online sewing forums** may be able to help with more immediate questions.

[!] BEGINNING SEWERS might want to **BUY A BIT OF EXTRA YARDAGE,** to have some in reserve in case of errors.

ERRORS AS FEATURES

Sometimes errors can **result in interesting new looks.** A recurring fashion trend involves having some or all pieces of fabric on a garment facing inside out. That idea may well have originally been inspired by a cutting error!

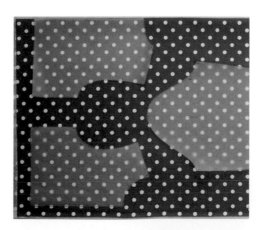

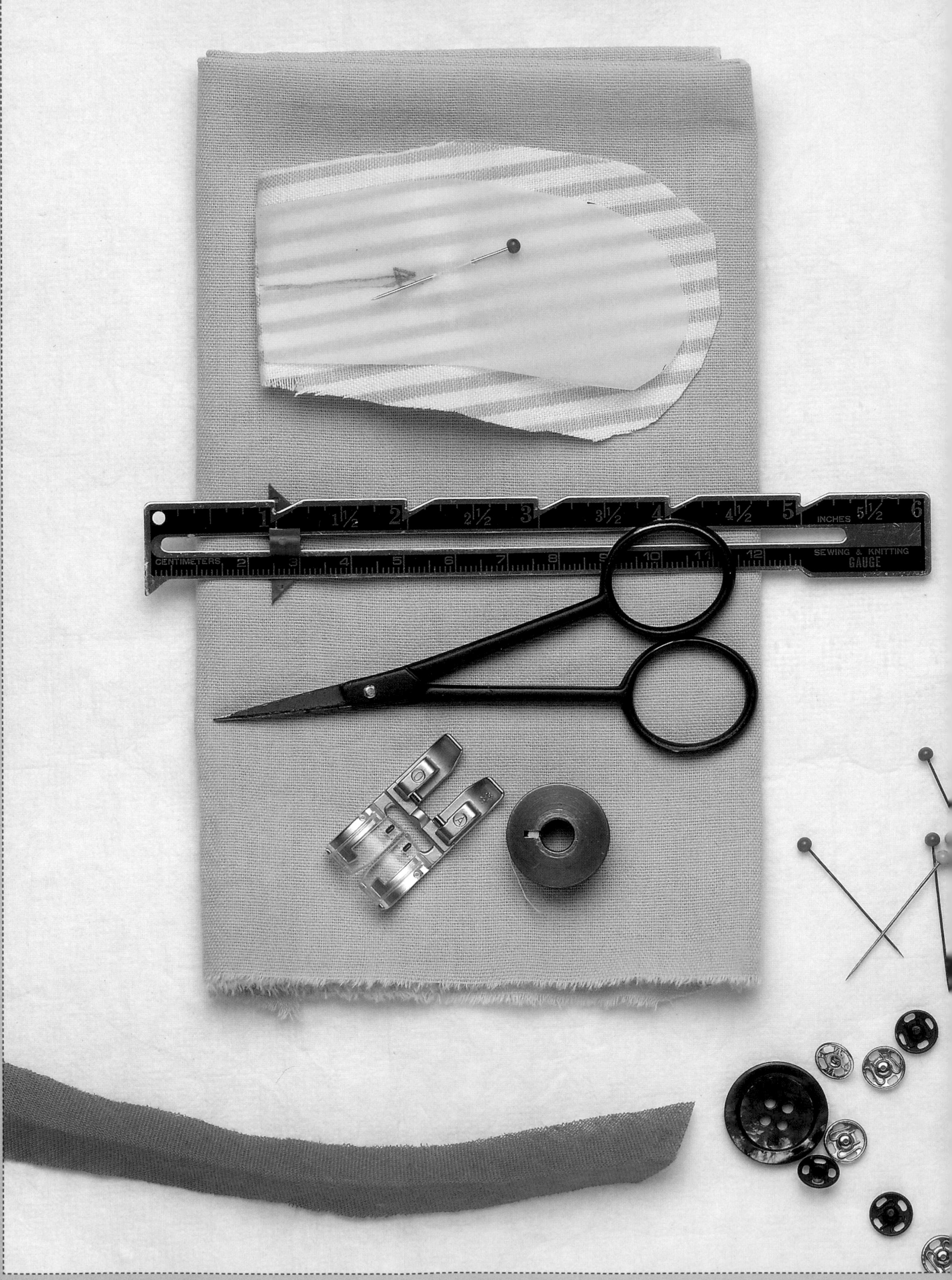
INCHES
SEWING & KNITTING
GAUGE
CENTIMETERS

creating a garment

CREATING YOUR OWN CLOTHING IS NOT ALWAYS SIMPLE. HOW DOES A COLLAR ATTACH TO A NECKLINE, OR A SLEEVE FIT INTO AN ARMHOLE OPENING? WHAT IS A FACING, A DART, AN UNDERLAP? THIS CHAPTER WILL SHOW YOU HOW TO REALIZE THE GARMENTS YOU IMAGINE, AND HOW TO MAKE OFF-THE-RACK ITEMS UNIQUELY YOUR OWN.

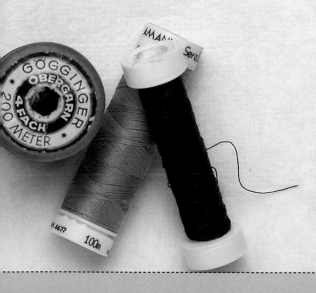

shaping
with darts

Darts are used to make certain areas of a garment narrower, to better follow the shape of the body. Darts are either triangular or diamond-shaped (*see page 172*).

ABOUT DARTS

There are various techniques for creating darts.
- **Mark the dart on the wrong side of the fabric** using a method appropriate for the material. Darts are sewn before individual garment pieces are put together. You can baste darts first to check the fit.
- Secure the beginning of the dart seam with backstitches. The stitching should run out **as flatly as possible** at the pointed end(s) of a dart to avoid any wrinkling or bulging there. Switch to slightly smaller stitches about ⅝" (1.5cm) before the end of the dart, and make sure the last couple of stitches are right along the fold line. **Secure the ends of the dart seam with backstitches,** or knot thread ends together. Trim any remaining thread ends.
- Carefully iron the completed darts. **First iron the dart flat along the fold,** without going past the ends (to avoid making wrinkles). Then lay the piece flat and, depending on the type of dart, **press it either open or to one side.** In general, horizontal darts are pressed downward and vertical darts are pressed toward the center of the garment. A tailor's ham is helpful for pressing darts smoothly.
- Darts **in linings should be pressed in the opposite direction** from those in the main fabric, to avoid creating bulky areas.

SIMPLE DARTS

>> TO HELP WITH ORIENTATION on darts, you can use a ruler and a disappearing-ink marker or tailor's chalk to draw a stitching/seam line. **ON STRAIGHT DARTS** you can use a strip of adhesive tape (for example, quilter's tape) as a quick guideline.

1 Mark the dart, using crosswise lines to mark the dart ends.

2 Fold the fabric right sides together down the middle of the dart so that the dart markings lie on top of each other; pin, starting at the point of the dart. **Sew the dart from the wide end to the tip,** securing the thread at the beginning and end of the dart seam.

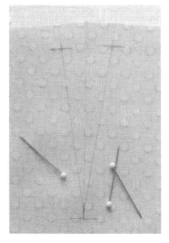
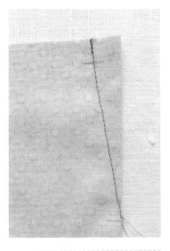

SIMPLE CUT DARTS

To prevent **wide darts or darts in heavy fabrics** from becoming bulky, they are **cut open and trimmed** after sewing.
Use a small pair of pointed scissors to **cut the dart up the middle, i.e., along the fold,** to about ⅝" (1.5cm) before the tip (see marking in photo); on narrow darts, stop cutting 1¼–1½" (3–4cm) before the tip. Wide dart allowances should be trimmed down to ⅜–⅝" (1–1.5cm). Press cut dart edges open and press the uncut section flat, as shown.

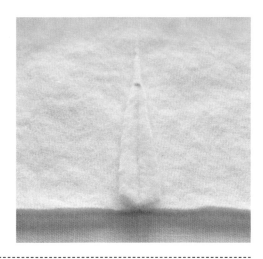

WAIST DARTS

Dresses and tops without waist seams are often given shaping with this type of dart. They are **vertical, diamond-shaped darts** that narrow down to a point at both ends.
Mark the dart lines and fold the fabric right sides together so that the dart markings line up. Sew the dart in two steps, **starting from the center each time and working toward the points;** begin the second line of stitching so that it **overlaps the first for ¼–⅜" (5–10mm), as shown.** To allow the dart to be pressed to the side, **snip it horizontally at the center almost to the stitching line.** Depending on the width of the dart, it may be necessary to cut it vertically toward each point as well.

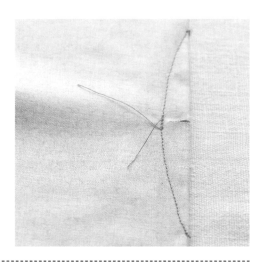

>> Always press darts FROM THE WRONG SIDE, since otherwise you may end up with shiny areas on the fabric.

specialized stitching lines

At certain times a special type of stitching line or seam is required to stabilize a piece of fabric or to sew two pieces together correctly.

EASE STITCHING

To connect two edges of slightly different lengths (for example, a sleeve cap in a set-in sleeve to the armhole), the **longer piece** must be **made slightly smaller** beforehand with the help of ease stitching. On pieces with **only a very small difference in size,** such as the back piece on a shoulder seam, it may be sufficient to merely pin the pieces together and skip the ease stitching. To ease stitch, reduce the top thread tension slightly. Stitch using a **long (about 6 spi*, or 4mm-long) straight stitch** directly next to the seam line; do not secure stitching at the beginning or end. Pull on the bobbin thread until the additional width is drawn in evenly and any matching symbols line up correctly. (Usually the longer edge is pinned to the shorter one before the bobbin thread is pulled.) The fabric will be slightly distorted, but **should not be allowed to form gathers or tiny folds.** Once the seam is stitched, **remove the ease stitching.**
*stitches per inch *(see pages 12–13, number 6)*

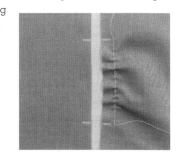

> **!** GATHERING will turn out more **EVENLY** if you sew a line of **EASE STITCHING** at ¹⁄₁₆–⅛" (2–3mm) on each side of the gathering line.

STAYSTITCHING

If staystitching is done on a single layer of fabric, for example, on a slit, neckline, or armhole, it is to **prevent the fabric from stretching out of shape while it is worked further.** Staystitching can also reinforce completed seams at points that will be heavily stressed. This may also be referred to as reinforcement stitching.
If a **fabric edge is to be stabilized,** sew with a normal straight stitch of about 13 spi (2mm long) next to the seam line within the seam allowance (as shown). To **strengthen an existing seam,** stitch directly next to the existing stitching using a slightly shorter straight stitch.

UNDERSTITCHING

To keep a facing from **rolling to the right side,** such as on a neckline or arm opening, the opening may be topstitched *(see page 17)* from the right side. If a visible stitching line is not desired, however, you'll need to **understitch the facing.** Sew the facing (shown here in light blue) to the main piece right sides together. Trim seam allowances, snip or notch curves, and press them toward the facing with the facing flipped upward. **Stitch the facing from the right side directly next to the seam line,** catching the seam allowances in the stitching. Turn the facing to the inside and press.

>  IF YOU NEED TO SEW MULTIPLE PIECES together in a row, you can save time and thread by feeding the pieces through one after the other without breaking the thread each time. Snip the thread between the pieces after you are finished stitching all of them.

facings

A facing is a piece of fabric that lines and finishes outer raw edges such as at necklines or arm openings. Depending on the shape of the edge, the facing may be part of the main piece or cut out separately.

OUTER EDGE WITH APPLIED FACING

For rounded or diagonal edges a facing is cut separately. (On some patterns, the facing will not be a separate pattern piece and instead will be indicated as a section of the main pattern piece. Cut the facing and interfacing with seam allowances all around (if not already included). Apply interfacing to the wrong side of the facing.

1 In cases where a collar will not reach to the end of the front edge, for example, when there are *lapels (see page 208)*, pin the facing right sides together along the edges of the main piece and **stitch to the marking** (collar start point). Trim seam allowances and corners and press them apart.

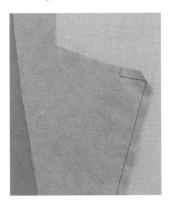 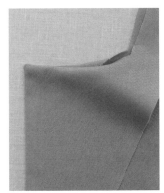

2 The opening edge of the garment is shown **from the right side** with the (still unfinished) facing applied and turned to the wrong side.

! AS A RULE, facings are cut out along the grain line to match the main fabric and are REINFORCED ON THE WRONG SIDE WITH INTERFACING to give the garment edges additional structure.

! ON UNLINED GARMENTS, the outer edges of the facing must be finished to avoid fraying.

OUTER EDGE WITH EXTENDED FACING

For straight edges on blouses and jackets, facings are often included as part of the main pattern piece and need only to be turned under to the wrong side. The facing will extend from the front opening edge and needs to include seam allowances (if not already included on the pattern). If the neckline will not have a collar, the back neckline will have an applied facing, as shown in step 1.

1 Apply interfacing to the wrong side of the facing sections and stitch, right sides together, at the shoulder seam. Press the seam allowances open and finish the edges if needed. **With right sides together, pin the facing onto the neckline edge and stitch;** the shoulder seams will lie on top of each other. Trim seam allowances and corners and snip curved sections if necessary.

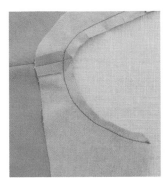 

2 Turn the facing to the inside and **tack it down by hand at the shoulder seams**; press.

! ON TOPS MADE FROM LIGHTWEIGHT FABRIC, an extended facing is often folded in double, in which case NO INTERFACING IS NEEDED. Facings must be completed before topstitching the front edges.

NECKLINE WITH SHAPED FACING

Round, oval, square, or V-shaped necklines may be finished with a shaped facing piece or facing strip. These facings will **usually be 1¼–2" (3–5cm) wide**, are easy to make, and provide a clean finish to the opening. If the facing consists of two pieces (front and back of garment), place the pieces right sides together and stitch at the shoulder seams. Press the seam allowances open and finish the edges. With **thick or heavy fabrics** the facing is often made from a bias strip, as that adds less bulk.

1 With right sides together, pin the facing to the neckline. Shoulder seams and center fronts and backs should line up; stitch. **Trim the seam allowances, snipping as needed.**

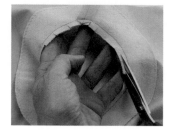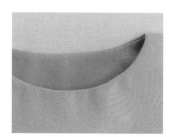

2 Understitch the facing (*see page 202*), or turn it to the inside and topstitch it from the right side. **Tack down the facing by hand on the inside at the shoulder seams; press.**

NECKLINE WITH COMBINED FACING

On sleeveless garments without collars, facings for the neckline and arm openings are usually made as a single piece, especially in cases where narrow shoulder straps would cause two separate facings to overlap. Apply facing pieces to the wrong sides of the facing pieces.

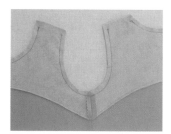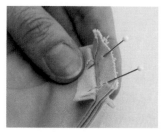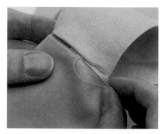

1 Sew the garment together at the side seams and press seam allowances open; do the same on the facing pieces. Finish seam allowance edges (*see page 102*) on all pieces, if needed. With right sides together, pin the facing to the garment along the neck and arm openings and **stitch**, *except at the shoulder seams* (see markings in photograph). Trim the seam allowances, snipping where necessary.

2 Turn the facing to the inside. **Pin the shoulder seams on the garment (only) right sides together** and stitch.

3 Working from the wrong side (inside), trim the facing shoulder seam allowances to about ¼" (6mm) and fold them under so that the folded edges abut at the seamline; **hand stitch the folded edges. Tack down the facing on the inside of the garment at the side seams,** making sure the stitching is not visible on the right side. Topstitch edges from the right side, if desired; press.

neckline *treatments*

Necklines are among the most noticeable details on a garment. In addition to clean necklines with faced finishes *(see page 204)* there are many other ways to finish necklines, from simple to complex. Some of the most common approaches are described here.

COLLARS

There are many different styles of collars, but all the variations are based on three basic shapes: **rolled, flat, and standing**. Rolled collars include shirt collars, shawl collars, and lapel collars; these stand up at the neckline and roll over toward the back. Flat collars are made without a separate collar band and lie flat against the garment; examples include Peter Pan collars and sailor collars. A basic standing collar (sometimes called a Mandarin collar) is easy to sew and consists of a narrow strip of fabric. Wide standing collars, such as turtlenecks, are folded to the outside.

- -

SEWING COLLARS

On **rolled collars** (for example, shirt collars and lapel collars), **the under collar should be cut about ¼" (6mm) smaller than the upper collar,** so that the upper collar will fall better due to its additional depth. The **type of interfacing** is determined by the fabric and style of the collar, and dictates how stiff or soft the collar will be. Usually the under collar is interfaced, but on lighter fabrics it may be preferable to interface the upper collar so that seams will not show through. If the collar is intended to be very stiff, all pieces should be interfaced. Pattern instructions will usually tell you which pieces of the collar should be interfaced, and will provide guidance on how to attach the collar.

1 Trim the corners of the interfacing so that they will just be caught in the eventual seams, then apply the interfacing to the wrong side of the appropriate collar piece(s). Place the collar pieces right sides together, pin, and stitch. The **long attachment edge you'll attach to the neckline remains open. Grade the seam allowances** so that the wider part is on the upper side; snip or notch curved edges as needed. Press seam allowances open.

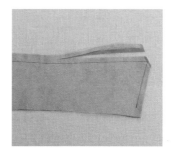

2 Turn the collar right side out and **use a point turner to carefully push out the corners;** press. Make sure that the seam line remains on the under collar side, directly next to the fold, **so that it will not be visible from the right side.** If desired, topstitch the finished collar edges near the edges or anywhere up to ¼" (6mm) away.

! **A COLLAR USUALLY CONSISTS OF TWO PIECES:** the visible upper collar and the unseen under collar (sometimes called the collar facing). **IF IT IS MADE FROM ONE PIECE,** it will be folded in half.

! **BEFORE ATTACHING A COLLAR,** complete any darts and seams that end at the neckline and sew a line of *staystitching (see page 202)* along the neckline edge. Any zippers in that area should also be inserted beforehand. Seam allowances on curved necklines should be snipped, if needed.

! **IF YOU ALTER THE WIDTH** of a neckline, you must change the shape of the collar accordingly.

» **THE SEAM** on a neckline is best ironed using a tailor's ham, rolled-up towel, or sleeve board.

» **COLLAR POINTS** will turn out better if you work **A SMALL DIAGONAL STITCH** across the pointed ends when sewing the pieces together. This is especially true when working with heavier fabrics.

! WHEN SEWING COLLAR PIECES TOGETHER, work all the way to the edges if the collar will later be sewn on through all thicknesses (upper collar and under collar), as on a Peter Pan collar. ON A LAPEL COLLAR, STITCH ONLY TO THE MARKINGS AT THE ATTACHMENT SEAM LINE.

» TO AVOID A VISIBLE ATTACHMENT SEAM LINE when using bias strips, work as follows: with right sides together, lay the flat strip along the collar edge, with the raw edges along the neckline aligned, then stitch. TRIM SEAM ALLOWANCES. Press the strip to the inside, then turn it under and stitch the raw edge.

» Use a shorter stitch length WHEN SEWING COLLAR PIECES TOGETHER around rounded edges; the finished collar edge will look better.

FLAT COLLARS

One of the best-known flat collars is the **Peter Pan collar**. It is easy to sew and is often finished with a shaped facing *(see page 204)* or a bias strip. If the garment has a **center back opening**, as described here, the collar is made in two pieces; when there is a **front opening**, it is worked as a single piece.

 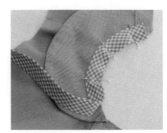 

1 Variation using a bias strip to finish: With right sides together, stitch the upper and under collar pieces together *(see page 205)*, **all the way to the outer edges**, leaving the attachment edges unstitched. Trim seams, clip corners, turn the collar right side out, and press. Repeat for the other upper collar and under collar. Overlap the two finished collar pieces at the center front, and **baste the overlapping seam allowances** or secure them with adhesive tape. Place the collar, upper collar facing up, on the right side of the neckline. **Turn the facings at the center back opening to the right side and lay them over the ends of the collar, as shown.** Baste the collar to the neckline using long machine or hand stitches. Trim seam allowances, clipping corners diagonally.

2 Make a 1⅛" (3cm)-wide bias strip *(see page 258)*, with the length equal to the neckline circumference minus about ¼" (5mm) *(see page 258)*, and press the strip in half lengthwise, wrong sides together. Pin the bias strip along the neckline collar so that the **folded edge of the strip lies over the seam line** (as shown), then stitch through all layers. Trim all seam allowances except the upper bias strip seam allowance.

3 Turn the facing to the inside. **Fold under the upper bias strip seam allowance** and stitch it down with hand stitches, or topstitch. Press.

STANDING COLLARS

Standing collars may be cut as one piece or can be made of an upper collar and an under collar. They are usually **straight, although two-piece versions can be curved,** as when part of a collar band is combined with a shirt collar. On **one-piece collars** made from fabrics that are not too thick, the entire wrong side is interfaced; on **two-piece versions,** the upper side should be interfaced. *Sew on the collar (see page 205),* **stopping at the marked seam line on the attachment edge** when sewing the two pieces together. Press under the inside attachment edge on the under collar. The easiest standing collar to sew is one in which the **ends of the collar align with the shirt opening edges** (as shown here).

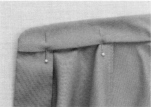

1 Snip the seam allowances on the neckline edge so that the collar will fit correctly. **Pin the upper collar to the neckline edge, right sides together,** and stitch. Grade seam allowances and clip corners diagonally.

2 Turn the collar to the right side (outside). Press the seam allowances open, and then up inside the collar. **Pin the folded edge of the under collar over the attachment seam** line and sew it down by hand, or topstitch around all edges from the right side, thereby catching in the folded bottom edge of the under collar.

3 **The standing collar** as seen from the right side. The pattern may call for a fastener of some type at the overlapping ends.

SHIRT COLLAR WITH COLLAR BAND

This collar, also called a **convertible collar,** is a type of **extended standing collar** and is used on blouses and shirts. The collar band is usually worked as a separate piece, but sometimes may be cut in one piece with the rest of the collar. As with other collars, it has an **upper collar and an under collar** and is interfaced in the same way (see above).

1 *Sew the collar (page 205, steps 1 and 2).* Place the collar band pieces right sides together and sandwich the collar between them, aligning raw edges. Place the collar between the collar placement symbols. **The interfaced collar pieces should be on the bottom, facing down.** Stitch the collar band pieces together, through all layers, all the way to the attachment edge, as shown, **Grade the seam allowances** and clip the corners diagonally. Press under the seam allowance on the under collar side of the band, as shown.

2 Turn the collar band over, then, **with right sides together, pin the upper collar side of the band (unpressed edge) to the neckline of the garment,** and stitch as you would a standing collar (above).

3 **Topstitch** the collar band **from the right side.**

4 The finished **shirt collar.**

» COLLAR BANDS can also be applied in reverse order by first SEWING THE WRONG SIDE OF THE UNDER COLLAR TO THE RIGHT SIDE OF THE NECKLINE, then turning under the seam allowance on the upper collar and topstitching it down from the right side.

NOTCHED/LAPEL COLLARS

Lapel collars (also called notched collars) are often found on blazers, jackets, and coats and come in different widths and lengths that vary according to fashion trends. They can be created in various ways. Here we describe a version on a blouse with a **square neckline and a neckline facing**; the collar attachment is done in two steps.

! If a garment WILL NOT BE LINED, the RAW EDGES OF THE FACING MUST BE FINISHED.

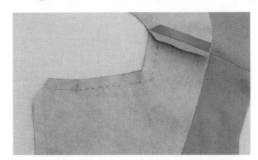

1 Apply interfacing to the wrong side of the neckline facing pieces, then **pin them, right sides together, to the front opening edges** of the garment. Stitch the facing and front opening edges together up to the collar attachment marking point, as shown *(see page 203)*. Then stitch the front and back together at the shoulder seams.

2 *Make the collar (see page 205, steps 1 and 2).* With right sides together, pin and sew the attachment edge of the under collar (only) to the faced neckline edge **between the collar attachment point mark and the horizontal marking at the notch** (on the neckline between the arrows). (In the photo at left, the attached facing and the shoulder seam are visible.) Snip the seam allowance of the front piece at the corner up to the attachment seam line (behind the right arrow).

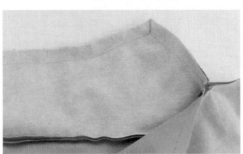

3 Snip the seam allowances on the neckline. With right sides together, **pin the remainder of the under collar attachment edge to the neckline** and stitch between the marked horizontal lines. Attach the upper collar to the facings the same way, in two steps.

4 Press seam allowances open, then flat. Pin the attachment seams together between the markings and stitch through all layers directly adjacent to the seam (in the seam allowance), then grade the seam allowances. **Turn the lapels and press the facing to the back.** Tack down the facings at the shoulder seams. If the garment will be unlined, **finish the facing edges.**

5 **Topstitch the collar** from the right side, if desired.

PLACKET NECKLINE

Some tops and dresses that do not open completely down the front will call for a **separately attached button placket**; it serves as both a closure and a finishing element. It can be used on garments **with or without collars** or neckbands. It is important to transfer all placket pattern markings carefully to achieve good results. The version shown here is on a **faced neckline.**

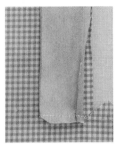

1 Mark the placket centerline on the garment and *stay stitch* (*see page 202*). Cut down the marked centerline, stopping ½–⅝" (10–15mm) before the bottom, and then snip diagonally to the bottom corners, creating a triangle. For the plackets, cut **two fabric strips** the same length as the opening and twice as wide, plus seam allowances all around. Depending on the fabric type, you may want to interface one lengthwise half of each strip on the wrong side. Fold each strip in half lengthwise, wrong sides together, and **stitch across the upper (short) end to the vertical seam line**; trim the seam allowance, clipping corners on the diagonal. Fold the long edge of the non-interfaced half of the placket to the wrong side and trim (the placket on the left shows the bottom side, the placket on the right the top).

2 Turn plackets right side out and press. **Right sides together, pin the raw edge of an interfaced placket to the opening edge on the garment** and stitch, ending exactly at the bottom corner marking. Repeat for the other placket on the other side of the opening edge. (If you sew the plackets on with the wrong side of the garment piece facing up, you can use the stay stitching as a guideline.) Trim the seam allowances.

3 On the left placket (as viewed from the right side—outside—of the garment), fold under the lengthwise seam allowance, wrong sides together, then stitch across the lower short edge; trim the seam allowance and snip the corner diagonally. **Turn the placket right side out.**

4 Fold the plackets over the opening and press the seam allowances inside the plackets. On the wrong side (inside), **pin the folded lengthwise placket edges over the attachment seams and sew down by hand,** or topstitch close to all edges from the right side. (If your placket buttons, this is the stage when you should make your buttonholes.)

5 Pin and sew down the **triangular piece at the bottom edge** of the left placket (viewed from the wrong side); finish edges.

6 Fold down the placket with the finished bottom edge and **hand stitch the two abutted lower edges together.**

7 **The placket viewed from the right side.** If desired, topstitch the placket edges from the right side and add **fasteners,** such as snaps. If the **placket is to be fastened with buttons and buttonholes,** it is best to create the buttonholes at step 4.

❗ ON STRETCH FABRICS it is a good idea to REINFORCE THE PLACKET ALONG THE MARKING LINES WITH HEM TAPE applied to the wrong side; iron the tape onto the seam allowance.

❗ FOR A MAN'S SHIRT, work the placket in mirror image to these instructions.

» WITH LIGHTWEIGHT FABRIC, you can sew the triangular allowances at the bottom of each placket together and FINISH them together (see step 5). This will eliminate the need for steps 3 and 6. This is INADVISABLE FOR HEAVY FABRICS, however, as it will create bulk at the bottom of the placket.

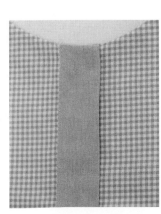

ELASTIC NECKBAND

On T-shirts and tops made of stretch fabrics, the necklines are often finished with a similarly stretchy band. It must be **wide enough to fit comfortably over the head**. The shoulder seams are sewn first and the raw edges finished. **The band is not reinforced with interfacing.**

! WHEN CHOOSING FABRIC FOR A NECKBAND, make sure it returns to its original shape after being stretched. You can also purchase READY-MADE BANDS, which are available in different lengths and widths.

! An overlock stitch is best FOR FINISHING AN ELASTIC NECK EDGE. If your machine does not have an overlock stitch, you can use an elastic/stretch stitch OR A NARROW ZIGZAG STITCH.

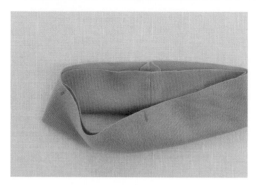

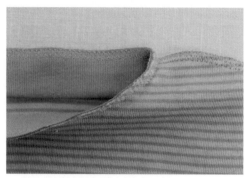

1 Cut a fabric strip on the bias (crosswise to the fabric grain): it should be twice the width of the finished band and, depending on elasticity, an inch or so (a few centimeters) shorter than the neckline circumference. **With right sides together, sew the strip together at the short end using a stretch stitch.** Trim and press seam allowances and clip corners diagonally. Fold the strip in half lengthwise with wrong sides together. Divide and mark both the band and the neckline **into quarters.**

2 With the wrong side of the garment facing out, place the band along the neckline, right sides together, and pin at the markings (and in between markings as needed). Stitch through all layers using a stretch or an overlock stitch; **stretch the band slightly to fit the neckline** as you go. Finish the seam allowances together and press the seam toward the garment.

3 Turn the garment right side out and **topstitch from the right side close to the attachment seam, if desired.**

faced yokes

Yokes can be made in various shapes and constitute a separate piece on blouses and shirts. The yoke spans the shoulder blades and often reaches over to the front of the garment (in which case there will be no shoulder seams). If the yoke is faced, the inside piece (that is, the facing) may be cut from the main fabric or from lining.

FACED YOKE WITHOUT SHOULDER SEAMS

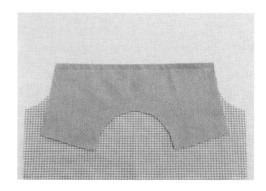

1 Lay the facing (shown here in solid blue) onto the outer yoke piece, right sides together, with the upper edge of the garment back inserted in between the facing and the yoke; the raw **edges of all three pieces are aligned.**

2 Pin all three layers together and stitch. **Grade seam allowances, leaving the yoke seam allowance widest.**

3 Press the yoke and facing upward. Topstitch close to the attachment seam line from the right side of the garment, if desired. **Pin the right side of the facing to the wrong side of the upper edges of the garment fronts** and stitch. Press seam allowances toward the facing.

4 Press under the unstitched front seam allowances on the yoke, then trim them; **pin the folded edges over the attachment seams of the facing** and topstitch close to the folded edges.

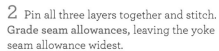 **AFTER STEP 1 YOU MAY** first stitch the yoke right sides together onto the front. On the wrong side (inside), handsew the folded-under seam allowance of the facing so that no seam is visible from the right side.

sleeves

Sleeves contribute a lot to the overall look of a garment, and their styling tends to vary with fashion trends. Whatever the style, sleeves usually consist of one or two pieces and are either set into an armhole or applied while still flat. Simple kimono sleeves are cut directly onto the front and back pieces of a garment.

GENERAL GUIDELINES FOR ATTACHING SLEEVES

Various matching symbols on your pattern will help you to set in sleeves properly (and on the correct side), so all markings should be transferred carefully to your fabric pieces. To discourage armholes from stretching out, **especially when using stretch fabrics**, the **seam line may be reinforced all around** with seam tape *(see page 214, kimono sleeves)*. A line of **reinforcement stitching or stretch stitching** can also help to stabilize armholes; sew these directly adjacent to the seam line, within the seam allowance *(see page 202)*.

If your fabric tends to **fray**, seams may be bound or worked as *French seams (see page 90)*. Before being sewn in, the sleeve should be basted along the arm opening. It is advisable to try on the garment to check the placement and drape of the sleeves. **Sleeves should always be basted and sewn from the sleeve side.**

! On SLEEVELESS GARMENTS we recommend you finish the armhole WITH A FACING *(see page 204)*, as this will create less bulk than a hem.

SET-IN SLEEVES

The most common sleeve shape may be made in **one or two pieces** and may have a **smooth, gathered, or pleated cap**; whatever the style, the method for setting in the sleeve is the same. Shoulder and side seams on the garment are completed first.

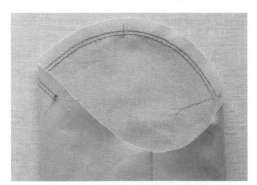

1 The **curved edge (sleeve cap)** is usually longer than the corresponding armhole edge on the garment, and **must therefore be ease stitched**. Sew two lines of 6–4 spi (4–6mm-long) stitches between the markings on the sleeve cap; leave the thread ends hanging. Fold the sleeve right sides together and stitch the sleeve seam (that is, from the bottom of the sleeve to the underarm). Press seam allowances open and finish all raw edges. Turn the sleeve right side out.

2 Place the sleeve in the armhole, right sides together; the wrong side of the garment faces out. The sleeve underarm seam and the garment side seam should align; **pin together at matching symbols first, then around the rest of the armhole edge.** Pull on the bobbin threads of the ease stitching **until the extra width in the cap is distributed evenly between the symbols.**

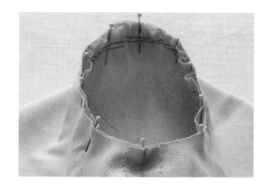

3 Stitch the seam, starting at the garment side seam. Smooth the excess sleeve cap fullness by hand as you go to prevent wrinkles from forming. After you've sewn in the sleeve, remove the ease stitching and, if needed, sew a **reinforcement seam** just inside the first seam. Trim seam allowances, snipping diagonally at the ends of the side and sleeve seams, then **finish the seam allowances together.** To preserve a rounded cap, do not press the seam allowances to one side or another, but rather just carefully press them open and flat using a sleeve board.

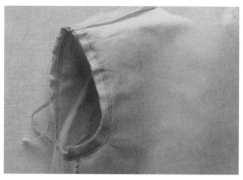

! DEPENDING ON THE SHAPE OF THE SLEEVE CAP, or, more precisely, if the cap is not centered in the armhole opening, the side and shoulder seams of the garment must be sewn before you set in the sleeves.

FLAT SLEEVES

Some types of shirts and children's pullovers have sleeves with relatively **flat, centered caps.** These are sewn to the front and back of the garment after the shoulder seam is completed, but **before the side and sleeve seams are sewn.**

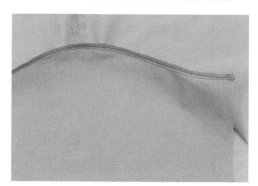

1 Pin the sleeve to the garment, right sides together, **distributing any slight fullness in the cap evenly,** and stitch. A **reinforcement seam** may be sewn close to the first seam, within the seam allowance. Trim the seam allowance and **finish the raw edges together;** press the seam allowance toward the sleeve.

2 Bring the front and back together, right sides facing, and **sew the side and sleeve seams in one step.** Trim all seam allowances and finish the raw edges together.

» AFTER SEWING THE UPPER SLEEVE EDGE, you can make a felled seam (*see page 90*) or finish the seam allowance edges by pressing them toward the garment and **TOPSTITCHING FROM THE RIGHT SIDE,** using contrasting thread if desired.

RAGLAN SLEEVES

This comfortable style is **usually found on tees, coats, and jackets.** On children's clothes, **sportswear, and leisurewear** it is common for the sleeves to be in a contrasting color. Raglan sleeves may be **made of one or two pieces,** and the attachment seams run **from the front and back neckband down to the side seams** at the underarm. Some **single-piece raglan sleeves** are rounded at the shoulder and shaped with a vertical dart *(see page 200).* On two-piece raglan **sleeves,** the upper sleeve seams are completed first; leave the underarm seams unsewn for now.

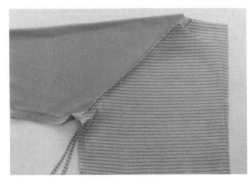

1 With right sides together, pin the sleeve (shown here in solid blue) to the **front and back arm opening edges, then stitch with the sleeve side facing up.** On stretch fabrics, trim the seam allowances, finish them together, and press the finished seam allowance toward the sleeve. With woven fabrics, press seam allowances apart and finish the edges separately.

2 Lay the shirt front and back with right sides together, and **sew the shirt side seams and sleeve underarm seams in one step.** Trim seam allowances and finish them together.

KIMONO SLEEVES

A **straight, wide sleeve** is typical on kimonos but is also found on other types of garments. Kimono sleeves are generally cut directly as part of the front and back pieces of a garment. Because of the rounding at the underarm, seam allowances should not be wider than ⅝" (1.5cm).

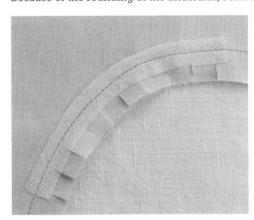

Place the front and back garment pieces with right sides together and stitch the upper sleeve/shoulder seam. **Depending on fabric type, it may be helpful to stabilize the underarm seam.** Iron on a 4–5" (10–12cm)-long piece of fusible reinforcement tape, centered along the seam line (there may be a line of stitching on the tape to guide you). Sew the side and sleeve seams in one step. Snip seam allowances at the underarm curve, press them open, and finish the raw edges. **On thin or stretchy fabrics,** the allowances may be trimmed and finished together, then pressed toward the garment back.

! A BATWING, OR DOLMAN SLEEVE, is a variation on the kimono sleeve. It is wide at the underarm but TAPERS TO A NARROW WRIST.

sleeve closures

Lower sleeve edges can take many shapes, from decorative to practical; but whatever the shape, the closure should match the overall style of the garment. Before cuffs or wristbands are attached, the sleeve seam must be finished and any pleats or gathers at the lower sleeve edge must be prepared.

SLEEVE SLITS

When a sleeve is finished with a cuff, it **requires a slit in the lower edge** to make the sleeve easy to get on and off. There are various ways to create slits; we show the most common ones here.

SLIT WITH BOUND EDGES

In this style (also known as a continuous bound placket), the **bound edges of the slit lie on top of each other.** Cut a strip of binding that is **twice the length of the slit and about 1–1½" (2.5–3.5cm) wide.** For thin, delicate fabrics, cut the strip along the straight grain line; for heavier fabrics or those that tend to fray, cut the strip on the bias *(see page 258).*

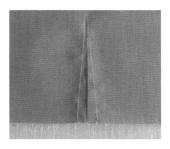  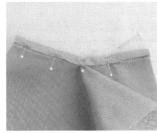

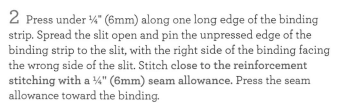

1 Mark the slit line at the bottom of the sleeve and stay stitch around it with small stitches (reinforcement stitching): **Start at the sleeve edge about ¼" (6mm) from the slit line** and work diagonally toward the top of the line. Make a crosswise stitch as close as possible to the top of the slit line, then sew back to the sleeve edge on the other side, mirroring the first side. Cut the slit.

2 Press under ¼" (6mm) along one long edge of the binding strip. Spread the slit open and pin the unpressed edge of the binding strip to the slit, with the right side of the binding facing the wrong side of the slit. Stitch **close to the reinforcement stitching with a ¼" (6mm) seam allowance.** Press the seam allowance toward the binding.

3 Fold the binding over the seam allowance to the right side of the sleeve, then pin the pressed edge of the binding so that it **covers the attachment seam;** stitch **close to the folded edge.**

4 On the inside of the sleeve, lay the bound edges together and **sew a small diagonal seam** at the center top of the binding. Press the bound edge on the upper part of the slit to the inside (overlap).

5 The bound slit as seen from the **right side.**

! IF YOU PREFER NOT TO HAVE A VISIBLE SEAM on a sleeve slit, first stitch the edging right sides together onto the slit edge, then FOLD THE EDGING UNDER AND SEW DOWN BY HAND ON THE INSIDE.

>> **WITH THIN FABRICS** we recommend you reinforce the lengthwise center of the facing on the wrong side with a stabilizer such as hem tape. **IF THE SLIT IS TO BE TAPERED,** sew diagonally toward the top and make a single stitch across the tip, as on a *slit with bound edges* (see page 215, photo 1).

>> ON A FINISHED **SLEEVE** with a hem you can retroactively reduce the width by **ADDING A PLEAT.** This style is attractive on pullovers and blouses and works best with light- to midweight fabrics. Try on the sleeve and pin a fold of the desired size, keeping in mind that your hand will need to fit through the reduced opening. **PRESS THE PLEAT BACK TOWARD THE SEAM.** Sew a large button through all layers, or several smaller buttons along the fold line.

FACED SLITS

Facing is a quick and simple method for finishing a slit; the **faced edges of the slit will abut.** It is appropriate for **all manner of cuff styles,** especially with heavily fraying or thick fabrics. With heavier fabrics, make the facing out of lining to prevent bulkiness.

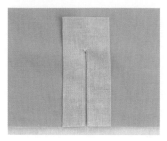  

1 Mark the slit line on the right side of the sleeve. Cut a facing strip that is 1½–2" (4–5cm) **wide and about 1¼" (3cm) longer** than the slit. Make a matching slit marking on the wrong side of the facing. Place the facing strip over the sleeve edge, **right sides together and with the slit markings aligned.** Stitch around the marking at a distance of ¹⁄₁₆" (2mm), using small stitches; work two to three crosswise stitches at the top of the slit. Cut the slit open with small, pointed scissors to about ¼" (5mm) before the tip, then snip diagonally toward the top corners, creating a small triangle.

2 **Pull the facing to the wrong side and press thoroughly.** Finish the facing edges and **topstitch close to** the slit edge from the right side, if desired. You can also fold under the facing edges and catch them in the topstitching.

3 The finished faced slit from the right side.

SLIT AT SEAMLINE

This is a quickly executed slit that requires no cutting.

1 Sew the sleeve seams, **leaving the bottom 2¾–3" (7–8cm) open.** Finish the seam allowances or press them under and topstitch. The seam allowances may also be fastened down with hem tape next to the slit.

2 Topstitch the slit from the right side. **For added stability, make a bar tack at the top edge** by sewing several stitches back and forth in one spot.

SLEEVE PLACKET

A classic slit treatment with an underlap and an overlap is typical on **men's shirts** but is also found on **blouses**; the finished width is about 1" (2.5cm). The placket can be made from the same fabric as the garment, or in a contrasting color. Make sure to work the plackets on the left and right sleeves in **mirror image.**

1 Cut 3" (7.5cm)-wide fabric strips for the overlap (cut two) and underlap (cut two); cut the underlap strip ⅝" (1.5cm) longer than the slit and the overlap strip 2¼" (5.5cm) longer than the slit. Include seam allowances of ⅝" (1.5cm) at the tops and ½" (1.3cm) along the long sides. Fold the **underlap** (left in photo) lengthwise with *wrong* sides together. Fold the **overlap** (right in photo) *right* sides together and sew a point at the top (the dotted lines indicate the slit outline). Trim the seam allowances beyond the markings as shown, then turn the strip right side out.

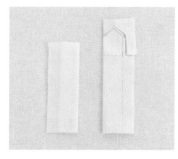

2 **Trim and press under the seam allowance along one long edge** of both the overlap and the underlap. Mark the slit line on the right side of the fabric—the distance between the vertical lines is 1" (2.5cm)—and topstitch all around *(see page 202, reinforcement stitching).* **Cut the slit line with small, pointed scissors up to ⅝" (1.5cm) from the top; snip diagonally from there to the corners,** creating a small triangle.

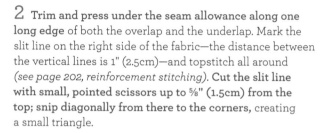

3 Press the triangle up toward the right side of the sleeve. Pin the **wrong side of the left (bottom) slit edge to the right side of the underlap's open raw edge** and stitch along the reinforcement stitching with a ½" (1.3cm) seam allowance. Trim the seam allowance.

4 Press the underlap over the seam allowance to the right side of the sleeve; pin, then topstitch close to the folded edge. Trim the top end of the underlap to a point. Pin the **wrong side of the right (top) slit edge to the right side of the overlap's open raw edge** and stitch with a ½" (1.3cm) seam allowance. Trim the seam allowance.

5 Press the overlap over the seam allowance to the right side of the sleeve and **pin so that it covers the attachment seam line,** then **topstitch in the direction of the arrows:** across the top of the slit, then up around the point and down the right edge, being careful not to catch the underlap as you are sewing downward beyond the crosswise arrow.

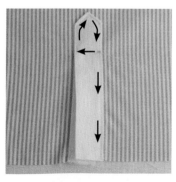

» ON A LONG PLACKET you can work a buttonhole in the center of the overlap and a button on the underlap, or add a no-sew snap.

CUFFS

A cuff consists of an upper side and a bottom side, and can be constructed from one or two pieces. Prepare the sleeve with an appropriate slit opening (*see pages 215–217*).

! On **MENSWEAR SHIRT CUFFS** the seam allowance on the interfaced upper side is pressed under, as those cuffs are attached to the sleeve in a different sequence. **ON FRENCH CUFFS** the bottom side is interfaced, since that side faces out when the cuffs are folded.

SINGLE-PIECE CUFFS

Straight cuffs with a classic width of 1¼–2" (3–5cm) are usually cut out as a single piece, as are wider, French (folded) cuffs.

1 **Apply interfacing to the wrong side of** one lengthwise half (the eventual upper side). Press under the seam allowance on the lengthwise edge of the bottom side of the cuff.

2 Fold the cuff right sides together; the seam allowance of the upper side will stick out past the bottom side's pressed edge. **Pin the short sides and stitch together.** Trim seam allowances and clip corners diagonally, then turn the cuff right side out and press. Repeat for the other cuff.

TWO-PIECE CUFFS

Cuffs can be made of two straight or diagonally cut pieces. Diagonal (pointed) cuffs are usually more than 2⅜" (6cm) wide and taper toward the wrist.

» **TWO-PIECE CUFFS** can be embellished with narrow piping inserted within the seam. You can make piping yourself (*see page 120*).

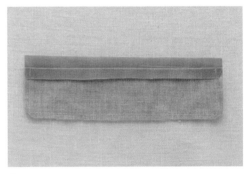

1 **Apply interfacing to the wrong side** of one cuff piece (the eventual upper side). On the remaining cuff piece, press under the seam allowance along one long side.

2 Pin the two cuff pieces right sides together and stitch, **starting and stopping at the seam line** of the cuff's attachment edge. Trim seam allowances and clip corners diagonally. Turn the cuff right side out and press. Repeat for the other cuff.

ATTACHING CUFFS

Depending on the type of slit used and the desired closure, cuff ends either are aligned with the slit opening edges or have an extended, underlapped tab on one side. French cuffs are extended at both ends.

- -

SIMPLE, ALIGNED CUFFS

Prepare the sleeve with a bound edge slit (*see page 215*) or a sleeve placket (*see page 217*). When finished, both sides of the cuff will be **aligned with the finished slit edges.**

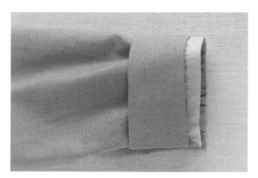 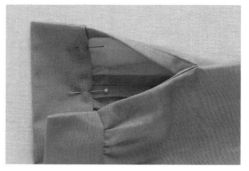

1 Apply interfacing to the wrong side of the upper side of the cuff. With right sides together, pin the upper side of the cuff to the **lower sleeve edge with raw edges aligned;** stitch. Trim seam allowances and clip corners diagonally at the ends of the vertical seams.

2 Turn up the cuff and press the seam allowances toward the cuff, then **pin the cuff's folded edge over the attachment seam line** or secure it with adhesive tape. Sew down the cuff's folded edge (on the inside of the sleeve) with hand stitches, or **topstitch it close to all cuff edges,** from the right side.

- -

CUFFS WITH AN UNDERLAP EXTENSION

Prepare the sleeves with a bound edge or faced slit. Prepare a one- or two-piece cuff, **leaving the short ends open.**

 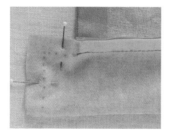 

1 Pin the interfaced upper side of the cuff, **right sides together,** to the lower sleeve edge. On the rear slit edge, the cuff extends past the slit edge (the underlap). On the front edge of the slit, only the cuff's seam allowance extends past the edge. **Stitch the upper edge of the cuff to the sleeve.**

2 Fold the cuff right sides together; pin the short ends **together and stitch, continuing around the corner to the attachment seam line on the underlap extension** (see dotted line). Trim seam allowances and clip corners diagonally.

3 Turn the cuff right side out and press the seam allowances toward the cuff. **Pin the folded inner edge at the attachment seam,** or secure with adhesive tape. Sew down the inner edge by hand, or **topstitch close to the fold around all cuff edges,** from the right side.

- -

! MENSWEAR CUFFS are attached in the opposite order from women's cuffs. **FIRST THE UNDERSIDE** of the cuff is sewn, right side to wrong side, onto the lower sleeve edge. **THEN THE UPPER SIDE OF THE CUFF** is pinned to the right side of the sleeve and topstitched close to the edges all around from the right side.

! ON A FRENCH CUFF, both ends are extended. Buttonholes are made in the extensions and the cuffs are fastened with cuff links. You can make your own cufflinks by joining two buttons with a thread shank (*see page 236, two-hole button*).

OTHER SLEEVE FINISHES

Beyond cuffs, there are many other ways to finish a sleeve edge. It is crucial to **consider your fabric's characteristics** when choosing a sleeve treatment to avoid bulky seams. Make sure to mark the sleeve length at the right point to work out correctly with your chosen finish.

SLEEVE HEM WITH ELASTIC BAND

For this type of stretchy sleeve hem, a ¼–⅜" (5–10mm)-wide elastic band is typically used. **The casing should be only about ⅟₁₆" (2mm) wider than the band** to discourage the band from twisting. A seam allowance of ¼" (5mm) is sufficient.

On the lower sleeve edge, mark the seam allowance and then the casing depth, pressing each to the inside (wrong side) in turn. Pin the folded seam allowance edge and stitch, **leaving an opening at the sleeve seam over the seam allowances.** Topstitch close to the lower folded edge from the right side. Cut the elastic to the desired length plus ⅝" (1.5cm) and pull it through the casing using a small safety pin or bodkin. Overlap the elastic ends by ⅝" (1.5cm) and, **to ensure a strong hold, stitch the elastic ends together in a square, then across the square in an X** (see page 261, reinforcing a strap attachment). Sew the opening closed, pulling the fabric flat at that point as you do so.

DARTED SLIT

This sleeve slit is appropriate for **especially narrow sleeves, for example, on suit jackets, coats, or dressy jackets.** The lower sleeve edge may be **hemmed, bound, or faced.** The slit may optionally be closed with **loop fasteners** (see page 234) or a **zipper** (see page 243, covered zipper).

1 Mark the dart on the bottom of the sleeve and fold the fabric right sides together so that the markings line up on top of each other. **Stitch from the crosswise marking to the tip,** securing the stitching at both ends. Snip the crosswise mark all the way up to the seam line, then **cut the dart up the middle (along the fold line)** from the lower edge to the crosswise marking.

2 Press the seam allowances to the sides; press the uncut part of the dart either flat or toward the front of the sleeve. **Trim the seam allowances to ⅝" (1.5cm)** and finish the edges if the sleeve will not be lined. Optionally, topstitch along the slit edges from the right side.

! ADDITIONAL SLEEVE FINISHES

The following methods can also be used to finish lower sleeve edges; general information about each method is found on the page indicated:

- Folded hem (see page 111)
- Visible or invisible faced hem (see page 112)
- Finishing with bias tape (see pages 103–104)
- Ruffle, single or double (see pages 118–119)

WRISTBANDS

Wristbands are sewn together at the short ends, so a **slit in the sleeve is not required.** Wristbands are popular on **children's clothing** and can be made from **either stretch or woven fabric.**

ELASTIC WRISTBANDS

This sleeve finish is appropriate for stretch fabrics such as **jersey and sweatshirt fabric.**

With right sides together, stitch the fabric strip for the wristband together at the short ends, using an elastic stitch (*see page 210, elastic neckband*). Trim seam allowances and press them open; clip corners diagonally. Fold the wristband in half lengthwise with wrong sides together; the wrong side of the sleeve is facing out. **Divide and mark both the band and the sleeve opening into fourths.** With right sides together, pin the band to the sleeve opening, starting by matching the markings. Stitch using an **elastic or overlock stitch, stretching the band as needed to fit the sleeve opening.** Finish the band and sleeve raw edges together.

>> Your wristbands will be finished LICKETY-SPLIT if you purchase ready-made elastic cuffs. Or try RECYCLING ORPHANED OR RETIRED SOCKS. Cut the leg bands to the desired size and sew to the lower sleeve edges.

INELASTIC/WOVEN WRISTBAND

If a wristband is made from an inelastic fabric, **the finished circumference must be large enough** to allow the wearer's hand to pass through. Apply interfacing to one lengthwise half of the band (the eventual upper side); on lightweight fabrics the entire band may be interfaced.

Fold under and press the seam allowance on the long lower (not interfaced) side of the band, then flip the seam allowance out again. Stitch the short ends of the band, right sides together; trim seam allowances, and press them open. **Pin the interfaced edge of the band along the sleeve opening, right sides together;** the band seam and the sleeve seam should be aligned. Stitch. Trim seam allowances and snip the ends of the band seam allowances diagonally. Press seam allowances toward the band. **Pin the folded bottom edge of the band over the attachment seam line on the inside,** or secure with adhesive tape. Hand stitch from the inside or **edgestitch from the right side.**

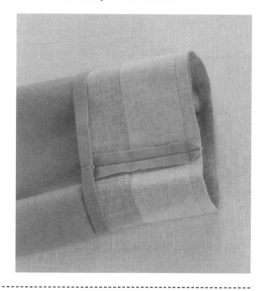

>> YOU CAN ALSO ATTACH THE WRISTBAND, once it has been connected into a circle, by sewing it right side to wrong side on the sleeve edge, then folding the cuff over the seam allowance and topstitching it from the right side.

comfortable waistbands

A waistband can serve as a focal point or can be inconspicuous, but it is always important for it to fit well and be comfortable. There are various techniques for creating a waistband, which can be cut straight or shaped to the body. It can close in front, in back, or at the side. An elastic waistband offers especially broad freedom of movement.

ALL ABOUT WAISTBANDS

The waistband should always be based on the **waist measurement**, and the remaining garment pieces should be adapted to that measurement. Do not excessively trim seam allowances in the waist area, or the band may pull apart. When using light- or medium-weight fabrics, trim waistband seam allowances to no less than ⅛" (3mm), and with heavy fabrics trim them to no less than ¼" (6mm).

When creating a **skirt with hanging loops**, attach these simultaneously with the waistband on the inside. Cut the hanging loops to end up about 3" (7–8cm) longer than the folded waistband height; fold them in half and place the raw ends flush with the top edge of the skirt at the inside side seams. Pin the loops in place on the seam allowances. **On lined skirts** place the loops over the lining and capture them when attaching the lining.

SHAPED WAISTBAND

When a waistband is **wider than 1½" (4cm)** it will often be fashioned as a shaped waistband. In order to conform better to the shape of the body, the pieces for the waistband are cut not at **straight angles but as gently curved lines.** If the band and facing (underside) are made of multiple pieces, they will be seamed together and the pieces for the outside waistband will be reinforced with interfacing before sewing.

  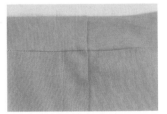

1 Place the waistband and facing with right sides together; pin and then sew around all non-attaching edges, **including the waistband tab to the point where it will attach to the garment (see arrow in photo).** Trim seam allowances and corners, clip into the seam allowances of any rounded edges, then press seam allowances open. Press up the seam allowance along the open edge of the inside facing.

2 Pin the front of the waistband along the garment waist edge, right sides together, then stitch. Grade seam allowances, trim corners, and press seams open. Continue following step 3 of the Straight Waistband *(see page 223).*

3 If desired, **topstitch all around the band.** Lastly, add a closure.

» ON A VERY WIDE WAISTBAND we recommend that you reinforce both the band and the facing with interfacing, so the waistband will remain sturdy.

! To avoid excess bulk WHEN USING HEAVY FABRICS, you should clean finish the bottom edge of the inside facing rather than fold it under. Pin the finished facing down or secure it with fabric adhesive tape, then sew from the right side directly in the ditch of the existing waistband attachment seam THROUGH ALL THICKNESSES, thereby catching the facing and securing it.

STRAIGHT WAISTBAND

The basic standard waistband for skirts and pants is usually worked in a width between 1–1½" (2.5–4cm). Since it must be **strong and stable,** the wrong side of the band fabric is reinforced with interfacing. There are specialized interfacings for this purpose; **premade waistband interfacing is** especially practical and comes in various styles and widths.

1 Cut the interfacing equal to the waist measurement plus about 1¾" (4.5cm). Of this, ⅝" (1.5cm) is for ease and 1⅛" (3cm) is to accommodate an overlapping tab closure. Press the interfacing onto the wrong side of the waistband fabric with the coated side facing down. Cut out the waistband along the edges of the interfacing, adding ½–⅝" (1–1.5cm) of plain (not interfaced) fabric at both short ends. **Pin the waistband to the waist edge, right sides together.** On one side the end extends past the edge by 1¼" (3cm) (the overlapping tab closure, see photo at right); on the other side only the seam allowance extends beyond the edge. Attach the band by sewing **exactly through the middle of the topmost row of perforations.**

2 Now fold the band lengthwise with right sides together, **pin the short edges,** and stitch together. On the side with the tab extension, **sew around the corner and over to the opening edge** of the garment. Grade seam allowances, trim corners, and press allowances open.

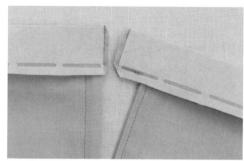

3 Turn the waistband right side out and press. **Fold up the bottom inside facing edge and pin it along the attachment seam** or use adhesive tape to secure it. On the inside, tack the facing by hand or machine stitch it from the right side through the ditch of the existing waistband attachment seam, thereby catching the waistband facing.

4 **Topstitch** around the finished waistband, if desired. Lastly, **add a closure.**

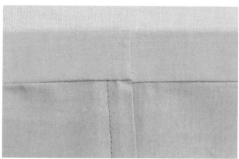

! Ready-made, easy-fold waistband interfacing is available with either different or equal-sized halves. **IF YOU ARE USING INTERFACING WHERE ONE SIDE IS NARROWER** by about ¹⁄₁₆–⅛" (2–3mm), that is the side along which the waistband should initially be attached to the garment.

» A STRAIGHT WAISTBAND can be worked more quickly if you **CUT ONE LONG EDGE ALONG THE SELVAGE OF THE FABRIC.** If the selvage is used as the lower edge of the waistband facing, it does not need to be finished and need only be folded under on the waistband tab. It can be sewn down from the right side through the ditch of the existing waistband attachment seam.

WAISTBAND WITH FACING

On a skirt or pair of pants where no waistband is visible, a facing will cover the raw edges on the inside. The facing may be extended (cut as part of the pattern pieces) or created separately, especially when the waistband is shaped. If a facing made from the main fabric would be too bulky, it must be made with lighter fabric. For a separately cut facing, include seam allowances and apply interfacing to the wrong side. Sew the facing pieces together and finish the lower edge.

1 Pin the facing **right sides together on the waistline edge** with the seam allowances at the short ends extending past the zipper opening edges; stitch. Grade seam allowances. Trim seam allowance corners diagonally at the vertical seams, and clip any curves.

2 Press the seam allowances toward the facing, then **understitch the facing** (see page 202). Fold under the seam **allowances** at the short ends of the waistband, pin the folded ends over the zipper seam allowance, and sew down to the zipper tape with hand stitches. Tack the **lower edge of the facing** by hand at the seams and darts.

3 The facing **cannot be seen** from the right side.

ELASTIC WAISTBAND

Garments with elastic waistbands are very comfortable to wear; the waist circumference is flexible due to the **elastic band concealed in the waistline casing.** The elastic waistband is used in children's clothing, sportswear, leisurewear, pajamas, and undergarments; it may also be used on blouses and shirts. **The casing should not be more than ¹⁄₁₆" (2mm) wider than the elastic band itself** to discourage the band from twisting. On pants and skirts an **elastic band can be combined with a flat waistband,** so that the elastic portion is limited to the back of the garment.

1 Mark the seam allowance and the casing fold line at the waistline edge, then press them under in that order. Pin down the lower folded edge and topstitch close to the edge, and then topstitch close to the fold at the upper casing edge, from the right side. Open one of the casing's side seams (on the inside) to the width of the elastic. Cut the elastic band to the desired finished length plus ⅝" (1.5cm) and pull the elastic through the casing with the help of a safety pin or bodkin. Overlap the elastic ends by ⅝" (1.5cm) and, **to ensure a strong hold, stitch the ends together in a square, then across the square in an X** (see page 261). Sew the side seam opening closed by hand.

2 **Distribute the fabric's fullness evenly** around the waistband, from the right side. To secure the elastic band and prevent it from twisting, you can sew vertically **through all thicknesses of the casing at the side seams.**

! To avoid creating excess bulk WHEN USING HEAVY FABRIC, THE LOWER SEAM ALLOWANCE IS NOT FOLDED UNDER, but rather finished and then stitched down on the inside.

» FOR A DRAWSTRING WAIST, make EYELETS AT CASING HEIGHT to the right and left side of center front. After the casing is sewn, pull the cord through one eyelet and around to the other; knot the ends or attach cord stoppers.

BELT LOOPS

Depending on the style of a garment, belt loops may be **very narrow to quite wide**. On **dresses, coats, and jackets** they are usually attached at the side seams. On **skirts and pants** they can be sewn in during waistband creation or may be applied afterward. They are generally made from the main garment fabric but can also be done in contrasting colors.

POSITIONING OF BELT LOOPS

Skirt (4 loops): two each in front and back, placed between the side and center or at the darts
Pants (5 loops): as with skirts, with an extra loop at the center back
Dress (2 loops): one at each side seam
Jacket, coat (2–3 loops): one at each side seam, optionally one at center back

CALCULATING BELT LOOP SIZE

For loops that will be **sewn in with the waistband or sewn on the side seams**, calculate loop length as follows: waistband width plus ¾–1" (2–2.5cm)—a ¼" (6mm) seam allowance at each short end, plus ¼–½" (6–10mm) to allow a belt to pull through easily. Loops that are **sewn onto a waistband** after the fact should be ⅝" (1cm) longer than the above. Increase seam allowance slightly when using **heavy fabric**.

MAKING BELT LOOPS

First cut a **long strip of fabric** (total length = length of one loop multiplied by the total number of loops required). The width should be double the desired finished width, plus seam allowances on the long sides.

1 Fold the strip in half lengthwise, right sides together; pin and stitch. **Move the seam to the middle** and press the seam allowances open.

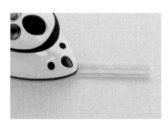
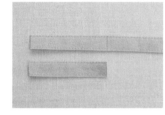

2 Turn the strip with a turning tool *(see page 262)* and **topstitch close to the edges**. Mark and cut the loops to the correct length.

SEWING BELT LOOPS INTO A WAISTBAND

With this method the belt loops are **attached at the waist edge before the waistband is sewn on**. Pin one end of each belt loop, right sides together, to the seam allowance of the waist edge at the desired locations. Apply the waistband, sandwiching the loops between the band and the waist edge, capturing the ends of the belt loops. Turn up each loop, **fold under the ¼" (6mm) seam allowance, and stitch in place close to the top edge of the waistband**. Loops may also be fastened with *bar tacks (see page 251)*.

ATTACHING BELT LOOPS TO A FINISHED GARMENT

Finish the garment completely and **position the belt loops at the desired points,** for example, at waist height at the side seam on a coat. If the **loops are being sewn onto a waistband,** fold under ¼" (6mm) at the **bottom of the loop** and pin (or secure with adhesive) ⅜" (1cm) below the lower waistband edge; stitch in place or use a bar tack *(see page 251)*. Lift **the other end of the loop** and attach it just underneath the top edge of the waistband in the same manner.

! **TRIPLE-LAYER BELT LOOPS** are common on **JEANS AND PANTS**. To make a belt loop, finish one long side of a fabric strip (three times as wide as the finished belt loop) with a zigzag or overlock stitch. Press under the unfinished edge and then the finished edge, then topstitch the strip close to the long edges. If you **CUT THE STRIPS ALONG A SELVAGE, FINISHING IS UNNECESSARY.**

» **BELT LOOPS** can be finished in **MANY WAYS.** For example, you could topstitch two lines down the center of the loop instead of stitching around its edges. Or use a decorative stitch, perhaps in a contrasting color.

! **TO SEW ON BELT LOOPS** made from heavy fabrics, it is best to use a **DENIM NEEDLE.** It is stronger and can sew through multiple layers better than a standard needle.

! **IF YOU ARE ATTACHING BELT LOOPS AFTER SEWING IS COMPLETE,** they can also be attached using a no-sew **RIVET,** if that matches the style of the garment. Punch a hole to start and then attach the rivet with the help of eyelet pliers.

sewing in linings

Lined garments are more stable and more durable. Additionally, garments made of coarser fabrics are more comfortable to wear when lined, and thinner fabrics are made less transparent. Thick linings, such as quilted linings, add extra warmth. Usually linings are prepared as a separate layer and sewn to the inside of a garment, so that no seams or raw edges are visible on the inside.

ALL ABOUT LININGS

Lining fabric should have **the same care requirements as the main fabric and usually match the color of the main fabric as well.** That said, a contrasting or patterned lining can create an attractive effect. It is best to buy your lining at the same time as your main fabric.

Lining should be **lighter in weight/thinner than the primary fabric** to avoid creating excess bulk. Garments made of stretch fabrics should have stretch linings.

Usually lining pieces are **cut from the same pattern pieces** as the main garment, **but without details** such as waistbands, facings, or pockets. Side seam pockets should be folded to the inside on **lining pattern pieces,** and the pattern pieces for hip yoke pockets should be taped together. *Important:* any alterations that were made to the main pattern **need to be reflected on the lining** as well.

On upper-body lining pieces an additional pleat at the center back may be added to allow better freedom of movement; **sleeve linings** may have gathering at the elbow.

The **fit of a garment should be tested** before a lining is sewn in.

LINING A SKIRT

Lined skirts drape better and are comfortable to wear. Complete the skirt except for the waistband and hem. **Lining pieces should be prepared: darts sewn and pressed** in the opposite direction from those in the main piece, to reduce bulk. Pin any **pleats and tucks** on the pattern pieces before cutting out the lining, as they would be too bulky if included in the lining as well.

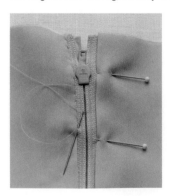

Sew all lining seams, except for those at the zipper and the slit, and press seam allowances open. Pull the lining wrong sides together over the main skirt, aligning all seams and darts. Pin top edges together. **Fold under the lining's seam allowances at the zipper opening,** pin folded edges to the zipper tape, and sew down using hand stitches. Optionally, **with wrong sides together, baste the lining to the skirt along the waistline edge; sew on the waistband,** treating the skirt and lining fabric as a single layer. Hem the skirt and lining, **making the lining ¾–1" (2–2.5cm) shorter.** The finishing of the skirt slit will vary depending on the skirt's design (*see pages 215–216*).

! Since there are so **MANY TYPES OF GARMENTS,** there are **SPECIALIZED APPROACHES TO CUTTING AND SETTING IN LININGS** that depend on the garment style. Most purchased patterns will have information in the instructions to assist you.

! **IF A SKIRT DOES NOT HAVE A SLIT,** like a wider skirt with pleats, leave 6–8" (15–20cm) **WALKING SLITS** open at the bottom side seams of the more narrowly cut lining. Work a narrow hem at the edges of the slits.

» **HANGING LOOPS** are placed over the lining at the top edge of a skirt and caught in when the waistband is sewn on. Fold the loops in half and **PIN THE LOOPS AT THE WAIST EDGE WITHIN THE SEAM ALLOWANCE,** with raw edges flush.

LININGS AT HEMS

To prevent jacket linings from showing, they should be **shorter than the garment pieces at the hem and sleeves.** To make sure the lining sits comfortably and does not tug, a **crosswise pleat** is added.

Handsew the lining hem to the jacket hem, at the same time adding an approximately ⅜" (1cm)-deep horizontal fold near the edge, as shown.

! ON COATS THE LINING USUALLY HANGS LOOSE AND IS HEMMED SEPARATELY. The finished hem is connected to any vertical seams on the main garment with a *thread chain (see page 78).*

LINING AT A SIMPLE HEM SLIT

On this type of slit the lining is **attached to the seam allowances of the main fabric.**

Press the lining seam allowances to the inside and secure them with hand stitches to the sides of the slit.

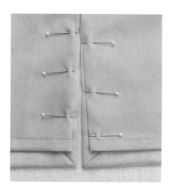

! ON SKIRTS THE LINING MAY BE LEFT HANGING LOOSE AT THE SLIT. First hem the lower edge, then work narrow hems along the slit edges. Connect the lining to the bottom and top of the slit, at the hem, and at seam allowances, respectively, with a *thread chain (see page 78).*

LINING AT AN OVERLAPPED SLIT

If the slit has **overlapped edges,** the lining is attached to these.

1 Align and pin the lining seam to the main fabric seam above the slit. Fold under the **lining seam allowance at the underlap edge** to ⅜" (1cm) and pin. **Trim the lining** so that only ⅜" (1cm) of seam allowance remains at the top and the other slit edge. Snip diagonally into the upper seam allowance corners.

 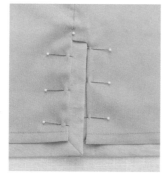

2 Fold under the allowances and **pin them to the underlap at the top and to the overlap along the side.** Attach the lining to the main fabric with invisible hand stitching.

! HEMS ON LOOSE HANGING LININGS should be kept as flat as possible. On thin fabrics a folded hem may be used. Heavier fabrics should be finished at the bottom edge with an overlock stitch or be reinforced with *stay stitching (see page 202)* near the edge and finished with pinking shears.

MACHINE-SEWN BUTTONHOLES

Automatic buttonholes are quick and convenient, but it is also possible to get good results using just a zigzag stitch and a standard presser foot *(see page 84)*. Buttonholes consist of two long rows of dense zigzag stitching. The top thread tension may need to be loosened slightly.

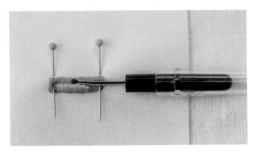

AUTOMATIC BUTTONHOLES

Modern sewing machines generally include an automatic buttonhole feature and a specialized buttonhole presser foot. Depending on the model of machine, it may create **two-, four-, or five-step buttonholes with straight or rounded ends.** If your machine is fully automatic, you can make a buttonhole in a single step. Stitch length and width are usually preprogrammed but may need adjusting depending on the type of fabric used. **Stretch buttonholes should be used on stretch fabrics.** Read the instructions in your user manual to see which types of buttonholes your machine is capable of, and how they are made.

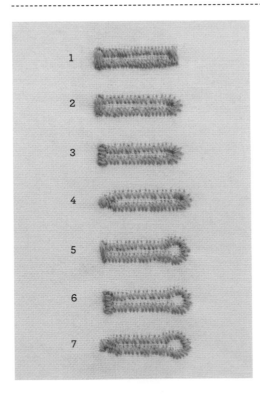

FULLY AUTOMATIC BUTTONHOLES

1 **STANDARD BUTTONHOLE WITH LENGTHWISE BAR** is used for the majority of garments, such as shirts, blouses, and dresses, and also on linens.

2 **ROUNDED BUTTONHOLE WITH LENGTHWISE BAR** is used on tops, such as blouses and jackets, made of lightweight fabrics.

3 **ROUNDED BUTTONHOLE WITH CROSSWISE BAR** is used on tops made from sturdy fabrics.

4 **ROUNDED BUTTONHOLE WITH POINTED END** is used on pants and sportswear.

5 **KEYHOLE BUTTONHOLE WITH LENGTHWISE BAR** is used on jackets, coats, and suits made from heavier fabrics.

6 **KEYHOLE BUTTONHOLE WITH CROSSWISE BAR** is used on pants, jackets, coats, and heavy-duty sportswear.

7 **KEYHOLE BUTTONHOLE WITH POINTED END** is used on jeans, pants, and sportswear.

HAND-GUIDED MACHINE BUTTONHOLES

This buttonhole is sewn using a standard presser foot and consists of two long, caterpillar-like sides with a short bar at each end. The stitch width for the bars is always double that of the sides. The machine is reset manually at each step.

1 Mark the position and length of the buttonhole on the right side of the fabric. Select a dense, 1/16–1/8" (2–3mm)-wide zigzag stitch. Raise the presser foot, position the fabric, and, using the handwheel, bring the needle down into the fabric at the right side of the beginning of the first long side of the buttonhole. Lower the presser foot and sew the first long side to the appropriate length. **Leave the needle in the fabric at the left side of the stitching.**

2 Lift the presser foot, turn the fabric 180 degrees, and lower the foot again. Bring the needle up and double the stitch width; sew four to six stitches to create the bar. Stop on the left side with the needle in the up position.

3 Reset the stitch width to 1/16–1/8" (2–3mm) and sew the second long side closely alongside the first, making sure that the stitches on the long sides do not cross into each other. Stop with the needle on the left side in the up position.

4 Once again, double the stitch width and sew the second bar. Then set the stitch width to 00 and sew a couple of stitches in place to secure the threads. Pull the thread to the back and fasten off. Cut open the buttonhole.

>> ON SOFT AND STRETCHY FABRICS, IRON ON a piece of embroidery stabilizer behind the buttonhole location before sewing to **PREVENT THE FABRIC FROM PUCKERING**. Once the buttonhole is completed, simply tear away any remaining stabilizer edges.

TOPSTITCHED BUTTONHOLE IN LEATHER

Since leather does not fray, buttonholes made in leather use a different technique. A quick and easy method is to **topstitch** around the buttonhole slit; this style is particularly well suited for faced opening edges.

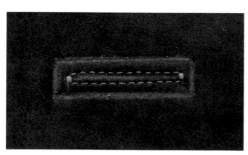 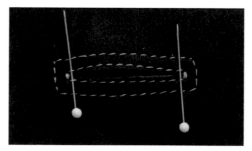

1 Mark the position, length, and outline of the buttonhole on the right side of the garment. Topstitch around the buttonhole's centerline about 1/16–1/8" (1.5–2mm) away from it, with stitch length at a minimum of 9 spi (3mm-long stitches). Work a bar at each end for added stability. To make the bar, sew five to seven stitches back and forth in place.

2 Topstitch the outline of the buttonhole. Pull the thread ends to the back and fasten them off. Stick pins through the two stitches at the ends just before the bars, and carefully cut the buttonhole along the centerline using a hobby knife or small, pointed scissors. Remove pins.

This buttonhole is **ESPECIALLY ATTRACTIVE** when **CONTRASTING FABRIC OR THREAD** is used for the binding.

BOUND BUTTONHOLES

On a bound buttonhole the slit's edges are bound with fabric. This classic method is used primarily on **jackets and bags.** The binding strips may be cut straight or on the bias; a bias strip is usually easier to work with and will sit better. Depending on the fabric, for example with plaids, the binding may create a noticeable contrasting pattern. **Reinforce the main fabric with interfacing at the buttonhole locations,** and finish the buttonhole before applying any facings.

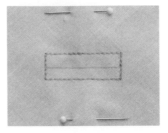

1 Mark the position and finished size of the buttonhole on the right side of the fabric. Cut a binding strip that is 1½–2" (4–5cm) wide and about 1⅛–1½" (3–4cm) longer than the buttonhole. Mark the buttonhole centered on the wrong side of the binding fabric. With right sides together, pin the binding onto the main fabric, lining up buttonhole markings. **Topstitch around the rectangular outline of the buttonhole with short stitches,** allowing the start and end of the stitching to overlap somewhat, as shown.

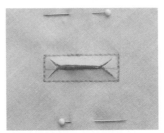

2 With small, sharp scissors, **cut the buttonhole slit up to ³⁄₁₆" (5mm) before the topstitching, then snip diagonally to the corners,** creating small triangles.

3 **Pull the binding through the slit to the wrong side.** On heavier fabrics, press the seam allowances open; on lighter fabrics, as shown here, press them toward the binding. Carefully press the corners flat.

4 Fold the long sides of the binding as inverted pleats toward the buttonhole opening, **so that the folded edges abut exactly in the center of the opening.**

5 To prevent the binding edges from shifting, secure them with **diagonal basting stitches** (*see page 73*) or with adhesive tape (such as quilter's tape).

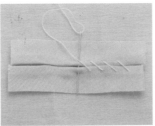

6 On the wrong side, **sew the little triangles onto the binding ends** using machine or hand stitches.

7 From the right side, **stitch the binding in the ditch of the seam (the seam line between the main fabric and the binding).** Press, then remove basting stitches.

8 If the garment will have a facing, mark the buttonhole position and outline on it and cut as in step 2. Press the edges to the inside. **Place the facing on the main piece, wrong sides together.** Slipstitch (*see page 75*) the buttonhole edges all around, catching only the back layer of the binding.

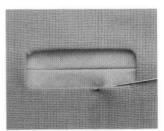

BOUND BUTTONHOLES

MAKING YOUR OWN CLOSURES

If you cannot find matching buttons, it is easy to make your own. Loop closures and frog closures take a little more effort and can be used in place of buttonholes. Depending on the materials used, they can **be compatible with many fashion styles.**

COVERED BUTTONS

You will need covered button blanks, which are available in various sizes and may be made from brass or plastic. They can be **covered with fabric, ribbon, or other flexible materials.** These are very easy to make with a special kit, including two plastic tools, that is available at sewing supply stores. Sometimes covered button packages include the tool along with the buttons.

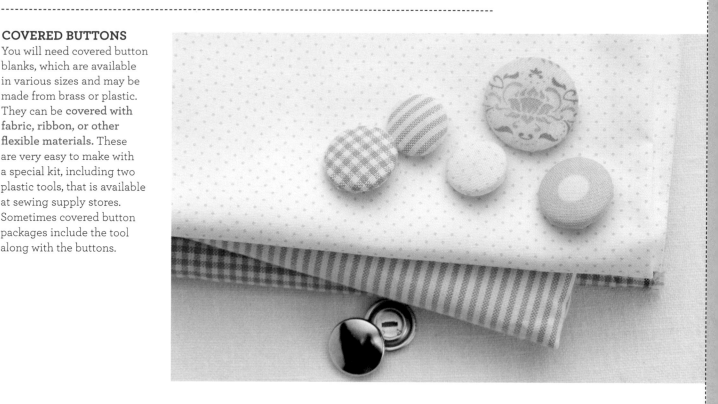

1 Cut out the template from the back of the covered button packaging. Trace the outline on the wrong side of the fabric and cut the fabric on that line. **Thin fabrics can be reinforced with an appropriate fusible interfacing.**

2 Lay the fabric, right side down, onto the white plastic piece that comes in the kit. **Press the button blank with the curved side down into the opening of the piece.** Push overhanging fabric edges to the inside and use a needle, if necessary, to help snag the fabric on the inner teeth.

3 Place the **back part of the button** into position.

4 Place the blue plastic cap on top of the button back and **press on it** until you hear the button back snap into place.

5 Push the finished button out of the plastic mold from the bottom.

>> ORIGINALITY FOR HOME TEXTILES: Bedding buttons made of linen can be DYED TO MATCH YOUR FABRIC. You can also draw designs on them using fabric markers.

>> TURN COVERED BUTTONS INTO TINY WORKS OF ART: After cutting, embellish the center of the fabric with BEADS, SEQUINS, OR RHINESTONES. TINY EMBROIDERY MOTIFS are also striking and can be done quickly using machine embroidery stitches.

LOOP CLOSURES

This type of closure consists of a series of loops on one side of the opening, captured between the main fabric and the facing, and buttons on the other side. Loops are mainly suited for **dresses and blouses, both front and back, and sleeve cuffs.** To create the loops, you can make your own fabric tubes/tiny rolls *(see page 262)*; these require bias strips about ¾–1" (2–3cm) wide.

  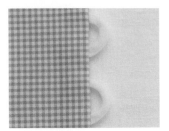

> **!** INSTEAD OF USING SINGLE LOOPS WITH SPACING BETWEEN THEM, you can put the loops directly adjacent to each other. This is an attractive look, especially on elegant garment pieces and on lightweight fabrics. Use NARROW ROLLS OF FABRIC COMBINED WITH SMALL SPHERICAL BUTTONS.

> **»** If you DO NOT WANT TO MAKE YOUR OWN FABRIC TUBES FOR LOOP CLOSURES, you can also use cording or prepared loop tape. The tape can be STITCHED ON UNDERNEATH THE FINISHED OPENING EDGE rather than caught within the seam.

1 To determine the required length of the loops, place a button on the closure's centerline. **Pin the loop around the button and mark where it meets the outer edge of the closure, add the button depth measurement, and mark the loop at that point.** Cut the loop at the marked point and cut as many additional loops as needed.

2 Mark equal distances for the placement of the loops: **the smaller the buttons, the shorter the distance between the loops.** Pin the loops to the garment edge, using an additional adhesive strip to hold the ends in place. Stitch the loops in place near the seam line, within the seam allowance. Remove pins and tape.

3 **Pin the facing on the main piece, right sides together,** with the loops sandwiched in between the two fabric layers. Sew on the facing, trim seam allowances, and press the facing to the inside. The loops will now stick out from the edge. Topstitch the edge from the right side, if desired.

LACED EYELET CLOSURE

Metal eyelets (also called grommets) come in assorted sizes and colors. Together with ribbon or cording they create a **decorative closure for corsetry and historical or festive dresses.** To prevent the sides from folding up against each other, corset boning or tape *(see page 54)* is worked into the edges, although this is not recommended for blouses. The edges can be given additional stability with an appropriate interfacing.

> **!** ON A LACED OPENING, the inner diameter of the eyelets should be ⅛–³⁄₁₆" (4–5mm). Eyelet packets purchased at sewing supply stores will have the metal or plastic eyelet pieces included, but you'll need your own hammer. APPLICATION OF EYELETS IS MADE SIMPLER WITH EYELET PLIERS (as shown), which work with the metal eyelet pieces.

> **»** IF YOUR CORSET BONING OR TAPE NEEDS TO BE SHORTENED, ROUND OFF THE EDGES to prevent the ends from poking through the fabric. You can also sometimes get special end caps, specially designed for placement on the ends of the boning.

1 If corset boning will be used, a **casing must be sewn along the opening edge.** Topstitch the casing close to the edge and then again at the width of the boning plus ¹⁄₁₆" (2mm); insert the boning. Mark the locations of the eyelets, spaced at about 1–1½" (2.5–4cm). Use eyelet pliers (shown) to make holes of the correct size.

2 Place the eyelet pieces in the pliers as shown on the packaging: the piece with the indentation on the bottom and the piece with the raised center on top. Hold the fabric with the right side down, then stick the piece with the cylindrical shaft through the hole from the bottom. Place the corresponding indented ring on top, then press the two pieces together using the pliers.

3 From the right side, **feed the lacing through the eyelets** in a **crisscross pattern,** similar to a shoelace.

FROG CLOSURES

Decorative frog closures typically embellish coats and jackets and can also be used on fabrics, such as very open lace, where buttonholes are difficult to sew. The closure is made from a **thin tube of fabric** (*see page 262*) or with purchased cording. **Handmade knotted buttons** look especially good with frog closures, but many standard buttons will work nicely as well.

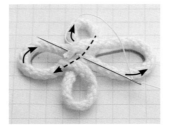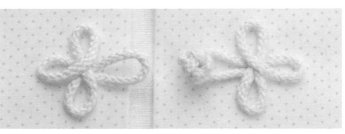

1 Draw the desired frog shape on a piece of graph paper, **making one loop somewhat larger than the others.** Lay down the end of the cord for the first loop, optionally holding it stable with a pin, and **secure it at the crossover point with short hand stitches.**

2 Create the remaining loops as pictured, one after the other, feeding the cord underneath the layers at the dotted arrow. Cut the cord end. **Handstitch the crossover points together** so that no stitches are visible; this will later be the top.

3 Remove the closure from the paper and place it on the garment edge **with the larger loop extending slightly past the closure edge** (left side of photo). Attach it to the garment with inconspicuous hand stitches. Make a knotted button (see below) and sew it to the opposite side.

» IF YOU ARE MAKING frog closures out of cording, brush the ends WITH FABRIC GLUE or wrap them with a narrow strip of adhesive tape. This will prevent the ends from unraveling.

KNOTTED BUTTON

Knotted buttons are made from materials such as **cording, narrow fabric tubes, or leather laces.** If they will be used as part of a frog closure, they should be made from the same material as the closure.

1 Depending on the weight of the cording, **cut a piece 8–10" (20–25cm) long** and create an initial loop. Optionally, pin the starting point to your work surface (for example, thick cardboard or an ironing board).

2 Make a second loop as pictured, following the directions of the arrows.

3 **Weave the long end of the cord** over and under the first two loops.

4 **Pull the loops together evenly** from both ends of the cord until they create a firm knot. Tie the cord ends together and **wrap them tightly with sewing thread** to create a short shank. The length of the shank will depend on the size of the frog closure. Cut the cord below the shank. The shank is sewn on at the desired position on the garment (see photo of frog closure, above right).

» CREATE A TEST VERSION of any FROG CLOSURE to make sure the relative size of the loop and button are correct.

» BODICES AND NECKLINES on blouses can look striking with a laced frog closure, where BOTH EDGES HAVE FROG LOOPS. On a back closure the distance between the edges should be no more then 3" (8cm); on a front closure no more than 2" (5cm). Leave about ⅝–¾" (1.5–2cm) between the top and bottom garment edges and the first/last loop. To finish, thread the lacing through the loops, as with an eyelet closure.

SNAPS AND HOOK-AND-EYE CLOSURES

These types of closures hold edges together without being visible from the right side. They are appropriate for use on areas where fabric is doubled and reinforced with interfacing. When sewing these on an overlap, it is important to take care that only the inner layer of fabric is pierced, so that no stitching is visible from the right. It is best to use heavy-duty thread.

SNAPS

Snaps are typically used as **supplemental closures** and are best for areas that will not be heavily stressed.

! CLOSE ANY ALREADY-ATTACHED SNAPS BEFORE MARKING THE PLACEMENT OF THE NEXT ONE. The bottom part of the snap may be sewn THROUGH ALL FABRIC LAYERS for a better hold.

Place the **upper half of the snap (the piece with the protruding center shaft) on the back (under) side of the overlap** about ⅛–¼" (3–6mm) away from the edge. Sew three to four stitches, depending on thread weight, through each hole all around the rim; direct the needle to the next hole by going in between the fabric layers. Sew the other half of the snap to the top (upper) side of the underlap at the corresponding position. To best determine the correct positioning, place the overlap on top of and aligned with the underlap; **stick a pin through the middle of the upper snap from the right side,** and mark the pin insertion point on the underlap.

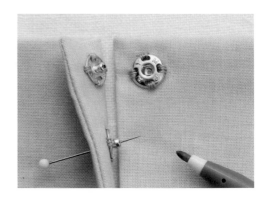

HOOK-AND-EYE CLOSURES

Hook-and-eye closures are usually used one at a time, often as a **secondary closure above a zipper.** Depending on the shape of the eye, they are appropriate for overlapping closures or abutted edges. Especially sturdy versions are available for waistbands.

» VERY SMALL CLOSURES can be difficult to hold while sewing. Secure the pieces with a small piece of adhesive tape, making sure it is smaller than the closure itself and that it does not obstruct the sewing area.

» SEWING SUPPLY STORES CARRY NO-SEW WAISTBAND CLOSURES that are inserted with the help of eyelet pliers. These closures are visible from the right side.

HOOK-AND-EYE CLOSURES FOR OVERLAPPED EDGES

These may also be called hook-and-bar closures. Place the **hook piece** about ⅛" (3mm) from the edge on the **underside of the overlap** and sew through each hole with three to four stitches. Place the overlap on top of and aligned with the underlap, and mark and pin the bar to the top side of the underlap in a corresponding position. Attach the bar in the same manner as the hook piece.

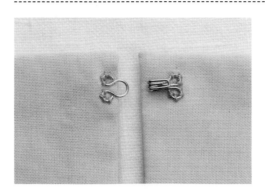

HOOK-AND-EYE CLOSURES FOR ABUTTED EDGES

Connect the hook and eye pieces and position them on the garment so that the **closed garment edges abut;** the hook will be about ¹⁄₁₆" (2mm) inside the edge, and the eye will extend somewhat past the edge, as shown. Insert a pin through each attachment ring, mark the positions, then unhook the two pieces and sew them on with a few stitches through each ring.

NO-SEW CLOSURES

If you want a closure without having to do additional sewing, you can use **riveted snaps.** Packages of snaps purchased at sewing supply stores will have the metal or plastic snap hardware included, but you'll need to supply your own hammer. Application is made simpler with eyelet pliers, which work together with the snap hardware. A **magnetic snap** can be used for closures on bags and totes. The location of a snap closure should be **reinforced with interfacing** appropriate to the fabric.

⏩ When you want to add closures to MATERIALS SUCH AS PLASTIC OR OILCLOTH, it is best to use no-sew snaps or zippers. Buttonholes can quickly tear out.

NO-SEW SNAPS

Snaps come in many different sizes and colors, and with **light, medium, or strong holding power.** They consist of top and bottom pieces, each of which has a corresponding back piece. For pronged snaps, such as those used on jackets, an appropriately sized hole must first be made at the installation point using eyelet pliers or an awl. For certain small-pronged snaps, such as those designed for use on jersey, prepunching a hole is not necessary.

APPLYING PRONGED SNAPS USING EYELET PLIERS

1 Mark the snap position on the overlap and underlap. **Application to overlap:** Place the snap hardware in the eyelet pliers as indicated on the packaging—the large, flat piece on top and the smaller piece with the indentation at the bottom. Place the top of the snap (the colored cap) in the upper piece and the pronged ring (the backing) in the bottom. **Press the pliers tightly together** at the marked location (right side of fabric facing up), until both pieces are solidly attached to the fabric.

2 **Application to underlap:** Turn the pliers around and set in the bottom part of the snap (with prongs and center shaft); the shaft sits in the indentation of the hardware. Set the backing piece in the bottom. Press the snap pieces together at the marking using the pliers.

MAGNETIC SNAP

This closure consists of an upper piece with a small center shaft and a lower piece with a corresponding indentation, each of which gets bound together with a backing disk. They should be attached **before any facings or linings are added,** so that the backings will not show on the finished item.

1 On the right side of the overlap, mark the position for the top part of the snap. Draw a line the same length **as the prong height, ³⁄₁₆"** **(5mm)** on each side of the mark (the slits for the prongs). Cut them open carefully with small, sharp scissors or a seam ripper. To prevent the slits from ending up too long, place a pin across each end.

2 Stick the top of the snap **into the fabric from the right side, inserting the prongs through the slits.**

3 Turn the fabric over and place the backing disk over the prongs. **Using pliers, bend the prongs toward the middle of the snap,** one at a time.

4 Attach the bottom part of the snap to the **underlap in the same manner.**

❗ ON LOOSELY WOVEN FABRICS the prongs can potentially be inserted without making holes in the fabric first; pull the fabric threads gently apart instead.

⏩ IF YOU WANT TO ADD A MAGNETIC CLASP TO AN ALREADY FINISHED ITEM, there are two-part versions that can be sewn on—but be aware that their holding strength will be somewhat weaker than with no-sew versions.

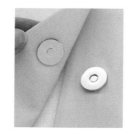

CLOSING TAPES

These two-part tapes are made with hook-and-loop fastener, snaps, or hook-and-eye closures and can be cut to the desired length. Take care that no metal or plastic parts end up in the way of later seam lines. Seam allowances on both closing edges need to be slightly wider than the tapes themselves. A doubled seam allowance will provide better strength.

HOOK-AND-LOOP FASTENER

Hook-and-loop fastener tape is useful on all kinds of overlapped closures and is practical **for adjustable waistbands.** Multiple shorter strips can be used for pieces such as removable hoods. The looped side is placed on the underside of the overlap, and the hooked side is placed on the top side of the underlap. This tape can be difficult to pin, so it is **best to secure it with a strip of adhesive tape** up the center. Topstitch tape edges with a zipper foot. To prevent stitching from being visible on the outside, sew on the upper tape by hand.

>> You can create your own **SNAP TAPE** by **APPLYING NO-SEW SNAPS TO STURDY SEAM TAPE OR RIBBON.** The tape will be even more stable if you first reinforce it with interfacing.

SNAP TAPE

Snap tape may have either **plastic or metal snaps** and is suitable for **overlapped opening edges.** You can choose from tapes with a variety of spacing between the snaps; pick the type that will work best with your finished item. To prevent the snaps from showing through the overlap on lightweight fabrics, reinforce the seam allowance with interfacing. Place the tape with the snap tops (with shafts) on the underside of the overlap, the other side (with indentations) on the top side of the underlap; pin or secure with adhesive tape. Topstitch closely around the edges of the tape using a zipper foot.

HOOK-AND-EYE CLOSURE TAPE

This tape is available in plain and decorative versions and with varied spacing between the hooks. It is used to **close abutted edges, such as on corsets and undergarments.** Before cutting to size, lay the tape against the garment to determine where the first and last hook will lie—if either will be in the way of seam allowances, they should be removed.
Mark a double-width seam allowance on each closing edge. Mark a centerline on the right side of the fabric. **Lay the hook tape, right side down, along this line** so that the hooks point away from the seam allowance and the bent ends of the hooks lie along the line. Pin the tape to the opening and stitch along the line of bent hook ends on the seam allowance.
Fold under the seam allowance, fold the tape in half wrong sides together, and stitch again close to the edge through all layers (see blue stitching).
Apply the eye tape to match the hooks on the opposite edge; the **eyes will extend across the centerline.**

SEWING IN ZIPPERS

Zippers, along with buttons, are the most frequently used textile closures. Depending on the desired style, placement, and look, there are various methods of applying a zipper. They may be covered and inconspicuous or made visible as a decorative detail.

ALL ABOUT ZIPPERS

A **zipper with cotton tape** should be prewashed to prevent it from becoming wavy when washed post-application. Press the tape flat before installing it. Before a zipper is inserted, the **edges of the zipper opening must be finished** in a manner appropriate to the fabric.

The **slider** should be pulled down somewhat below the seam line while the zipper is being sewn in: about ¹⁄₁₆" (2mm) below for lightweight fabrics, up to ³⁄₁₆" (5mm) on heavier fabrics. If a waistband or collar will be placed above the zipper, the slider should similarly be positioned ¹⁄₁₆" (2mm) below the seam line. On **thin or stretch fabrics**, seam allowances should first be reinforced on the wrong side with seam tape, or the seam line should be given a line of *reinforcement stitching (see page 202)*; this will make it easier to sew in the zipper.

Whenever possible, **baste and stitch the edges of the zipper opening in the same direction**, ideally from the closed (seamed) end of the zipper opening to the open end, to help prevent tiny folds from forming at the closed end when machine stitching. To **secure the zipper's position for stitching**, use a textile glue stick or double-sided *wonder tape (see page 33, figure 6)*; this will eliminate the need for pinning and basting and will hold the zipper flat during application. This is especially advisable with materials such as leather and oilcloth where pin and needle holes remain permanently visible.

On **curved zipper openings**, sew a line of reinforcement stitching about ¼" (6mm) from the fabric edge to discourage stretching.

Separating zipper
1 Insertion pin
2 Retainer box
3 Reinforced patch

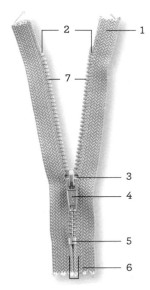

Standard zipper
1 Tape
2 Upper stops
3 Slider
4 Pull
5 Lower stops
6 Teeth (or spiral) width
7 Teeth/Spiral

SHORTENING A ZIPPER

Zippers come in many different lengths, but not in every length—depending on the type, they are generally offered in ¾" (2cm) or 2" (5cm) increments. If you cannot get one that is the correct length for your project, buy a slightly longer one and shorten it using the appropriate method from below.

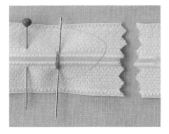

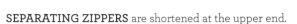

STANDARD ZIPPERS are shortened at the lower end: determine and mark the desired length down from the upper stops, then **sew a bar tack across the closed zipper** about ⅜–¾" (1–2cm) below the marking, using hand or machine stitching (zigzag stitch: stitch length 0, stitch width equal to the zipper teeth/spiral width). Trim the tape ends to about ⅝" (1.5cm) below the stitching.

SEPARATING ZIPPERS are shortened at the upper end.

1 Mark the desired length of the zipper, measuring upward from the retainer box. **Remove any superfluous teeth above the marking, using pliers to break them apart.** Also remove the first tooth below the marking.

2 Trim the tape to about ⅝" (1.5cm) **above the topmost remaining tooth**, preferably using **pinking shears**. Sew a bar tack on both tapes above the topmost tooth. On some zippers the **upper stops can be pried off and pinched back** onto the shortened tape.

>> STICKY ZIPPERS WITH METAL TEETH will zip more smoothly if the teeth are RUBBED WITH SOAP OR WAX. On plastic zippers, use HAIRSPRAY OR SILICONE GREASE. Cover the fabric portion of the zipper completely, or APPLY THE LIQUID WITH A SMALL BRUSH.

LAPPED ZIPPER

This style of zipper application is frequently found in **seam openings on women's pants or skirts.** One edge (the overlap) covers the zipper, so its seam allowance should be at least ¾" (2cm) wide.

! ON WOMEN'S CLOTHING WITH A FRONT ZIPPER, a lapped zipper will feature the right side of the zipper opening as the overlap, as shown here. A zipper in a left side seam is applied in the same way. For a ZIPPER IN A RIGHT SIDE SEAM, work the DESCRIBED STEPS IN MIRROR IMAGE.

1 **Mark the centerlines on each edge** on the right side. Press under the seam allowance of the right zipper opening (the overlap, at left in photo) along this line. On the left zipper opening (at right in photo), mark the fold line for the very narrow underlap ⅛" **(3mm) from the centerline.**

2 At about ¾" (2cm) below the bottom of the zipper opening, **snip the left seam allowance almost to the seam line** and press under along the fold line.

3 Place the zipper, right side up, beneath the underlap and baste or secure with adhesive tape, positioning the overlap so its **folded edge lies directly next to the zipper teeth.** Install a zipper foot to the left of the needle. Start at the bottom end of the zipper opening and stitch alongside the zipper teeth through all layers. Shortly before the top, open the zipper slightly and maneuver the slider past the presser foot. Complete the stitching to the open end with the zipper open.

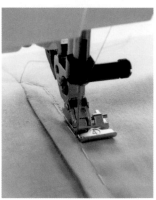

4 Close the zipper. Position the overlap so that the **seam sewn in step 3 is covered.** Pin the overlap's edges along the centerline **and baste or use adhesive to secure the zipper to the overlap.**

5 Install the zipper foot to the right of the needle. Start at the bottom end of the zipper opening and **stitch along the basted line to the top open edge.** The lower end of the seam (that crosses the zipper) **may be sewn in a slight curve instead of straight across.**

CENTERED ZIPPER

A centered zipper is topstitched from the right side at equal distances from the fabric edges of the zipper opening; the spiral lies directly under the abutted edges and is not visible. The method is straightforward and can be used at the **center back or center front of dresses and skirts, as well as on sleeve slits.** We advise that you use zippers with plastic spirals for the centered **method,** as they are more flexible than zippers with teeth. The lower zipper stops need to be covered by the seam so the zipper opening should be ⅛" (3mm) shorter than the zipper length.

❗ **IF A ZIPPER IS INSERTED IN A SEAM** that is closed both above and below the zipper, the length of the opening corresponds to the length of the zipper teeth/spiral between the stops. **INSERT USING THE CENTERED ZIPPER METHOD,** but sew the tapes together above the pull.

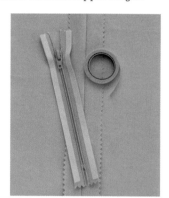
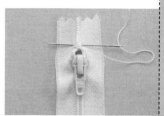

1 Right sides together, pin the two edges of the zipper opening together and **baste using long machine stitches.** Snip the basting stitches every 1⅛–1½" (3–4cm) to make them easier to pull out later. Press the seam allowances open.

2 Mark the stitching lines on the right side of the zipper opening; they should **run parallel to the basted seam about ¼" (6mm) to each side** of it (or possibly wider, depending on the width of the zipper spiral). Join lines at the bottom with a crosswise line.

3 **Place adhesive tape along the right sides of the zipper tape** and peel off the backing.

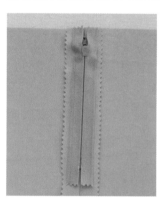

⏩ **WHEN APPLYING A CENTERED ZIPPER,** you can stitch a flat "V" at the bottom of the zipper rather than working straight across; this is especially attractive when done in decorative topstitching.

4 With the zipper opening facing wrong side up, place the zipper right side down on top of the opening's seam allowances so **the spiral and the basted seam lie on top of each other.** Flip the zipper pull upward.

5 When there is a very small distance between the topstitching attaching the zipper and the zipper's spiral, it may be necessary to **undo the basting at the top of the zipper opening** for about 2" (5cm), so the slider can be moved aside. You will topstitch the left side of the zipper with the fabric facing right side up. Install the zipper foot to the left of the needle; the needle will enter the fabric to the right of the foot. Starting at the center bottom of the zipper opening, work two to three stitches across the zipper to the vertical stitching line. Turn the work 90 degrees, leaving the needle in the down position in the fabric, then stitch along the sewing line up to the top edge of the zipper opening. **Shortly before reaching the top, open the zipper slightly,** lifting the presser foot to move the pull past it but leaving the needle in the down position in the fabric, then finish stitching to the end.

⏩ **CENTERED ZIPPERS** are suitable for handsewn application on fabrics such as velvet, silk, brocade, and lace. Sew using *dot stitches (see page 76)* about ³⁄₁₆–¼" (5–6mm) from the opening edges.

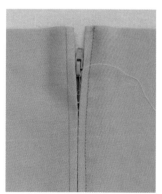

6 Install the zipper foot to the right of the needle. **Topstitch the other side of the zipper opening in the same manner, at the same distance from the center.** Remove the basting.

ZIPPERED FLY OPENING

With this method the zipper is covered by an overlap; this style is usually found as a **front closure on men's and women's pants and on casual skirts.** A supplemental underlap beneath the zipper is advisable on close-fitting garments to prevent the zipper slider from catching on any clothing beneath it, but it is not strictly necessary.

! ON WOMEN'S CLOTHES the right zipper opening edge lies atop the left, as shown here; on men's clothing it is the opposite. **WHEN MAKING A MEN'S GARMENT,** follow the instructions **IN MIRROR IMAGE.**

   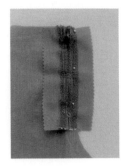

1 Mark the front centerline on both front zipper-opening pieces. Then mark the curved topstitching line on the right front (the overlap, at left in the photo). On the left front piece (the underlap, at right in the photo), mark the fold line for the very narrow underlap, about ¼" (6mm) from the centerline. Stitch the center front seam of the pants from the bottom of the zipper opening to the crotch.

2 On the underlap, snip the facing at the bottom to ¼" (6mm) before the seam, then fold the facing along the marked fold line (*see page 242, photo 2*). Use adhesive to secure the closed zipper, right side up, under the underlap so that the fold line lies directly alongside the zipper teeth. Install the zipper foot to the left of the needle. Starting at the bottom of the zipper opening, stitch alongside the zipper teeth through all thicknesses. Shortly before reaching the top, open the zipper slightly, lifting the presser foot to do so but leaving the needle in the down position in the fabric, then finish stitching.

3 On the overlap, press the overlap facing to the inside along the marked fold line. Lay the folded edge of the overlap over the zipper and pin the overlap edge to the underlap along the centerline.

4 Working from the wrong side, pin the remaining half of the zipper to the facing (underside) of the overlap, **being careful not to catch the main fabric, and stitch through the center of the zipper tape.**

5 Working from the right side, topstitch the overlap along the marked curved line starting at the bottom of the zipper.

6 For the supplemental, attached underlap, cut a strip of fabric 2½–3" (6–8cm) wide and 1⅛" (3cm) longer than the zipper opening. Fold right sides of the strip together and stitch a curved seam at the lower edge—it should **match the curved end of the topstitching on the overlap.** Trim excess fabric at the curve.

7 Turn the supplemental underlap right side out and press. **Finish the long open edges together.**

8 On the wrong side (inside) of the pants, secure the supplemental underlap to the left front overlap facing (the flap at left in photo) so that the **zipper is completely covered.**

9 Using the zipper foot, **sew the flap to the underlap directly alongside the zipper attachment seam.**

10 On heavily stressed garments, it is advisable to **reinforce the bottom of the opening with a bar tack** (*see page 251*); the underlap is caught in the stitching.

INVISIBLE ZIPPER

Invisible (or concealed) zippers are used primarily on **skirts, women's pants, and dresses** where a visible zipper is undesirable, and with **plush fabrics** such as velvet, where topstitching would damage the fabric. Creating this closure requires a **special invisible zipper** that has the spiral on the underside, and a **specialized invisible zipper presser foot,** which can be purchased as a supplemental accessory for many machines. The zipper should be about ¾" (2cm) longer than the planned zipper opening. The seam that connects the fabric pieces is worked after the installation of the zipper, to prevent a bulge from forming at the bottom of the zipper opening.

» OPEN INVISIBLE ZIPPERS BEFORE APPLICATION and press on the wrong side. This will make the tapes smoother and allow the special zipper foot to glide over them more easily.

! THE ZIPPER PICTURED HERE was shortened, which is why a hand-sewn bar tack *(see page 241)* is visible at the bottom.

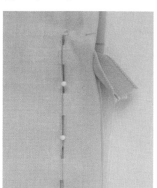

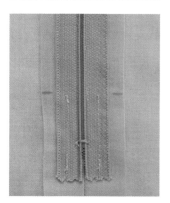

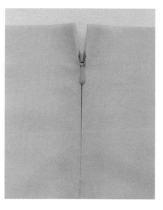

1 Mark the centerline and the bottom end of the zipper opening on the right sides of both fabric pieces. Open the zipper and baste one tape, right sides together, onto the opening's seam allowance so that the **spiral lies directly on the centerline;** allow the bottom of the zipper to extend ¾" (2cm) past the marked end of the opening. Install the special zipper foot so that the groove on the bottom will glide over the spiral and the **needle will insert very close to the spiral.** Stitch the zipper to the fabric, starting at the top, down to the marked end of the opening.

2 Sew the **remaining half of the zipper to the other fabric piece in the same manner.**

3 Close the zipper. Stitch the seam beneath the end of the zipper opening, using a regular zipper foot. **Sew from the bottom of the zipper to the lower edge, moving the zipper tapes gently aside at the start** so that the first section will sew smoothly. A gap of about ⅛" (3mm) will remain between the zipper attachment seam and the center garment seam.

4 Sew the zipper tapes through the lengthwise center onto the seam allowances, as shown, so that they will lie flat, being careful not to catch the upper fabric.

5 This is an invisible zipper viewed **from the right side.**

EXPOSED ZIPPER

In areas where there are no seams, zippers can be **installed in an opening that is cut directly into the fabric and faced.** Depending on the desired finished look, you may want to consider using a novelty zipper with prominent teeth. The length and width of the opening depend on the length of the zipper and the width of the teeth/spiral.

EXPOSED ZIPPER IN A SEPARATING CLOSURE

If a zipped closure separates at the top, as on a neckline, the zipper can be installed as follows:

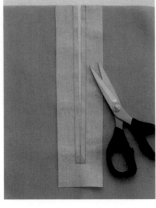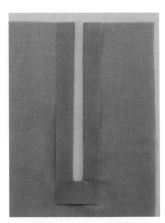

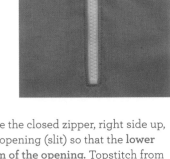

>> WITH LIGHTWEIGHT ZIPPERS you can calculate the opening length so that the lower stops will not be visible. If you are installing a zipper with metal teeth, make sure that IT IS EXACTLY THE RIGHT LENGTH. If you sew across a metal zipper that is too long at the bottom, the needle may encounter a metal tooth and break off.

1 Mark the slit opening on the right side of the fabric; the length corresponds to the length of the zipper teeth to below the bottom stops, plus a ⅝" (1.5cm) seam allowance at the neckline. Cut a strip of fabric that is 1½–2½" (4–6cm) wide and about 1⅛" (3cm) longer than the slit marking; apply interfacing to the wrong side of the strip, then mark an identical slit line on the wrong side, along with parallel stitching lines at the same width as the teeth plus ¹⁄₁₆" (2mm). **Stitch the lines across the bottom.** With right sides together, pin or baste the strip to the main fabric and stitch along the outer marking lines.

2 Cut the slit line with small, sharp scissors to about ⅜" (10mm) above the bottom, then **snip diagonally to the corners,** creating a small triangle of fabric.

3 **Fold the facing strip along the stitching lines to the wrong side** and press completely flat; press from the right side afterward as well.

4 Center and then pin or tape the closed zipper, right side up, under the folded edges of the opening (slit) so that the **lower stops are visible at the bottom of the opening.** Topstitch from the right side using a zipper foot; sew across the bottom edge. Optionally, topstitch again somewhat farther away, so that the zipper tapes will lie flat.

EXPOSED ZIPPER IN AN INTERNAL OPENING

When both ends of a zippered opening are non-separating, **such as on a pocket opening,** install the zipper just the same way you would an exposed zipper that separates at the top, with the following exceptions: **the opening length corresponds to the length of the teeth to the bottom of the lower stops.** The facing strip is 1½–2½" (4–6cm) wide and about 2½" (6cm) longer than the opening, so that it extends past both ends.

Sew the zipper tapes together at the top *(see page 243, far right photo).* **Mark the stitching line all around the zipper opening and stitch.** Snip the corners at both ends of the opening as shown. Finally, topstitch all around the zipper from the right side, close to all edges *(see page 255, figure 3).*

SEPARATING ZIPPER

Separating zippers can be completely opened and are used primarily on **jackets, anoraks, sportswear, and leisurewear**. They may be concealed or, especially with decorative zippers, exposed.

APPLIED SEPARATING ZIPPER

In this quick and simple method, the zipper is applied to the reverse side of the garment's **already finished opening edges**; the tapes are visible from the inside (wrong side). The teeth/spiral may be concealed from view on the right side (edges abut) or not (edges are separated by a small gap).

1 **For a concealed zipper**, baste or tape the closed zipper, right side up, underneath the finished zipper opening edges; the upper stops lie about ⅟16–⅛" (2–3mm) below the upper edge, and the pull is flipped upward. The teeth lie directly under the zipper-opening edges of the garment. **Fold under the tops of the zipper tapes so that they lie between the zipper and the underside of the garment edge.** At the bottom, the zipper tape ends at the garment's hemline.

2 Undo the zipper and **topstitch** each side of the zipper opening, from the right side, ¼–⅜" (6–10mm) **away from the teeth through all layers.** Install the zipper foot once to the left and once to the right of the needle, as appropriate for the side of the zipper you are stitching. Stitch another line of stitches somewhat farther away, if desired, so that the tapes lie flat.

ENCLOSED SEPARATING ZIPPER

With **jackets and vests in particular**, you can install a separating zipper so that it lies between the main fabric and the facing, with the zipper tapes concealed on the wrong side; **the teeth, however, are visible from the right side.**

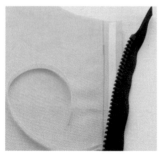

1 Mark the centerline on the right side of both fabric pieces. Press the seam allowances to the wrong side on both the main fabric and the facing; baste (optional). Using adhesive tape, stick one half of the zipper, right side down, on the seam allowance of the main fabric, as shown; **the teeth extend about ⅟16" (2mm) past the centerline marking.**

2 Place the facing right sides together with the main fabric and secure with tape or basting stitches. **Stitch along the centerline from the wrong side of the main fabric through all thicknesses.**

3 Turn the facing to the wrong side; the zipper teeth are now visible along the garment closing edge, as shown. Press the edges, pin, and topstitch along the front edge either very close or farther away from the edge, as desired. **Trim the excess zipper tape.** Stitch the remaining zipper half to the other opening edge in the same manner.

! **IF THE ZIPPER TEETH** are intended to be visible, a gap remains between the closing edges. The ends of the tape are folded back behind the zipper.

» **SEPARATING ZIPPERS** are also available with narrower teeth or finer spirals. They can be used in corsets, bodices, lightweight jackets, blouses, and bridal fashions.

practical pockets

Pockets are not only functional; they can also serve as decorative elements or even design features on a garment. There are many variations of both external and internal pockets, the most important of which are described below.

ALL ABOUT POCKETS

To guarantee the correct positioning of pockets, it is important to **precisely transfer all pocket attachment lines and/or matching symbols from the pattern to your fabric.** Depending on the style of pocket, some of these markings may need to be made on the right side of the main fabric. Pocket positioning, especially when primarily decorative, should be adjusted to **best suit the wearer.** Grade the seam allowances on pockets to lessen bulk. When applying patch pockets, **always bring the thread ends to the back** and tie them off. To strengthen the bottom of a side seam pocket, add a **bar tack or triangular reinforcement stitching** *(see page 251).*

PATCH POCKETS

Usually patch pockets are made from the same fabric as the rest of the garment, but when made in a contrasting color they can add a **striking accent.** They may be embellished with decorative topstitching, ribbon, appliqués, pintucks, ruffles, button closures, or a flap. Depending on the type of pocket and the fabric used, they may be **lined or unlined.**

RECTANGULAR POCKET WITH FACING

This simple, unlined type of pocket is quickly sewn and is used on **shirts, jeans, aprons, and children's clothing.** The opening edge will be sturdier if the wrong side of the facing is **reinforced with interfacing** up to the fold line; on lightweight fabrics the entire pocket may be interfaced.

1 Cut out a pocket of the desired dimensions, including an additional ¾" (2cm) at the top for the facing and ⅜–½" (1cm) all around as seam allowance. **Finish the edges all around. Press the pocket facing along the fold line to the right side** and stitch together at the sides. Trim edges diagonally.

2 **Turn the facing to the wrong side.** Press under the remaining pocket edges; **on heavy fabrics, make mitered corners** *(see page 281).* If desired, topstitch the facing from the right side, then sew on the pocket *(see page 251).*

» WHEN THE POCKET ON A PATTERNED GARMENT is intended to blend seamlessly with the garment's fabric design, make a TEMPLATE OUT OF TRANSPARENT PLASTIC. Place the template on the intended location of the pocket on the garment and use a marker to copy the pattern onto the plastic. Place the template on your leftover fabric, matching the pattern, then cut out the pocket using the template.

» IF THE LOCATION OF A POCKET is clearly predetermined, you can SEW ON THE POCKETS BEFORE THE GARMENT IS COMPLETED. This way you can avoid wrestling with a potentially too-large finished piece.

! DEPENDING ON THE TYPE AND WEIGHT of your fabric, you may be able to fold under and stitch the pocket's facing seam allowances rather than finishing them with zigzag stitches.

» Patch pockets are ESPECIALLY ATTRACTIVE when their edges are bound beforehand with bias strips *(see pages 103–106).*

ROUNDED POCKET WITH FACING

Rounded pockets are made just like rectangular pockets. To create evenly rounded edges, use the pattern piece to make a **pocket template (excluding seam allowances)** out of thin cardboard.

Lay the cardboard pattern on the fabric and mark the seam allowances. Cut out the pocket and work the upper facing as for a rectangular pocket *(see page 248)*. **Stitch along the curves near the cut edge** using a 6–4 spi (4–6mm-long) straight stitch (a gathering stitch); do not secure either end of the stitching. Center the template on the wrong side of the pocket, matching the seamlines. Hold it down and pull the bobbin threads, **gathering the fabric at the curves until it lies flat against the template**; on heavier fabrics, notch the corners almost to the seamline. Tie off the threads and remove the template. Topstitch the pocket onto your garment.

>> IF YOU WANT YOUR POCKET TO BE ROOMIER, you can add a pleat. Work a BOX PLEAT OR INVERTED PLEAT into a piece of fabric and then cut the pocket so that the pleat is centered down the middle. Work a facing at the top, fold under the remaining edges, and sew on the pocket.

LINED POCKET

Patch pockets can be cleanly finished on the inside using a lining, a method that is particularly advisable for **heavier fabrics.** On **sheer and loosely woven fabrics,** the lining and the top facing should be reinforced with interfacing. The lining is cut without a top facing but is otherwise the same as the outer pocket piece.

1 Place the pocket facing edge and the top edge of the lining right sides together and stitch the top edge only, **leaving an opening in the middle for turning.** Press the seam allowances open, or toward the bottom of the pocket on heavier fabrics.

2 From the wrong side, pin the side and bottom edges together and stitch. **Trim seam allowances,** notch curves, and trim upper corners diagonally.

3 Push the pocket through the opening at the top to turn it to the right side. Press, making sure the **lining is not visible from the front.** Close the turning hole with *slipstitches (see page 75),* then sew on the pocket *(see page 251).*

>> POCKETS CAN BE MADE FROM A DOUBLED LAYER OF FABRIC; the eventual entry edge of the pocket will be along the fold. This is especially practical for rounded pockets, provided the fabric is not too heavy. Sew the pocket, right sides together, leaving a hole for turning at the bottom center. AFTER TURNING THE POCKET RIGHT SIDE OUT, CLOSE THE HOLE using hand stitches or while topstitching the pocket to the garment.

BELLOWS/EXPANSION POCKET

Bellows (expansion) pockets are popular for use on **jackets, sportswear, leisurewear, and work clothes**, where **functional pockets** are especially important. The larger volume of the pocket is achieved via pleated sides, which can be created in a variety of ways. The following describes a simple technique involving separately cut side strips for the pleats. **Light- to midweight densely woven fabrics** will work best.

>> BELLOWS (EXPANSION) POCKETS also look good with rounded lower corners, which you can shape with a line of gathering stitches at the corners *(see page 249)* before attaching to the upper fabric.

>> THIS STYLE OF POCKET allows for many variations. You could work an inverted pleat down the center and/or add a pocket flap *(see page 252)*, or USE CONTRASTING FABRIC FOR THE SIDE PLEATS.

1 Cut a rectangular pocket with a ¾" (2cm) upper facing and a ⅜" (1cm) seam allowance all around. For sides with a ¾" (2cm) pleat depth, cut a 2½" **(6cm)-wide strip.** Calculate the pleat strip length as follows: add together the lengths of the two sides and the bottom of the pocket piece, and from this total subtract 1½" (4cm). Fold the side strip in half lengthwise, right sides together, and press the fold line. Fold under and press ⅜" (1cm) along one of the long sides of the pleat strip. **Pin the long unpressed side of the strip around the pocket,** right sides together, snipping seam allowances at ⅜" (1cm) above the lower corners. **Stitch the side strip (pleat) to the pocket edge.** Trim seam allowances diagonally at the corners and top, then finish the allowances together; press the pocket.

2 Fold under (to the wrong side) and **press** the top edge of the pocket (the facing), first by ⅜" (1cm) and then by ¾" (2cm); **stitch along the lower folded edge.**

3 **Topstitch narrowly around all but the entry edge** of the upper pocket. Place the pocket in position on the garment and sew to the garment along the long **folded edge of the bottom layer (only) of the side strip/pleat** *(see page 263)*. Pin down the upper ¾" (2cm) at each side edge (see arrow) and topstitch through all layers.

SIMPLE MITERED CORNERS

Instead of folding lower pocket edges at right angles, you can make mitered corners. This should be done especially with **heavier fabrics, to reduce bulk in the seam allowances.**

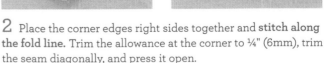

1 **Press** the corner seam allowance to the wrong side at a **diagonal,** then open the fold.

2 Place the corner edges right sides together and **stitch along the fold line.** Trim the allowance at the corner to ¼" (6mm), trim the seam diagonally, and press it open.

3 Turn the corner right side out and **press flat.**

SEWING ON A POCKET

Patch pockets can be sewn on **invisibly by hand or topstitched by machine**; machine stitching is faster and more durable. To make sure the pocket attachment lines are visible on the right side of the fabric, they can be transferred using **machine basting stitches of 6–4 spi (4–6mm-long) stitch length or with a marker.** Decorative elements such as embroidery stitching, appliqués, and ribbons can be added before the pocket is attached.

1 Apply adhesive tape to the garment just **inside the pocket attachment marking lines.** Place the pocket on top of the adhesive, right side facing up.

2 **Topstitch close to all edges except the opening edge;** on thicker fabrics, the distance from the edge may be somewhat wider. **Reinforce the upper corners/seam ends** (see below).

>> ON HEAVILY STRESSED sportswear, children's clothing, and work clothing—or simply when the look is desired—pockets can be sewn with a second line of topstitching at some distance from the first, or sewn with a twin needle.

REINFORCING SEAM ENDS

Once the pocket is sewn on, the **seam ends at the entry edges are reinforced** to discourage them from tearing. On only lightly stressed pockets, such as on blouses, it is sufficient to secure the seams with back stitching at the seam ends. Additional reinforcement can be provided with **narrow triangles or bar tacks;** these can be decorative elements when sewn with contrasting thread. Always pull thread ends to the back and tie them off.

BAR TACKS

A bar tack is a **short seam made of dense zigzag stitches;** it is typically about ⅜" (1cm) long and is used frequently to reinforce seams on **children's clothing, sportswear, and leisurewear.** Many modern sewing machines have a programmed bar tack. On areas that will be especially heavily stressed, the main fabric is **additionally reinforced with a piece of interfacing** on the wrong side before the pocket is attached.

Reduce the thread tension slightly to ensure well-formed stitches. **Sew diagonally across the corner** using dense, ⅟₃₂–⅛" (1–3mm)-wide zigzag stitches.

! BAR TACKS can also be made parallel to the side edges, directly next to the side seam.

TRIANGLES

Triangular reinforcements are used mainly on **tops,** such as on shirt pockets; they help to **evenly distribute stress at corners.** Start at the end of the lengthwise stitching and sew **three to four stitches horizontally across the upper pocket edge,** then **diagonally downward,** so that a small triangle is formed.

>> ON JEANSWEAR, pocket-opening edges are typically SECURED WITH NO-SEW RIVETS, which simultaneously add a design element. Pre-punch holes and then install rivets with the help of eyelet pliers.

POCKET FLAPS

As a rule, a pocket flap will fully cover the open edge of a pocket. Flaps may be various shapes, and when combined with patch pockets the shape should complement the pocket and be about ¼" (6mm) wider. The flap is typically made from **the same fabric as the pocket,** though the underside may be made of lining when needed, as with heavier fabrics. **A snap, button, or clasp closure may be added.** Flaps can also be used as purely decorative elements, such as when a pocket would normally be placed but would add too much bulk.

>> WHEN VISIBLE TOPSTITCHING is not desired on the pocket flap, trim the seam allowances after turning the flap and finish them together. After attaching and pressing down the flap, SEW THE UPPER FLAP CORNERS TO THE MAIN FABRIC WITH INVISIBLE HAND STITCHING, so that the flap will lie flat.

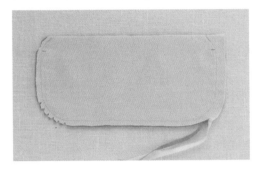
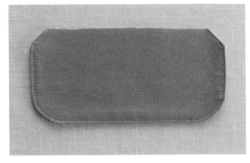
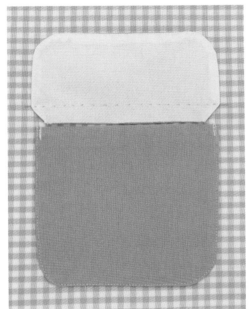

1 Depending on fabric type, optionally reinforce the upper part of the flap with interfacing (on the wrong side). Pin the flap pieces (bottom piece shown here in white) with right sides together around the outer edges and **stitch together, starting and stopping at the upper attachment seam line. Grade seam allowances,** leaving the upper flap's allowance wider. If needed, trim corners diagonally and/or notch rounded edges.

2 Turn the flap right side out and press, making sure that the **underside is not visible from the front. Topstitch the outer edges,** if desired. If the pocket was applied using a twin needle, the flap should be finished the same way.

3 Mark a line ⅝" (1.5cm) parallel to the pocket opening edge. **Pin the attachment line of the flap (see dotted line) along this marking, right sides together,** or secure with adhesive tape. The sides of the flap extend ⅛" (3mm) to each side of the pocket. Stitch. Trim the seam allowance to about ⅛–³⁄₁₆" (4–5mm). **Press the flap downward** and topstitch ¼" (6mm) from the upper edge.

SET-IN POCKETS

Set-in pockets are concealed within the garment and are often made of **densely woven lining fabric**, so that they will add as little bulk as possible. They are located **either along a seam or at a separately cut opening**; hip yoke pockets may also be created between the waist and side seams. Opening edges may optionally be embellished, for example, with contrasting decorative stitching.

HIP-YOKE POCKETS

Hip-yoke pockets are located **on the garment sides directly beneath a pant or skirt waistline**, and are simple to construct. The opening edges run from the waist to the side seam and can be diagonal, curved, or squared. They consist of a **yoke piece with an attached pocket section and a separately cut pocket facing section** that can be made of lining when the primary fabric is heavy. Transfer the pocket opening line to the right side of the yoke piece.

1 Reinforce the opening edge on the front piece of the garment on the wrong side; seam tape works well. Pin and sew on the pocket facing, right sides together, along the opening edge of the garment front. Trim seam allowances, grading them if the fabric is heavy (the allowance on the pocket side should be narrower), and snip curves.

2 Turn the pocket facing to the wrong side, press, and (optionally) topstitch the pocket opening with one or two stitching lines. Pin the yoke section under the front (right side of yoke facing wrong side of front), with the pocket opening aligned with the marking on the yoke.

3 On the wrong side, pin the pocket edges together except for the top and side seams; stitch, then finish the edges together. Baste the top edge of the pocket at the waistband seam and catch it into the waistband when it is applied. The side pocket seam is later caught in with the side seam.

！ THE SET-IN POCKET is made using two different pattern pieces: the pocket section with the visible yoke attached is part of the main garment and is made of the primary fabric; the smaller, hidden pocket section (also called the pocket facing) finishes the opening edge and is often made of lining. **ON VERY HEAVY FABRICS** the larger pocket section may be pieced together from two different fabrics: the yoke area from the main fabric and the lower pocket area from the lining.

SIDE SEAM POCKETS

These types of pockets are **concealed inconspicuously in the side seams of skirts, pullovers, jackets, coats, and pants.** Side seam pockets are easy to construct, and depending on fabric type they may be cut as extensions on the main garment pieces or made separately. Each pocket requires two pieces to create the pocket "bag."

Extended pocket pieces (a) work best with light- to midweight fabrics. Attachment seams are not needed, but yardage requirements will be increased. **Separately attached pockets (b)** are made from the outer garment fabric, or, if that would be too bulky, they can be pieced from an approximately 1⅛" (3cm)-wide extended facing strip and additional sections made of lining fabric (c).

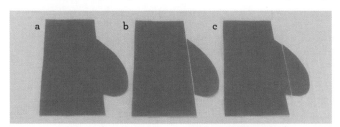

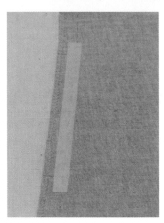
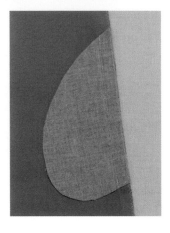
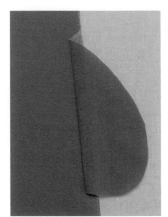

❗ WHEN USING HEAVIER FABRICS you can make one half of the pocket out of the main fabric and the other out of lining (variation b); **THE LINING PIECE IS ATTACHED TO THE FRONT OPENING EDGE.**

❗ TO KEEP THE SEAM ON A PIECED POCKET (variation c) from adding too much bulk, place the lining section, right side up, **UNDER THE FACING STRIP** and sew them together using an overlock or zigzag stitch.

1 Finish the seam allowance edges on the front and back garment pieces, as well as on the straight long edges of the pocket pieces (variation b is shown here); the side seams will be closed later. **Reinforce the front piece with a strip of interfacing or seam tape,** to prevent the opening edge from stretching.

2 With right sides together, pin the pocket bag sections between the pocket opening markings on both the **front and back** garment side seams. **Stitch close to the seam line.**

3 Press the bag sections **outward over the attachment seam.**

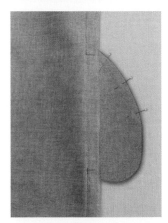

4 With right sides together, pin the front and back garment pieces together; the pocket sections stick out to the side. Stitch the side seams above and below the pockets **exactly to the pocket opening markings,** securing seams with back stitching at the beginnings and ends (see blue seam). Press open seam allowances, thereby **flipping open the pocket sections so that they lie right sides together against the garment pieces.** Optionally, topstitch along the pocket opening edges.

5 Press the rear pocket piece toward the garment front and trim the extending piece of seam allowance from the pocket. Pin the **pocket sections with right sides together and stitch;** finish the edges together.

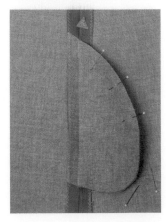

ZIPPERED POCKETS

Zippered pockets are a popular detail on **sportswear and leisurewear;** the openings may be **positioned diagonally, vertically, or horizontally.** The components are a zipper and two pocket sections. A **decorative zipper pull** can be added, if desired. These are available separately in many designs and colors.

1 **Mark the pocket opening** on the wrong side of the project fabric: first the slit, which should be as long as the zipper teeth including the lower stops, then a stitching line on each side of the slit line, each at a distance of the zipper teeth width plus ⅟₃₂–⅟₁₆" (1–2mm). Connect the ends with a short line across, as shown. **Transfer the stitching line markings to the right side of the project fabric.** On the wrong side, **apply a strip of fusible interfacing** on top of the marked lines.

2 On one pocket section make identical markings about 1–1⅛" (2.5–3cm) below the top edge on the wrong side. Pin or baste this pocket section, right sides together and with markings lined up, onto the main fabric and **stitch along the marked seam line.** Cut the slit open with small, sharp scissors **to about ⅜" (10mm) from each end. Snip diagonally to the corners,** creating small triangles.

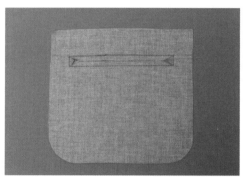

3 Pull the pocket section through to the wrong side and press thoroughly. Sew together the upper zipper tapes *(see page 243, upper far right photo).* Pin or baste the closed zipper, right side up, under the opening edges **with the lower stops visible at the end of the opening.** Topstitch narrowly all around the zipper from the right side. If desired, topstitch again somewhat farther away.

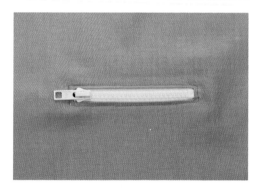

4 On the wrong side, pin the second pocket section to the first, right sides together, and **stitch all around.** If the garment will be unlined, finish the pocket edges.

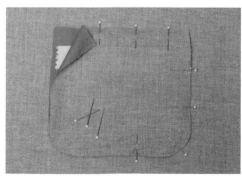

⚠ **WHEN USING HEAVIER FABRIC,** make the pocket section that will be finished together with the pocket's opening edge out of lining fabric to decrease bulk. On very heavy fabrics, both pocket sections can be made of lining, or out of thinner fabric.

⚠ **IF YOU ARE INSERTING A LIGHTWEIGHT ZIPPER** you can calculate the opening length so that the lower stops will be concealed.

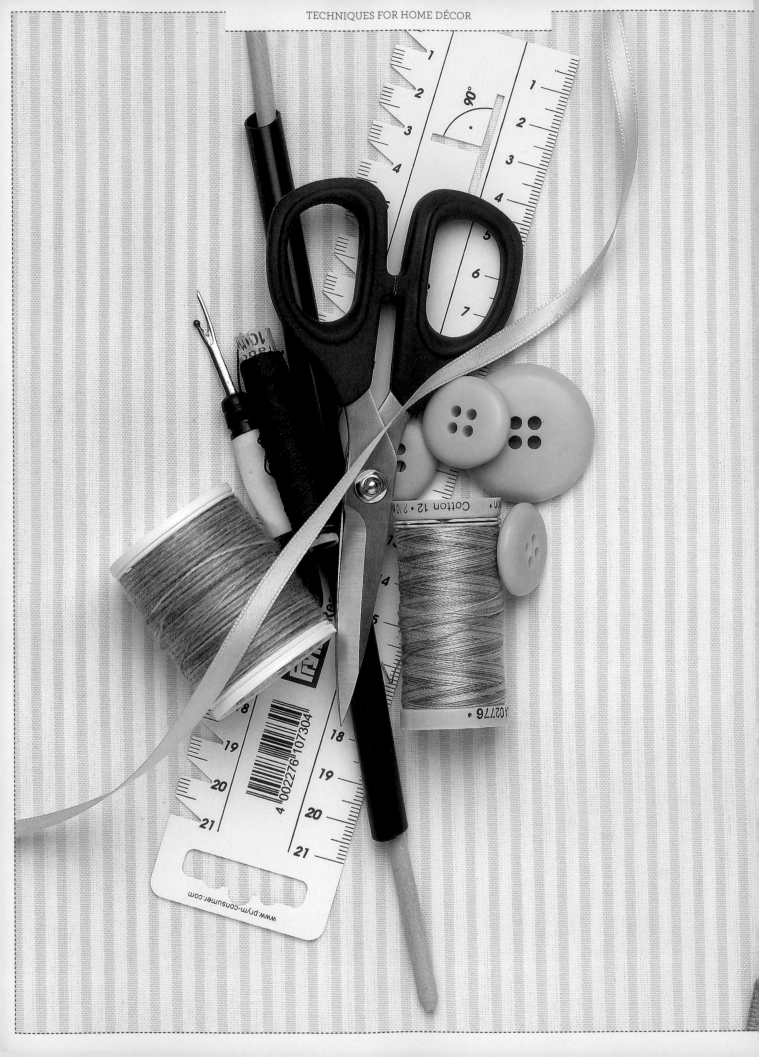

techniques for home décor

SAY HELLO TO PILLOWS, CURTAINS, AND TABLECLOTHS! IN THIS CHAPTER YOU WILL FIND A WIDE RANGE OF DECORATING IDEAS TO HELP TURN YOUR HOME INTO A COMFORTABLE AND COLORFUL OASIS. TAKE INSPIRATION FROM THE OPTIONS YOU FIND HERE, AND LEARN HOW TO TURN SIMPLE ITEMS INTO UNIQUE SHOWSTOPPERS WITH THE HELP OF DECORATIVE SEWING TECHNIQUES.

handsewn trims and tapes

There is a vast assortment of ready-made tapes available in stores. You can make your own, too, if you want them in the same fabric as your project or if you have a specific color, width, or unusual pattern in mind.

BIAS TAPE

Depending on the intended application, it is often necessary to cut fabric strips on the bias, i.e., diagonal to the fabric grain. Bias tape conforms well to shaping and is primarily used for binding raw edges. It is especially well suited for use on curved edges in place of a facing. Simply fold under its raw edges and it can be sewn directly onto fabric pieces as embellishment. Bias strips work best when made from lightweight cotton or jersey.

CUTTING BIAS STRIPS

A bias strip used for binding an edge must be four times the width of the finished binding visible on one side of the fabric edge. So, if the visible finished binding will be ½" (1.25cm) wide, cut a bias strip that is 2" (5cm) wide. Cut it the desired length plus seam allowances at the short ends.

1 Fold one straight-grained edge of the fabric diagonally so the selvage edge aligns with the cut (crossgrain) edge. This is the bias grain. Press the fold.

 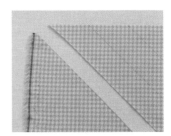

2 Unfold the fabric and mark lines of the desired width parallel to the fold line until you have the total length you need for your finished bias strip. Cut out the strips along the lines, ideally using a straightedge and rotary cutter on a cutting mat.

CONNECTING BIAS STRIPS

If a long bias strip is required, you will often need to connect several shorter strips together. The short ends are pieced together on the grain so that the strip does not lose any elasticity.

1 Pin together the slanted ends of the strips at a right angle and with right sides facing; small ends of the seam allowances will stick out on each side. Stitch.

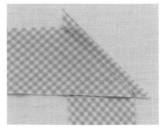 

2 Trim seam allowances to about ¼" (5–6mm), press open, and snip off the excess corners to be flush with the strip edges.

>> IF YOU WANT TO MAKE BIAS STRIPS out of satin, spray the fabric WITH SPRAY STARCH BEFORE CUTTING, and press flat—this will discourage the fabric from slipping and make it easier to work with.

>> It is QUICK AND EASY TO MARK EXACT DISTANCES between lines with the help of an omnigrid ruler (see page 32, figure 6). It can also be used as a guide for a rotary cutter. A large triangular ruler works well, too.

! The instructions for USING BIAS STRIPS to finish edges are on page 103.

PRESSING BIAS STRIPS

Depending on the application, bias strips may be used flat (unfolded) or folded. A bias tape maker is a practical tool to help with pre-folding; an iron is also needed.

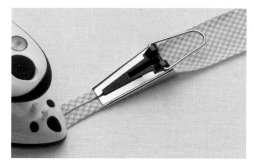

WITHOUT BIAS TAPE MAKER
Fold the strip in half lengthwise, wrong sides together, and lightly press the fold. Open the strip and press each long edge, wrong sides together, to the center.

WITH BIAS TAPE MAKER
Insert the cut strip, wrong side up, into the wide end of the tool and then press the folded strip that emerges from the narrower end.

>> BIAS TAPE MAKERS come in a variety of sizes (see page 47, figure 4). The measurement shown on the tool indicates the WIDTH OF THE COMPLETED TAPE. If the measurement given is 1" (25mm), cut 2" (48mm)-wide strips. Add 1/16" (2mm) for very thin fabrics. The visible binding on the right side of an edge will end up ½" (12.5mm) wide. Instructions are printed on the packaging.

WELTING

Welting strips are flat or have a rounded edge (this version may also be called piping) and are used as a decorative element. Welting is less voluminous than cording. Welting strips are made from bias-cut strips, often in a contrasting color. They can be inserted into seams or used to finish and strengthen edges.

! WELTING IS INSERTED INTO A SEAM OR APPLIED TO EDGES just like piping and cording (see pages 120–122); you can use a zipper foot or edging foot.

DETERMINING WELTING WIDTH

To make welting, *cut bias strips (see page 258)*. Determine the width for flat welting as follows: twice the desired finished visible width plus two times the seam allowance; for example, for a ⅝" seam allowance, ⅝" (1.5cm) x 2 = 1¼" (3cm). The length is as needed.

FLAT WELTING
Fold strips lengthwise, wrong sides together, and press. You may topstitch along the seam line, although this is not absolutely necessary.

ROUNDED WELTING

1 To calculate the width of rounded/piped welting, add together the circumference of the filler cord and two times the seam allowance. To determine the cord circumference, lay the cord as pictured and fold a small corner of the fabric over it; pin in place. Mark a ⅝" (1.5cm) seam allowance, cut through both fabric layers along the marks, and unfold (this is the width for the starting bias strip). Depending on its fiber content, the cord may need preshrinking.

2 Wrap the bias strip wrong sides together around the cord and use a zipper foot to stitch closely along the cord.

FABRIC STRAPS

Flat fabric straps have many potential uses—as ties, hanging loops, or bag handles—and can be made from either one or two fabric pieces. Usually both ends are straight, but depending on the application or the desired look, they may also be rounded or pointed. Ties are usually made without interfacing, so that they can be more easily knotted.

SEWING FABRIC TUBES

For flat straps you first sew a tube, right sides together, which then gets turned right side out. Usually at least one end remains open for turning. If both ends will be attached in a seam, the tube is stitched only along the lengthwise edges. If the tube is made from two fabric pieces, they may be contrasting.

MADE FROM A SINGLE PIECE

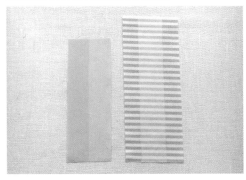

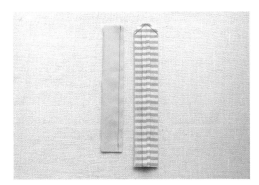

>> IF YOU NEED A FABRIC STRAP WITH BOTH ENDS CLOSED, sew around all sides, leaving a small opening unsewn for turning (a turning hole) at the center of one long edge. After turning, close the hole during topstitching or USING INVISIBLE HAND STITCHING.

1 Cut the strip: the length as needed (including seam allowance), the width double the finished visible width, plus two times the seam allowances. Depending on fabric type, reinforce the wrong side with interfacing: one lengthwise half if the seam is to be on the side (left), or down the center if the seam is to be centered (right). The interfacing is the width of the finished strap.

2 Fold strips lengthwise, right sides together, then stitch along the long edge. Trim seam allowances and snip corners diagonally. For the tube on the right, move the seam to the center and press seam allowances open. Stitch one end of the tube closed as desired (straight across or to a point). *Turn the fabric tube right side out (see page 261).*

MADE FROM TWO PIECES

1 Cut two strips of the required length and width (see step 1 above), with seam allowances added all around. Depending on the fabric type and application, reinforce one strip from the wrong side with interfacing.

2 Pin strips right sides together, then stitch together along both long sides and (optional) across one short end. Trim seam allowances and snip corners diagonally. *Turn the fabric tube right side out (see page 261).*

TURNING A FABRIC TUBE

You can turn a fabric tube with the help of special accessories like loop turners and tube turner sets, but it also can be done using just a bodkin or safety pin.

! A LOOP TURNER (see page 262) can be used to turn a tube whether or not one narrow end is closed.

WITH A TUBE TURNER SET

Even very narrow fabric tubes can be turned easily with a tube turner set; one narrow end of the tube must be stitched closed. The set, available at sewing supply stores, includes three plastic tubes in various sizes, each with a corresponding wooden or metal rod (see page 47, figure 3b). The smallest size turns tubes from ⅜–⅝" (9–16mm), the middle size from ¾–1" (19–25mm), and the largest size handles pieces wider than 1" (25mm).

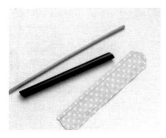

1 Assemble the stitched fabric tube and the corresponding-sized tube turner pieces.

2 Insert the plastic tube into the fabric tube all the way to the end. Press the rod onto the closed narrow end of the fabric tube so that it begins to push the fabric into the plastic tube positioned inside. Continuing pushing, thereby turning the fabric right side out.

3 Press the resulting strap thoroughly; topstitch close to the edges, if desired.

SEWING A FOLDED FABRIC STRAP

Long straps such as apron ties are best sewn together along folded edges, since turning such long pieces would be difficult. Straps used as ties are usually not interfaced, so that they will knot more easily.

1 Cut a strip: the length as needed, the width double the finished size, plus two times the seam allowances. Fold the strip lengthwise, right sides together. Mark one end at a diagonal and press seam allowances to the wrong side.

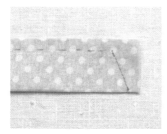

2 Turn the strip and pin together the folded edges, with seam allowances together; stitch, leaving the square narrow end open (it will later be caught in a seam).

REINFORCING A STRAP ATTACHMENT POINT

Heavily stressed straps such as ties or bag handles can be further reinforced at their attachment points. Topstitch the area in a square, then across the square in an X. Pull the threads to the wrong side and tie them off.

NARROW TUBES

Narrow fabric tubes can be made in varying widths out of bias tape. They are suitable for use as thin ties and hanging loops, and for making frog closures or loop closures. When made with filler cord they hold a nicely rounded shape. They can be made with purchased bias tape, or you can *cut your own bias strips (see page 258)*.

WITH FILLER CORD

These are made using a bias strip the width of the cord circumference plus 1" (2.5cm). Depending on its fiber content, the cord may require preshrinking.

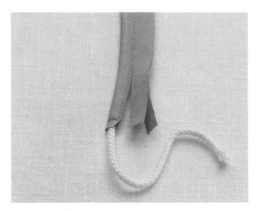

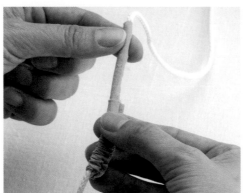

1 Cut a bias strip to the desired finished length (plus seam allowances) and cut a piece of filler cord double the desired finished length plus ⅜" (1cm). Wrap the strip, right sides together, around one half of the cord length, leaving ⅜" (1cm) of cord sticking out at the beginning end. Use a zipper foot to stitch narrowly alongside the cord (although not too tightly, or else it will be impossible to turn); sew across the cord at the end of the bias strip. Sew a second line of stitching ¹⁄₃₂–¹⁄₁₆" (1–2mm) away from the first to reinforce the seams. Trim seam allowances close to the second line of stitching.

2 Pull the fabric over the other half of the filler cord, starting from the center. Trim exposed cord ends.

WITHOUT FILLER CORD

For very narrow fabric rolls, use a bias strip 1–1¼" (2.5–3cm) wide. *A loop turner (see page 47, figure 3a)* may be used for turning, or, depending on the size of the tube, a small safety pin.

» **IF YOU WANT TO TURN A NARROW TUBE WITHOUT A FILLER CORD** using a bodkin or safety pin, leave long thread ends attached after sewing. Feed one thread end through the bodkin or pin and knot it tightly to the other end. Feed the pin through the tube, thereby turning it right side out.

Fold the bias strip lengthwise in half, right sides together, and stitch at presser foot width. To reinforce the seam, stitch again ¹⁄₃₂–¹⁄₁₆" (1–2mm) away from the first line of stitching. Do not trim the seam allowance, as it will help give the tube a fuller shape. Turn the tube with the loop turner. Insert the turner into the fabric tube and catch the fabric at the opposite end with the hook; close the hook. Carefully pull the hook back through the tube, thereby turning it right side out.

WALL ORGANIZER POCKETS

Hanging wall organizers need pockets that have enough room to hold all sorts of small items. A simple way to increase a pocket's volume is to add expanding pleats between the front (outside) and back (inside) pocket. Pockets such as this are known as bellows pockets *(see page 250)*. Cotton and fabrics with a high natural fiber content are ideal for these pockets because they respond better to pressing and hold folds longer than do synthetics.

1 Cut a pocket, extending the width to accommodate the desired fold depth and seam allowance: for a fold depth of ⅝" (1.5cm), add an additional 1¼" (3cm) to each side. Also include the following seam allowances: at the top, ¾" (2cm) for a facing, plus ⅜" (1cm) all around (here shown as dotted lines). Mark the side fold lines. Finish side and bottom edges. Press under ⅜" (1cm), then ¾" (2cm) at the top edge; topstitch.

2 Press the seam allowances to the wrong side on the bottom and sides of the pocket; then press in the folds along the marked fold line. Topstitch close to the outer side edges; this will stabilize the fold.

3 Mark the pocket position outline on the main fabric piece. Secure the side pleats at the marked location using adhesive tape and topstitch the bottom pleat (only) over the previous stitching *(see page 251)*.

4 Pin the pocket's bottom edge to the main fabric and topstitch as you did the sides. Pin the upper sides for ¾" (2cm), starting from the top edge, and stitch through all layers. As an option you can reinforce the pocket opening edges with a *bar tack (see page 251)*.

>> BELLOWS POCKETS with extended side facings can be used on shirts and pants alike.

pillow talk

PLAIN (OR BLANK) PILLOWS are often available for very low prices at furniture or discount stores. Fitted with **NEW COVERS**, they can become unique décor pieces.

! **COORDINATE PILLOW FABRICS** with the textiles already in your home.

Pillows are probably the most prevalent and most popular home accessory. With their different shapes, colors, and patterns, they can continually add new accents inside the home or on a porch or in the yard. They are easy to swap out to match seasons, meet changing needs, or keep up with the latest fashion and color trends. Pillows come in many shapes and materials—toss or accent pillows, wedges or tubes, heart-shaped pillows, pillows for children, and floor pillows, to name a few.

PILLOW EMBELLISHMENTS

Cases for accent pillows are quick and easy to sew, and changing them can instantly refresh the look of sofas, chairs, stools, and beds. There is almost no limit to the embellishments that can be made to pillowcases (generally added before completing the case itself). Embellishments might include decorative stitching (*see page 86*), applied braids or ribbons (*see page 131*), appliqués (*see pages 123–124*), embroidery (*see pages 132–133*), tucks (*see page 115*), or pintucks (*see pages 114–115*). The edges of a pillow can also be embellished, by incorporating decorative elements such as cording (*see pages 120–122*), ruffles (*see pages 118–119*), lace (*see page 113*), fringe (*see pages 126–127*), or pompom trim in the seams between the front and back fabric pieces. Flanged hems (*see page 268*) are especially attractive on pillows and add a nostalgic charm when sewn with a wing needle. Three-dimensional embellishments, rhinestones, and quilting can also add interest. Pillowcases can also be made using many different closure methods.

PILLOWCASE WITH ENVELOPE CLOSURE

The quickest and easiest pillowcase closure is the envelope closure, where the pillow back is made of two overlapping sections. The case is usually made from a single piece of fabric; you can also cut contrasting front and back pieces—don't forget to add ⅝" (1.5cm) seam allowances to the single front piece and two back pieces.

1 For a pillow measuring 16" x 16" (40.5cm x 40.5cm), cut a fabric piece 16" (44cm) wide by 44" (112cm) long. Make a 1" (2.5cm) *deep folded hem (see page 111)* on each narrow end, and topstitch close to the folds using straight stitches. Fold over the hemmed sections, right sides together, so that they overlap by about 8" (20cm) in the center back of the case.

2 Pin side edges and stitch together with a ⅝" (1.5cm) seam allowance. Trim corners diagonally and finish seam allowances.

3 Turn the pillowcase right side out, square out corners, and press.

>> **EMBELLISH THE FOLDED HEMS** with embroidery stitching or iron an appliqué onto the front of the case.

! **EMBELLISHMENTS** such as appliqués, decorative stitching, embroidery, or ribbons should be applied before sewing the front and back of the case together.

! **CASE MEASUREMENTS SHOULD ALWAYS INCLUDE** ⅝" (1.5cm) seam allowances. A 16" x 16" (40.5cm x 40.5cm) pillow requires pieces that are 17¼" x 17¼" (44cm x 44cm).

ZIPPERED PILLOWCASE

Zippers are a practical pillowcase closure and can be positioned either at the lower third of the back panel or in a side seam. If a zipper is placed on the back, the back must be cut in two pieces.

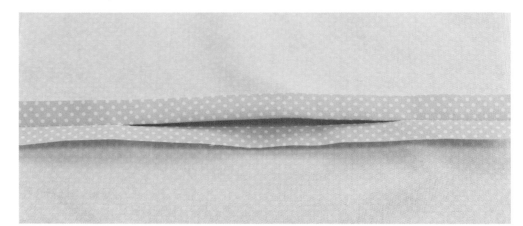

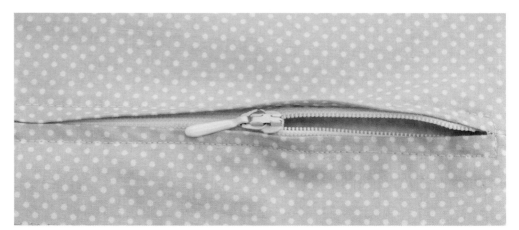

>> You can ADD INTEREST TO PILLOWCASES simply by using different fabrics for the front and back.

! IF THE ZIPPER is in a side seam, the front and back are cut to the same size; for example, for a 16" x 16" (40.5cm x 40.5cm) pillow, cut 17¼" x 17¼" (44cm x 44cm) pieces. The zipper is then sewn in the side seam as described. Choose a zipper 2–4" (5–10cm) SHORTER THAN THE PILLOW WIDTH.

! BEFORE SEWING THE PILLOW PIECES TOGETHER, make sure to open the zipper so that you will have an opening through which to turn the completed pillowcase right side out.

1 For a 16" x 16" (40.5cm x 40.5cm) pillow, cut a fabric piece 17¼" x 17¼" (44cm x 44cm) for the front; for the back pieces, cut one that is 17¼" (44cm) x 11½" (29cm) and one that is 17¼" (44cm) x 7½" (19cm). On both back pieces, finish one long edge with zigzag stitching and place these edges right sides together. Stitch a 2½" (6.5cm)-long seam at each end so that an opening of approximately 12" (30cm) remains for the zipper. Press allowances apart.

2 Place the joined fabric right side up and center the zipper under the open seam allowances so that it is concealed when closed. Pin the zipper in place and *sew in using the centered zipper method (see page 243)*. Open the zipper, then pin the front and back pieces right sides together and sew all around with a ⅝" (1.5cm) seam allowance. Trim the corners diagonally, finish the seam allowance edges, pull the pillowcase right side out through the zipper opening, square out the corners, and press.

PILLOWCASE WITH BUTTON BAND CLOSURE

A button band may be worked on either the front or the back of a pillowcase. If the closure will be on the front, decorative buttons, bows, or other embellishments can be used.

1 For a 16" x 16" (40.5cm x 40.5cm) pillow, cut a fabric piece 17¼" x 17¼" (44cm x 44cm) for the front; for the back pieces, cut one that is 17¼" x 16" (44cm x 41cm) and one that is 17¼" x 7" (44cm x 18cm). On one long edge of both back pieces, fold under 1⅛" (3cm) to the wrong side, then fold under again the same amount and sew a deep folded hem (see page 111).

2 In the hem of the larger back piece, make three long buttonholes, approximately ¾" (2cm). The first and third buttonholes are positioned about 4½" (11.5cm) from the respective edges. Pin the hem with the buttonholes over the hem of the smaller back piece, right sides facing up, as shown; stitch the bands together ⅜" (1cm) away from the edge. Pin the back and front, right sides together, and stitch together all around with a ⅝" (1.5cm) seam allowance.

3 Finish the seam allowances, trim the corners diagonally, turn the pillowcase, square out the corners, sew on the buttons to match the buttonholes, and press.

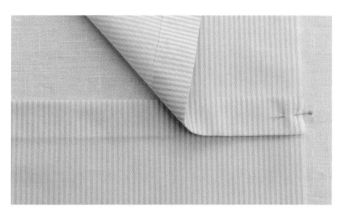

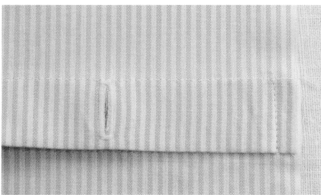

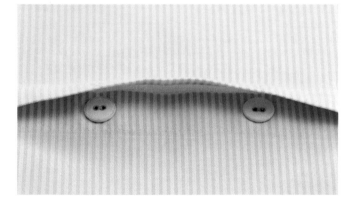

! INSTEAD OF SEWING buttons and buttonholes, use NO-SEW SNAPS, or sew on hook and loop tape (see pages 239–240).

» THE PILLOW can be embellished with DECORATIVE BUTTONS or with ribbons sewn onto the underlying fabric (see pages 268–269).

QUILTED PILLOWCASE WITH CORDING AND 3-D APPLIQUÉ

Pillowcases with a sewn-in quilted layer are soft, lofty, and warming. Those that are quilted on both sides are especially cuddly. Extra touches such as a 3-D appliqué or cording will make the pillowcase truly unique.

» A ROLLER FOOT *(see page 22, figure 4)* works well for creating QUILTED FABRIC.

! FOR MAKING QUILTED FABRIC, use THIN, FUSIBLE FLEECE INTERFACING.

QUILTING/WADDING

Apply fusible fleece interfacing to the front and back pieces for a pillowcase with an *envelope closure (see page 265),* leaving the edges—about 1½" (4cm)—free of interfacing. Using a 9 spi (3mm-long) straight stitch, quilt the material at 2" (5cm) intervals *(see page 134).*

If your interfacing does not have a diamond pattern built in, use tailor's chalk or a marker to draw a line on the interfacing at the desired angle. This will be the first sewing line, which will be the guideline for the remaining lines to be worked in parallel or at a right angle, spaced at identical distances. We recommend you use a straightedge for drawing the lines. Work until the entire piece is quilted in a grid pattern.

Sew the envelope closure, making a 1½" (4cm)-deep folded hem on the long edge of the overlap (upper piece) and a ¾" (2cm) hem on the other piece. Pin pieces together so that the upper piece overlaps the remaining lower piece, right sides facing up. Stitch together ⅜" (1cm) away from the side edges.

CORDING

Round off the pillowcase corners slightly to make it easier to sew the cording around the corners. Install a cording foot or zipper foot in the machine and cut the fabric strips for the cording.

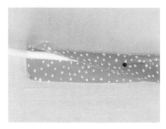  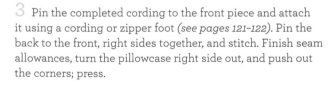

1 Fold the fabric strips lengthwise with wrong sides together, enclosing the filler cord at the fold line *(see page 120).*

2 Pin the edges of the fabric strip and sew together closely alongside the filler cord using a straight stitch.

3 Pin the completed cording to the front piece and attach it using a cording or zipper foot *(see pages 121–122).* Pin the back to the front, right sides together, and stitch. Finish seam allowances, turn the pillowcase right side out, and push out the corners; press.

3-D APPLIQUÉ

3-D appliqués distinguish themselves from other appliqués both in their appearance and in the way they are created. They are not applied directly onto the main fabric, but rather made separately and attached to an item such as a pillow or blanket at selected positions using hand or machine stitches. Alternatively, they can be buttoned on. The appliqués have a sculptural look, and when they are attached with hand stitching or with buttons they can easily be removed or interchanged.

1 Two pieces of fabric are used for the petal appliqués. Apply a fusible interfacing/ stabilizer to the wrong side of the fabric. Draw the outline of the flower on the wrong side of one fabric piece; cut it out.

2 Place the cut piece, wrong sides together, against the second piece of fabric and cut out a second flower. Pin the two together, matching raw edges.

3 Stitch the edges of the flower together with a satin stitch, using machine embroidery thread for both top and bobbin. Make a second, smaller flower out of coordinating fabric. Center the flower pieces on top of each other and fasten them together with a button.

4 Attach the flower to the pillowcase by hand or with the machine.

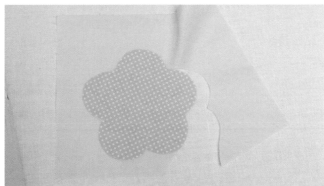

» TO MAKE THE FLOWER PIECES INTERCHANGEABLE, make buttonholes in the center, SEW A BUTTON TO THE PILLOWCASE, and button the flower pieces to the case.

! FABRICS CAN BE CUT AS EASILY AS PAPER when they are backed with fusible, tear-away stabilizer (see pages 57–58). Motifs can be DRAWN beforehand on the UNCOATED SIDE OF THE STABILIZER. CUT the stabilizer piece generously, then IRON it onto the wrong side of the fabric and CUT IT OUT ALONG THE MOTIF OUTLINES. Once motifs are cut, REMOVE THE STABILIZER. It can be used as a template up to five more times.

BOX CUSHION

Box cushions are essentially miniature mattresses, and the classic edge treatment used on them is called a mattress edge. They are popular to use for seating on floors or steps, or in the garden or for picnics. They may be stuffed with foam, kapok filling, or fiberfill. Typical design details include topstitching, buttons that are sewn on through all layers, and a carrying handle. The fabric choice should be guided by the cushion's intended usage—whether it will be indoors or outdoors, heavily used or primarily decorative, et cetera. They are especially handy in 16" x 16" (40.5cm x 40.5cm) or 20" x 20" (50.75cm x 50.75cm) sizes.

>> MATERIALS
FOR A BOX CUSHION
15¾" x 15¾" (40cm x 40cm),
4" (10cm) depth

Measurements include
⅝" (1.5cm) seam allowances

• 2x 17" x 17" (43cm x 43cm) fabric pieces (cushion top and bottom)
• 4x 17" x 5⅛" (43cm x 13cm) fabric pieces (cushion side panels)
• 3" x 9" (8cm x 25cm) fabric piece (handle)
• 8 ⅝" (1.5cm) buttons to cover
• Colorful fabric scraps for covering buttons

>> USE COARSE
LINEN and attach a leather handle and leather buttons (*see page 97*).

>> TO SEW ON THE
BUTTONS use THIN
COTTON CROCHET
THREAD.

! BOX CUSHIONS
CAN ALSO BE STUFFED
WITH A PIECE OF CUT
FOAM, in which case,
instead of a turning hole, you
will need to install a zipper
in one of the side panels
(for example, a 14" (35.5cm)
zipper for a 16" (40.5cm)
square cushion. INSTALL
THE ZIPPER BEFORE
SEWING TOGETHER THE
SIDE PANELS.

1 *Create the handle and reinforce the handle attachment points (see page 261).* Fold under one narrow end of the handle fabric strip by ⅜" (1cm) and press; fold the strip lengthwise in half, right sides together, and pin; stitch with a ⅜" (1cm) seam allowance, starting at the unfolded narrow end. The folded end is not sewn shut, as the opening is needed to turn the strap. Turn the handle right side out, press, and topstitch close to the edges all around. Attach the handle to the center of one side panel.

2 Sew the side panels together to create a large continuous circle by placing the short ends right sides together and stitching with a ⅝" (1.5cm) seam allowance; start and end ⅝" (1.5cm) away from each edge.

3 and 4 Pin one cushion piece, right sides together, to the sewn-together side panels. Pin or baste the edges together precisely at the corners; stitch the pieces together with a ⅝" (1.5cm) seam allowance, sewing back and forth one time at each corner.

5 Stitch the remaining cushion piece to the other edge of the side panels, leaving an opening for turning at the edge opposite the handle. Press seams and press under the ⅝" (1.5cm) seam allowance at the turning hole.

6 Trim corners diagonally and turn the cushion cover right side out. Stuff the cover firmly with your chosen filler, making sure to distribute the filling evenly. Close the turning hole by hand using *slipstitches (see page 75)*.

7, 8, and 9 Create a welt *(see page 259)* around all edges of the cushion by handsewing doubled backstitches *(see page 72)* 1" (2.5cm) from the edges, including at the corner edges of the side panels.

10 *Cover the buttons with fabric (see page 233).* Use a marker to indicate button placement 5" (12cm) from the cushion's corners, four times, on both sides of the cushion. With a long needle (upholstery or doll-making needle) and heavy-duty thread, pull the thread through the metal eye of a button and down through all layers of the cushion, emerging at the marking on the opposite side.

11 Thread a second button onto the working thread, pull the thread back through the cushion to the first button, and pull hard enough on the thread to create an indentation in the cushion; knot the thread multiple times and cut off. Repeat for all buttons on both sides.

12 This is the finished box cushion.

curtains
and drapes

It is truly not difficult to sew curtains. There are myriad fabrics available, and your own ideas about color, pattern, curtain type, and hanging style can be easily and quickly realized.

! IF PLEAT TAPE IS MARKED "3:¼ pleats," the tape has an allowance of 3, meaning the curtain fabric must be the window width multiplied by three + seam allowances for any panels to be sewn together + allowances for folded hem borders at the curtain edges.

MEASURING FOR YOUR CURTAINS

Before you purchase fabric for curtains or drapes, you must measure your windows and/or glass doors, as well as consider which hanging technique is most suitable. A long folding ruler or measuring tape is best for measuring; do not use a yardstick, as the measurements will be too imprecise. The width of the windowsill, if there is one, is a good starting width; otherwise measure the inside width of the window frame.

PLEAT TAPE AND CURTAIN WIDTH

The width of the curtain fabric is dependent not only on window width, but also, when pleat tape is used, on the pleat tape—that is, on whether the band creates double, triple, or quadruple pleats. Guidelines for fabric allowance are noted on curtain tapes, and a drapery store employee can help with these calculations as well. Curtains without pleat tape as a rule must be twice the window width + seam allowances for any fabric panels that will be sewn together + seam allowances for doubled side borders.

CALCULATING CURTAIN LENGTH

Curtain length is calculated in accordance with the window height, the curtain style, the hanging technique, the distance between the curtain rod or rail and the top edge of the window frame, the doubled top border of the curtain, which should be at least 2" (5cm) deep, and the hem, which should always be doubled and be at least 2" (5cm) deep.
Curtain fabrics that might shrink should always be prewashed; otherwise, increase both width and length by 10% when sewing.

! WE RECOMMEND before sewing that you finish the edges of your fabric all around with zigzag or overlock stitching.

! AS A RULE, FOR SEWING CURTAINS use standard thread for both top and bottom, matching in color to your fabric, and sew with straight stitches at a length of 9 spi (3mm).

GENERAL GUIDELINES

When purchasing fabric for curtains, avoid the cheapest offerings, as they are almost guaranteed to pucker and become misshapen. Always have the fabric cut with scissors rather than ripped. (Fabrics are ripped toward a single direction and thus get pulled out of shape.) Consider at the time of purchase whether you may at some point want to make matching pillows or similar items. Fabrics can shrink; inquire about this when you buy it. You may wish to purchase additional yardage and/or wash the fabric before cutting your pieces. Lightweight, smooth cotton fabrics are easy to work with and care for. Consider having your fabric pre-cut to your required length, making your next steps at home easier. When calculating yardage and when cutting, always remember to include seam allowances. Always use high-quality, brand-name sewing thread. Do not pull or stretch your fabric while pressing or sewing; you can easily end up with seams that no longer line up. Be careful to keep all seams the same width. A stitch length between 9 spi and 7.5 spi (3 and 3.5mm) will remain more elastic, and the seam will not pull. Inexperienced sewers may wish to use an edging foot to maintain exact sewing lines.
Always press corners well after turning; this will make sewing them easier. Likewise, always press seams after sewing them. Save hemming as the last step so that you can do a trial hang first to determine the ultimate correct length.

» DEPENDING ON YOUR DÉCOR PREFERENCES, you can sew using contrasting thread or make BORDERS AND HEMS WITH DECORATIVE STITCHING.

CURTAINS WITH A ROD POCKET

A rod pocket (also known as a rod casing or rod pocket) at the top of a curtain is a quick and easy curtain treatment variation. The curtain rod is inserted through the pocket. With lightweight fabrics, the fabric can be gathered along the rod; heavier fabrics tend to lie flatter.

CALCULATING FABRIC REQUIREMENTS

Length = Distance from curtain rod to top of windowsill in inches (cm) + window height in inches (cm) + pocket (2x width of curtain rod) + ⅝" (1.5cm) seam allowance + 4" (10cm) hem

Width = double width of window + 5" (12cm) seam allowance

 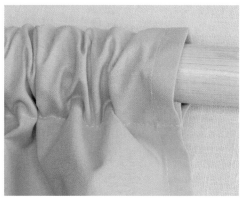

! WHEN MULTIPLE FABRIC PANELS ARE SEWN TOGETHER *(see page 276)*, an ADDITIONAL ⬚" (1.5CM) SEAM ALLOWANCE PER PANEL must be included to end up with the correct width. Fabric panels are sewn together with a French seam *(see page 90)*, where the first seam is ¼" (0.5cm) wide, and the second is ⅜" (1cm).

1   Cut the fabric along the straight/lengthwise grain. To achieve the desired width, two or more fabric panels can be sewn together using a *French seam (see page 90)*. Fold in the seam allowances at each side edge and sew a 1¼" (3.5cm)-wide doubled border. At the top of the curtain, fold under the calculated depth for the rod pocket plus a ⅝" (1.5cm) additional fold to the inside. Sew the pocket, stitching the seam closely along the lower folded edge.

2   On the lower curtain edge, sew a 2" (5cm) doubled hem: fold the hem to the wrong side 2" (5cm), then fold it again the same amount.

ROD POCKET WITH RUFFLE

A pretty variation on a plain rod pocket features a supplemental ruffle. This requires additional fabric equal to twice the ruffle height.

The sewing technique for a ruffled rod pocket is identical to that described above. The difference is that more fabric is folded over at the top: the calculated amount for the pocket + double the ruffle height + ⅝" (1.5cm) seam allowance. For example, if the ruffle is to be 1⅛" (3cm) tall, an additional 2½" (6cm) of fabric must be included in the total fabric. After the rod pocket is sewn closely along its lower folded edge from the reverse side, the ruffle is stitched. In this case, measure 1⅛" (3cm) down from the top fold line and stitch along that line to form the pocket.

» Sew over THE ROD POCKET SEAM WITH A DECORATIVE STITCH.

CURTAINS WITH CLIPS

Curtains that hang with clips from a curtain rod **(also known as ring top curtains)** are quick to sew and hang. This style is appropriate for shorter curtains, such as at a kitchen window, or for longer curtains made from lightweight fabric such as batiste or sheer linen. The rod will require appropriate end caps or some other retaining mechanism to keep the clips in place. This style is well suited to both short and long bistro curtains.

CALCULATING FABRIC REQUIREMENTS

Length = Distance from curtain rod to top of windowsill in inches (cm) + window height in inches (cm) + 8" (20cm) hem + length of clips

Width = double width of window in inches (cm) + 5" (12cm) seam allowance

! IF MULTIPLE FABRIC PANELS ARE SEWN TOGETHER to create a curtain, a ⅝" (1.5cm) SEAM ALLOWANCE PER PANEL MUST BE ADDED.

! The fabric panels are sewn together using a *French seam (see page 90)*, whereby the first seam is ¼" (0.5cm) wide and the second is ⅜" (1cm).

≫ ATTACH A LACE BORDER OR WOVEN RIBBON to the UPPER CURTAIN EDGE. This is an easy way to give a curtain a particular feel (romantic, country farmhouse, or urban modern, for example).

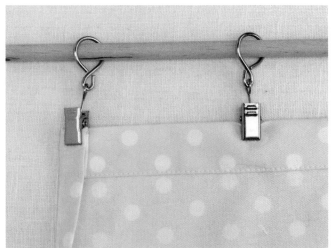

1 Cut the fabric along the straight/lengthwise grain. If needed to create the curtain width, connect two or more fabric panels with a *French seam (see page 90)*. Turn the seam allowances at both side edges to the wrong side and finish with a 1⅛" (3cm) *doubled hem (see page 275)*. On the remaining raw edges make a 2" (5cm)-wide doubled hem. Fold under 2" (5cm) twice and stitch close to the fold. Turn back each side edge once and fasten it with a clip.

2 Determine the midpoint between the two side edge clips and fasten the next clip there. Determine the midpoint between this center clip and each side, attaching the next clips at those points. Continue to attach remaining clips in this manner.

CURTAIN WITH ARCHED TABS

Create a coffeehouse atmosphere with these (typically) short curtains with arched tabs that hang by the tabs from a rod. They work well as short kitchen curtains or as longer drapes made of cotton; depending on the fabric chosen, they can convey a quaint farmhouse feel.

CALCULATING FABRIC REQUIREMENTS

Length for a short curtain = Window height in inches (cm) + 12" (30.5cm) fold + 3" (8cm) hem
Length for a long curtain = Distance from curtain rod to top of window + window height in inches (cm) + 12" (30.5cm) fold + 4" (10cm) hem
Width = 1.5x width of window in inches (cm) (each arch plus tab requires 7½" [19cm] of fabric) + 1⅛" (3cm) seam allowance

1 Cut a 5½" (14cm) x 8" (20cm) piece of light cardboard; starting 5⅛" (13cm) from one short end, use a compass at the centerline to draw a rounded edge that ends at the same point on each side. Cut out the curve.

2 Cut out the fabric along the straight/lengthwise grain line. Sew multiple panels together to achieve the needed width, using a *French seam (see page 90)*. Finish the top and bottom edges of the curtain panel with zigzag or overlock stitching. Fold over 10¼" (26cm) at the upper edge, press, and pin. Position the arch template 2½" (6.5cm) from one side edge and use a disappearing-ink marker to draw the arch on the doubled fabric. Reposition the template 2" (5cm) from the first outline and mark another arch; continue across in this manner. There must be 2½" (6.5cm) of fabric left beyond the final arch. Once all arches are marked, sew along the outlines. Cut out the arches ¼" (0.6cm) from the stitching lines.

3 Turn the arch/tab section right side out, press seams, fold back 2½" (6cm) on each tab strap and topstitch in place. Make a 1½" (4cm) or 2" (5cm) (for longer curtains) hem at the lower edge.

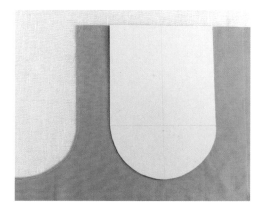

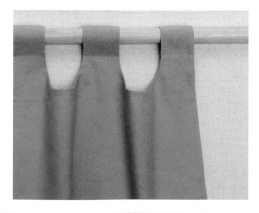

! **THE YARDAGE** must be calculated so that there are 2½" (6.5cm) beyond the last arch; numbers will need to be rounded off.

EXAMPLE: Window width 31½" (80 cm) x 1.5 = 47¼" (120cm); 74¼" (120cm) – 1⅛" (3cm) seam allowance = 46" (117cm); 46" (117cm) ÷ 7½" (19cm) = 6.13; so the curtain will have six arches. **ADDITIONAL FABRIC MAY BE TRIMMED FROM THE SIDES.**

! **IF MULTIPLE FABRIC PANELS NEED TO BE SEWN TOGETHER** to make a sufficiently wide curtain *(see page 276)*, a ⅝" (1.5cm) **SEAM ALLOWANCE PER PANEL MUST BE ADDED.** The panels are sewn with a French seam *(see page 90)*, whereby the first seam is ¼" (0.5cm) wide and the second is ⅜" (1cm).

» **INSTEAD OF SEWING THE LOOPS CLOSED IN BACK**, hang the curtain using clips.

! **MAKE THE CURTAIN WITHOUT THE TOP FOLD**; instead, make it from a double layer of fabrics in two different patterns. This way the curtain can have **EITHER SIDE FACING OUT.**

CURTAIN WITH TIES

Tied curtains can look refreshingly unconventional, especially when the ties are made from a combination of fabrics. The curtains are hung from a rod using fabric strips that are tied into bows or knots.

CALCULATING FABRIC REQUIREMENTS

Length = Distance from curtain rod to top of window + window height in inches (cm) + 4" (10cm) for the hem
Width = Double the width of window in inches (cm) + 5" (12cm) seam allowance
Facing: Length = 3" (8cm), width as for curtain, 1⅛" (3cm) seam allowance
Fabric for ties: 34" x 2½" (86.5cm x 6.5cm) per tie; alternatively, use purchased ribbons

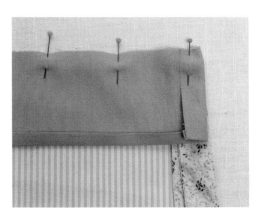

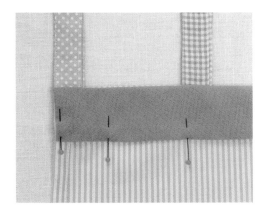

! **THE NUMBER OF TIES** is based on the **WIDTH OF THE FINISHED CURTAIN** and the desired distance between each tie.

! **IF MULTIPLE FABRIC PANELS NEED TO BE SEWN TOGETHER** (see page 276) to make a sufficiently wide curtain, a ⅝" (1.5cm) **SEAM ALLOWANCE PER PANEL MUST BE ADDED.** The panels are sewn with a *French seam (see page 90)*, whereby the first seam is ¼" (0.5cm) wide and the second is ⅜" (1cm).

» **LOOPS INSTEAD OF TIES:** Shorten the ties somewhat and pin the short ends at the upper edge between the curtain panels and facing; stitch. This will create loops.

1 Cut the fabric for curtain, facing, and ties along the straight/lengthwise grain line. Sew multiple panels together to achieve the needed width, using a *French seam (see page 90)*. Fold in the seam allowances at both side edges and make 1⅛" (3cm) hemmed borders. To make ties: Fold under ⅜" (1cm) at one narrow edge, pin the strip in half lengthwise, right sides together, stitch with a ¼" (0.6cm) seam allowance on the long edge and the remaining (unfolded) narrow edge.
Turn the tie, press, and topstitch close to all edges. Fold finished ties in half crosswise and pin the folded edge flush with the upper edge of the curtain. The first and last ties are placed directly at the side edges, and the rest are spaced evenly between. To make ties with contrasting fabrics, cut ties in half and pin the raw edges of nonmatching halves onto the curtain edge to be sewn on together. Fold under and press ⅝" (1.5cm) along one long side of the facing. Place the other long side, right sides together, over the ties, leaving ⅝" (1.5cm) of facing extending past each side edge.

2 Stitch the facing to the curtain with a ⅝" (1.5cm) seam allowance, press the seam, turn the facing to the wrong side, fold in the ⅝" (1.5cm) seam allowances at the facing side edges; pin, and topstitch the facing to the curtain close to the edge.

3 Make a 2" (5cm) *doubled hem (see page 275)* at the lower edge of the curtain.

GATHERED CURTAINS

To easily create curtains that are evenly gathered or pleated, sew an appropriate pleating tape onto the upper part of the curtain. The folds are created when the ties on the tape are pulled together after application. Various types of pleating are possible. Pleat tape can be found in specialty stores or in the home décor section of most sewing shops. It is available in a variety of widths and comes in white, cream, or transparent versions. Pleat tape also has tiny loops for attaching curtain sliders or hooks that can then be integrated with traverse curtain rods. To conceal the curtain hooks, a header of at least 1" (2.5cm) must be included when sewing the curtain.

CALCULATING FABRIC REQUIREMENTS
Length = Distance from curtain rod to top of window in inches (cm) + window height in inches (cm) + header: 2x desired header height in inches (cm): min. 2x 1" (2.5cm) + ⅝" (1.5cm) seam allowance + 4" (10cm) hem
Width = 2x to 3x the width of window in inches (cm) + 5" (12cm) seam allowance

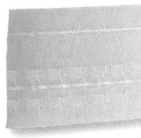

Cut curtain fabric on the straight/lengthwise grain line. Sew multiple panels together to achieve the needed width, using a *French seam (see page 90)*. Fold and press the upper edge of the joined curtain panels to the wrong side by the appropriate number of inches/cm (the header height). From the wrong side, pin the pleat tape over the inside fabric edge starting and ending 2½" (6.5cm) from each curtain side edge; sew the pleat tape to the curtain closely along the tape edges. Pull the pleat tape strings until the curtain is the desired width. Knot strings to secure them, but do not trim off the ends, as they can be untied to allow the fabric to be pulled flat for washing. Make 1⅛" (3cm)-wide *doubled hems (see page 275)* at each side edge, making sure that the ends of the pleating strings remain free.

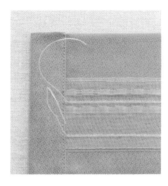

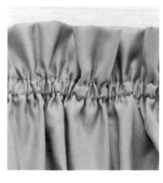

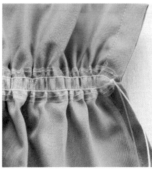

! IF MULTIPLE FABRIC PANELS NEED TO BE SEWN TOGETHER *(see page 276)* to make a sufficiently wide curtain, a ⅝" (1.5cm) SEAM ALLOWANCE PER PANEL MUST BE ADDED. The panels are sewn with a *French seam (see page 90)*, where the first seam is ¼" (0.5cm) and the second is ⅜" (1cm).

» YOU CAN ADJUST THE ARRANGEMENT OF FOLDS with gathering tape by switching between a few centimeters of heavy gathering and a few centimeters of no gathering at all.

PLEATING AND SMOCKING TAPES
Pleat tape can be used in many decorative ways. The amount of pleating is variable.

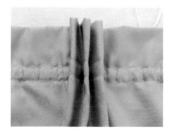

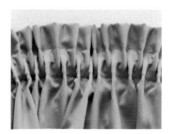

Narrow pleat tape 3:⅓   Narrow pleat tape 3:¼   Smocking tape

---

patches and repairs

YOUR JEANS ARE TOO LONG AND YOUR FAVORITE
TABLECLOTH HAS A HOLE? IN THIS CHAPTER YOU
WILL LEARN ABOUT THE SEEMINGLY MIRACULOUS
FIXES YOUR SEWING MACHINE CAN HELP YOU
ACHIEVE. AND WHEN A REPAIR IS NOT TOTALLY
INVISIBLE, MAKE A VIRTUE OF NECESSITY—A PATCH
CAN BE VERY DECORATIVE.

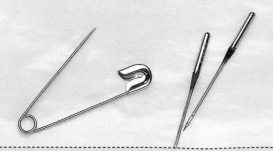

mending *with a* sewing machine

Darning and mending are not exactly everyone's favorite activities. But who isn't familiar with the frustrations of small holes or tears in clothing, worn spots on jeans, defective zippers, holes at the knees, moth holes in sweaters, ripped seams, or fallen hems? Professional repairs and alterations can be costly and take time, so it can be worth it to engage your imagination and take on certain clothing repairs yourself.

AIDS FOR PATCHING AND MENDING

Patched and mended jeans are frequently in fashion. Designer jeans with intentional patching and frayed holes can be found everywhere.
All manner of materials and techniques can be employed to repair clothing items. It can be helpful to give garments that are no longer in rotation a second life as a source of patches and appliqués. Other helpful items are spray adhesives, textile glues, fusible fabric tape, double-sided fusible interfacing, fusible bi-stretch interfacing, iron-on or sew-on appliqués, and iron-on patches.

MENDING CLOTHING

Tears or holes in jeans and jackets can be repaired in a number of ways. On children's pants a hole can quickly and easily be patched with a sew-on appliqué, and look cheerful to boot. If the damaged area needs to be invisibly mended, matching thread combined with freehand embroidery or darning is used. A hole can also be subtly accented by patching it with a piece of fabric in a matching color but a slightly different pattern.

A few basic guidelines: A damaged spot should be reinforced before mending with similar fabric or with a piece of interfacing. On delicate fabrics, use embroidery and darning thread. Patches are best secured with double-sided fusible interfacing, so that they cannot shift during application.

REPAIRING A HOLE USING AN APPLIQUÉ

This technique works on most densely woven fabrics. Additional stitching with a machine or by hand will increase the durability of the patch.

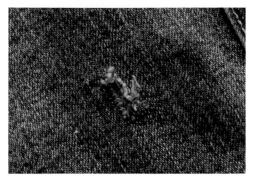

1 Trim away any frayed threads from the damaged spot.

2 To reinforce the fabric around the hole, apply fusible interfacing to the wrong side of the fabric, following manufacturer's instructions.

3 Choose an appliqué about ⅜" (1cm) larger than the damaged area, so that the hole will be fully covered. If the appliqué is not an iron-on, apply it using double-sided fusible web: iron the web to the back of the appliqué, peel off the paper backing, and then iron the appliqué over the hole and allow to cool. Alternatively, glue on the appliqué with a textile adhesive.

>> SELF-STICK APPLIQUÉS should be fastened with some hand stitches for extra security.

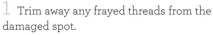

REPAIRING A TEAR USING A FABRIC BACKING

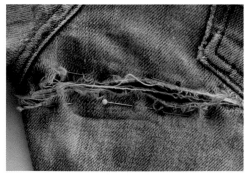

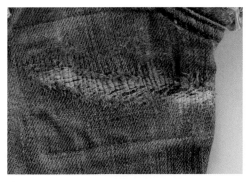

1 Cut a patch of fabric about 1⅛"–1½" (3–4cm) larger than the damaged area. Pin the patch underneath the torn section, or apply double-sided fusible web to the wrong side of the patch: peel off the paper backing, iron the patch onto the wrong side of the garment, and allow to cool.

2 On the right side of the garment, sew back and forth over the damaged area in ¹⁄₁₆" (2mm) intervals using straight, zigzag, or elastic zigzag stitches, extending occasionally past the edges of the tear in order to optimally secure the patch (see page 288).

SEWING ON A FRAYED SURFACE PATCH

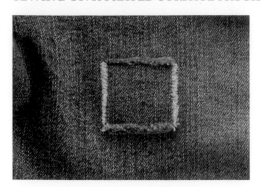

Cut a patch about ⅜" (1cm) larger than the damaged spot, then cut a piece of double-sided fusible web about ⅛" (3-4mm) smaller than the patch. Apply fusible web to the back of the patch, peel off the backing, and iron the patch to the damaged area. For added durability, sew around the patch using straight stitches. Brush the patch edges so that they begin to fray.

DECORATIVELY MENDING A HOLE USING AN UNDER LAYER

1 Cut a patch somewhat larger than the hole, place it behind the hole, and pin.

2 Use zigzag or decorative stitches—some in contrasting colors—to sew on the patch.

MENDING A HOLE USING A CONTRASTING UNDER LAYER

If you would like your patch job to be especially emphasized, the patch can be cut in an unusual shape and sewn with either matching or contrasting thread, using straight, zigzag, or decorative stitches.

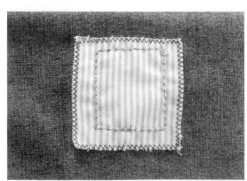

1 Make a double-layered patch and finish the edges together with a zigzag stitch. Place the patch underneath the hole and pin; sew on the patch as desired from the right side (wrong side shown at left).

2 As an option, sew or glue on small fabric flowers or beads for further embellishment.

>> IF A DAMAGED SPOT is in a hard-to-reach area, such as the middle of a pant leg, the INSEAM MUST BE OPENED ALONG ONE SECTION in order to make a patch accessible for sewing. Use a seam ripper (see page 31, figure 4) or a small pair of scissors to open the seam.

>> USE BUTTONHOLE THREAD to sew on a patch.

286

REPAIRING A TORN POCKET LINING

Pocket linings are often made of thin cotton and are not up to the task of enduring constant stress; holes and tears are frequent. Iron-on patches are a quick fix for small holes and tears, and may be found in the notions department of sewing shops as well as online. They are simply ironed over the damaged spot, and the pocket is instantly ready to use again.

>> **MAKE A PATCH**
from a scrap of fabric. Apply double-sided fusible web to the wrong side of the patch. Peel off the paper backing and iron the patch over the damaged area.

REPLACING A TORN POCKET LINING

If the damage is too extensive to patch, the pocket lining can be replaced with an iron-on repair pocket. These are available in sewing shops or online.

1 Cut away the damaged pocket lining.

2 Pin on the replacement lining and iron to attach it.

3 The pocket may be stitched afterward for extra reinforcement.

MACHINE DARNING

Worn spots and small holes and tears can be quickly repaired using the freehand embroidery technique or the programmed darning stitch on your machine.

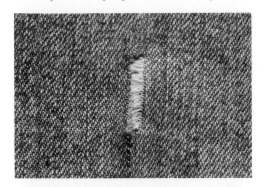

>> THE DARNING will be almost invisible if you choose a thread that BLENDS IN WITH THE FABRIC.

1 Cut a piece of bi-stretch fusible interfacing slightly larger than the damaged area and iron it on to the damaged area from the wrong side.

2 Install the darning foot and, depending on the machine, select the freehand embroidery or darning setting; lower the feed dogs. Use matching thread and a size 12 (European 80) needle. Place the damaged area in an embroidery hoop. Stitch back and forth over the damaged fabric in the direction of the weave, using a straight stitch and the freehand darning method, i.e., *moving the embroidery hoop slowly backward and forward (see page 83)*. Begin sewing at an undamaged spot, then across and beyond the damaged area; this will help the repair to be almost invisible. By sewing beyond the damage at irregular distances, you will avoid repeatedly piercing the fabric directly around the repaired spot, which might otherwise tear out again quickly.

! Sew over DAMAGED AREAS ON THIN FABRICS with embroidery and darning thread.

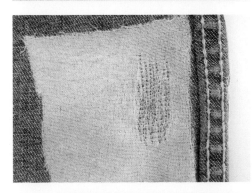

3 This is the wrong-side view of the darned area.

4 If you would prefer to give the repaired area a decorative character, you can use zigzag stitching and contrasting thread.

SHORTENING JEANS WHILE PRESERVING
THE ORIGINAL HEM

Your jeans are too long, but shortening them will cause you to lose the perfectly weathered hemline. Here we show you a way to shorten jeans while preserving the original hem.

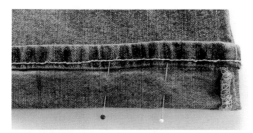

1 Determine the desired new hem location, wearing shoes to make sure the length is correct. On the inside of the leg, use a disappearing-ink marker to indicate half the length of the desired adjustment. For example, if you want the pants shortened by 3" (8cm), mark off 1½" (4cm).

 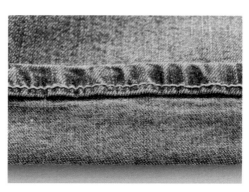

>> FINISHING with an overlock machine will create a professional-looking edge while simultaneously cutting away the excess hem.

! ON FLARED-LEG JEANS the legs will first have to be made narrower, since the width at the original hem will be wider than at the shortened hem. PARTIALLY OPEN THE INSEAMS and re-stitch a narrower seam to make up for the difference in width, so that the technique described here will work.

2 Turn up the pant leg inside out (right sides together) at this new marking. Pin, making sure the side seams are aligned, and press. Install a zipper foot and denim needle in the machine. Align the left edge of the zipper foot with the original hem edge and set the needle to the left side so that it will enter directly alongside the original hem seam.

3 Pull the pant leg over the free arm of the machine and stitch alongside the original seam using all-purpose or denim thread to match the fabric (illustrated here with contrast thread). Select a stitch length of 9 spi (3mm). Press the fold, then turn it to the inside (wrong side). Press the folded section upward and tack in place with a few hand stitches at the inner side seams.

4 If the pants have been shortened considerably, trim the folded section to ⅜–¾" (1–2cm). Finish the cut edge using zigzag stitches.

5 The hem edge can be supplementally topstitched from the right side in the ditch of the seam, using an edging foot or a standard foot.

REPLACING A JEANS ZIPPER

Jeans generally have topstitching that cannot be exactly replicated with a home machine.

1 Open only the seams that actually hold in the zipper, leaving the topstitched seams undisturbed.

2 Exception at waistband: Here only a couple of stitches need to be broken in order to free the top of the zipper tape. Use a seam ripper.

3 Open the zipper seam on the opposite side of the zipper.

4 The old zipper may now be removed.

5 On the underlap, insert the top of the zipper tape into the opening at the waistband and pin the remaining tape between the fabric layers exactly as the old zipper was; baste. Install the zipper foot and use all-purpose thread in the machine. Stitch as closely as possible along the zipper teeth from top to bottom.

6 Insert the top end of the zipper tape into the waistband on the opposite side and attach the zipper tape by hand to match the old zipper position, using backstitches *(see page 74)*. Be sure to catch only one fabric layer, so that the stitching remains invisible from the right side. Stitch the bottom of the zipper thoroughly, as this is the spot that endures the most stress. Sew the waistband closed.

! MARK THE EXCESS ZIPPER LENGTH, trim it off, and SECURE THE END: Set the machine to zigzag stitching with a stitch length of 00 and a width to match the width of the zipper teeth. Lower the feed dogs, or, alternatively, use the button attachment setting. Sew back and forth across the zipper teeth multiple times using standard or denim thread *(see page 41)*. THE NEEDLE ENTERS THE ZIPPER TAPES TO THE RIGHT AND LEFT OF THE TEETH, creating a new lower stop. Tie off the thread ends.

! IF THE NEW ZIPPER needs shortening, this is done at the lower edge.

» INSTEAD OF BASTING, use double-sided, water-soluble wonder tape or a temporary adhesive stick *(see page 33, figure 6, or page 55)*.

» ZIPPERS FOR JEANS or work pants should have metal teeth.

IRONING HEMS INSTEAD OF SEWING

Fallen hems on skirts, dresses, coats, or pants can be repaired quickly without sewing. Fusible hemming tapes bind fabric together with the application of heat *(see page 109)*.
On the wrong side (inside), place a sufficiently long piece of hemming tape between the hem and the garment. Set the iron to medium heat and press for about 8 seconds. Allow to cool.

! VERIFY FIRST whether the garment can withstand medium heat.

! FUSIBLE HEM TAPE is washable up to 140°F (60°C).

GLUING INSTEAD OF SEWING

Modern textile adhesives allow for the quick repair of small tears or holes in garments. Fallen hems can also be swiftly fixed without needle and thread *(see page 109)*. Thinly apply textile glue on the inside of the hem, allow it to dry, then press the hem firmly against the garment. Ironing the hem afterward will strengthen the bond (follow manufacturer's instructions).

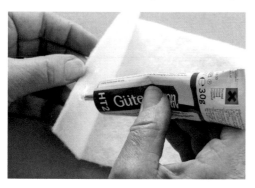 

! SMALL DOTS OF GLUE are sufficient.

! TEST THE GLUE on a hidden part of the garment first.

TEARS AND HOLES

Holes and tears can be covered with matching fabric, an appliqué, or a piece of leather. Apply textile adhesive to the back of the patch, allow it to dry, and place it over the damaged area, overlapping the damage by at least ¾" (2cm). Ironing the patch afterward will strengthen the bond (follow manufacturer's instructions).

For very small tears or holes, take some fabric from the same item (from a seam allowance, inside pocket flap, or hem) and glue it underneath the tear. Snip off any thread ends sticking up on the right side.

SIMPLE REPAIRS ON LINENS

This patching technique can be used on larger holes and tears in bed linens, tablecloths, or dish towels; it is quick and easy to do with a machine.

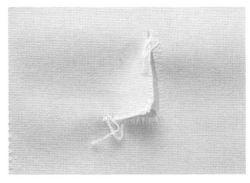

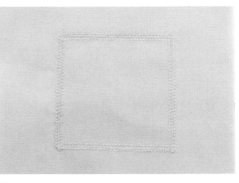

» Use an EDGING FOOT to SEW ON the patch.

1 Cut a patch approximately ⅜" (1cm) larger all around than the damaged spot.

2 Center the patch over the damage on the right side and pin. Sew along the edges of the patch with an elastic stitch or narrow zigzag stitch. The damaged area is no longer visible.

3 and 4 On the back side, cut away the damaged original fabric close to the stitching.

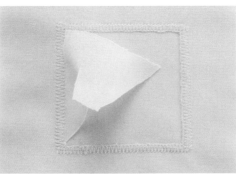

5 This is the finished back view.

REPAIRING A RIPPED-OUT BUTTON

To repair the damage caused by a ripped-out button, reinforce the back of the fabric at the button position with a piece of bi-stretch fusible interfacing. Sew together the damaged area with a few hand stitches from the right side. Afterward, the button can be sewn back on at the repaired spot.

» THE BUTTON MAY also be sewn on using your machine.

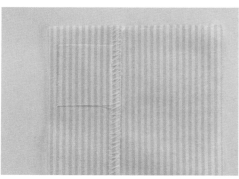

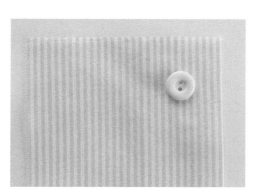

REPAIRING A TORN BUTTONHOLE

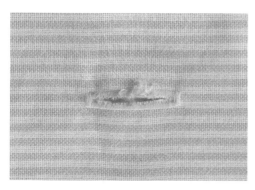

On the back of the damaged buttonhole iron on a piece of bi-elastic fusible interfacing. Sew a new buttonhole of the same length over the original buttonhole from the right side and carefully cut open with a seam ripper. Alternatively, sew over the torn leg of the buttonhole only, using a dense zigzag stitch.

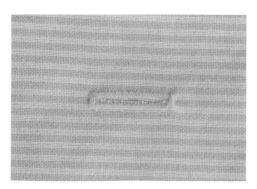

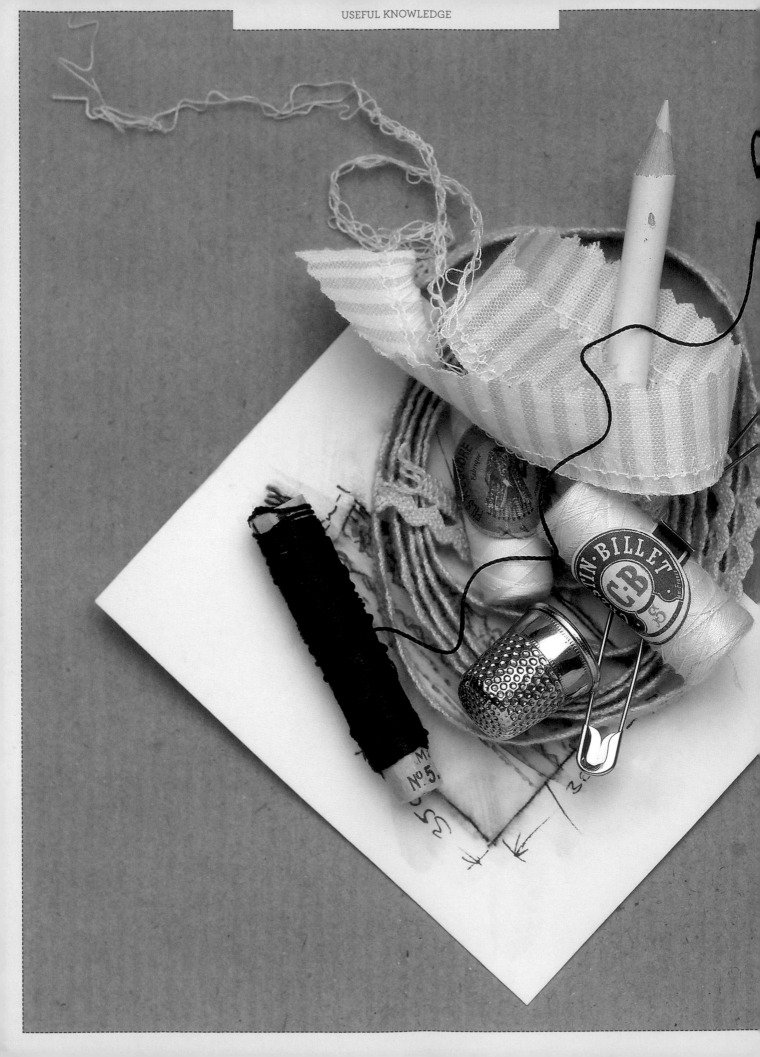

useful
knowledge

THIS CHAPTER OFFERS EVEN MORE INFORMATION
THAT MIGHT INTEREST SEWING ENTHUSIASTS:
TIPS FOR MARKETING YOUR CREATIONS,
FREQUENTLY ASKED QUESTIONS, AND A GLOSSARY
WITH IMPORTANT TERMS.

INTERNET

Another increasingly popular marketing approach is to put your work up for sale on the Internet. The advantages are obvious: you can reach a broad, nationwide audience of potential customers at very little cost. However, to be successful you must have a good grasp of computer technology and digital media.

The Internet offers a variety of possibilities for marketing your products. Patterns and instructions are typically sold in the form of PDF documents. For the buyer, these offer the advantage of instant access and no shipping costs. Some designers, however, prefer to ship hard copy patterns in order to make any illegal copying and distribution more difficult—though piracy can never be completely eliminated.

! Software for **CREATING PDFs** is available for free.

YOUR OWN ONLINE SHOP

The most professional way of selling on the Internet is to open your own online shop, but bear in mind that the maintenance of such a business takes a large time commitment and requires a fairly sophisticated grasp of digital technology. A shop needs space on a Web server, which will cost varying amounts, depending on the amount of storage needed.

EBAY, ETSY, ET CETERA

! **THE MORE SIZES** you offer, the better your chances are of selling.

You can also market your products on existing sales platforms. The biggest are eBay and Etsy. They have the advantage of being well-known and relatively easy to use, even for those who may be less computer savvy. Disadvantages include the selling fees charged by the platforms and the existence of a lot of competition from other designers. You run the risk of your products getting lost in the crowd, perhaps never reaching the eyes of potential customers. On the other hand, the platforms offer various types of sales promotion assistance, though these also have associated costs.

>> Have someone else **TEST SEW** an item based on your instructions, or at the very least proofread them.

BLOG

You can also set up an online journal or blog (short for weblog) to help market your wares. The online handcrafts community is huge and well connected. The customer base for new and interesting products is expanding very rapidly.

You can set up a blog using any of a number of free services. It is fairly simple once you familiarize yourself with the format, assuming you are generally comfortable with computers. However, blogs were not originally designed as sales platforms, so if you want customers to be able to order and purchase directly from your blog site, it will require a bit of additional online savvy on your part to arrange those services.

» Fill out your blog with interesting supplemental content, such as TIPS OR TUTORIALS.

PRESENTATION ON THE INTERNET

A picture is worth a thousand words—and that is true when it comes to the sale of handcrafts as well. Sharp, high-quality photographs are critical to your sales success. The photos should be large enough to show details, and the colors should be as true as possible. Since different monitors will display colors differently, it is a good idea to describe colors in detail as part of your product description.

Photograph your items in front of a neutral background or an attractive backdrop. A striped dress on a floral bedspread or a blouse hanging from a hanger on the kitchen door (perhaps with a dirty dish or two in the background) looks unprofessional and does not motivate people to buy. Take inspiration from relevant magazines. Show your items from different angles and take close-ups of the fabric pattern or any interesting design details.

Garments should be photographed on a dress form or—better yet—a live model, so that the fit and shaping can be evaluated. If you do use live models, you must get their permission to display the photographs on the Internet. To show the garment to its best advantage, your model should have good posture. Generally, photographs that include the model's head (and perhaps a glowing smile) come across better than ones where the head is cut off for the sake of anonymity.

The item description should be clearly organized and contain all the important information for a potential customer, including details about the materials used, size, color, et cetera. It is also important to provide clear information about shipping costs and the payment methods you accept. As a rule, you should not ship any items before you have received full payment. Also give some thought to how you would prefer to deal with complaints and returns/exchanges.

» WHEN PHOTOGRAPHING CLOTHING, consider that HEELED SHOES improve a model's posture—even if the shoes do not appear in the photo.

» Pay attention to CORRECT SPELLING AND GRAMMAR when participating in forums to look more professional.

ADVERTISING

The best advertising for your designs will be word of mouth, which can work astoundingly well on the Internet. Happy customers will show off the items they purchased from you, or that they made from your instructions, on their own websites and link to you, the source. Ideally, your products will soon be the talk of the Web community.

You can help out a bit by having a solid Internet presence, for example, by actively participating in relevant forums and commenting on other blogs. Avoid heavily promoting your own site in forums and in commentary on other people's blogs, however, as this is broadly frowned upon. A link to your shop in your signature file will suffice; curious readers will do the rest. If you want to sell patterns/instructions, it can help to offer a few for free. These are very popular for downloading and can quickly help you develop a good reputation as a designer. You can also offer your designs for inclusion in online collections of free patterns: these sites are used by many people and will help you gain name recognition.

If you are using a sales platform, you can take advantage of their promotional tools. Search engines such as Google also offer advertising services and/or assistance with search engine optimization to help your shop appear higher in search results. All of these options, however, are associated with potentially nontrivial costs that may make sense only for a more extensive business.

» News of CONTESTS and GIVEAWAYS spreads quickly and can raise your profile.

» THE GREATER YOUR PRESENCE on the Internet, THE FASTER you will start appearing in search engine results.

FAQs —
100 common questions

SEWING MACHINES

1   How can I clean out thread ends from in between the tension disks? Move a piece of thin crochet cotton back and forth between the disks to loosen and remove thread remnants. A soft paintbrush or tiny stiff-bristled brush can also help.

2   What should I do when my machine is skipping stitches and my thread keeps breaking? This problem can have a number of causes, namely: The needle is bent or dull, in which case replace the needle. / The needle is not appropriate for the fabric (*see pages 36–39*). / The thread is not appropriate for the needle (*see pages 40–42*). / The needle is not inserted correctly in the needle shaft. / The machine is not threaded properly. / The bobbin is not installed correctly. / The thread is of poor quality. Cheap thread often has loose fibers with pills or knots, and breaks easily during sewing. Use brand-name thread.

3   What should I do if the machine keeps sewing in place? Engage the feed dogs. Remove any dirt from between the teeth of the feed dogs. Double-check your stitch length setting.

4   What is the difference between an overlock machine (serger) and a sewing machine? An overlock machine is a special machine that can stitch, finish, and trim seams in a single pass. On the other hand it cannot, for example, make buttonholes or sew in a zipper, so it is not a replacement for a sewing machine but rather a supplement.

5   Which presser feet are essential to own? Here are the essentials: A standard (also called zigzag) foot, which can be used for many types of seams and stitches. / A zipper foot that can be set with the needle to either side, so you can sew directly alongside the zipper teeth. (A zipper foot is also good for edge stitching on hems or to sew on beaded or sequined ribbons.) / A buttonhole foot for creating buttonholes. Its ability to include a supplemental thread on a buttonhole can also be used to attach elastic threads used for gathering.

6   What stitches can be made using a blind stitch foot? With a blind stitch foot and zigzag stitch, you can finish the edges of thin fabrics. The stitching is guided over the peg on the foot, giving it more thread per stitch, which in turn allows the fabric edge to lie flat instead of rolling in. A blind stitch foot is also advisable for overlock stitching, as the overlock stitches contain extra thread per stitch.

7   What is a walking foot used for? A walking foot is used to sew together two or more layers of fabric without any shifting as they are being fed through the machine, from both top and bottom. These feet are popular for use on patchwork and quilted items and for stitching very thick layers.

8   Is it worth investing in an edge stitch foot? Together with the correct needle positioning, an edge stitch foot guarantees straight, parallel topstitching on edges and hems, and around curves. Narrow hems can be made with ease. It is especially good for machine quilting, as it makes stitching in the ditch very easy.

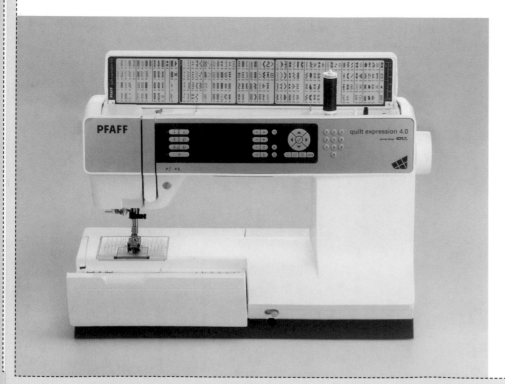

SEWING EQUIPMENT

9   Why should needles be replaced regularly? Frequent sewing, sewing speed, fabrics, and thread all affect your needles. The tip becomes dull over time, and the eye can develop sharp edges. The consequences are torn thread, poorly formed stitches, pulled threads in your fabric, and uneven seams.

10   What should I do if the seams in a T-shirt are wavy? For an elastic seam, sew T-shirt fabric with an elastic stitch or a narrow zigzag stitch, using a ballpoint needle.

11   What are twin needles used for? A twin needle can be used to sew elastic seams in stretch fabrics. It can also be used to create decorative topstitching on clothing and home décor items. Narrow stitches result in parallel lines, while wider stitches may overlap. The upper thread tension should be reduced slightly when sewing with a twin needle.

12   What is the right needle spacing for a twin needle? Twin needles with a distance of ⅛" (4.0mm) or greater are used on heavier fabrics. Choose a smaller spacing for lighter fabrics.

13   Can a twin needle be used in any sewing machine? Yes. Home machines use needles from the 130/705 needle system, and twin needles are among these.

14   Can a twin needle be used with any presser foot? No! It can be used only with a standard (zigzag) foot. As a rule, the machine should be set for straight stitching before you start to sew with a twin needle. If decorative stitches are to be used, the stitch width must be adjusted so that the needles do not hit the presser foot. The needle position should always be centered. Modern machines have a twin needle limiter.

15   How do you sew around a corner with a twin needle? A slight curve may be sewn instead of a regular corner; the curve should be pre-drawn with a disappearing-ink marker. Adjust the stitch length to 24 spi (1mm) shortly before reaching the curve, then sew slowly around, using the handwheel as needed and pulling slightly on the fabric. Return to the original stitch length after completing the curve. If the corner needs to be sewn at a right angle, sew to the corner, and then sew backward for a distance equal to the needle spacing. Bring the needle to the highest position and turn the fabric by 90 degrees. Bring the

needle back down almost into the fabric, adjust the position so that the right needle enters at the last stitching point at the upper right, and continue sewing.

16   What different kinds of threads are there? "Thread" is a catchall term that can cover various types of sewing thread. Individual fibers are twisted or spun together to make thread. Multiple single threads (or plies) may in turn be twisted together to create heavier thread. When many threads are twined together it creates a tear-resistant thread. Commonly used thread types for sewing include cotton, cotton-polyester, mercerized cotton, silk, wool and acrylic, embroidery, nylon (invisible), metallic, and quilting.

17   What should I watch out for when I am using two spools of thread on the machine at once? The spools must be installed in mirror image to each other, so that one feeds from the front and one feeds from the rear. If only one spool can be attached to the machine, the second spool can be placed in a drinking glass behind the machine. The attached spool gets threaded to the left of the tensioning disk; the other spool is threaded to the right of the tensioning disk.

18   Is there special thread for jeans, backpacks, and other heavy materials? For these materials it is advisable to use extra strong, 40-weight thread. It is especially tear-resistant but still easy to work with.

19   What is heavy buttonhole thread good for? It is suitable only for large buttonholes in thick fabrics, or for whimsical, exaggerated buttonholes that are sewn by hand. However, it can also be used to create very attractive decorative stitches and topstitching.

20   What do I do if my embroidery stitching is not dense enough? Use 30-weight machine embroidery thread. It is heavier than 40-weight thread and will fill out your stitching.

21   What should I do if my metallic thread gets tangled or keeps breaking? Metallic thread and flat metallic thread are more brittle than normal machine embroidery thread. The spools should be installed vertically on the machine with a piece of netting pulled over them. Also reduce the upper tension slightly, and sew slowly.

54 What are warp knit fabrics? These are machine-knit fabrics such as jersey, often simply called knits, where the thread runs vertically and on the diagonal rather than horizontally, as with traditional knits.

55 Can lining fabrics be used as primary fabrics? In principle there is no reason why not, but be aware that there are many types of linings. Some are very prone to wrinkling, some may retain pin and needle marks, some have no elasticity and are not very durable, and some may not be colorfast. Examine a lining fabric carefully to determine whether it has the correct properties to work with your intended project.

56 On some fabric bolts and on patterns, measurements are given in millimeters, centimeters, and meters (mm, cm, and m). How do I convert them to inches and yards? There are many free (and instant) conversion calculators on the Internet, just search "mm to inches," "cm to inches," and "meters to yards." You can also refer to the small conversion chart on page 156.

57 What should I watch out for when buying fabric online? Colors can appear different on your monitor than they do in person, and there are other characteristics (hand, drape, heft, et cetera) that can be neither seen nor felt in cyberspace. If you require a large quantity of fabric, it is best to get a fabric swatch from the seller before ordering.

58 Are there any fabrics, such as those for children's garments and toys, that are guaranteed to be free of contaminants? Pay attention to quality marks on the label when purchasing fabric. These ensure that the fabric meets certain manufacturing and content guidelines. Look for the abbreviation "KbA" or the GOTS (Guaranteed Organic Textile Standard) symbol on fabrics, which indicates that the cotton is certified organic.

ALL ABOUT PATTERNS

59 Can I take my own measurements? Of course, but it is much easier to have someone else take yours.

60 Are the instructions really that important? Yes! Sewing instructions can be compared to a recipe. All the ingredients are listed, the workflow is laid out, and any unusual steps are described. All this is important toward achieving an optimal result and avoiding mistakes.

61 The pattern sheets that come in books and magazines are gigantic, and sometimes there are even two sets of patterns together on a single sheet. How can I make them easier to handle? It is helpful to cut the sheets apart at designated spots (look for a scissor symbol) to make the pieces smaller.

62 I have opted to make a particular variation from a purchased pattern; can I dispose of the irrelevant pattern pieces? Better not to. Perhaps you will want to make a different variation sometime later. Even if not, you can use the extra pieces as tracing paper for other patterns.

63 When tracing a multi-size pattern, can I just trace off the next biggest size instead of adding seam allowances? Never do this! It will yield a very poor result. Your garment will almost certainly not fit correctly.

64 Is it really as easy as it sounds to make a multi-size pattern one size larger or smaller? Yes! You just need to make sure that all the altered pieces match up correctly in length where they will be sewn together (and adjust if needed).

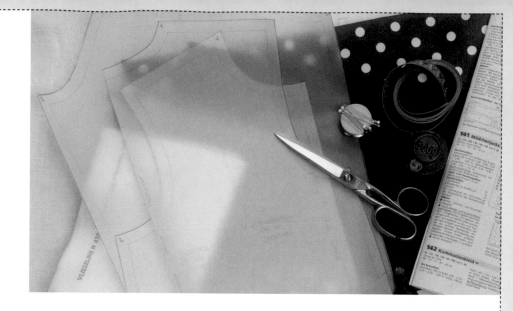

PREPARING TO SEW

65 Do all fabrics need to be prewashed? Not necessarily. When deciding whether or not to prewash a fabric, consider how much it is likely to shrink and whether it will be frequently washed later (as in the fabric for a blouse). Woolens and fabrics with protective finishes should preferably not be prewashed.

66 Do I have to have a tailor's square to straighten fabric ends? No. A large piece of cardboard with clean corners (90-degree angles) can serve the same purpose.

67 At the fabric store they often tear fabrics, especially cottons, instead of cutting them. Is the torn edge then on the grainline? Unfortunately, usually not. This will become obvious when lining up the selvages.

68 Is it bad if I accidentally switch the right and wrong fabric sides when cutting/sewing? It can be. On dyed wovens where the right and wrong sides look identical (making them easier to confuse in the first place), and when a piece is rectangular, it may be completely unnoticeable. But if you accidentally reverse a sleeve piece, it will hang crooked in the armhole. The mistake may go unnoticed until the garment is worn.

69 I have never sewn before. Can I still start right off using the more complicated seam allowance method of tracing and cutting patterns? Of course! Then you will never have to "unlearn" the stitching line method (*see page 186*). The seam allowance method/ cutting line method (*see page 186*) is a clear, simple, and time-saving way to cut patterns that don't already include a seam allowance.

70 Pattern weights or pins? What are the relative advantages? Weights are quicker to use: position pattern piece, secure them with weights, cut, and immediately use the weights for the next piece. Unlike pins, weights also will not potentially damage delicate fabrics.

71 Do they have to be purchased weights? No—you can use any small, heavy objects as pattern weights.

72 Why is it so important to observe grainline markings when cutting out fabric pieces? The finished garment will otherwise not drape properly. Pieces not cut out as specified will not sit optimally, and on pants it may even cause the legs to twist.

73 Does the grainline have to be precisely determined, or is there some leeway? The more exact, the better. Deviation of a few millimeters is tolerable.

74 Do I have to buy specialized tracing paper? No, but be sure that whatever paper you use is really transparent. Possibilities include blueprint paper, tissue paper, and rolled parchment.

75 Are there tricks to adding seam and hem allowances to paper patterns that do not include them? This task goes well using a triangular ruler and a sharp pencil. Mark and cut the desired hem allowance, fold the allowance up at the hemline, mark the seam allowances at the sides, and trim them from the folded section. The hem will now be the correct width.

76 Is it difficult to use electric scissors? Not at all. The scissors cut only as quickly as they are pushed: slowly on complex edges, more quickly on straight ones. Test the scissors before buying. Cordless versions are very comfortable to use, since there is no cord to get in the way.

77 Why is it important to transfer all the markings from a pattern? Having these marks will help you enormously when sewing. They indicate things such as where zippers are to be positioned, where sleeves should meet the shoulder seam, and where there are fold lines.

78 I am a beginner and so far have used only solid-color fabrics. I would like to branch out to patterned ones. What sort of fabric should I choose? We recommend fabrics with patterns that do not have a specific direction, in other words, where the pattern cannot end up on its head or running vertically instead of horizontally. But if a directional pattern is widely spaced and does not need to be exactly matched up, it can be a good choice to gain some experience.

79 Can I skip the interfacing? No. It is very important! It is also inexpensive. Buy one or two yards of assorted types, in both black and white, so you will always have some at hand.

80 Basting seems really time-consuming and not worth it. Can I skip this step? Indeed you can! It isn't always worth the time spent; instead, you can use pins to secure pieces together. Insert them parallel or perpendicular to the seam, but never sew over them—that will frequently end up damaging your machine needle.

CREATING A GARMENT

81 Why does every seam need to be pressed? A firm pressing bonds the thread with the fabric and smoothes out any tiny wrinkles. If seams are not pressed flat before you continue to sew, they can get pulled out of shape and create unattractive bulges.

82 Are there alternatives to basting and pinning? For some tasks, such as sewing on ribbons and positioning zippers and pockets, you can use a special double-sided, water-soluble basting tape, making basting or pinning unnecessary.

83 What is surplus? Example: for a collar to drape more attractively, the upper collar requires surplus width, meaning it is about ⅛–¼" (3–6mm) larger than the undercollar. This size difference is not visible on the finished collar; it just helps the upper collar lie more smoothly. Some sleeves have surplus width at the cap to make them fit better.

84 Is a sleeve always sewn on first, before the side and sleeve seams are closed? Whether or not a sleeve is set in an already-finished armhole depends on the shape and position of the sleeve cap. A straight sleeve with no surplus and a centered cap can be sewn directly to the front and back garment pieces, after which the side and sleeve seams can be closed in one pass. On sleeves with a rounded, slightly offset cap and surplus width, the shoulder, side, and sleeve seams all must be sewn first.

85 What is a shaped facing? A shaped facing can be used to finish places such as armhole and neckline edges. It is cut out to match the shape of the edges and is invisible from the right side when completed *(see page 204)*.

86 What does it mean to stitch at "presser foot width"? Presser foot width means that a folded edge or an existing seam is sewn with the edge aligned exactly with the outer edge of the presser foot. The distance between the stitching and the edge (or previous seam) is thus actually half the width of the foot.

87 What is the difference between topstitching close to the edge and edge stitching? Edge stitching is done directly at the edge, whereas topstitching may be as much as ⅛" (4mm) away from the edge.

88 What is a decorative facing? A decorative facing is a separately cut fabric piece that is used to finish open edges such as necklines. It can be made from the primary fabric or from contrasting fabric and is visible from the right side.

89 What is understitching? Understitching can be used to keep an inside facing from rolling to the outside. The seam allowances are sewn down on the right side of the facing near the attachment edge, so that the seam is not visible from the right side.

90 Can a facing made from crushed fabric be stabilized with fusible interfacing? Fabrics with a wrinkled or crushed effect should be stabilized with sewn-in interfacing to preserve their unusual structure.

91 What is patchwork? This is a technique where multiple small pieces of fabric are pieced together to create a larger surface, usually in multiple colors and/or different patterns. Patchwork fabric is used for garments as well as bags and home accessories.

92 Is there a quick and easy way to turn narrow tubes of fabric? Specialized tools are very helpful for this task. A loop turner or a turning rod and tube set allow for easy turning of even narrow fabric tubes *(see pages 261–262)*.

93 What is bar tacking? Bar tacks are sewn to reinforce seam endings at heavily stressed points, such as the sides of pocket openings. Depending on the amount of reinforcement required and the type of fabric, there are different ways to make bar tacks. A very stable version is a zigzag bar tack *(see page 251)*.

94 What is a gusset? A gusset is a piece of fabric that is inserted to allow for more freedom of movement, such as at the underarm of a kimono sleeve.

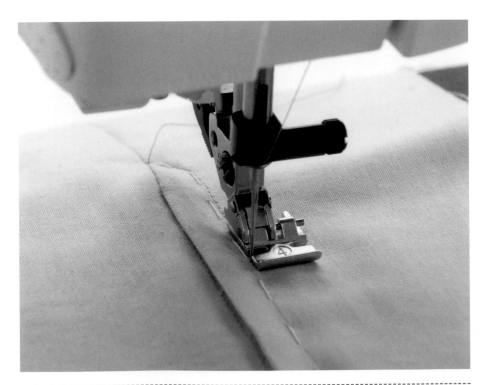

TECHNIQUES FOR HOME DÉCOR

95 How much fabric is required to make a curtain hang loosely? Depending on the hanging arrangement, you will need at least twice the width of the window plus seam allowances for doubled hems on the side edges, plus seam allowances on every panel that may need to be sewn together to create a wide-enough fabric piece (*see page 274*).

96 What is shrinkage allowance? Fabric can shrink with washing, so it is important to purchase about 10 percent more fabric than originally calculated to account for this possibility. The fabric should be washed before cutting.

97 What does it mean if it says "3:¼" on a pleating tape? This indicates how much fabric is required if the pleating tape will be used on a curtain. The "3" means you need a piece of fabric that is 3x the width of the window. The "4" means that when the pleating tape is pulled to window width, sets of four pleats will form at equal intervals.

PATCHES AND REPAIRS

98 What do I do if the machine stops moving at thick seams or if my fabric doesn't want to feed? Make a roll of scrap fabric that is the same height as the thick seam. Place the roll behind the needle under the presser foot. The foot can then sew through multiple layers of fabric easily. Alternatively, there are bi-level feet available at sewing shops (*see page 98*).

USEFUL KNOWLEDGE

99 How can I get labels to put into the handmade items I want to offer for sale? Labels made to your custom specifications can be ordered from specialty retailers on the Internet.

100 Can stuffed animals be filled with regular batting? Normal batting tends to get clumpy when it is washed. Washable fiberfill is preferable for this use. Alternatively, you may be able to find inexpensive pillows and use the poly filling from them.

from A to Z — glossary

Abutted seam Two non-fraying fabric edges that are abutted and sewn together using a zigzag stitch or symmetrical embroidery stitch, creating a flat seam.

Accessories A catch-all term used in both home décor and fashion to describe decorative, stylish supplemental items such as a scarf for a dress or a pillow on a sofa.

Appliqué A motif or patch that can be cut from various materials, including fabric, leather, vinyl, knitting, or felt, and that serves as a decorative addition to a background fabric. Appliqués may be sewn on by hand or machine, or ironed or glued on.

Attachment line Marking on a pattern piece indicating that two pieces will be sewn together at/along that location. Also called the seamline and/or stitching line.

Band collar Also called a Mandarin collar, used as a neck finish on items such as shirts, blouses, dresses, and traditional jackets.

Bar tack A small line of narrow, dense zigzag stitching, used to reinforce heavily stressed areas, such as pocket openings or the ends of zippers.

Basting The provisional connection of two pieces of fabric using long hand or machine stitches.

Bias grain See Grainline.

Bias strips See Bias tape.

Bias tape A fabric strip cut at a 45-degree angle to the grainline, used to bind edges.

Bias tape maker A tool to help with folding bias tape.

Binding Fabric edges and seam allowances are bound by hand or machine with sewn-on fabric strips to prevent fraying. Ribbons and tapes can be used for binding, as well as bias strips, which are suited for finishing curved edges.

Blind hem A machine-stitched, nearly invisible hem seam.

Bodkin A needle-like tool with an oversized eye and a blunt tip, used to pull ribbon, elastic, cording, et cetera through fabric casings.

Bound buttonhole A buttonhole with edges that are bound with small fabric strips.

Box pleat Also called an inverted pleat. A pleat made with two folds that abut. Popular on skirts and as a back pleat on jackets and dresses.

Casing Also called a tunnel casing. A tunnel made in a double layer of fabric, delineated by two stitching lines, through which elastic bands, drawstrings, ribbons, et cetera can be pulled. Frequently used as the waist finish on athletic wear.

Center back Paper patterns will have the garment center back line indicated; it is usually parallel to the grainline.

Center line On a pattern, indicates the center line of a garment front or back.

Chalk marker Tailor's chalk in pencil form, used to transfer pattern markings to fabric.

Chalk tracing A technique using a tracing wheel and chalked tracing paper to transfer seam lines and other construction markings from a pattern sheet onto fabric.

Chenille A soft, plush yarn; or a velvety woven fabric made of four to six layers that are topstitched on the diagonal throughout and then sliced open between the stitching lines.

Combination machine Sewing machine with an embroidery module for creating professional-quality embroidered motifs.

Couched thread gathering Strong thread is sewn over with zigzag stitches and can then be pulled to create gathers in heavy fabrics.

Cross grainline See Grainline.

Cuff Additional length at a pant or sleeve hem that is folded up at a line indicated on the pattern.

Curved ruler A special ruler with various curves for creating pattern pieces and marking curved lines; also available in flexible versions.

Cut edge The raw edge of a pattern piece cut from fabric.

Cutting layout See Pattern layout.

Cutting mat A plastic mat used to protect the work surface when using a rotary cutter or hobby knife.

Darning A way to repair worn or damaged areas in fabric, done either by hand or with the machine, using freehand embroidery stitching or a programmed stitch.

Darts Wedge-shaped folds that end in a point, used to give a three-dimensional shape to fabric so that it fits better to the body.

Decorative facing A facing that is attached to the wrong side and then turned to the outside of the garment and topstitched.

Easing When two pieces of different widths are sewn together, the excess fabric (the ease) must be lightly pulled in and evenly distributed to prevent the formation of gathers or small pleats.

Elastane A synthetic elastic fiber, often used in exercise clothing and stretch fabrics.

Elastic stitch An elastic machine stitch for sewing together stretch fabrics.

Entredeux A sewing technique that creates the appearance of an inserted lace or border strip between two fabric pieces. Entredeux is found on blouses, linens, bodices, and lingerie.

Extended facing A facing cut as part of the main garment piece; the facing section is reinforced with interfacing and folded to the inside.

Eyelets Small holes, finished by hand or with the machine, or small riveted metal rings; used in garments and accessories for lacing.

Fabric pattern A design printed onto the right side of a fabric.

Facing (n.) A fabric piece, often interfaced, attached to a raw edge to finish it and keep it from stretching out of shape. Cut in the same shape as the section to which it is attached, it is folded to the wrong side after stitching. Facings can be used on opening edges, collars, lapels, waistbands, necklines, armhole openings, and slit openings.

Facing (v.) Turning a section of fabric to the inside after stitching two pieces together along an edge, so that the seam allowances are concealed between the fabric layers.

Feed dogs The component of the sewing machine that transports the fabric underneath the presser foot as stitches are formed.

Felled seam Also called a denim seam. A sturdy, double-stitched, flat seam used on jeans, work clothes, and sportswear. This seam involves overlapping and folding one seam allowance over the other and then topstitching; the seam allowances as such are no longer visible.

Fiber The raw material for thread and fabric; it may be of plant, animal, or synthetic origin.

Filler cord The filling for piping; may be cord, lacing, or string.

Finishing Preventing the fraying of raw fabric edges by sewing over them with zigzag or overlock stitches or by cutting them with pinking shears.

Flap See Pocket flap.

Fly facing A double-layered flap of fabric, often to cover a zipper, usually on the front of a skirt or pants.

Fold line Also called the fold or the folded edge. The line along which a piece of fabric is folded and upon which any pattern piece that is to be "cut on the fold" should be placed.

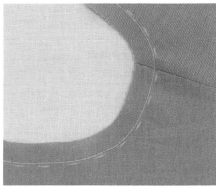

Freehand embroidery Sewing technique that can be done with either straight or zigzag stitches, with the feed dogs either lowered or covered.

Front facing Extended or separately cut fabric section, which may be interfaced, used to finish garment front opening edges.

Fullness adjustment A pattern alteration that adds width to a piece for additional freedom of movement.

Fusible interfacing A heat-bonded material, usually nonwoven, that is used to reinforce and stiffen fabrics; also available in stretch versions for use with stretch fabrics (see Interfacing).

Fusible web Double-sided, heat-adhesive material that is ironed between two pieces of fabric; the web melts, creating a durable bond.

Gathering Two or more rows of long straight stitches are pulled together from the ends, thereby reducing the fabric width by creating gathers (see Couched thread gathering).

Gathering tape Cotton or synthetic tape with eyelets and cording, used to regulate the gathering and width of curtains.

Grading To grade a seam allowance means to trim its multiple layers to different widths to help prevent bulkiness.

Grainline Straight/lengthwise grain refers to the direction of the warp threads, which run parallel to the selvages. The straight grainline is indicated on pattern pieces with an arrow. Cross grainline is the weft thread that runs perpendicular (at a 90-degree angle) to the selvages; cross grainline runs at a 45-degree angle to the selvages.

Gusset A piece of fabric, often diamond-shaped, inserted into a seam to provide added freedom of movement, for example, at an underarm.

Hand stitches Stitches that are sewn by hand.

Header A doubled, gathered section above a tunnel or rod pocket casing, frequently used on curtains, drapes, and accessories.

Hem Bottommost finished edge on a garment or a folded, sewn edge on any type of textile item.

Hem, fused A hem that has been secured with double-sided fusible webbing ironed between the hem allowance and the main fabric.

Hem allowance The width between the marked hemline and the lower cut edge of the fabric.

Hemline The line where a hem is folded to the inside.

Hong Kong seam A seam binding technique using fabric strips, used in unlined garments.

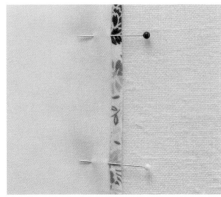

In-seam pocket An internal pocket that is sewn in on a seam line.

Interfacing Used to give structure and strength to areas such as collars, cuffs, and garment opening edges. Interfacings come in many types, designed for different uses.

Interlining See Underlining.

Invisible zipper A zipper concealed in a seam.

Keyhole buttonhole A buttonhole with a rounded "eye" at one end that resembles a keyhole. (The eye provides extra room for thicker button shanks and prevents buttonhole stretching.) It is usually worked horizontally on heavier fabrics.

Lacing Braided or twisted ties, used for closing edges or applied as an embellishment.

Lapels Folded flaps of cloth, usually attached to a collar, found on the fronts of jackets, coats, shirts, and shirt dresses. Preferred lapel sizes and shapes tend to shift with fashion trends.

Lengthwise grain See Grainline.

Lining Separately prepared fabric layer that is sewn into a garment to cover inside seams and interfacings. Lined garments are more comfortable to wear.

Locking/securing Fastening a seam line by starting and ending with a few back stitches or by knotting the thread ends.

Machine basting The provisional connection of two pieces of fabric with long straight stitches or a programmed basting stitch, using reduced upper tension, optionally with a water-soluble basting thread.

Machine quilting Sewing together two layers of fabric surrounding a layer of batting, using straight stitches, machine embroidery stitches, and/or embroidery motifs.

Machine stitches The various stitches that are executable by a particular sewing machine.

Marking Transferring symbols from paper pattern pieces to the corresponding cut pieces of fabric.

Mitered corner A single- or double-folded hem corner found on items such as linens, duvet covers, and unlined jackets that provides a cleaner finish and reduces fabric bulk at corners.

Mock felled seam In contrast to a true felled seam, the seam allowances are finished together and then topstitched.

Multi-size pattern A pattern that comes in multiple sizes that are indicated using different types or colors of outlines on a single pattern sheet.

Nap The direction of the pile on fabrics with a plush surface. The direction of the nap can be determined by running a flat hand over the fabric and noting which direction feels smoother. Fabrics with nap are cut so that all pieces have the nap running in the same direction (usually downward from the perspective of the wearer).

Notions Supplies and components needed for sewing, for example, needles, thread, and buttons.

Overlap Overlap is a section of fabric that lies atop another fabric section (the underlap) at a garment opening. Typically it will be double-layered and have interfacing. An overlap may have buttonholes matched to buttons sewn on the underlap.

Pattern layout A diagram in the pattern instructions that shows how the pattern pieces should be most efficiently arranged on the fabric for cutting.

Pattern markings Symbols such as triangles, circles, numbers, or lines on a pattern. Helpful when sewing together pattern pieces. A legend in the pattern instructions explains the symbols, which should be transferred to the wrong side of the fabric.

Pattern notches Small triangles marked on the edges of pattern pieces, indicating where pieces will match up during sewing.

Pattern outline On multi-pattern sheets, the colored and/or numbered and differentiated lines indicating the outlines of a particular pattern.

Pattern overview A section in the pattern instructions showing a line drawing of each pattern piece, providing an overview of which pieces are required for a particular item.

Pattern repeat A motif or design on fabric that repeats at regular intervals, such as flowers, stripes, or checks.

Pile Raised fibers or loops incorporated into the fabric surface during manufacturing. Typical piled fabrics include terrycloth, velvet, corduroy, minky, and velour. They all have a nap that must be considered when cutting out a pattern.

Pintucks Narrow tucks—about ¹⁄₁₆" (2mm) wide or smaller—are sewn before fabric pieces are cut. Usually stitched in parallel groupings, they are often used to embellish linens, dresses, and blouses.

Piped pocket A pocket where one or both opening edges are finished with piping.

Piping A corded strip of fabric, bias tape, or leather that is folded lengthwise in half and inserted in a seam or otherwise used to embellish an item.

Placket Fabric strips that finish a slit edge, visible from the right side.

Pleat tape A prepared tape to sew on curtains and drapes. Pleats are formed when the tape is pulled together using the attached cord.

Plissé Small, regular, permanent pleats that are mechanically pressed into fabric.

Pocket flap A flap that conceals the opening edges of a pocket.

Pocket lining The concealed, bag-like portion of a pocket sewn in at a seam or behind a cut opening. Often made of thin cotton.

Point turner A special plastic or bamboo tool to push out corners on collars or seams.

Preshrunk fabric Prewashed fabric that will not shrink further after being sewn.

Presser foot Sometimes simply called a foot. An interchangeable component of the sewing machine that holds fabric down against the stitch plate during sewing. Specialty feet are available for various decorative sewing purposes.

Prick stitching An invisible way to hand stitch interfacing onto fabric to reinforce collars, lapels, and fronts on jackets and coats. Used almost exclusively on hand-tailored garments.

Raw edge Unfinished edge on a piece of fabric.

Reinforcement stitching A line of stitching sewn along an edge, for example, a neckline or arm opening, to prevent it from stretching out of shape. Also called stay stitching.

Reinforcing Strengthening stressed areas on a garment, such as button plackets, with an additional layer of interfacing or interlining.

Right side The front, outside, or public side of a fabric.

Ruffles Gathered strips of fabric used to embellish edges on hems, sleeves, collars, pillows, et cetera.

Satin stitch A dense zigzag stitch used to finish hems, fill in spaces in embroidered motifs, and create the limiting bars on buttonholes.

Seam The line of stitching that connects two or more pieces of fabric together.

Seam, overlapped A flat seam created by sewing two lines of stitching on the overlapped edges of two fabric pieces.

Seam, piped A seam where piping has been inserted between the layers of fabric.

Seam, self-finished A seam where the method of creation encloses the edges of the seam allowances (see Felled seam).

Seam allowance The fabric between the seam line and the fabric edge; usually between ⅜–⅝" (1–1.5cm).

Seam clipping Small clips and/or notches made in the seam allowances of concave and convex edges that allow the excess fabric to fit better along the curves, so that the seams there will lie flat.

Seam ditch To "stitch in the ditch" means to sew directly along a finished seam line from the right side in order to catch in an additional layer of fabric that is underneath.

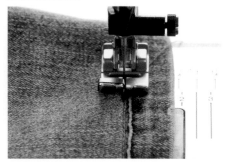

Seam line Also called the stitching line; the line along which one sews. (See Attachment line.)

Seam numbers A type of pattern marking; seams with identical numbers end up sewn together.

Seam ripper Forked tool for cutting open the stitches in seams.

Seam roll A stuffed fabric tube to help with pressing seams on narrow, circular pieces that cannot be pulled over an ironing board. One can easily be made at home using fiberfill and terrycloth.

Selvage The nonfraying, inelastic lengthwise edge of a piece of fabric; it may have manufacturer's information printed on it.

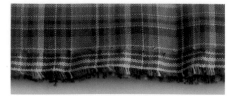

Shawl collar An extended upper collar that folds over gently in a slight roll, often found on coats, jackets, blouses, and dresses.

Shoulder pads Inserts at the shoulders of a garment to provide additional shaping. The popularity of shoulder pads follows fashion trends.

Sleeve cap The upper, rounded edge of a sleeve.

Sleeve slit Slit opening at the lower edge of a sleeve.

Slit A cut opening with finished edges that provides additional freedom of movement on a garment (as on a slit skirt).

Sloper A basic pattern that is fitted to the individual wearer. Slopers can be used as a basis for other patterns.

Smocking A traditional technique for reducing fabric width with multiple rows of topstitching, to then be embellished with decorative stitching. Smocking may be done by hand or machine.

Snaps A type of closure made of plastic or metal, to be sewn or riveted on. The two pieces of the snap are pressed together to close.

Spray adhesive A temporary adhesive to hold pieces of fabric together; the bond diminishes over time.

Stabilizers Nonwoven materials that are ironed or glued on, sometimes temporarily, to stabilize thin fabrics and prevent them from being pulled out of shape. Some are water-soluble or can be torn away after use.

Stay stitching See Reinforcement stitching.

Stitching line See Attachment line.

Straight grainline See Grainline.

Straight stitch Fundamental machine stitch, useful in almost all projects.

Tailor's chalk Used for transferring pattern markings to fabric.

Tailor's tracing paper Special paper for tracing pattern outlines and markings onto fabric; used in combination with a tracing wheel.

Tension control Regulates the interlocking of the upper and lower sewing machine threads and plays a role in creating correctly formed stitches.

Textile adhesive A permanent adhesive used to bind textiles or leather.

Thread Thread is made by spinning animal, plant, synthetic, or mineral fibers.

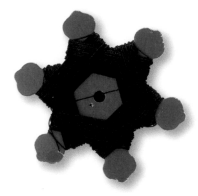

Thread chain A chain made from loops of thread, similar to a crochet chain; used to hold together pieces of fabric that hang next to each other, such as the lining and outer fabric of a garment.

Thread marking A method of transferring pattern markings to fabric using a doubled thread and hand stitches. It is used when other methods of transferring markings are not suitable for the fabric type.

Thread snippers A tool similar to scissors, with two sharp blades and a spring mechanism, used for cutting thread.

Topstitching Stitching along edges, hems, or folds that is used to secure and/or embellish them. It can be done with all-purpose, buttonhole, heavy-duty, or machine embroidery thread. Topstitching may also be done using a twin needle.

Tracing paper See Tailor's tracing paper.

Tracing wheel Tool with a single or double, smooth or serrated wheel (sometimes with a chalk holder); used in combination with tailor's tracing paper to transfer markings from patterns to fabric.

Tucks Tucks are folds that can both restrict and add fullness. For example, a skirt may have tucks at the waist area that flare open farther down to give more freedom of movement.

Turning See Facing (v.).

Turning a corner When stitching a seam around a corner, the fabric itself is turned while the needle remains in the down position in the fabric, serving as the turning point.

Undercollar Also called the collar facing. The underneath or inside section of a collar, depending on collar style, usually cut slightly smaller than the upper collar.

Underlap See Overlap.

Underlining Additional fabric cut from the same pattern pieces and sewn or fused to the fashion fabric before construction; often used with sheer or lace fabrics. Also called interlining.

Upper collar The part of the collar that faces up, on the outside.

Waistband Strips of fabric, usually interfaced, set at the waist edge on garments. Waistbands may be elastic, straight, or shaped.

Warp threads The lengthwise threads in a woven fabric, running parallel to the selvages.

Weft threads Crosswise threads in woven fabric, running at a 90-degree angle to the selvages; the cross grain.

Weighted hem tape Small lead beads encased in a synthetic casing, sewn inside curtain hems to weigh them down and help ensure proper drape of the curtain folds.

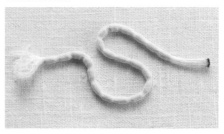

Welt pocket A set-in pocket, usually on jackets and coats, whose opening edges are finished with a fabric binding.

Wristband Applied fabric piece that finishes a lower sleeve edge, frequently closed with a button placket. See also Cuff.

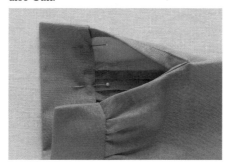

Wrong side the back, underside, or inside (non-public side) of the fabric, sometimes also called the reverse side.

Yoke A panel made of single or doubled fabric, usually at the shoulders or waistband. The remaining part of the garment is sewn to the yoke.

Index

BRIGITTE FRIEDERIKE BINDER

lives and works in Freiburg, Germany, and is the mother of two adult sons. Even as a schoolgirl she was interested in fashion, design, and interior decorating, and sewed dresses and home décor items for her friends. She went to college and focused on textiles (among other subjects), and was a teacher for many years. Today she works as a contractor with creative firms and various book and magazine publishers and media outlets. She has been designing embroidery motifs since 1997 for prominent companies and leads workshops on digital embroidery. Further information can be found on her website: www.bfb-creativeconcepts.de.

JUTTA KÜHNLE

worked for a children's clothing company after finishing her degree in design, and later went into business with her own small studio, where she specialized in bridal fashions, menswear, and custom-made items. Her love of children's clothing remained as well, and once a year she would design and produce a limited collection of whimsical children's garments. Together with her husband, she now runs a small hotel in Stuttgart-Berg, where in 2009 she began a small dirndl rental business—which has even made an appearance in the novel *Brezeltango*. The Bavarian designer works under the motto "Bound by tradition, unleashed by modernity."

KARIN ROSER

is a freelance editor, designer, and author who designs and produces pieces for numerous craft and home and garden magazines from renowned publishers. She has a particular weakness for secondhand items and flea market finds, which she restores and revamps with great imagination and detail, often converting them for entirely different uses. No materials are safe from her clutches!

12/14- WS

161 Avenue of the
Americas
New York, NY 10013
sixthandspringbooks.com

Editorial Director
JOY AQUILINO

Developmental Editor
LISA SILVERMAN

Art Director
DIANE LAMPHRON

Editorial Assistant
JOHANNA LEVY

Page Designer
ARETA BUK

Translator
KAREN BAUMER

Copyeditor
MARTHA MORAN

Illustrations
OTTO HABLIZEL
URSULA SCHWAB

Photography
MICHAEL RUDER/
LICHTPUNKT

Vice President
TRISHA MALCOLM

Publisher
CARRIE KILMER

Production Manager
DAVID JOINNIDES

President
ART JOINNIDES

Chairman
JAY STEIN

Cataloging-in-Publication Data is available from the Library of Congress.

ISBN: 978-1-936096-72-5

Manufactured in China

1 3 5 7 9 10 8 6 4 2

First Edition